SYSTEMS
OF
ETHICS AND VALUE THEORY

SYSTEMS OF ETHICS AND VALUE THEORY

WILLIAM S. SAHAKIAN, Ph.D.

PHILOSOPHICAL LIBRARY
New York

© Copyright, 1963, by
Philosophical Library, Inc.
15 East 40th Street, New York, N.Y.

All rights reserved

Library of Congress Catalog Card Number: 63-11487

ISBN 978-0-8065-2949-3

Printed in the United States of America

DEDICATED TO:

The aesthetic soul, who loves truth
and pursues the good.

"If God held all truth concealed in his right hand, and in his left hand the persistent striving for the truth, and while warning me against eternal error, should say: Choose! I should humbly bow before his left hand, and say: Father, give thy gift; the pure truth is for thee alone." (Lessing, Werke, Vol. X, 53.)

TABLE OF CONTENTS

SELF-REALIZATIONISM

ARISTOTLE 1
(Self-Realizationism)
1. Nicomachean Ethics. 2. Definition of Ethics and Related Terms. 3. The Self-Realization School of Ethics. 4. The Three-Fold Nature of Man. 5. The *Summum Bonum*. 6. The Contemplative Life. 7. Moderation in All Things. 8. A Schematic Representation of the Mean. 9. A List of Aristotelian Virtues and Vices. 10. The Right Act. 11. Virtue. 12. The Relation of the Soul to Virtue. 13. Freedom of the Will. 14. Analysis of the Cardinal Virtues: (a) Courage (b) Temperance (c) Liberality (d) Magnificence (e) Magnanimity (f) Unnamed Mean of Ambition (g) Gentleness (h) Friendliness (i) Truthfulness (j) Wittiness (k) Shame and Continence (l) Justice. 15. The Intellectual Virtues. 16. Moral Character. 17. Slaves by Nature. 18. Evaluation of the Aristotelian Ethic. 19. Further Reading in Aristotle.

ETHICAL INTUITIONISM

IMMANUEL KANT 44
(Deontological Ethics)
1. Intuition School of Ethics. 2. Nothing Good Except a Good Will. 3. Autonomy of the Will. 4. Heaven and Hell as Moral Motivation. 5. Morality and Prudence. 6. What is Right for One is Right for All. 7. The Categorical

Imperative. 8. Will and Inclination. 9. Dignity. 10. Kingdom of Ends. 11. Deontological Ethics. 12. I Ought Implies I Can. 13. Virtue. 14. The *Summum Bonum*. 15. Evil as Parasitic. 16. Man's Nature as Basically Good. 17. Primacy of Pure Practical Reason. 18. Metaphysics of Ethics. 19. Kant's Social Ethics. 20. Evaluation of the Kantian Ethic. 21. Further Reading in Kant.

JOSEPH BUTLER 76
(Classical Intuitionism)
1. Classical Intuitionism. 2. The Nature of Virtue and Vice. 3. The Supremacy of Conscience in Adjudicating Moral Issues. 4. Self-Love, Benevolence, and Appetite. 5. The Social Nature of Man. 6. Evaluation of Butler's Intuitionism. 7. Further Reading in the Ethics of Butler.

JAMES MARTINEAU 87
(Classical Intuitionism)
1. Idiopsychological ethics. 2. Duty. 3. Criterion of Right Action: Moral Motives. 4. Moral Springs of Action. 5. Table of Springs of Action. 6. Evaluation of Martineau's Intuitionism.

HEDONISM AND UTILITARIANISM

JEREMY BENTHAM 97
(Egoistic Hedonism)
1. Utilitarianism (a) Psychological Hedonism (b) Quantitative Hedonism (c) Egoistic Hedonism (d) Qualitative Hedonism. 2. The Right and the Good. 3. The Hedonistic Calculus. 4. The Four Sanctions. 5. The Pig Philosophy. 6. The Greatest Good of the Greatest Number. 7. Everybody to Count for One, Nobody for More Than One. 8. The *Summum Bonum* and the Right Act. 9. Temptation. 10. The Proof of Hedonism. 11. Evaluation of

Bentham's Ethic. 12. Further Reading in the Philosophy of Bentham.

JOHN STUART MILL 121
(Ethical Hedonism)
1. Utilitarianism. 2. The *Summum Bonum* and the Right Act. 3. Everybody to Count for One, Nobody for More Than One. 4. The Two Sanctions. 5. Justice. 6. The Proof of Utilitarianism. 7. Comparison of the Ethics of Bentham and Mill. 8. Evaluation of Mill's Ethic. 9. Further Reading in the Philosophy of Mill.

EPICURUS 138
(Epicureanism)
1. Epicureanism. 2. The *Summum Bonum* (Prudence) 3. Selected Proverbs of Epicurus: (a) From the *Principle Doctrines* (b) From the *Vatican Collection* (c) From the *Symposium* (d) From *On the End of Life* (e) From the *Letter to Anaxarchus* (f) From the *Letter to Idomeneus* (g) From *Letters to Unknown Recipients* (h) From *Fragments from Uncertain Sources*. 4. Further Reading in the Philosophy of Epicurus.

STOICISM AND CYNICISM

EPICTETUS 146
(Stoicism)
1. Stoicism. 2. Contentment. 3. The Unconquerable Will. 4. Resignation. 5. Virtue. 6. Cynicism. 7. Sex. 8. Evaluation of Stoicism. 9. Further Reading in Epictetus.

SOCRATES 158
(The Socratic Ethics)
1. Major Ethical Principles. 2. The Socratic Method. 3. Virtue Is Knowledge. 4. Know Thyself. 5. Virtue. 6. The Unexamined Life Is Not Worth Living. 7. Further Reading in Socrates.

RELIGIOUS ETHICS

MOSES 171
(Ethics of Israel)
1. The Decalogue. 2. The *Lex Talionis* and the Concept of Justice 3. The Great Commandment and the Golden Rule. 4. Diverse and Sundry Ethical Principles.

JESUS 181
(Christian Ethics)
1. The Christian Ethic. 2. The Sermon on the Mount: (a) The Beatitudes (b) Murder and Anger (c) Lust, Adultery, and Divorce (d) The Swearing of Oaths (e) Retaliation (f) *Agape* (Christian Love) (g) Ostentation (h) Anxiety (i) Censoriousness (j) Golden Rule. 3. The Great Commandment. 4. The Christian Mandate. 5. Human Dignity and the Brotherhood of Man.

ST. PAUL 199
(Pauline Ethics)
1. The Greatest Virtue (Love). 2. The Good Life. 3. The Moral Law of Compensation. 4. Interim Ethics. 5. Miscellaneous Moral Teachings.

ST. AUGUSTINE 208
(Augustinian Ethics)
1. Natural Goodness of all Things. 2. Evil as the Privation of Good. 3. Freedom of the Will. 4. *Summum Bonum* (God). 5. The Greatest Virtue (Love of God). 6. Confessions of St. Augustine. 7. Further Reading in St. Augustine.

ST. THOMAS AQUINAS 220
(Scholastic Ethics)
1. Sypnopsis of the Thomistic Ethic. 2. Self-Realizationism: (a) Good, Evil, and the *Summum Bonum* (b)

Will vs. Intellect (c) Happiness. 3. The Seven Cardinal Christian Virtues: (a) The Intellectual Virtues (b) The Moral Virtues (c) The Cardinal Virtues (d) The Theological Virtues (e) Outline of the Thomistic Virtues. 4. Venial and Mortal Sin. 5. Further Reading in the Philosophy of St. Thomas.

EVOLUTIONARY NATURALISM

FRIEDRICH NIETZSCHE 237
(Ethics of Power)
1. Outline of Nietzsche's Evolutionary Naturalism. 2. The Genealogy of Morals. 3. Master-Morality vs. Slave-Morality. 4. Critique of the Ethics of Christianity. 5. The Superman. 6. The Will for Power. 7. Evaluation of the Nietzschean Value Theory.

HERBERT SPENCER 264
(Ethics of Survival)
1. Ethics of Survival. 2. The Evolution of Conduct. 3. Psychological Hedonism and Optimism. 4. Evaluation of the Spencerian Ethic. 5. Further Reading in the Philosophy of Spencer.

ETHICAL PESSIMISM AND EXISTENTIALISM

ARTHUR SCHOPENHAUER 276
(Ethics of Pity)
1. The Ethics of Pessimism. 2. Evil as Positive. 3. The Vanity of Existence, Suicide and Death. 4. Ethical Salvation. 5. Ethics of Pity. 6. Evaluation of the Schopenhauerian Ethic. 7. Further Reading in the Philosophy of Schopenhauer.

SOREN KIERKEGAARD 294
(Dialectical Ethics)
1. Dialectical Ethics. 2. Either/Or. 3. Purity of Heart. 4. The Individual. 5. The Self, Freedom, and Will. 6. Evaluation of the Ethics of Kierkegaard. 7. Further Reading in the Philosophy of Kierkegaard.

ETHICAL PRAGMATISM

JOHN DEWEY 318
(Ethical Instrumentalism)
1. Ethical Inquiry. 2. Reconstruction of Moral Conceptions. 3. Moral Growth. 4. Value Theory. 5. Rights, Duties, and Moral Standards. 6. Morality as Social. 7. Evaluation of the Ethics of Dewey. 8. Further Reading in the Philosophy of Dewey.

ETHICAL REALISM

G. E. MOORE 341
(Ideal Utilitarianism)
1. Ideal Utilitarianism. 2. The Right Act. 3. The Doctrine of Ethical Realism. 4. The Indefinability of Good. 5. Evaluation of Ideal Utilitarianism. 6. Further Reading in G. E. Moore.

ETHICAL IDEALISM

JOSIAH ROYCE 352
(Ethics of Loyalty)
1. The Philosophy of Loyalty: (a) The Ethics of Loyalty (b) The Definition of Loyalty (c) The Need of Loyalty (d) The Intrinsic Value of Loyalty (e) Loyalty to Loyalty (f) Loyalty as the Transmutation of All Moral Values. 2. Evaluation of the Ethics of Loyalty. 3. Further Reading in the Philosophy of Royce.

ETHICAL SUBJECTIVISM

DAVID HUME 362
(Ethical Subjectivism)
1. Ethics as Sentiment. 2. Moral Approbation as Social Opinion. 3. The Criterion of Right Conduct (The Disinterested Spectator). 4. Evaluation of the Ethics of Hume.

EDWARD WESTERMARCK 373
(Ethical Relativity)
1. Ethical Relativity. 2. The Emotional Origin of Moral Judgments. 3. The Nature of Moral Emotions. 4. Ethical Subjectivism. 5. Evaluation of Ethical Relativity.

ETHICAL NATURALISM

RALPH BARTON PERRY 381
(Ethical Naturalism)
1. Ethical Naturalism. 2. The Interest Theory of Value. 3. The Criteria and Calculus of Value. 4. The *Summum Bonum*. 5. Evaluation of the Ethics of Perry. 6. Further Reading in the Philosophy of Perry.

THOMAS HOBBES 392
(Egoistic Naturalism)
1. Might Makes Right. 2. The Social Contract. 3. Natural Moral Law. 4. Evaluation of Ethical Naturalism. 5. Further Reading in the Philosophy of Hobbes.

MORITZ SCHLICK 401
(Ethical Naturalism)
1. Ethical Naturalism (a) Analysis of Moral Value (b) Moral Value as Desire (c) Ethical Relativity (d) Moral Value as Social Survival (e) The Role of Kindness. 2. Critique of the Ethics of Schlick. 3. Further Reading in the Philosophy of Schlick.

ETHICAL SKEPTICISM AND VALUE NIHILISM
(Logical Positivism)

A. J. AYER 410
(Emotivism)
1. The Emotive Theory of Ethics. 2. Ethical Emotivism *vs.* Ethical Subjectivism. 3. Critique of the Ethics of Ayer. 4. Further Reading in A. J. Ayer.

BERTRAND RUSSELL 425
(Ethical Skepticism)
1. Ethical Skepticism. 2. Russell's Critique of His Own Theory of Moral Value. 3. Further Reading in the Philosophy of Russell.

CHARLES L. STEVENSON 434
(Non-Cognitivism)
1. The Non-Cognitive Theory of Ethics. 2. Ethics as Attitude. 3. The Resolution of Ethical Disputes. 4. The Dual Function of Language. 5. Critique of the Ethics of Stevenson. 6. Further Reading in the Philosophy of Stevenson.

INDEX 445

PREFACE

The present work is not a book of readings: it constitutes a thorough summary, explanation, and critical evaluation of the classics in ethics and value theory with profuse quotations lavishly interspersed throughout the entire book, equipping the reader with an explanation which he can understand plus the flavor of the classical philosophers speaking for themselves. It is the author's hope that the reader will be inspired, once having completed the present work, to seek out the primary sources in their entirety and gain a first hand experience and mastery of them on his own initiative, once he realizes himself to be in a position to cope with such.

The present work is a synthetic approach designed to remedy the dilemma posed to previous authors of texts of this nature. In the past, the approach has been to select one of two antitheses: (a) that of the traditional type of text which is painfully lacking in quotations, hence shares little or none of the primary sources with the reader, consequently the words of the classical author and the manner in which he expresses his cherished and original concepts are not shared with the reader; (b) the second approach, which has become popular in recent years, has been to clip pages from the original classics, paste them together with pages torn from other great works, and then hand the product to the reader with the unwarranted expectation that he can contend with it. The psychological experience confronting the average reader of the "book of readings" type of text is the bewildered feeling of having entered a theatre an hour late for the performance in which a mystery drama is being enacted, and being required to leave the theatre an hour before the conclusion of the performance with the preposterous expectation that the individual in this perplexed state of mind has a coherent grasp of the subject matter as an integrated whole. The present book resolves the difficulties encountered by the other two methods by bringing both into a harmonious synthesis, enabling the reader to profit in having entire systems of a multiplicity of types of value theory plus the added advantage and satisfaction of having read much of the original masterpiece with all of its inflections for himself. E.g., to be told that Nietzsche is a satirist with a command of language par excellence is enlightening, but to read his own phraseology gives it a savor that renders all else bland. Read the following scathing caricatures by him of illustrious personalities:

> *Schiller*: or the Moral-Trumpeter of Säckinger.
> *Dante*: or the hyena who *writes poetry* in tombs.
> *Victor Hugo*: or the pharos at the sea of nonsense.
> *Lizst*: or the school of smoothness — with women.
> *George Sand*: or *lactea ubertas* — in translation, the milk cow with "a beautiful style."
> *Carlyle*: or pessimism as a poorly digested dinner.
> *John Stuart Mill*: or insulting clarity.
> *Les freres de Goncourt*: or the Ajaxes in battle with Homer — music by Offenbach.
> *Zola*: or "the delight in stinking."

The same holds true for the Socratic injunction: "The unexamined life is not worth living;" also for Epictetus' Stoicism: "Anytus and Melytus have power to put me to death, but not to harm me;" and a final one from Mill: "It is better to be a human being dissatisfied than a pig satisfied; better to be Socrates dissatisfied than a pig satisfied."

The book of readings type of text often produces the demoralizing effect that one lacks the necessary intellectual acumen to understand the classic author; the second which is grossly deficient in quotations is incapable of creating the confidence necessary to encourage the reader to proceed directly to the unabridged original book. It is hoped that the present synthetic approach will prove a satisfactory resolution to the prior confronting obstacles.

To facilitate matters for the reader, an outline of each man treated in the body of the text is found in the table of contents; in many cases an outline summary is provided in the initial section treating each philosopher — this is intended to provide a bird's eye view or synopsis to orientate one and prevent his becoming lost after embarking into the detailed material.

The men treated do not appear in chronological order for some good reasons: First, it seemed more logical to arrange the philosophers according to schools of ethical thought and orientate the reader from this standpoint; second, a chronological ordering has a tendency to prejudice the reader in favor of later writers to the detriment of earlier ones. Dates also have been avoided to detour this bias.

Technical ethical terms used freely by philosophers in a light unfamiliar to the layman have been carefully defined wherever the word makes its first appearance in the body of the text. It is primarily for this reason that the earlier men covered in the text require a fuller treatment than those appearing subsequently, and for this reason should be studied first.

In numerous instances, extended quotations have been worked into the normal body of the text wherever this was deemed advisable for the sake of continuity, *i.e.*, in order not to interrupt the even flow of thought, rather than submitting to the customary practice of indentation or the use of diminutive type.

One's attention is called to the striking quotations immediately under the name of each philosopher treated; they are provided and inserted at this particular point because they do in a sense summarize the thought of the ethical theory under consideration.

WILLIAM S. SAHAKIAN

Boston, Massachusetts

ACKNOWLEDGMENTS

The writer is indebted to the following authors and publishers for inclusion of copyrighted material into this text: Aristotle, *Nicomachean Ethics* tr. by W. D. Ross, Oxford University Press; Immanuel Kant, *The Fundamental Principles of the Metaphysics of Ethics* tr. by Otto Manthey-Zorn, Appleton Century Crofts; *Kant's Critique of Practical Reason, and Other Works* tr. by Thomas Kingsmill Abbott, Longmans, Green and Co.; Plato, *Philebus* tr. by Harold N. Fowler, and Xenophon, *Memorabilia* tr. by E. C. Marchant, Harvard University Press; *The Interpreter's Bible*, Abingdon Press; *Basic Writings of St. Thomas Aquinas* ed. by Anton C. Pegis, Random House, Inc.; Friedrich Nietzsche, *Beyond Good and Evil* tr. by Marianne Cowan, Henry Regnery Co.; *The Birth of a Tragedy* and *The Genealogy of Morals* tr. by Francis Golffing, Doubleday and Co.; other quotations from Nietzsche's works are translated by Walter Kaufmann, Princeton University Press; Soren Kierkegaard, *The Sickness unto Death*, and *Either/Or* tr. by Walter Lowrie, Princeton University Press; *Concluding Scientific Postscript*, tr. by David Swenson and Walter Lowrie, Princeton University Press; *Journal* tr. by Alexander Dru, Oxford University Press; *Purity of Heart* tr. by Douglas V. Steere, Harper and Brothers; John Dewey, *Reconstruction in Philosophy* and *Human Nature and Conduct*, Henry Holt and Co., *Problems of Men*, Philosophical Library, *The Quest for Certainty*, Minton Balch and Co., "Theory of Valuation" in *International Encyclopedia of Unified Science*, University of Chicago Press, *Ethics* with J. H. Tufts, Henry Holt and Co.; G. E. Moore, *Ethics*, Oxford University Press, *Principia Ethica*, Cambridge University Press; Josiah Royce, *The Philosophy of Loyalty*, the Estate of Josiah Royce, Harvard

Trust Company, Cambridge, Mass.; Edward Westermarck, *Ethical Relativity*, Routledge & Kegan Paul, Ltd.; Harcourt, Brace and Co., *The Origin and Development of the Moral Ideas*, Macmillan and Co. and St. Martin's Press; Ralph Barton Perry, *General Theory of Value* and *Realms of Value*, Harvard University Press; Moritz Schlick, *Problems of Ethics* tr. by David Rynin, Prentice Hall, Inc.; A. J. Ayer, *Language, Truth and Logic*, Victor Gollancz Ltd. and Dover Publications, Inc., Bertrand Russell, *Religion and Science*, Oxford University Press; *The Philosophy of Bertrand Russell* ed. by Paul A. Schilpp, Northwestern University Press; Charles L. Stevenson, *Ethics and Language*, Yale University Press; C. E. M. Joad, *Critique of Logical Positivism*, Victor Gollancz Ltd.; Epictetus, *Discourses* and *Fragments*, tr. by P. E. Matheson, Oxford University Press; and *Epicurus' Extant Writings*, tr. by Cyril Bailey, Oxford University Press.

The author wishes to express his gratitude to the many persons who assisted him in this undertaking, but particularly to Dr. Mabel Lewis Sahakian of Northeastern University who labored many hours to see this work to its completion and to whom this book is affectionately dedicated, and to Dean Charles W. Havice of Northeastern University whose constant encouragement and advice transformed what would have been a laborious task into a pleasurable adventure.

W. S. S.

SYSTEMS
OF
ETHICS AND VALUE THEORY

SELF-REALIZATIONISM

ARISTOTLE

"Those who love in excess also hate in excess."

(A saying quoted by Aristotle)

1. Nicomachean Ethics

The ethical school of thought of Aristotle is termed the *Self-Realization School of Ethics*, but one is cautioned not to confuse it with the name of Aristotle's university, viz., the *Lyceum*. The principal interest of the present discussion is in his book entitled: *Nicomachean Ethics*, named after Aristotle's son, Nicomachus. Scholarly opinion regarding the naming of the book differs; the discrepancy arising from the fact that Aristotle himself did not personally write the book, at least, not the finished product which constitutes a compilation of the notes of Aristotle. The conclusion arrived at by some scholars is that the book was merely dedicated to Nicomachus, while others surmise that Nicomachus edited the work. There are those who go so far as to conjecture that it was Nicomachus who wrote the book rather than Aristotle, at least, this was Cicero's intimation.[1] Other philosophers contend that the notes, if not the finished treatise, may represent a collective endeavor involving a multiplicity of contributors. Some scholars maintain that the works attributed to Aristotle are considerably more than a single man could possibly have accomplished through unaided efforts; consequently, they feel entitled to infer that it is the product of his university's combined faculty. For present purposes, it need only be regarded as the direct and sole work of Aristotle.

At this point, it is probably worth mentioning that besides the *Nicomachean*, there are two other versions: *Eudemian* and *Magna Moralia*; the *Magna Moralia* is ignored by most professors because its content is merely a collection of excerpts from the former two that a *Peripatetic* used for lecture notes. Aristotle's school was referred to, colloquially, as the *Peripatetic School of Philosophy* because its members would promenade about as they discussed and lectured on philosophy; peripatetic literally means to *walk about*. Some scholars reject the *Eudemian* version as spurious,[2] but this controversy will not affect the present treatment as it will be restricted to those ten books which compose the *Nicomachean Ethics* together with pertinent excerpts from the *Politics*.

A proper treatment of the ethics of Aristotle should include a study of the *Politics* since this book is the logical continuation of his efforts in moral theory. Aristotle takes the position that politics is social ethics and one cannot attain an ethical goal except in a society: "the complete science of 'politics' falls into two parts which may for convenience be called ethics and politics. Aristotle's ethics, no doubt, are social, and his politics are ethical; he does not forget in the *Ethics* that the individual man is essentially a member of a society, nor in the *Politics* that the good life of the state exists only in the lives of its citizens."[3] The concluding books of the *Nicomachean Ethics* constitute a discussion on friendship followed by one on happiness both of which serve as a transition into his social ethics, viz., the *Politics*.

2. Definition of Ethics and Related Terms

At this point, some definitions, together with their reciprocal relationships, appear to be in order, particularly for terms such as: *ethics, morals, social ethics, politics, sociology*. *Ethics* has been defined as *the study of the right and the good*, i.e., right conduct and the good life; whereas, *morality* is the *practice* of what one believes to be right and good. Ethics is a study, hence is theoretical, whereas, morality is pragmatic;

2

it involves doing, acting, behaving. An expert in ethics is not *necessarily* a highly moral person; his morals may border on mediocrity or suffer complete deterioration; on the other hand, the moral person may be incapable of passing a simple examination in ethical theory. Summarily, ethics applied becomes morality; and morality theorized or studied is ethics.

Etymologically, the word moral comes from the Latin: *mos, mores,* which means customs or manners; ethic comes from the Greek: *ethike* and means the science of character;[4] "moral virtue comes about as a result of habit, whence also its name *ethike* is one that is formed by a slight variation from the word *ethos* (habit)."[5] The term, ethics, usually pertains to personal morality; when the word is used collectively in application to groups, then it becomes the study of social ethics, *i. e.*, the manner in which a society *ought* to behave. Politics and sociology are social sciences and as *sciences,* their province is restricted to a *description* of the facts; scientists do *not evaluate, i.e.*, pass moral judgments, such as philosophers do; however, political theory as it is studied today in many universities is social ethics, *i. e.*, social or political philosophy.

3. The Self-Realization School of Ethics

Self-realizationism is self-explanatory for its meaning is implicit in the term. Explicitly, it denotes that the attainment of high ethical goals consists in realizing oneself, *i. e.*, one must develop his true nature; he must take his *potentialities and actualize them*; he must take his innate talents, abilities, special capacities and fulfill them to completion. Securing complete actualization is accompanied by a dual satisfaction: it not only makes one a virtuous person, but a felicitous one as well. "The happy man lives well and does well; for we have practically defined happiness as a sort of good life and good action."[6]

Aristotle lays heavy emphasis on nature, stressing that good is the fulfillment of nature, whereas, evil is its perversion. The criterion of morality is behavior which is natural for "nothing which is contrary to nature is good."[7] He who fulfills his true nature will avoid frustration, the principal cause of unhappiness; moreover he will find the road to contentment and happiness unimpeded, but a perverse person vainly seeks lasting happiness or blessedness. The following implication could be drawn from Aristotle's philosophy: Only man seems to be able to pervert his nature, whereas, animals and vegetables behave according to their given natures. The apple tree has no desire to become a rose bush nor does the tomato plant strive to become an oak tree. The tiger does not seek to become a mosquito nor does the fly want to become a dog. Of all nature's creations, man alone seeks to be other than the being he was created. The naturally born talented artist seeks to become a lawyer, the lawyer wants to become a dentist, the dentist desires to become a musician, the musician aspires to become a surgeon, and the surgeon covets the life of a clergyman. The reason for their misery and search for another field of endeavor is that they have pursued an interest which is incongruous with their fundamental natures, *i. e.*, their talents lie in another direction. Such persons have entered a field foreign to their personality make-up, consequently, feel "like fish out of water." The probable reason for their entrance into a field for which they have no natural calling is ignorance, misguidance, the glamour of the profession, etc. Nevertheless, misfits, with a disdain for their work, constantly suffer a sense of frustration and are malcontent. Such persons needlessly suffer endless friction, similar to a cylinder in operation without any lubrication.

The principle underlying the foregoing is explained by Aristotle: "The function of man is an activity of soul which follows or implies a rational principle . . . *e.g.*, the function of the lyre player is to play the lyre, and that of a good lyre player is to do so well: if this is the case . . . the function of the good man to be the good and noble performance of these, and if any action is well performed when it is performed in accordance with the appropriate excellence: if this is the case, human good turns out to be activity of soul in accordance with virtue, and if there are more than one virtue, in accordance with the best and most complete."[3] It is notable that for Aristotle one is morally compelled to live a full life, not merely one that satisfies but a single potentiality. In order to be in a position to fulfill every phase of one's life, it is necessary to know the constituents of a complete life, *i. e.*, a comprehension of the various aspects of human nature treated in the following section.

4. The Threefold Nature of Man

Much of current scientific knowledge, at least, the layman's grasp of it, emanates from Aristotle. For over a thousand years, Aristotelian thought dominated the academic world, during which period whenever reference was made to "the philosopher," it signified Aristotle; in modern times the same appellation applies to Hegel.[9] A great number of persons unversed in the sciences of psychology and physiology still think of the human with only five senses, instead of over twice that number. This misconception stems from Aristotle along with the average layman's definition of the word *man*, viz., "Man is a rational animal."

The preceding discussion provides a suitable basis for a proper understanding of the three-fold nature of man as envisaged by Aristotle. Man's three natures are: *vegetable, animal,* and *rational*; *e. g.*, one's hair and fingernails grow as vegetation; his animal emotions are shared in common with the brute; but his rational nature is unique and private. Man's multiple nature creates the necessity of defining him as animal as well as rational; to be consistent, vegetable should be incorporated in order to derive a complete definition: Man is a *rational animated vegetable.* His rationale is: "Life seems to be common even to plants, but we are seeking what is peculiar to man. Let us exclude, therefore, the life of nutrition and growth. Next there would be a life of perception, but *it* also seems to be in common even to the horse, the ox, and every animal. There remains, then, an active life of the element that has a rational principle."[10] Man's uniqueness lies in his possession of an intellect.

One could question the relevance of the three-fold nature of man to the Aristotelian ethic, but would find the challenge met when the point is made that the moral goal is attainable only when one has developed each area of his multiple nature to its maximum. Since man's nature is three-fold, all three must be considered and exhaustively exploited; most particularly his supernal self, viz., the rational via which one surmounts the pinnacle of the ethical life. Furthermore, the lower natures of the individual ought to be developed in accord with his rational nature: *any man can live, i. e., exist; the task of life, however, is to live well.* Hence, man has the responsibilities of: (1) the care and proper development of his physical body, (2) the more important task of cultivating his emotional and psychological life, (3) the most important undertaking of all, viz., the unfolding of the intellectual self, *i. e.*, a life devoted to science, philosophy, religion, culture, etc. The actualization of any potential is a guarantee of happiness, but it is found in differing grades in the following ascending order: *pleasure, honor, meditation*; its highest degree is the *summun bonum*, viz., *contemplation*.

5. The Summun Bonum

Aristotle contends that the *summun bonum* (greatest good) is happiness: "Happiness then is the best, noblest, and most pleasant thing in the world;"[11] its superlative form is contemplation or meditation. It is interesting to note his rationale in arriving at this conclusion. The *Nicomachean Ethics* open with the statement: "Every art and every inquiry, and similarly every action and pursuit, is thought to aim at some good; and for this reason the good has rightly been declared to be that at which all things aim."[12] Aristotle's teleological orientation toward life is extraordinary; purpose is inherent in every object animate or otherwise, because nature decreed it so: "Nature makes nothing incomplete, and nothing in vain."[13] Obedience to nature is a moral dictate; one's ethical goal is the fulfillment of his intended nature. States antithetic to happiness result from thwarted goals; this disruption of mental tranquility is arrested only by properly expediting nature's proposals.

Aristotle keenly observed that everything in the world is sought and pursued, not for itself alone, but as instrumental to one's goal or objective; but in the final denoument, there is something desired for its "dear sweet sake alone," viz., *happiness*. *E. g.*, college students usually seek an education to enhance employment opportunities, but often the position is not the desired ultimate end; its desideratum is contingent upon earning a respectable salary, but salary is not the terminal point; "the life of money making is one undertaken under compulsion, and wealth is evidently not the good we are seeking; for it is merely useful and for the sake of something else."[14] Financial earnings are valued instrumentally for their purchasing power, *e. g.*, necessities and luxuries for one's family, but the desirability of a family is contingent upon its efficacy to yield happiness. Ultimately happiness alone is the end which is intrinsically sought; all else is relegated to a subservient position, and rightly so, since happiness is the supreme good:

> There is some end of the things we do, which we desire for its own sake (everything else being desired for the sake of this) [happiness] ... clearly this must be the good and the chief good. ... Now such a thing happiness, above all else, is held to be; for this we choose always for itself and never for the sake of something else ... every virtue we choose indeed for themselves but we choose them also for the sake of happiness, judging that by means of them we shall be happy. Happiness, on the other hand, no one chooses for the sake of these, nor in general, for anything other than itself.[15]

The designation of happiness as the greatest good, or to translate Aristotle literally, "the aristocrat of goods," rests in its intrinsic and definitive value, hence its unqualified goodness: "The chief good is evidently something final, therefore, if there is only one final end, this will be what we are seeking. Now we call that which is in itself worthy of pursuit more final than that which is worthy of pursuit for the sake of something else ... therefore we call final without qualification that which is always desirable in itself and never for the sake of something else."[16] Happiness fits this prescription well; but its accomplishment is not as easily facilitated as is the road to perdition.[17]

A logical contradiction, viz., the *hedonistic paradox,* is encountered when one attempts to maintain the cogency of the position that happiness is obtainable by direct pursuit; this fallacy is bared in the section treating critical evaluations. Evidently, Aristotle is aware of the fact that the person who sets happiness as his mark, has set up a very difficult goal for himself. He stresses this issue, utilizing the figure of the master archer whose accuracy in striking the bull's eye is an achievement requiring great talent and skilled precision. The same holds true of life, whose ultimate mark is happiness, but the superior knowledge and innate ability required to succeed, commands all of one's resources and skill.

In fairness to Aristotle,[18] it should be noted that happiness and hedonism (the philosophy of pleasure) are not equivalent. In the mind of the Greek philosophers, pleasure and happiness were not considered identical experiences nor is the same word used: the word pleasure in Greek is *hedone,* from which is derived the term hedonism, whereas, the Greek word for happiness is *eudaimonia,* which denotes a beautiful state of mind. Happiness is a felicity which results from a life of activity in accordance with reason; it is a mental or spiritual condition, whereas, pleasure is a bodily or sensual state.

6. The Contemplative Life

The life of enjoyment is preferable for three fundamental reasons: (1) *the intrinsic value of enjoyment,* (2) *political reasons,* (3) *the contemplative life.* The first group compose the vulgar and the youth who are victimized by the dictates of the masses and enslaved by their passions: the "mass of mankind are quite slavish in their tastes, preferring a life suitable to beasts."[19] Those whose pursuit of enjoyment is politically channeled, *i.e.,* who elected this option, were prompted by fine breeding couched in rich culture: "A consideration of the prominent types of life shows that people of superior refinement and of active disposition identify happiness with honor; for this is, roughly speaking, the end of the political life."[20]

The third and supernal form of enjoyment issues from the contemplative life, and ensues from a dedication to the thought life, *i. e.*, philosophizing, creative activity, scientific endeavor, cultural pursuits, etc.; this constitutes the royal road to happiness. Although it is the duty of man to realize his three-fold nature: vegetable, animal, rational, his chief efforts must be devoted to his supreme and divine-like self, viz., the rational; his remaining nature holds an ancillary position and must be ordered according to the rational life. The highest form of happiness entails the meditative or thoughtful life since "perfect happiness is a contemplative activity."[21] The contemplative life is that which most resembles the activity of God and is the "most divine element in us," for this reason, the pinnacle of the virtuous life issues from it, viz., happiness in its sublimest form. "Therefore the activity of God, which surpasses all others in blessedness, must be contemplative; and of human activities, therefore, that which is most akin to this must be most of the nature of happiness."[22]

There are numerous techniques employed by Aristotle to prove that the realization or actualization of the contemplative life insures happiness. One has been mentioned, *i. e.*, that nature in man which is uncommon to the animal kingdom; the *sine qua non* of happiness, viz., a life of creative thought, contemplation, or scientific endeavor; "animals have no share in happiness, being completely deprived of such activity."[23] To share in the sublimest form of happiness necessitates a life that completely exploits even the hidden regions of the soul, developing fully even the smallest talent in order to reap the pleasures known only to the human intellect. "Happiness extends, then, just so far as contemplation does, and those to whom contemplation more fully belongs are more truly happy, not as a mere concomitant but in virtue of the contemplation; for this is in itself precious. Happiness, therefore, must be some form of contemplation."[24]

To recapitulate: "The happy life is one lived according

to reason. Anyone can live, only few can live well. For man, therefore, the life according to reason is best and pleasantest, since reason more than anything else *is* man. This life therefore is also the happiest."[25] Thus, the good life is not readily accessible to everyone alike; it is reserved only for the disciples of reason who compose the community of the blessed: "Now he who exercises his reason and cultivates it seems to be both in the best state of mind and most dear to the gods."[26] Who best answers this description and requirement? "That all these attributes belong most of all to the philosopher is manifest. He, therefore, is the dearest to the gods. And he who is that will presumably be also the happiest; so that in this way too the philosopher will more than any other be happy."[27]

7. Moderation in All Things

Two fundamental principles underlying all of Aristotle's philosophy are: (1) *In all things, moderation,* (2) *Nature does nothing in vain.*[28] The second principle signifies that every created object, human and otherwise, has been fashioned for a purpose; the whole universe and its inhabitants are teleologically orientated and until or unless this purpose is satisfactorily fulfilled, frustration is inevitable.

"In all things moderation" defines right action to be the middle course: the *via media*; this mean has since been coined the *aurea mediocritas* (golden mean). Evil lurks in extremes: "excess and defect are characteristic of vice, and the mean of virtue."[29] Virtue is located as a mean between two extremes: the vice of deficiency found on the one side, and the vice of excess on the other; but in between *est modus in rebus.*[30] "Virtue, then, is a state of character concerned with choice, lying in a mean . . . It is a mean between two vices, that which depends on excess and that which depends on defect; and again it is a mean because the vices respectively fall short of or exceed what is right in both actions and passions, while virtue both finds and chooses that which is intermediate."[31]

8. A Schematic Representation of the Mean

                      MEAN
                      Right Act
                      Habitually practiced becomes virtue
                      Virtuous actions
                      E.g., courage

EXTREME OF DEFICIENCY   EXTREME OF EXCESS
Immoral act   Immoral act
Habitually practiced becomes vice   Habitually practiced becomes vice
Vicious actions   Vicious actions
E.g., cowardice   *E.g.*, foolhardiness

Note from the above diagram, that the mean because it lies mid-way between the two extremes, is closer to either vice than the vices are to each other and that "the middle states are excessive relatively to the deficiencies, deficient relatively to the excesses, both in passions and in actions."[32] The British, who are fairly well entrenched in Aristotelian philosophy, often express moral censure by saying that "one has gone to excess" in lieu of other expressions of condemnation.

Aristotle, realistically recognizing the impossibility of infallible obedience to the mean, offers the suggestion that when facing perplexing situations, one should lean to the extreme that is in greater compatibility with the mean; the reason is that one "of the extremes . . . is more erroneous, one less; therefore, since to hit the mean is hard in the extreme, we must hit second best, as people say, take the least of evils."[33] Thus, an intimation of pragmatism looms up in Aristotle's philosophy; nevertheless, the middle course is deemed preferable.[34]

9. A List of Aristotelian Virtues and Vices

VICE OF DEFICIENCY	VIRTUE OF MEAN	VICE OF EXCESS
1. Cowardice	Courage	Foolhardiness
2. Insensibility	Temperance	Licentiouness
3. Illiberality	Liberality	Prodigality
4. Meanness	Magnificence	Vulgarity
5. Humility	Magnanimity	Vanity
6. Lack of Ambition	Unnamed	Ambitiousness

7. Unirascibility	Gentleness	Irascibility
8. Self-depreciation	Truthfulness	Boastfulness
9. Mock-modesty, irony or boorishness	Wittiness	Buffoonery
10. Contentiousness	Friendliness	Obsequiousness (when no ulterior motive, otherwise) Flattery
11. Shamelessness	Modesty	Bashfulness
12. Maliciousness	Righteous Indignation	Envy

10. The Right Act

Since men of principle live by rules and their ethics constitute their code of moral principles, it follows that they would supply a criterion of morality, *i. e.*, a rule for discriminating between a right and wrong action. They must provide an answer to the question: How can one determine whether or not the act he is about to commit is moral? Kant responds with the classical *categorical imperative;* Bentham offers his ingenious *hedonistic calculus;* and Aristotle's guide is the *golden mean*: "moral virtue is a mean . . . a mean between two vices, the one involving excess, the other deficiency."[35] It is an easy matter to say that the right act is the mean or the middle road, but how is one to pin point exactly the golden mean? Aristotle, sensitive to this problem, expounds: "For in everything it is no easy task to find the middle, *e.g.*, to find the middle of a circle is not for every one but for him who knows,"[36] so, too, the ignorant person is incapable of reaching the summit of the virtuous life, that is reserved for the man of knowledge and wisdom. The intellectually inferior, the unlearned and the vicious are incapable of making accurate moral judgments and readily confuse the mean with the extreme, "For the brave man appears rash relatively to the coward, and cowardly relatively to the rash man."[37]

A simple moral exercise, *e.g.*, a monetary donation properly contributed to charity, is not within the province of every individual. Its correct performance, virtuously executed, is not merely to "give or spend money; but to do this to the right person, to the right extent, at the right time, with the right motive, and in the right way, *that* is not for everyone, nor is it easy; wherefore goodness is both rare and laudable and noble.'"[38]

The constituent features of moral behavior are easily perceptible in the following recapitulatory definition: *the right act is to do the right thing to the right person, to the right extent, at the right time, with the right motive, and in the right way*.[39] Note that the mere discharge or performance of an act in some cursory fashion does not render the act moral; equally vital is the consideration of *when, why, how, to whom, and how much*: An ill-timed statement is tantamount to a deception; an ill-prompted impulse perniciously affects a moral act; the manner in which assistance is offered, *e. g.*, the absence of alacrity, can destroy the virtue of the deed; an insufficient gift may prove harmful. Consequently, ethical superiority and moral excellence necessitate innate discernment and learning of the highest magnitude. To dispute Aristotle's formidable position would inevitably result in inviting difficulty which few persons can afford to do.

11. Virtue

The execution of a right act is an accomplishment in itself; unfortunately, it does not constitute virtue. An isolated moderate act is unquestionably a moral one, but for the individual who would soar to the lofty heights of virtue, a solitary right act will not suffice unless rooted in the depths of one's being and prompted *ex animo*. The performance of a right act divorced from an internal propensity is a mere formal exercise which will not serve in the cultivation of virtue since virtue is a *state* of character. The regular practice of moderate acts can be instrumental in acquiring habits of moral worth which are capable of changing the individual internally to the point of augmenting his spiritual disposition, thus enabling him to respond to acts of moderation naturally, *i. e.*, effortlessly. An adequate definition of virtue includes more than mere moderation; it connotes *habitual moderation*; "moral virtue comes about as a result of habit.'"[40] Aristotle voices an optimistic note sufficiently encouraging to enlist one's efforts in the task of cultivating virtuous habits, *i. e.*, it is considerably less strenuous to generate noble habits than it is to breed villainous ones, remarkably enough, for the reason that virtue is in cohesive harmony with human nature, whereas vice is discordant with it. It is natural to be virtuous and "nothing that exists by nature can form a habit contrary to its nature... For instance the stone which by nature moves downwards cannot be habituated to move upwards, not even if one tries to train it by throwing it up ten thousand times; nor can fire be habituated to move downwards."[41] The celerity of moral growth is augmented by being carried in the currents of nature. Fortunately, when habits of moderation have been seasonably bred, their concomitant by-product is happiness; consequently, "with those who identify happiness with virtue or some one virtue our account is in harmony."[42]

The two fundamental kinds of virtue are: *intellectual* and *moral*; intellectual virtues are transferrable via the medium of instruction; whereas, the formation of moral virtue accompanies habit. "Moral virtue comes about as a result of habit, whence also its name *ethike* (ethic) is one that is formed by a slight variation from the word *ethos* (habit)."[43]

Morality cannot be predicated of an individual at birth; he possesses merely the potentiality of being moral. Constant activity in the practice of moderation is rewarded by moral virtue; even with reference to the moral life, the old adage "practice makes perfect" holds true.[44] "Virtues we get first by exercising them ... *e.g.*, men become just by doing just acts, temperate by doing temperate acts, brave by doing brave acts."[45] Aristotle constantly reminds one that the virtuous and natural road is a mean, but that vices can develop if allowed to crystallize as a result of constant repetition. Therefore, one must be regularly on his guard to recoil from any coercive tendency that forces him to an extreme course; moderate living is best suitable for man; Aristotle accentuates this point well:

> It is the nature of ... things to be destroyed by defect and excess, as we see in the case of strength and health ... both excessive and defective exercise destroys the strength, and si-

milarly drink or food which is above or below a certain amount destroys the health, while that which is proportionate both produces and increases and preserves it. So too is it, then, in the case of temperance and courage and the other virtues. For the man who flies from and fears everything and does not stand his ground against anything is a coward, and the man who fears nothing at all but goes to meet every danger becomes rash; and similarly the man who indulges in every pleasure and abstains from none becomes self-indulgent, while the man who shuns every pleasure, as boors do, becomes in a way insensible; temperance and courage, then, are destroyed by excess and defect, and preserved by the mean.[46]

12. The Relation of the Soul to Virtue

The importance of the nature of virtue is sufficiently compelling to enlist Aristotle's efforts in conducting a thorough analysis of virtue and defining its precise relationship to the soul. The investigation which is divisible in two parts includes the prolegomenon which led to the inference that the human soul consists of three major qualities: (1) *passions*, (2) *faculties*, (3) *states of character*; and that virtue is necessarily associated with one of these. A definitive finding resulted in the identification of virtue with states of character. *Passion* is used in a broader sense than its familiar use in common parlance; it encompasses the gamut of pathetic feelings, appetites, as well as character traits, *e.g.*, confidence. Faculties include much of the subject matter treated in contemporary psychology, *in re* sensation and perception. States of character constitute material familiar to the ethicist: "By passions I mean appetite, anger, fear, confidence, envy, joy, friendly feeling, hatred, longing, emulation, pity, and in general the feelings that are accompanied by pleasure or pain; by faculties the things in virtue of which we are said to be capable of feeling these, *e.g.*, of becoming angry or being pained or feeling pity; by states of character the things in virtue of which we stand well or badly with reference to the passions."[47]

Aristotle's conclusion has the essence of virtue weighted in favor of states of character over passions because he is convinced that the stability of emotions is a legacy from birth, whereas, the mutability of states of character is at the disposition of the individual. Consequently, one is absolved from all moral responsibility for the governance of his passions; furthermore, passions, provided they have not been perverted, are not to be implicated with vice. Passion, *per se*, lacks moral significance; however, its misuse has moral import, *e.g.*, sex, *per se*, is morally neutral, its vitiated practice is censurable. "We feel anger and fear without choice, but the virtues are modes of choice. Further, in respect of the passions we are said to be moved, but in respect of the virtues and the vices we are said not to be moved but to be disposed in a particular way."[48] Mental or psychological dispositions are of moral consequence since they lie within the province of choice, but emotional responsibility is restricted to its perverse expression. The limitations of moral liability extend no further than the degree to which emotions can be manipulated: "virtue is concerned with passions and actions, and on voluntary passions and actions praise and blame are bestowed."[49]

Inasmuch as virtues are not innate, they cannot be faculties of the soul; moreover, a further inference from the preceding discussion is that passions must also be eliminated: "If, then, the virtues are neither passions nor faculties, all that remains is that they should be states of character."[50] The moral life has its inception subsequent to birth and its development into a state of character is a responsibility which the individual cannot escape.

13. Freedom of the Will

Among Aristotle's firm convictions is the belief in freedom of the will; this is not to be construed as signifying that one has omnipotent powers in the sense that every phase of his nature is subject to his command through sheer volition, *e.g.*, the ability to transgress natural law by flying unaided through the air at will. This is an abuse of the concept of free will. The intended meaning of the term is that in certain instances man does have a choice; he is not completely disenfranchised: "Man acts voluntarily; for the principle that moves the instrumental parts of the body in such actions is in him, and the things of which the moving principle is in a man himself are in his power to do or not to do. Such actions, therefore, are voluntary."[51] Aristotle is adamant in drawing a sharp distinction between *volition* and *choice,* and disavows their reciprocal use. Those instances in which a man has choice, he acts voluntarily, but the inverse is not true because choice is not equivalent to volition. All choices are voluntary, but not all voluntary actions are choices: "acts done on the spur of the moment we describe as voluntary, but not as chosen."[52] Choice implies rational deliberation, a quality peculiar to the human, but totally absent on the subhuman level. Animals exhibit a semi-voluntary ability, but want choice: "choice is not common to irrational creatures . . . but appetite and anger are. Again, the incontinent man on the *contrary* acts with choice, but not with appetite,"[53] *e.g.*, the obese man, fully cognizant of his excessive indulgence of appetite, has *voluntarily* exceeded appropriate bounds of self-gratification, and his servile compulsion to appetite is tantamount to a deprivation of choice. The tiger that seeks, kills and devours its prey is, in a sense, mentally conscious of his actions, but nevertheless, void of choice; "choice seems to relate to things that are in our power.[54] Choice involves a rational principle and thought."[55]

Choice and *wish,* as well as *choice* and *deliberation* must be differentiated: a wish is essentially telic; it implies a goal or desire, whether or not within reach, *e.g.*, one may wish for immortality in spite of the fact of his impotence in effecting its realization. Deliberation implies the possession of the requisite cognitive faculty to attain one's goal: "the end, then, being what we wish for, the means what we deliberate about and choose, actions concerning means must be according to choice and voluntary."[56]

Aristotle's fascination for the discriminate use of terms is captivating; note his treatment of *voluntary, nonvoluntary* and *involuntary*. When one acts voluntarily, he is the sole agent of a conscious act; when rational discrimination is added, volition is transmuted to choice. Nonvoluntary actions are divested of volition, *i.e.*, they fall outside the realm of will, *e.g.*, the swaying of a tree with the breeze is a deterministic act; a second example is that of a man who is completely ignorant of the fact that he has perjured himself. *Involuntary* signifies a transgression of one's own will, connoting disapprobation of one's personal behavior: *e.g.*, "if a tyrant were to order one to do something base, having one's children or parents in his power, and if one did the action they were to be saved, but otherwise would be put to death,"[57] illustrates involuntary behavior provided it were cowardly not to do so, otherwise, it is an example of voluntary. Nonvoluntary acts are not cause for embarrassment or remorse since the actions are innocently committed out of ignorance. Compunction being present in involuntary behavior, remorse, contrition, or guilt is experienced. Involuntary actions are prompted from external forces extraneous to the will; "actions are so when the cause is in the external circumstances and the agent contributes nothing. . . . Those who act under compulsion and unwillingly act with pain. . . . Everything that is done by reason of ignorance is *not* voluntary, it is only what produces pain and repentance that is *in*voluntary."[58] Aristotle's intrigue for subtle distinction in terms continues: to act *from* ignorance is not equivalent to acting *in* ignorance: *e.g.*, the inebriated person does not act from ignorance, but in ignorance as a result of his intoxication, "for the man who is drunk or in a rage is thought to act as a result not of ignorance . . . but in ignorance."[59] An act committed from ignorance discloses an uninformed or ill-informed state, viz., one bereft of knowledge; an act contrived in ignorance denotes one who is well informed or enlightened, yet his antithetical behavior contradicts his moral principles, *e.g.*, "the person who should know better" is acting in ignorance together with the individual who persists in odious behavior in spite of his better judgment. The following illustrates both terms: A proprietor discovering a sum of money stolen from the safe, mistakenly fires an innocent, but suspected, employee; such action proceeds out of or *from* ignorance; however, should the employer, on discovering the money stolen, lose his temper and in a fit of fury fire a man he knows to be unquestionably innocent then such action is grounded in ignorance.

Aristotle, reminiscent of the Socratic equation: *knowledge is virtue,* substantiates it by assigning a sizable portion of reprehensible behavior to ignorance; ignorance is often the cause of injustice and a multitude of other sins. "Every wicked man is ignorant of what he ought to abstain from and it is by reason of error of this kind that men become unjust and in general bad."[60] Misunderstanding, rather than ill intent, is often the source of harm.

14. Analysis of the Cardinal Virtues

Somewhat similar to the recurrence of a theme in a symphony is an underlying Aristotelian dictum: *natura non frustrata* (nature does nothing in vain). This hypothesis: everything in nature has a purpose is deeply imbedded as an indispensably integral part of his entire system. Since this is a focal point in Aristotle's philosophy, it is imperative to be constantly cognizant of it in order to gain a proper orientation and coherent understanding of the thought of this philosopher. One connotation of this postulate involves the necessity of defining the precise purpose of an object, human or otherwise, before one is in a position to derive a definitive explanation. At least, by locating the purpose one is better situated to offer an adequate and accurate explanation.

Man's essential function is the actualization of his potentialities, *i.e.,* an exhaustive realization of oneself; and from this premise, the inference drawn is that man ought to accept this as a moral obligation. The complete realization of man must be subject to the intellect, inasmuch as, the ideal moral life is one that is well ordered. Virtues are within man's power to cultivate and in the well ordered life they are noticeably prevalent.[61] The following treatment of the particular

Aristotelian virtues includes Aristotle's version of the Platonic four, viz., temperance, courage, wisdom, justice.

a) COURAGE

Throughout the following discussion, one must be mindful of the fact that virtues are mean or middle states existing between two extreme conditions which are defined as vices: one deficient and the other excessive. Courage occupies a median state in respect to the sentiments of fear and confidence, but proof of its virtuous goodness is contingent upon the purpose it serves; "each thing being defined by its end. Therefore it is for a noble end that the brave man endures and acts as courage directs."[62]

An insensitivity to a fearful situation is not a proper concept of courage since it exceeds its limitations and encroaches the bounds of foolhardiness. To designate as courage, fearlessness in the face of portentous situations is a misnomer as is intimidation when fortitude is warranted; "nor is a man a coward if he fears insult to his wife and children . . . nor brave if he is confident when he is about to be flogged."[63] In a well ordered life a man lives a life under the direction of reason, *i.e.*, "the man, then, who faces and who fears the right things and from the right motive, in the right way and at the right time, and who feels confidence under the corresponding conditions, is brave."[64] The often erroneous interpretation of passion as courage, *e.g.*, a man in a fit of anger plunging head-long into a hazardous situation is not to be construed as bravery; "lust also makes adulterers do many daring things."[65] At times, ignorance has been misinterpreted as courage, *e.g.*, persons unaware of impending danger manifest actions that are confused with daring; actions committed under the influence of alcohol can be misunderstood as daring. It is necessary to draw a sharp distinction between those who are in fact courageous and those whose actions merely resemble fortitude; the quintessence of valor is exemplified in the person who exhibits courage in the face of death, fully aware of its ominous perils. The courageous man's disposition compels him to do what is noble in spite of the fact that such a course of action is attended by sacrifice or pain because the heroic soul is inspired by a majestic love of nobleness or a fear of disgrace.

b) TEMPERANCE

Since *temperance* is a virtue, then it necessarily follows, in order to cohere with the rationale of this philosophical system, that it is a medium of two extreme states; the middle position that temperance occupies is one pertaining to pleasure, viz., physical and sensual pleasure. Aristotle cautions against fusing the meaning of the terms *sensual* and *sensuous*: the former, which is the excessive state of temperance, pertains to sensual pleasures, but not sensuous ones; the sensual are voluptuous, *i.e.*, appetitive gratification, whereas, the sensuous pertain to the activity of the specific senses, *e.g.*, beautiful sounds, such as music, and delightful objects of vision, such as scenery and paintings. The sensual pleasures do not command the dignity of the sensuous, on the contrary, their baseness is indicated in that they are shared in common with the animal. The excessively self-indulgent man is a victim of licentiousness whose ravenous appetite and temptations prove unconquerable obstacles; such a person regularly succumbs or suffers acute pain whenever compelled to forego the satisfaction of his pleasures. Reasonableness should serve as the proper guide in selecting those pleasures that are appropriate and wholesome. "As the child should live according to the direction of his tutor, so the appetitive element should live according to rational principle. Hence the appetitive element in a temperate man should harmonize with the rational principle; for the noble is the mark at which both aim, and the temperate man craves for the things he ought, as he ought, and when he ought; and this is what rational principle directs."[66] To exist is a relatively simple matter; the task required of man is to live well.

c) LIBERALITY

The mean or virtuous state in reference to an individual's monetary condition or property is *liberality;* its accompanying extremes are: miserliness or stinginess on the side of deficiency; and flanking it on the extreme of excess is prodigality. The spendthrift is the prodigal and the skinflint is his complement in the opposite direction. Liberality and its opposed vices are easily perceptible in charitable participation, viz., almsgiving: "the liberal man, like other men, will give for the sake of the noble, and rightly; for he will give to the right people the right amounts, and at the right time, with all the other qualifications that accompany right giving; and that too with pleasure and without pain."[67] The prodigal gives his money or property away irrationally while the niggardly person is selfishly grasping with little or no regard for others; his life is enriched at another's expense by stooping to manipulations, exploitations and devious tactics; such a person and others like him "exceed in respect of taking by taking anything and from any source, *e.g.*, those who ply sordid trades, pimps and all such people, and those who lend small sums and at high rates."[68] These persons have an avaricious love of gain and obtain their possessions by descending to base and ignoble tactics.

d) MAGNIFICENCE

The virtue *magnificence* is bounded by meanness and vulgarity as its opposed vices. Liberality is subalternately related to magnificence. Magnificence is the prerogative of the privileged wealthy for they alone have the necessary means by which to exercise the virtue; such individuals can always be liberal, if they so choose, but the liberal man hampered by financial limitations is disqualified from performing the role. Magnificence entails lavish expenditures in princely fashion, thus eliminating the liberal man of limited means.

Large scale expenditures on the part of the excessively rich are not necessarily indicative of magnificence; the practice can degenerate into vulgarity which is the pitfall of the indvidual who overshoots his mark to the point of ostentation, *e.g.*, in the presentation of inappropriate gifts. On the other hand, men of wealth whose efforts prove deficient deteriorate to a meanness or miserliness that springs from petty economy.

The liberal man restricts his expenditures to what is absolutely necessary, but the magnificent man, moved by a magnanimous spirit, spends bountifully, "and the magnificent man will spend such sums for honour's sake; for this is common to the virtues. And further he will do so gladly and lavishly; for nice calculation is a niggardly thing."[69] The magnificent man, being selfless and altruistically motivated, spends munificently for the common good; while the vulgar, lacking *savoir faire* and the cheap, who gives stintingly, present a marked contrast to him. Aristotle depicts each:

> The man who goes to excess and is vulgar exceeds ... by spending beyond what is right. For on small objects of expenditure he spends much and displays a tasteless showiness; *e.g.*, he gives a club dinner on the scale of a wedding banquet, and when he provides the chorus for a comedy he brings them on the stage in purple. ... And all such things will he do not for honour's sake but to show off his wealth, and because he thinks he is admired for these things, and where he ought to spend much he spends little, and where little, much. The niggardly man on the other hand will fall short in everything, and after spending the greatest sums will spoil the beauty of the result for a trifle, and whatever he is doing he will hesitate and consider how he may spend least, and lament even that, and think he is doing everything on a bigger scale than he ought.[70]

e) MAGNANIMITY

Magnanimity holds an exalted position by being designated the crown of the virtues. Literally, the original Greek term used by Aristotle is *megalopsuchia* (great-souledness); the analysis of which is *mega* (large or great) and *psuchia* (soul or mind), hence great-souledness, big-heartedness, or still better, a magnanimous spirit. W. D. Ross in his translation of the *Nicomachean Ethics* renders it pride, but in his magnificent work *Aristotle,* he interprets it as *self-respect* or a proper sense of pride.

Listed below are the many laudable characteristics of the magnanimous individual:

1. He is a good man blessed with "nobility and goodness of character."
2. He possesses the "crown of virtues" which excells them all.
3. The magnanimous man treats no one wrongfully.
4. The kindnesses received from others are enjoyed, but repaid with interest for the magnanimous man "returns more than he receives in benefits."
5. There is no shrinking from great dangers since "there are conditions on which life is not worth having."
6. This type of person is self-reliant and independent; because he is capable of standing on his own two feet, of others he asks for nothing.
7. The magnanimous individual is capable of maintaining his dignity with persons of the highest rank, but with social inferiors, he is unassuming.
8. His mental tranquility is relatively unaffected by life's provocative vicissitudes, either joyous or tragic.
9. He will stand his ground and speak for what is right; his disdain for and refusal to be a party to *sub rosa* dealings is a badge of his nobility.
10. He projects his self-respect to others, holding them with equal esteem.
11. This virtue behooves one to bear no grudges and to forget the wrongs suffered.
12. He is above being affected by both praise and criticism because in his eyes nothing is spectacular; he is completely emancipated from self-conceit or narcissism, consequently is not victimized by flattery.
13. His disposition is such that he prefers spiritual values to utilitarian profit.
14. His unhurried gate is an indication of self-confidence, but above all, for being virtuous he has captured the coveted prize of honor.

The magnanimous man is one of high self-respect; he is a person who is sufficient unto himself, for he possesses what Aristotle describes as "honor on a grand scale." The relative vices of magnanimity are *vanity* and *humility*; humility is a free rendition of the Greek, *mikropsuchia* (small-souledness). Neither extreme is recognized as malicious, consequently, they are not particularly heinous. The person who succumbs to the vice of defect is unduly humble and retiring, comparable to what the contemporary psychologist designates as an inferiority complex, *i.e.*, one who is plagued with severe bashfulness or shyness or other traits that imprison him within a retiring personality.

"Vain people, on the other hand, are fools and ignorant of themselves, and that manifestly; for, not being worthy of them, they attempt honourable undertakings, and then are found out; and they adorn themselves with clothing and outward show and such things, and wish their strokes of good fortune to be made public, and speak about them as if they would be honoured for them."[71] Vanity displays itself through ostentation, consequently, one succeeds only in making a dishonorable spectacle of himself; such persons are deficient in sincerity. As a result of their pompous attitudes, they flaunt their meager successes before those less fortunate.

f) UNNAMED MEAN OF AMBITION

Ambition is a neutral concept which is regarded at times as a vice and at other times as a virtue; this inherent ambivalent factor creates a condition in which ambition oscillates from the median to excess. The bi-polar nature of this virtue, *i.e.*, its vacillations to and fro, is responsible for the intermittent disappearance of the mean of ambition and "the extremes seem to dispute for its place as though that were vacant by default." Sometimes the ambitious man is praised for this characteristic trait and other times he suffers censorship; the same maintains in the case of deficiency, at times it is viewed with disdain and at other times esteemed as noble.

g) GENTLENESS

Gentleness, which denotes good temper, is a mean in respect to anger. Its concomitant vices are: irascibility, *i.e.*, a proneness to anger, and a "sort of inirascibility," as Aristotle put it after being thrown into a quandary and at a loss for a better term. Such an individual is phlegmatically disposed and his opposing counterpart is defined as choleric.

The gentle good tempered man, as prescribed by the Aristotelian formula for moderation, becomes angry at the right things, to the right extent, at the right time, in the right manner, etc., such as becoming indignant at unjust social conditions, viz., racial prejudice and religious bigotry. Moreover, "the good tempered man is not revengeful, but rather tends to make allowances."[72] The individual, who is deficient in the virtue, will not defend himself, his ideals, nor will he fight for noble causes, on the contrary, he will endure insult because he is a truckling character. In marked contrast to this, is the person at the opposite end of the pole, viz., the irascible fellow characterized by: sulkiness, wronging the innocent, a hot temperament, implacability, sternness, sullenness, unrestrainedness, revengefulness, unfair retaliatory methods. "By reason of excess *choleric* people are quick-tempered and ready to be angry with everything and on every occasion; whence their name. Sulky people are hard to appease, and retain their anger long; for they repress their passion. But it ceases when they retaliate; for revenge relieves them of their anger. . . . We call *bad tempered* those that are angry at the wrong things, more than is right, and longer, and cannot be appeased until they inflict vengeance or punishment;"[73] the excess is the more baneful of the two extremes.

h) FRIENDLINESS

Aristotle's research in the direction of ascertaining a name for the median state lying between the person who is *compliant* and the one who is *contentious* proved futile. *Friendliness* seems to approximate it best, "for the man who corresponds to this middle state is very much what, with affection added, we call a good friend.'"[74] On the deficient side, the vice is obsequiousness, *i.e.*, "yes men," "viz., those who to give pleasure praise everything and never oppose, but think it their duty 'to give no pain to people they meet';"[75] such persons are motivated by expediency and readily acquiesce to the will of others. Obsequiousness and flattery are not identical qualities for "the man who aims at being pleasant with no ulterior object is obsequious, but the man who does so in order that he may get some advantage in the direction of money or the things that money buys is a flatterer.'"[76]

The extreme contradiction of obsequiousness is churlishness or contentiousness, viz., the reactionary who opposes everything, is quarrelsome and insensitive to another's hurt. "The states we have named are culpable and plain enough, and that the middle state is laudable — that in virtue of which a man will put up with, and will resent, the right things and in the right way; but no name has been assigned to it, though it most resembles friendship.'"[77]

Significantly, two of the ten books comprising the *Nicomachean Ethics* are devoted to friendship. To be friends, persons "must be mutually recognized as bearing goodwill and wishing well to each other.'"[78] Qualities indicative of friendship are: similar tastes, reciprocity *in re* emotions, mutual concern for each other's well being, promoting each other's good. Goodwill is a friendly quality, but differs in that "it does not involve intensity or desire, whereas these accompany *friendly feeling;* and friendly feeling implies intimacy.'"[79] Goodwill is only a superficial love because it is capable of being summoned instantly without prior preparation, *i.e.*, one may exhibit goodwill even towards strangers.

Three types of friendship are distinguishable: *utility, pleasure, good* or *perfect*. Friends of the first category lack intrinsic value; their worth consists in the utilitarian or exploitative value that either one provides for the other or both provide reciprocally, *e.g.*, business friends and associates. Friendships of pleasure exist when one or both parties narcissistically derive pleasure through the instrument of the other; such friendships are deeper in intensity and intimacy than the utilitarian mode, *e.g.*, a couple romantically in love. Both forms are hedonistic and egoistic and survive for expediential reasons; friendship, *per se*, is only incidental, "it is not as being the man he is that the loved person is loved, but as providing some good or pleasure."[80] The tenuous and volatile basis on which such friendships are founded is usually the cause of their brevity and the legerity of their dissolution.

"Perfect friendship is the friendship of men who are good, and alike in virtue;"[81] its dominant features are altruism and the intrinsic value of the friend *suo jure;* utility is an ancillary consideration, while enhancement of the friend's cause is paramount. The rarity of perfect friendships is attributable to the paucity of the type necessary to engender such; furthermore, considerable time is required for seasoning and breeding love and trust. A wish for friendship may arise impetuously, but perfect friendship must undergo a mellowing process. Only the good man has the necessary qualifications for a perfect friendship; evil men are limited to friendships of utility or pleasure; "bad men do not delight in each other unless some advantage come of the relation."[82] Good friendship is categorically grounded; while other forms rest on a conditional basis, *i.e.*, friendship is only incidental, opportunism is the important factor.

The majority of persons, being self-seeking and selfish, enjoy having a friend in preference to being one for this entails responsibilities and obligations. Flattery is not indicative of genuine friendship "for the flatterer is a friend in an inferior position, or pretends to be such and to love more than he is loved; and being loved seems to be akin to being honoured."[83] Friendship for utility's sake is compensatory in nature and transpires between opposites, *e.g.*, rich and poor (the wealthy need servants and the poor need employment), uneducated and learned, etc. Although friendship does not occupy a position of pre-eminence in the Aristotelian system, it is recognized as one of life's cardinal values "for without friends no one would choose to live, though he had all other goods; even rich men and those in possession of office and of dominating power ... for what is the use of such prosperity without the opportunity of beneficence, which is exercised chiefly and in its most laudable form towards friends.'"[84]

i) TRUTHFULNESS

Truthfulness is the mean state existing between boastfulness and self-depreciation or irony. The boastful man is disposed to making pseudo-claims for his own glorification, hence is given to exaggerations; his contemptibility eventuates in futility rather than evil. His deficient correlate is the mock-modest individual who disclaims his accomplishments, belittles them, dislikes publicity and is given habitually to making understatements which serve to avoid calling attention to himself. In marked contrast to boastful persons, "mock-modest people, who understate things, seem more attractive in character; for they are thought to speak not for gain but to avoid parade. . . . But those who use understatement with moderation and understate about matters that do not very much force themselves on our notice seem attractive."[85]

The virtuous state, viz., truthfulness, is exemplified in the manner in which a person behaves as well as what he utters; the truthful man is equitable, free from ulterior motives and maintains his veracity even when he has nothing to lose, therefore, *a fortiori*, he would be even more so if there were something valuable at stake.

j) WITTINESS

Remarkably, there is a virtue pertaining to relaxation and amusement, viz., wittiness; its encompassing vices are boorishness *in re* deficiency, and buffoonery is its complement. Overdone humor degenerates into vulgarity, *e.g.*, the buffoon who sacrifices refinement in attempting to be humorous at all costs; due to his perverse sense of humor he goes to great length in order to induce laughter.

The boorish individual, unpolished, devoid of a wholesome sense of humor, is clumsy at telling jokes. Because of this inability plus the covetous desire to be witty, he is intolerant and envious of those who master the art. The boor, coarse and lacking in social graces, makes a worthless or feeble contribution to a conversation because of his censorious attitude: "the boor ... is useless for such social intercourse; for he contributes nothing and finds fault with everything."[186]

The virtuous man is blessed with a wholesome sense of humor, *i.e.*, a *bel esprit*; he is quick witted and his jokes are in good taste. He is tactful and is party only to such conversations that befit a man of breeding and refinement, hence, he has earned the status of being "as it were a law unto himself." "To the middle state also belongs tact; it is the mark of a tactful man to say and listen to such things as become a good and well-bred man; for there are some things that it befits such a man to say and to hear by way of jest, and the well-bred man's jesting differs from that of a vulgar man, and the joking of an educated man from that of uneducated."[187]

k) SHAME AND CONTINENCE

At this point in his treatise, Aristotle's attention is turned to the topics: shame and continence; the outcome of his deliberation is that they are not virtues, but feelings:

> Shame should not be described as a virtue; for it is more like a feeling than a state of character. It is defined, at any rate, as a kind of fear of dishonour, and produces an effect similar to that produced by fear of danger; for people who feel disgraced blush, and those who fear death turn pale. Both, therefore, seem to be characteristic of feeling rather than of a state of character.... Continence too is not virtue, but a mixed sort of state.[88]

The feeling of shame is becoming only to youth; a proneness to a sense of shame functions as an effective restraining harness in curbing nefariousness and delinquency.

1) JUSTICE

Justice, "that kind of state of character which makes people disposed to do what is just and makes them act justly and wish for what is just,"[189] consumes a major portion of the discussion allotted to the specific virtues. Justice, which can properly be said to be the aggregate of all the virtues, is essentially that which is lawful and fair: "Justice is the summary of all Virtue." The eulogy in praise of justice continues: "Justice is often thought to be the greatest of virtues, and 'neither evening nor morning star' is so wonderful."[190] This singular virtue will prove effective as an all-sufficient guide or rule for whatever intercourse one finds necessary to conduct with his neighbor.

Although, justice and virtue are alike, they are not *essentially* the same. Justice is a social ethic, consequently it has relevancy in relations pertaining to one's neighbor, it serves as a guide or rule. "The rule will show the man," *i.e.*, unveils the man, *e.g.*, the manner in which one treats his neighbor, not only reveals a man's rule of justice, but exposes his entire personality. Justice springs from virtue, with a majestic quality of sufficient magnitude and splendor to encompass the entire body of virtue.

Justice is a virtue reserved for the chosen few whose unrelenting and valorous spirit insures that ideals of justice will be upheld in all phases and levels of a complex social life regardless of how fraught with vicissitudes. The *hoi polloi* can conceivably negotiate a life of virtue with a fair degree of competence when confined to a solitary existence, but chances of success are minimal when encountering social situations.

Inevitably, justice will triumph; the culprit's position is precarious due to the fact that his noxious activities will boomerang, causing damage to himself; the nature of justice will insure this. Good cannot be predicated of the selfish person whose pseudo-virtuous deeds are intended to benefit himself primarily. The goodness that issues from one must not be to the exclusive benefit of its author, otherwise, it will give rise to the peculiar state of being *selfishly good*. Aristotle endorses the Platonic thesis that justice is " 'another's good:' The worst man is he who exercises his wickedness both towards himself and towards his friends, and the best man is *not* he who exercises his virtue towards himself but he who exercises it towards another: for this is a difficult task. Justice in this sense, then, is not part of virtue but virtue entire, nor is the contrary, injustice, a part of vice but vice entire."[91]

Aristotle recognizes two forms of justice: *fairness* and *lawfulness*; the former pertains to a fair sense of proportional quantities, viz., a principle which obligates one to restrict himself to no more than what is justly his fair share. Proceeding on the premise that laws are just, it necessarily follows that the criminal behavior of the outlaw is unjust. Legal justice assumes two subdivisions; (1) the equitable distribution of honor, wealth, and other goods among the citizens; (2) correction of inequities privily transpired, such as, theft, assault, murder, rape, and business transactions.

Justice as a median state is identical to fairness or equality; its extreme is an ambivalent unfairness which may take the form of either excess or deficiency. Fairness is a social ethic inasmuch as it necessitates a minimum of two persons to become activated, otherwise it remains dormant.

Retaliation must not be construed as justice; the *lex talionis* (law of retaliation), *e.g.*, an eye for an eye and a tooth for a tooth, is not uniformly fair because it neglects to take under advisement a person's circumstances, character and position, moreover, it fails to consider the part played by the will, viz., the motive or intent. "Men seek to return evil for evil — and if they cannot do so, think their position mere slavery — or good for good — and if they cannot do so there is no exchange. . . . Now 'reciprocity' fits neither distributive nor rectificatory justice.'"[92]

At this point in his discussions, Aristotle elucidates, in a most engaging manner, on the subtleties that lie hidden in the meaning of injustice. Injustice implies both *volition* and *deliberation*: "A man acts unjustly or justly whenever he does such acts voluntarily. . . . By the voluntary I mean . . . any of the things in a man's own power which he does with knowledge. . . . Of voluntary acts we do some by choice, others not by choice; by choice those which we do after deliberation, not by choice those which we do without previous deliberation. . . . A man *is just* when he acts justly by choice; but he *acts justly* if he merely acts voluntarily.''[93] A voluntary act is not necessarily elicited by choice; one may voluntarily perform an exercise not of his own choosing, *e. g.*, the victim of an armed bandit delivering his money voluntarily to his captor constitutes an act of volition, but not of choice, forasmuch as choice implies autonomy, thoughtful and deliberate action. To *act* unjustly does not imply *being* unjust, inasmuch as the possibility exists wherein one may commit an unjust act and yet be a just person, as indicated by acts of volition unaccompanied by choice:

> Since acting unjustly does not necessarily imply being unjust, we must ask what sort of unjust acts imply that the doer is unjust with respect to each type of injustice, *e. g.*, a thief, an adulterer, or a brigand. Surely the answer does not turn on the difference between these types. For a man might even lie with a woman knowing who she was, but the origin of his act might be not deliberate choice but passion. He acts unjustly, then, but is not unjust; *e. g.*, a man is not a thief, yet he stole, nor an adulterer, yet he committed adultery; and similarly in all other cases.[94]

The foregoing analysis bears a strong resemblance to the Kantian position, viz., actions rooted in emotion, sentiment, or any other force extraneous to the will, reduces them to a morally neutral state, viz., amoral. Inasmuch as man is subject to passions from which many unjust acts are educed, accordingly, one should not ''allow a *man* to rule, but *rational principle*, because a man behaves thus in his own interests and becomes a tyrant.''[95] Since justice is acquired or fully developed as a virtue when it has been thoroughly rooted deep within the personality, enabling just deeds to flow freely, painlessly, effortlessly and naturally from the individual, it would be presumptuous to conclude that the just and unjust persons are equally susceptible to deleterious behavior. "Men think that acting unjustly is characteristic of the just man no less than of the unjust ... for he could ... wound a neighbor; and the brave man could throw away his shield and turn to flight.... But to play the coward or to act unjustly consists not of doing these things, except incidentally, but in doing them as the result of a certain state of character.'"[196]

The perpetration of injustice or the suffering of its incommodious effects is to be eschewed, but of the two, the latter is preferable since the one who suffers injustice is not guilty of any vice.

Equity and *justice* are neither identical nor are they generically different terms; although both are laudable qualities, equity enjoys the position of eminence in that it functions in a justificatory capacity, *i.e.*, a correction of legal justice. Its pragmatic applicability is of value in certain anomalous cases that are not subject to adjudication according to existing principles or laws. Laws are universal generalizations, the validity of which does not extend to exceptional instances; in such extraordinary cases, one resorts to equity. "It is evident also from this who the equitable man is; the man who chooses and does such acts, and is no stickler for his rights in a bad sense but tends to take less than his share though he has the law on his side, is equitable, and this state of character is equity, which is a sort of justice and not a different state of character.'"[197]

15. The Intellectual Virtues

The intellectual virtues, unlike moral virtues, pertain to the rational aspect of the soul, which is dichotomously divided into rational and irrational. The rational in turn has two subdivisions: the scientific, which includes knowledge and invariable principles, and the ratiocinative, *i.e.*, the logical phase. The five states by virtue of which the soul or mind arrives at or possesses truth are: 1, art (technique), 2, scientific knowledge, 3, prudence (practical wisdom), 4, wisdom (philosophical sagacity), 5, intuitive reason. The soul or mind has three qualities which control action and obtain truth: (a) sensation, (b) reason, (c) desire or appetite. Man's sensuous nature plays no role in the moral life inasmuch as it is common to the animal kingdom, but desires are implicated because moral virtue is a state of character involving moral choice, *i. e.*, deliberative desire. The following outline serves to elucidate the foregoing:

I. Soul (mind)
   1. The irrational
   2. The rational
      a. Scientific
      b. Ratiocinative
   3. Possession of truth (cognitive processes)
      a. Art (technical ability)
      b. Scientific knowledge
      c. Prudence (practical wisdom)
      d. Philosophical wisdom
      e. Intuitive reason
   4. Faculties that determine action and truth
      a. Sensation
      b. Reason
      c. Desire or appetite

Philosophical wisdom is a combination of intuitive reason and scientific knowledge. Practical wisdom (applied logic) and philosophical wisdom are equally important and vital, but a position of relative priority is given to the practical. Political wisdom, like practical wisdom is concerned with morality and both stem from the same mental state, but differ in essence.

16. Moral Character

Three species of moral character ought to be shunned, viz., *vice, incontinence, brutality*; vice is opposed to virtue, incontinence to continence, but the opposite of brutality is detectable with less alacrity or clarity than the former two, however analysis reveals it to be a supernal virtue, *i.e.*, a heroic or divine nature. "With regard to the pleasures and pains and appetites and aversions arising through touch and taste . . . it is possible to be in such a state as to be defeated even by those of them which most people master, or to master even those by which most people are defeated; among these possibilities, those relating to pleasures are incontinence and continence, those relating to pains, softness and endurance. The state of most people is intermediate, even if they lean more towards the worse states."[98] The continent person lives a life of reason manipulated with extreme care, he inhibits the gratification of improper desires; all this in contrast to the incontinent individual who, failing to live by his convictions, sinks to the enslavement of emotion and the degradation of indiscretions. Apparently, he is aware of the deleterious effects of his nocuous behavior, but appears to stand by impotently. This is an evident repudiation of the Socratic thesis, viz., a man who knows what is right will automatically do it. There are two phases of incontinence, viz., impetuosity and weakness, the former indicates lack of emotional control and the latter stems from ignorance: "some men after deliberating fail, (owing to their emotion), to stand by the conclusions of their deliberation, others because they have not deliberated are led by their emotion."[99]

Incontinence does not imply vice "because incontinence is contrary to choice while vice is in accord with choice."[100] The self-indulgent man is implicated in vice inasmuch as he is confronted with the option to choose an alternative course, but the incontinent individual, a prostrate, helpless victim of compulsion, manifests contrition. The former is in an incurable state whereas the latter is remedial.

17. Slaves by Nature

One of the most bewildering and shocking aspects of the Aristotelian philosophy, particularly for one whose *Weltanschauung* is democratically orientated, is the thesis: *slavery is natural, hence morally right.* On the other hand, if slavery were contrary to nature then it would be a mere convenient convention, consequently, immoral.

Whatever nature decrees is moral; she ordained the male superior in stature and the female his ancillary; the same is applicable to slavery: "the male is by nature superior, and the female inferior; and the one rules, and the other is ruled; this principle, of necessity, extends to all mankind."[101] Some human beings are incapable of choice; they are happier when decisions are made for them. Although they understand reason, they do not possess it; "he who participates in rational principle enough to apprehend, but not to have, such a principle, is a slave by nature."[102] Natural slaves, out of role, are miserably discontented and frustrated individuals, *e. g.*, when forced to deliberate and make decisions. Their serenity is contingent upon their servile obedience. Slaves forced to participate in the rational life would find it a cruel hardship and a warping of their natures. Such persons are alien to the world of creative mental activity, *e. g.*, philosophy, science, politics, religion, etc.; thoughtful effort in these fields must be made on their behalf since they are perfectly content only when allowed to follow like sheep. "That some should rule and others be ruled is a thing not only necessary, but expedient; from the hour of birth, some are marked out for subjection, others for rule."[103]

Aristotle held that much of the slavery existing in his day was detestable because it was a distortion of nature; such persons are not natural slaves, but captives who have been taken in conquest. Nevertheless, the procurement of slaves through the instrument of war is justifiable. A slave, who has been so endued by nature, enjoys a pleasant relationship with his master for common interests are shared; the simile of the body and its members may be applied to the pair, *e. g.*, the slave is like an extra arm; "the slave is part of the master, a living but separated part of his bodily frame. Hence, where the relation of master and slave between them is natural they are friends and have a common interest."[104] The relationship between master and slave is not to be confused with that which maintains between ruler and his subjects for citizens are not without franchise since those in authority officiate subject to constitutional decree. The slave's status is not assigned by legislative decree only; his role is prescribed by nature; consequently, "there is in some cases a marked distinction between the two classes, rendering it expedient and right for the one to be slaves and the others to be masters; the one practising obedience, the others the authority and lordship which nature intended them to have. The abuse of this authority is injurious to both."[105]

18. Evaluation of the Aristotelian Ethic

This section's arrangement is divided pro and con, opening with the critically destructive comments for it seems more appropriate to end on a positive note.

There is a fair degree of probability that the most common criticism of the ethics of Aristotle is that which is termed the *hedonistic paradox, i. e.*, the quest of happiness culminates in an ironic paradox, viz., happiness will never be found if directly pursued. Peculiarly, happiness is a by-product and if sought directly proves elusive; this inherent fleeting quality of happiness is demonstrated by the fact that the universe contains no object which can be labelled happiness. It would prove absolutely futile and ludicrous to attempt to seize happiness by mechanically acting as if one were happy. No royal road to happiness exists as though it had an existence of its own *suo jure*. It issues as a concomitant, a reward as it were, *e. g.*, for a job well done, for an invention or discovery, for a noble deed, such as being fortunate enough to be the discoverer of the cure of cancer.

A second aspersion from which this ethic suffers at the hands of its critics is that of its being one of *propriety* rather than one of duty. F. H. Bradley referred to it as the ethics of doing the duties of your station; the right act for a nobleman is to give according to his rank and station; in short, it substitutes diplomacy for morality. Karl Marx would discredit the system as being the ethics of the bourgeoisie, *i. e.,* a code contrived to keep the masses in check; a code to inhibit revolt, viz., a police force.

A third criticism that is lodged is in reference to the requirement: "live according to nature." Proceeding on the basis of this premise it would follow that all impulses are of *equal* value; no single impulse has a moral priority, not to mention a moral monopoly over any other; yet certain impulses are recognized as noble and others as ignoble. John Stuart Mill objects: "That a feeling is bestowed on us by nature, does not necessarily legitimate all its promptings."[106]

The impossibility of realizing fully all of one's powers and developing them equally is a fourth objection.

The most serious stricture levied against this ethic concerns its most objectionable feature, viz., *slavery*; this incongruous note in Aristotelianism has been vehemently censured by subsequent philosophers such as Bentham: "Tyranny has taken advantage of its own wrong, alleging as a reason for the domination it exercises, an imbecility, which, as far as it has been real, has been produced by the abuse of that very power which it is brought to justify. Aristotle, fascinated by the prejudice of the times, divides mankind into two distinct species, that of freemen, and that of slaves. Certain men were born to be slaves, and ought to be slaves.—Why? Because they are so."[107]

Turning attention to the favorable aspects of this system, the following evaluation is ascertained: (1) The Aristotelian ethic is one that is easily grasped and mastered; therefore, it has the capability of winning a widespread following. (2) Aristotle's moral theory is readily practicable; it neither requires extensive nor intensive study, nor a mastery of any complex network of facts. (3) Danger of excessive deviation from the moral course is diminished by following a middle of the road philosophy, *e. g.*, when in doubt, the *aurea mediocritas* is the best policy. (4) The self-realization ethic is one that can be incorporated into an existing philosophy or religion since it readily lends itself to religious interpretation. Religiously, it is attractive and well suited in its adaptability to religious values, viz., God, soul, immortality, etc.; the facility of its assimilation into theology has been exemplarily demonstrated by St. Thomas Aquinas for the Christian world and by Averroes for the Arabian religious community.

19. Further Reading in Aristotle

For the student interested in venturing further into Aristotle's philosophy, the following of his works may be explored: *Organon* (logic), *Physica* (physics), *De Caelo* (on the heavens), *De Generatione et Corruptione* (on generation and corruption), *De Anima* (on the soul), *Parva Naturalia* (physical treatises), *Historia Animalium* (history of animals), *De Partibus Animalium* (on the parts of animals), *De Generatione Animalium* (on the generation of animals), *Metaphysic* (metaphysics), *Ethica Nicomachea* (ethics), *Politica* (politics), *Rhetorica* (rhetoric), *De Poetica* (poetics).

NOTES
ARISTOTLE

1. Werner Jaeger, *Aristotle*, tr. by Richard Robinson (Oxford: Clarendon Press, 1948, 2nd ed.), 230.
2. For a discussion of the matter, see *ibid.*, 228ff.
3. W. D. Ross, *Aristotle* (London: Methuen and Co., Ltd., 1937, 3rd ed.), 187.
4. Aristotle, *Politics*, 1261^a 31. See W. D. Ross, *op. cit.*, 187.
5. Aristotle, *Nicomachean Ethics*, tr. by W. D. Ross (Oxford: University Press, 1915), 1103^a 16-19.
6. *Ibid.*, 1098^b 21, 22.
7. Aristotle, *Politics*, 1325^b 9.
8. Aristotle, Nicomachean *Ethics*, 1098^a 7-18. In the field of psychology this is known as *functionalism*.
9. Classical philosophers, such as Kierkegaard and Marx, have made such references.
10. Aristotle, *Ibid.*, 1098^a 1-4.
11. *Ibid.*, 1099^a 24-25.
12. *Ibid.*, 1094^a 1-3.
13. *Ibid.*, *Politics*, 1256^b 20.
14. *Ibid.*, *Nicomachean Ethics*, 1096^a 5, 6.
15. *Ibid.*, 1094^a 18-20, 1097^b 1-6.
16. *Ibid.*, 1097^a 27-35.
17. *Facilis descensus Averno*, (descent to Avernus (hell) is easy, *i.e.*, the road to hell or evil is easy).
18. The hedonistic paradox is a common criticism launched against the Aristotelian ethic *in re* happiness.
19. *Ibid.*, 1095^b 19, 20.
20. *Ibid.*, 22, 23.
21. *Ibid.*, 1178^b 8.
22. *Ibid.*, 22, 23
23. *Ibid.*, 24.
24. *Ibid.*, 28-32.
25. *Ibid.*, 1178^a 6, 7.
26. *Ibid.*, 1178^b 23, 24.
27. *Ibid.*, 29-32.
28. *Ibid.*, *Politics*, 1253^a. (*Natura non frustrata*).

29. *Ibid., Nicomachean Ethics,* 1106^b 34.
30. There is a proper measure, *i.e.,* a golden mean.
31. Aristotle, *op. cit.,* 1107^a 1-5.
32. *Ibid.,* 1108^b 17.
33. *Ibid.,* 1109^a 31-35.
34. *Medio tutissimus ibus,* (in a middle course you will go most safely).
35. *Ibid.,* 1109^a 20-21.
36. *Ibid.,* 24, 25.
37. *Ibid.,* 1108^b 19, 20.
38. *Ibid.,* 1109^a 26-29.
39. It is interesting to compare these many features with the Kantian categorical imperative which is unconditional. Cf. Kant, section 5, the categorical imperative.
40. *Ibid.,* 1103^a 17.
41. *Ibid.,* 18-23.
42. *Ibid.,* 1098^b 30, 31.
43. Aristotle, *op. cit.,* 1103^a 16-18.
44. *Abuent studia in mores,* (practices zealously pursued become habits).
45. *Ibid.,* 1103^a 33-1103^b 2.
46. *Ibid.,* 1104^a 12-25.
47. *Ibid.,* 1105^b 21-25.
48. *Ibid.,* 1106^a 3-6.
49. *Ibid.,* 1109^b 30.
50. *Ibid.,* 1106^a 10.
51. *Ibid.,* 1110^a 15-17.
52. *Ibid.,* 1111^b 9.
53. *Ibid.,* 11-13.
54. *Ibid.,* 29.
55. *Ibid.,* 1112^a 16, 17.
56. *Ibid.,* 1113^b 3-5.
57. *Ibid.,* 1110^a 5-8.
58. *Ibid.,* 1110^b 2, 11, 17.
59. *Ibid.,* 25.
60. *Ibid.,* 27-29.
61. *Ibid.,* 1113^b 6.
62. *Ibid.,* 1115^b 23.
63. *Ibid.,* 1115^a 22-24.
64. *Ibid.,* 1115^b 18, 19.
65. *Ibid.,* 1117^a 1.
66. *Ibid.,* 1119^b 15-19.
67. *Ibid.,* 1120^a 24-26.
68. *Ibid.,* 1121^b 30-32.
69. *Ibid.,* 1122^b 6-8.
70. *Ibid.,* 1123^a 19-23.
71. *Ibid.,* 1125^a 28-33.
72. *Ibid.,* 1126^a 3.
73. *Ibid.,* 17-27.
74. *Ibid.,* 1126^b 20, 21.

75. *Ibid.*, 13-15.
76. *Ibid.*, 1127ᵃ 8-10.
77. *Ibid.*, 1126ᵇ 17-19.
78. *Ibid.*, 1156ᵃ 5.
79. *Ibid.*, 1166ᵇ 34.
80. *Ibid.*, 1156ᵃ 19.
81. *Ibid.*, 1156ᵇ 6.
82. *Ibid.*, 1157ᵃ 19.
83. *Ibid.*, 1159ᵃ 13, 14.
84. *Ibid.*, 1155ᵃ 5-9.
85. *Ibid.*, 1127ᵇ 23-25, 29-31.
86. *Ibid.*, 1128ᵇ 1, 2.
87. *Ibid.*, 1128ᵃ 18-22.
88. *Ibid.*, 1128ᵇ 10-14, 35.
89. *Ibid.*, 1129ᵃ 8, 9.
90. *Ibid.*, 1129ᵇ 26-30.
91. *Ibid.*, 1130ᵃ 6-10.
92. *Ibid.*, 1132ᵇ 24, 1133ᵃ 1, 2.
93. *Ibid.*, 1135ᵃ 15, 23, 1135ᵇ 9, 10, 1136ᵃ 4.
94. *Ibid.*, 1134ᵃ 16-22.
95. *Ibid.*, 35, 36.
96. *Ibid.*, 1137ᵃ 17-23.
97. *Ibid.*, 1137ᵇ 33 - 1138ᵃ 3.
98. *Ibid.*, 1150ᵃ 9-15.
99. *Ibid.*, 1150ᵇ 19-21.
100. *Ibid.*, 1151ᵃ 6.
101. *Politics, op. cit.*, 1254ᵇ 13-15.
102. *Ibid.*, 21.
103. *Ibid.*, 1254ᵃ 22, 23.
104. *Ibid.*, 1255ᵇ 11-13.
105. *Ibid.*, 7-9.
106. John Stuart Mill, *Utilitarianism* (London: Longmans, Green, and Co., 1907), 62.
107. Jeremy Bentham, *An Introduction to the Principles of Morals and Legislation* (New York: Hafner Publishing Co., 1948), 268.

ETHICAL INTUITIONISM

IMMANUEL KANT

*"With all his failings, man is still
Better than angels void of will."* (Haller)

1. The Intuition School of Ethics

Intuitionism is the term by which the Kantian system of ethics is identified, but the word as it is used in ethical theory should never be confused with the meaning it acquires in the common parlance of laymen *i.e.*, "hunch" or "womanly intuition." In the ethicist's universe of discourse it signifies that morality is intuitively apprehended, more specifically, it denotes that moral value is inner, within the personality exclusively, *not* in overt actions issuing in the form of human behavior. Overt actions lack moral content, they are foreign to what the Intuitionist recognizes as morality, since essential moral qualities are will, intent, motive, etc.

As far as consequences are concerned, the intuitionist takes the following stand: "Let the chips fall where they may," right is right and must be pursued without regard to consequences. It matters not whether consequences are favorable; duty's mandate is to will the right even though the heavens fall; *fiat justitia ruat callum.*[1] Moral obligation stems from an imperative which carries the weight of a command: "this imperative is CATEGORICAL. It has nothing to do with the matter of action or with that which results from it . . . and its essential good consists of the state of mind irrespective of what may result from it.'"[2]

For purposes of camparison, it would be well to consider the relative positions of two diametrically opposed schools of ethical thought, viz., *Intuitionism* and *Ideal Utilitarianism, i. e.*, the philosophy of one who believes that morality is essentially found in the consequences resulting from human choice. Good consequences imply a moral person, evil consequences, an immoral one. Not intentions, motive, will, but consequences serve to determine the moral status of an individual. It now becomes apparent that the intuitionist with his stress upon intention or will and the ideal utilitarian objecting to this stand with equal emphasis on his philosophy of consequences are in opposing camps, mutually contradictory. The Ideal Utilitarian's stand that a man's moral character must be judged in the light of the results that flow from his actions is counteracted by the Intuitionist's contention that a person's will is the sole significant moral factor. When a will is divorced from human action, moral activity ceases; external to will, morality terminates. Since will is a form of intention, the Ideal Utilitarian criticizes the intuitionist with the old adage: "hell is paved with good intentions," but the Intuitionist, ignoring this retort, insists that good intention or good will is the stairway that leads to heaven. The position of each school of thought is easily illustrated: For the Ideal Utilitarian, murder is immoral because of the baneful consequences of killing; for the Intuitionist, murder is immoral because it stems from an ill will.

The foregoing raises some important questions: Do *particular sins* exist or just *sinners*? Can one speak of an immoral *act* or are all actions morally neutral? The intuitionist claims that there are no sins, only sinners because a sin is an act and an act is a natural occurrence. To be sure, many acts of nature are initiated by a person; nevertheless, all acts are natural, hence cannot be termed immoral *per se*. After a person criminally shoots and kills another, one does not condemn the bullet that damaged the heart of the human being; nor does one indict the gun, or the finger that pulled the trigger. What then is said to be immoral? Is it not the *motive* or *intent* within a person? Therefore, the only permissible conclusion is that there are not particular sins, *per se*, but only sinners; "good and evil ... can only be a manner of acting, the maxim of the will, and consequently the acting person himself as a good or evil man that can be so-called, and not a thing;"[3] hence, only persons can be properly designated as good for only persons have a will.

2. Nothing Good Except A Good Will

The opening and oft quoted sentence of one of Kant's ethical classics entitled: *The Fundamental Principles of the Metaphysic of Ethics*, is: "It is impossible to conceive of anything anywhere in the world or even anywhere out of it that can without qualification be called good, except a Good Will."[4] From the previous discussion in respect to ethical intuitionism, it should be relatively simple to make the logical transition into this Kantian concept. Assuming that all morality is to be found in the inner personality and is exclusively a matter of motive or will, then it becomes impossible for anything extraneous to a human personality to be deemed good in and for itself, without qualification. The only intrinsic good, *i. e.*, a good that is not merely a means to another, must reside within a person. The moral good within a human being is attributed to the will, for only the will has the prerogative and liberty to make moral choices. In ethical theory, this concept of "freedom of the will" is referred to as the *autonomy of the will*; "the principle of autonomy is the sole principle of morality."[5]

3. Autonomy of Will

Autonomy of will signifies that a human individual is free to make choices because he possesses a will; "only a rational being has the faculty to act *according to the conception* of laws, that is, according to principles, in other words, has a will."[6] An analysis of the word *autonomy* results in the following finding: *auto* is the Greek word that means self, and *nomy* is the term for govern or law; hence autonomous means self-governed, self-ruled, self-legislated, or in Kantian terms: *freedom of the will.* "Man is bound under law by duty ... the *universal* system of laws to which he is subject are laws which he *imposes upon himself,* and that he is only under obligation to act in conformity to his own will, a will ... which prescribes universal laws. ... The supreme principle of morality I shall therefore call the principle of the *autonomy* of the will.'"[7] The autonomy of the will is the *raison d'etre* of morality.

The concept of autonomy dominates the Kantian system of ethics; he maintains that every person has a free will regardless of age or circumstance, *i.e.*, whether he is a child or an adult, a slave or a conqueror. One can coerce a child, even his own child, to do his bidding, but one cannot make him *will* to do it; one can force a slave to do his bidding, but cannot make him *will* to do it; one can force a prisoner to wash floors, but cannot make him *will* to do it. *E. g.*, one's own young child who refuses to eat his spinach can by intimidation be forced to eat, but he cannot be forced to *will* to eat. Inasmuch as the will is autonomous, the child must will for himself, consequently one has no control over the will of another, even the will of his own young child. The only possible and legitimate method to induce a child, or for that matter anyone, to will according to one's preference, is to convince him through rational persuasion because only reason can direct the will; "reason has been alloted to us as a practical faculty, that is to say, a faculty which is meant to influence the will.'"[8] A rational good will is the sole responsible agent in making choices. The Kantian claim, that one should be moral for the sake of morality, stems from reverence for moral law and not for the sake of any reward; "it is of no use to give children rewards; this makes them selfish, and gives rise to an *indoles mercenaria'*"[9] (mercenary disposition). Kant thinks that to train the child with incentives such as rewards will contribute to his becoming a spiritual invalid since a truly moral person acts out of reverence for moral law and not out of a desire for reward or fear of punishment.

> If you punish a child for being naughty, and reward him for being good, he will do right mere-

ly for the sake of reward; and when he goes out into the world and finds that goodness is not always rewarded, nor wickedness always punished, he will grow into a man who only thinks about how he may get on in the world, and does right or wrong, according as he finds either of advantage to himself.[10]

Kant sternly opposes those who use heavenly reward as moral motivation, moreover, the threat of future punishment in hell in order to keep a person morally astute is equally repugnant to him. A fuller treatment of the relation of heaven and hell to morality follows.

4. Heaven and Hell as Moral Motivation

Kant refutes the contention of those who claim that heaven and hell are valid reasons for being moral; the Kantian countermand is that when a man "recognizes a thing as his duty, he needs no other spring than this conception of duty itself."[11] Kant's objection can be illustrated by the case of a student who said that although he believed in immortality, he wished that death ended all; the reason being that he lived a questionable moral life and would prefer to spend the rest of it in similar pursuits without paying any penalty for it. In the estimation of Kant the foregoing form of motivation is fit only for animals, not for moral agents.

Kant is diametrically opposed to this mode of thought; he contends that one is moral for the sake of morality, *i.e.*, because of *reverence for moral law*. Moral impetus stems from the fact that persons are moral agents and will autonomously; one's morality stems from the endowment of a rational good will. In a sense, "virtue is her own reward." Since the will is autonomous, *i. e.*, free, only autonomously willed actions are moral. Actions committed out of duress are morally neutral, *i.e.*, they are neither moral nor immoral; such actions fall outside the moral domain, hence are termed *amoral.*

The words *nonmoral* and *unmoral* are used interchangeably with *amoral* without variation in meaning. The prefixes *a, non,* and *un* express negation; *non* and *un* are Latin derivatives, whereas *a* is from the Greek; each expresses negation. Since moral is derived from the Latin *mos, mores* (customs or manners), some individuals object to the use of *a*moral, claiming that a Greek prefix should not be affixed to a Latin word; however, in usage, amoral seems to be the favored term. The nonhuman kingdom is considered amoral, *e.g.*, a tree falling and killing a man is a tragedy not an immoral act; a rat lethally attacking an infant is also an amoral incident for neither possesses moral agency. Actually most human actions are amoral since they do not stem from choice, *i.e.*, the function of an autonomous will. Moral actions are grounded in a *rational good will*; morality cannot be present in the absence of will. Such a situation is considered amoral, *e. g.*, individuals forced into committing actions against their will. The coercion may be internal, such as overpowering emotions, or external such as threats from hostile individuals. Whenever the will is restrained, moral responsibility ceases.

If heaven or hell serves as one's moral motivation then his ensuing behavior cannot be deemed virtuous, but amoral, since it is not autonomous. Motivation which is emotive in nature, *e. g.*, fear, desire, feeling, love, etc., renders the act amoral for one is incapable of moral agency under these conditions. Coercive action of every nature, external or internal, renders the will impotent, hence lacks moral significance. Kant summarizes: "Here again then, all remains disinterested and founded merely on duty; neither fear nor hope being made the fundamental springs, which if taken as principles would destroy the whole moral worth of actions."[12]

Not only must morality be distinguished from force such as reward and punishment, but a distinction must be drawn between morality and prudence, or more technically, between ethics and aesthetics.

5. Morality and Prudence

A merely clever or prudent maneuver is not to be construed as morality such as Socrates taught; acts of wisdom are not necessarily moral. *The prudent man makes the wisest use of consequences, whereas the moral command warrants one to make the most equitable choice.* Prudence requires technical ability, 'scientific know-how,' and factual knowledge; "skill in the choice of the means to one's own greatest well-being may be called prudence."[13] Prudence belongs to the province of aesthetics,[14] whereas, morality is the study of ethics. Aesthetics, the study of beauty, is a study of excellence in superior attainment; ethics is the study of moral excellence, *e.g.*, to say, "Don't kill the pianist, he is doing his best," is to make a moral judgment; however, to say, "Kill the pianist, for his best is not good enough," is to make an aesthetic judgment.[15]

One may admire the cleverness of the plans of a bank thief with his technique of flawless accuracy and brilliant mental ingenuity, but may censor the same thief for his moral callousness; his aesthetic achievement may warrant praise, but his moral behavior evokes contempt. One must not lose sight of this fundamental difference between prudence and morality inherent in Kantian thought.

Is it ever right to break a promise? *E. g.*, under extenuating circumstances, when it would prove detrimental to everyone concerned if one kept it and beneficial if one broke it. *E. g.*, two youngsters deciding to play in a neighbor's yard to which they were expressly forbidden entrance, trespass in spite of caustic parental warnings. To exit from the yard, one of the two unsuccessfully attempts to scale the barbed wire fence, gashing his leg, and wounding him seriously. The injured boy extracts a solemn promise from his friend, swearing him to absolute secrecy. After a lapse of several hours the worried friend asks to have his promise rescinded, convinced that unless immediate medical attention is given the wounded leg, it will have to be amputated or possibly result in loss of life. For the sake of his friend's life, *ought* the promise be broken? *Morally* speaking, can the promise be broken? Kant's emphatic reply is, *no!* Prudence might dictate that the promise be broken, but the moral imperative would prohibit it. Kant speaks in his own defence:

May I, for instance, under the pressure of circumstances, make a promise which I have no intention of keeping? The question is not, whether it is prudent to make a false promise, but whether it is morally right. To enable me to answer this question shortly and conclusively, the best way is for me to ask myself whether it would satisfy me that the maxim to extricate myself from embarrassment by giving a false promise should have the force of a universal law, applying to others as well as to myself. And I see at once, that, while I can certainly will the lie, I cannot will that lying be a universal law. If lying were universal, there would, properly speaking, be no promises whatever. I might say that I intended to do a certain thing at some future time, but nobody would believe me, or if he did at the moment trust to my promise, he would afterwards pay me back in my own coin. My maxim thus proves itself to be self-destructive, so soon as it is taken as a universal law.[16]

6. What is Right for One is Right for All

The foregoing may indicate severe austerity on the part of Kant, but a definitive judgment should be held in abeyance pending the discussion on the "categorical imperative."

The categorical imperative implies the existence of an inherent moral democracy binding on all mankind, viz., the "Golden Rule," *i. e.*, "Do unto others, as you would have them do unto you."[17] Kant believed that he was giving philosophical expression or formulation to the Golden Rule. The categorical imperative and the Golden Rule imply, "what is right for one is right for all," *e. g.*, the *agent provocateur* who feigns friendship with criminals in order to expose them is immoral. If it is right for government men to lie, then every man is entitled to deceive; if it is wrong for *one* man to lie, then it is immoral for *all* others. Moral laws are universally binding; they are valid for all persons and the criterion by which they are detected is termed the *categorical imperative*.

7. The Categorical Imperative

The categorical imperative is a moral measuring device, facilitating the determination of a right act; the rule requires that one *"act in conformity with that maxim, and that maxim only, which you can at the same time will to be a universal law,"*[18] *e. g.*, to determine the rightness of one's action, check its underlying principle; if the principle underlying the deed is stealing, then inquire whether it can be willed that stealing become a universal law binding upon everyone. If the answer is in the affirmative and free from encountering any contradictions, then stealing is permissible, but if the answer is negative, then no one including oneself has a moral right to steal. Kant repudiates the claims of those persons who justify stealing in exceptional instances, *e. g.*, a father stealing for his hungry children (a permissible act according to the Mohammedan moral code). The question is not: "Is it right to steal just this one time?" nor is the question: "Is it permissible to steal under dire circumstances?" The question raised by the categorical imperative is: "Can I will that all men steal?" "Can I will that stealing be a universal law?

Note that the categorical imperative makes one a *moral legislator*; furthermore, the imperative is *categorical; i.e.,* not limited by temporal or spacial restrictions. One is cautioned not to confuse categorical as signifying classification; its fundamental Kantian meaning, is *unconditional, i. e.*, without qualifications, independent of time and space, without any "ifs." Imperative connotes command and in the present context it is a moral command; hence, the *categorical imperative is a moral command that is autonomously willed out of reverence for moral law.* "The conception of an objective principle in so far as it is obligatory for the will, is called a command (of reason), and the formula of the command is called an IMPERATIVE."[19]

Inasmuch as the categorical imperative occupies a fundamental position in Kantian theory, further elaboration is warranted. There are times when one feels that it is not only proper to lie, but that lying is the only moral course of action, such as, the experience that a heart specialist often encounters when attending a neophyte who is unaware that he is suffering from his first heart seizure. The crisis is heightened by the fact the patient normally suffers from a nervous disposition and it now becomes the responsibility of the physician to apprise his patient of the seriousness of his condition without incurring shock. Hopefully, the patient diagnoses his case as a virus attack and seeks the doctor's confirmation by asking haltingly: "It is not my heart, is it, doctor?" The doctor, fully cognizant that the critical phase of the disease has not subsided, guards against any emotional shock capable of killing him. Consequently, the physician concurs with the erroneous lay diagnosis in the interest of saving life. His plans are to see the patient through the crisis period with the least possible disturbance to him and with the diminution of the crisis, gently to inform his patient of the nature of the malady. The doctor is faced with the repugnant choice of either shocking his patient to death or saving his life by condescending to deception. Although some persons would praise the doctor for being *splendide mendax*, Kant's position is: "In that manner I soon realize that I may will the lie, but never a universal law to lie."[20] Thus, one may succumb to lying and even willingly, but one can never bring himself to will that lying become a universal law practiced by all mankind. The categorical imperative would forbid lying under any condition on the grounds that one cannot will that lying become universally practiced. Therefore, no one, including physicians, has a right to lie, regardless of circumstances including exceptional ones. However, the Kantian ethic would not censure the physician on the grounds that he acted amorally, *i.e.*, under coercion, hence lacked moral agency.

8. Will and Inclination

Moral life is grounded in the will; all other existence is *a*moral; therefore, actions motivated out of inclinations, such as: feeling, love, sympathy, kindness, joy, fear, hate, anger, hunger, etc., must be categorized as amoral. This submoral region in which moral distinctions and judgments are inapplicable is akin to the animal kingdom. An animal has no will, yet sometimes kills when motivated by anger or hunger, but when a man is similarly motivated, his will is temporarily held in abeyance and he ceases to be a moral agent during the period of motivation by animal inducements or impulses.

The following is an example that illustrates the point in question well: Suppose that as a result of a storm, a huge cargo ship is wrecked and grounded on an island in the warm South Seas with only two survivors who are crew men who swore an oath against stealing from the ship's cargo. Rescue is assured eventually, but the delay could involve several weeks and possibly months; the men could survive for years provided they stole food from the ship's cargo. The moral problem is: Do they have a right to rescind the promise earlier made and steal from the cargo? The question is not: "*Will* they steal from the cargo?" The question is: "Are they morally entitled to steal?" *i.e.*, "Is stealing moral?" According to Kant, it would be immoral to *will* to steal. Why? Apply the categorical imperative: Can I will that stealing be a *universal* moral law? If the answer is yes, then I must permit people to steal my prized possessions, which to me would be unthinkable. Although I could will to steal in this particular instance, I could never allow stealing to become a universal law.

It would be safe to assume that the shipwrecked men, due to hunger and fear for their lives, would break into the cargo. Would Kant censor the action of the crewmen? No! Why? Because such actions, motivated *a corps perdu*, are amoral. The act of stealing was not autonomous, but in response to inclination or feeling, *i.e.*, animal impulses. Animal impulse is a force temporarily suspending freedom, a force that can be likened to the experience of having rogues place a gun in a man's back and force him to steal.

The reason Kant dismisses feelings, inclinations, and propensions from the moral realm is that universal moral laws are not deducible from them, but issue from a rational good will implementing the categorical imperative. It is possible to detect a principle in an act prompted by feeling, but all attempts will prove futile in locating one containing a moral command, *i.e.*, one that is categorically valid.

> Whatever is deduced from the particular natural characteristics of humanity, from certain feelings and propensions, nay, even, if possible, from any particular tendency proper to human reason, and which need not necessarily hold for the human will of every rational being; this may indeed supply us with a maxim, but not with a law; on a subjective principle on which we may have a propension and inclination to act, but not with an objective principle on which we should be enjoined to act, even though all our propensions, inclinations, and natural dispositions were opposed to it.[21]

Feelings and inclinations, man shares with the animal kingdom; but man's autonomy, that is, his possession of a rational good will, which renders him capable of value judgments and moral decisions is the key factor which differentiates him from the animal kingdom. Man's capability of sensing and responding to duty and of being a moral legislator by formulating categorical imperatives endows him with *dignity*.

9. Dignity

Kant's use of the term *dignity* has technical connotations unfamiliar in common parlance, where the word is associated with esteem and rank, such as, a dignified person. Dignity comes from the Latin, *dignitas,* meaning worthy; the Kantian denotation is infinite worth or infinite intrinsic value. Since persons are autonomous, *i.e.*, moral legislators or evaluators who impute value to other objects in the universe, they are said to be invested with dignity. "Reason . . . relates to every maxim of the will as legislating universally.... It does not do this because of some other practical motive or some future advantages, but from the idea of *dignity* of a rational being who obeys no law but that which he himself also gives."[122] Whereas man possesses dignity, everything else in the world has *exchange value,* that is, has a price tag on it; consequently if someone would offer a price sufficiently enticing, then the item would be sold. Only persons are priceless, *i.e.,* they cannot be replaced. To the person who fancies: "Every man has his price,"[23] Kant would quickly countermand by saying, if a person sold himself for a price, then he sold himself short, *i.e.,* he was short changed.

> Everything either has Price or Dignity. Whatever has a price can be replaced by something else as its equivalent. But what is raised above all price and therefore admits of no equivalent, has a dignity. That which relates to general human inclinations and needs has a *commercial price* ... but that which constitutes the condition under which alone something can be an end in itself, has not a mere relative value, that is a price, but an intrinsic value, that is dignity.[24]

Suppose you were God,[25] himself, and you were creating two worlds: one was ugly, vile, evil, bad, vicious, undesirable, etc., and the second was beautiful, wonderful, attractive, desirable, virtuous, good; would it make any difference which one you created if there were no persons involved? Since God is a person also, he would have to absent himself from the two worlds as well. Actually, it would not make one iota of difference if no persons were involved since persons give the universe its value and moral content. The universe is dignified by the presence of man in that value, including moral value, exists in and for persons; outside of personality, there is no morality.

Man as an evaluator endues the universe with value and by virtue of this fact is gifted with dignity. "*Autonomy* then is the basis of the dignity of human and of every rational nature."[26]

Because man possesses dignity, i. e., he is a being endowed with intrinsic value, he is an end in himself and must be so treated, never as a means only. "The creatures . . . if they are non-rational, have merely a relative value as means and therefore are called *things*. On the other hand, rational beings are called *persons* because their very nature distinguishes them as ends in themselves . . . and moreover an end that cannot be replaced by any other end for which they would serve as means *only*, because that would make it impossible to find anything of absolute value anywhere."[27] Since every rational autonomous being is a member of the kingdom of ends by virtue of his possession of dignity, he is to be regarded as valuable as any other human being. This non-instrumental use of persons is the Kantian "kingdom of ends."

10. The Kingdom of Ends

Since persons are autonomous and thereby endowed with dignity, they belong to a kingdom of ends; "a rational being belongs as member to this realm of ends if he shares in the making of the universal laws but also is himself subject to these laws. He belongs as sovereign to this realm if he makes the laws and is not subject to the will of any other."[28] It is as if the universe were subject to man, especially created for him, and man, as a member of the kingdom of ends, is to be free from exploitation; "man and every rational being anywhere exists as end in itself, not merely as means for the arbitrary use by this or that will."[29] There is no place for utilitarianism where man is concerned; he must not be treated as a mere commodity on the market.[30]

The kingdom of ends is not a categorical imperative, but a practical imperative: "Act so that in your own person as well as in the person of every other you are treating mankind also as an end, never merely as a means."[31]

11. Deontological Ethics

Kant employs the technical form deontological[32] to designate his mode of ethical thought; the word's derivation is the Greek *deon* (duty or obligation); hence a deontological ethic is an ethics of duty. The concept, duty, plays a major role in the Kantian system, so much so, that all ethics is reducible to *reverence for duty*. Action resulting from motivation that does not issue from a sense of duty cannot licitly be considered moral in spite of the fact it may have all the characteristics of morality, *e. g.*, a politician who is instrumental in the acquisition of a desperately needed community hospital may have as his primary concern the promulgation of his political interests, the community's welfare being only an ancillary consideration. Such an individual acts in *accord* with morality, but not *out* of it. "Although many a thing demanded *by duty* may be done *in accordance* with it, yet there is always reason to doubt that it has actually been *done out of it*."[33] Kant's observation is reminiscent of St. Paul's contention that an act is morally deficient unless accompanied by love: "And though I bestow all my goods to feed the poor, and though I give my body to be burned, and have not love, it profiteth me nothing."[34] However, for Kant, the obligation does not include love, but only good will, forasmuch as one can and ought to command good will, but is incapable of summoning love at will. This point may be illustrated by the adolescent, whose parents were divorced in his infancy, who, meeting his mother for the first time and being introduced by his father and expected to kiss his mother, may find himself incapable of registering any feeling of affection or love in spite of his attempts to evoke this emotion.

Although attempts to summon love prove vain, one is capable of exhibiting good will:

> That undoubtedly is the true interpretation of the scriptures, where we are commanded to love our neighbor, even our enemy. For love from inclination cannot be commanded; but to do good out of duty, even though no inclination at all impels toward it, yes, even when a natural and uncontrollable disinclination opposes it, is a practical and not a pathological love. Such a love lies in the will and not in some propensity of affection, in the principles of action and not in

tender sympathy. And such love alone can be commanded.[35]

Obligation can be predicated only to that which is subject to the will; inasmuch as feelings, emotions, etc. are extraneous to it, they cannot be considered morally significant. "It is a duty to preserve one's life and, besides, everyone has an immediate inclination to do so. But the frequently anxious care which most men take of it has no intrinsic value and their maxim no moral content. They indeed preserve their life dutifully, but not out of duty."[36] Contributions or benefactors do not qualify as moral, unless their actions are prompted from a sense of duty; should their actions issue from a desire for glory, prestige, esteem, etc., they would be of doubtful moral worth.

One may recapitulate the preceding by saying moral promptings ought to emanate from a pure will whose sole motivation is duty or obligation; "*duty is obligation to act from reverence* for law. . . . Thus there arises the maxim, to obey the moral law even at the sacrifice of all my natural inclinations."[37]

Duty and *obligation* are inversely related to *right*; one's obligations become another's rights and vice versa, *e. g.*, if one has a right to property, then it is another's duty and obligation to respect that right or if one has a right to free speech, then others are indebted to respect that right. Note the fine shade of meaning that distinguishes duty and obligation: "The dependence of a will . . . on the principle of autonomy . . . is *obligation*. . . . The objective necessity of an action from obligation is called *duty*."[38] In Kantian moral theory, duty and obligation constitute the *sine qua non* of all ethics.

12. I Ought Implies I Can

It would be a tragedy if the duties and obligations were impossible of fulfillment; fortunately this is not the case for when a person says, "I ought to do my duty," the implication is, "I can." Self-imposed obligations which are incapable of execution would result in an impossible ethic; a feasible ethic is one in which the obligations incurred are practicable, e. g., one does not obligate himself to jump over the moon for the simple reason that it is humanly impossible. Whenever one responds to duty by saying, "I ought," the possibility of its successful accomplishment invariably follows, e. g., to say, "we ought to become better men resounds with undiminished force in our soul; consequently, we must be able to do so."[39] One does not contract the moral obligation of regenerating his personality if he is incapable of redeeming the debt; one is amenable to the obligation because of its feasibility, hence, "if the moral law commands that we *shall* now be better men, it follows inevitably that we also *can* be better."[40] Aristotle, too, concurs with this thesis: "Now no one deliberates about things that . . . it is impossible for him to do,"[41] such as being morally bound to live a thousand years. On the other hand, the evasion of duty cannot be countenanced under any conditions; each person must be the judge of the extent of his own liability:

> The impulses of nature then contain *hindrances* to the fulfilment of duty in the mind of man, and resisting forces, some of them powerful; and he must judge himself able to combat these and to conquer them by means of reason, not in the future, but in the present, simultaneously with the thought; he must judge he *can* do what the law unconditionally commands that he *ought*."[42]

Often, "I ought" is accompanied with a strong sense of moral determination; this intense moral constraint which is often erroneously confused with duty, Kant identifies as *virtue*

13. Virtue

Virtue is defined as the power behind the will which is its driving force; "virtue signifies a moral strength of Will."[43] The Aristotelian concept of virtue, viz., habitual moderation, is unacceptable to Kant on the grounds that it is solely of legal value; its unsuitability stems from the fact that it "does not require any *change of heart*, but only a change of morals."[44] Kant contends that virtue is not an acquired habit, as Aristotle taught, but innate strength; *"virtue* is the strength of the man's maxim in his obedience to duty.'"[45] Kant epitomizes:

> Virtue then is the moral strength of a man's Will in his obedience to duty; and this is a moral *necessitation* by his own law giving reason, inasmuch as this constitutes itself a power *executing* the law. It is not itself a duty, nor is it a duty to possess it (otherwise we should be duty bound to have a duty), but it commands, and accompanies its commands with a moral constraint.[46]

Note that it is not considered a duty to have virtue, for Kant dislikes the circularity of being duty bound to have a duty. Kant's defence rests on his claim that virtue is innate; some persons are born with an abundance of it while others are impoverished; to attempt its generation is futile. Virtue cannot be considered a moral mandate, inasmuch as it cannot be summoned into existence at will. Nevertheless, virtue does have a pertinent role in the ethical life, viz., the duty of perfecting one's own moral life (not others) and the responsibility of promoting the happiness of others (not one's own), as the following schematicism indicates:[47]

THE SCHEME OF DUTIES OF VIRTUE
The Material Element of the Duty of Virtue

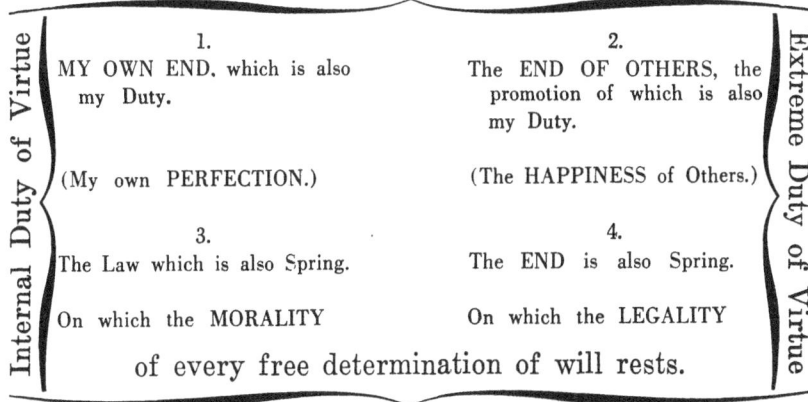

	Internal Duty of Virtue	Extreme Duty of Virtue
	1. MY OWN END, which is also my Duty. (My own PERFECTION.)	2. The END OF OTHERS, the promotion of which is also my Duty. (The HAPPINESS of Others.)
	3. The Law which is also Spring. On which the MORALITY	4. The END is also Spring. On which the LEGALITY

of every free determination of will rests.

The Informal Element of the Duty of Virtue

14. The *Summum Bonum*

The *summum bonum* (greatest good) for Kant is a *pure will*, *i. e.*, a will which is in perfect accord with moral law; "but in this will the *perfect accordance* of the mind with the moral law is the supreme condition of the *summum bonum*."[48] Aristotle's *summum bonum*, viz., happiness, particularly in its highest form, namely, meditation or contemplation, is comparable to Kant's at one point only; for Aristotle, happiness, *per se*, is the *summum bonum*, whereas, for Kant, the virtuous person is *entitled* to happiness. In Aristotle's thinking, a virtuous man is happy *de facto*, but for Kant, a virtuous man is worthy of happiness, *i. e.*, is entitled to it *de jure*; "It has been shown in the Analytic that *virtue* (as worthiness to be happy) is the *supreme condition* of all that can appear to us desirable, and consequently of all our pursuit of happiness, and is therefore the *supreme* good."[49] This point is carried a step further by Kant for he contends that when one is in possession of both virtue and happiness jointly, then he is, *ipso facto*, in possession of the *summum bonum*:

> Now inasmuch as virtue and happiness together constitute the possession of the *summum bonum* in a person, and the distribution of happiness in exact proportion to morality (which is the worth of a person, and his worthiness to be happy) constitutes the *summum bonum* of a possible world; hence this *summum bonum* expresses the whole, the perfect good, in which, however, virtue as the condition is always the supreme good, since it has no condition above it; whereas happiness, while it is pleasant to the possessor of it, is not of itself absolutely and in all respects good, but always presupposes morally right behavior as its condition.[50]

Happiness, *de jure*, belongs to the moral individual who is fully entitled to it.

15. Evil as Parasitic

Evil is incapable of self-existence, self-support, or sustenance, *i.e.*, it is not self-contained, it merely survives a parasitic existence; an entirely good world, completely emancipated from evil, can thrive, but a totally evil world would devour itself cannibalistically. Since the universe more than survives, *i. e.*, steadfastly progresses, then it is permissible to infer that the world is basically moral; had the universe been fundamentally evil, its destructive quality would have malignantly eaten away at the good and in the final denouement virulently destroyed itself. The survival of evil is dependent upon a symbiotic relationship to the good, such as the cheat whose success is contingent upon the fact that the vast majority of persons are trustworthy; if everyone were to cheat, then no one would be trusted, hence the cheater's efforts would prove futile, regardless of the extent of his craftiness or the number of persons who contrived the connivance. The rationale is uncomplicated; the hypocritical cheat or liar is commensally thriving on the reputation of the trustworthy and innocent whose actions are prompted in all sincerity, *ex animo*. A second suitable illustration is that of the relative success of counterfeiters who find the bad checks they pass honored only because the vast majority of checks in circulation are valid. A further example is that of businessmen who safeguard the value of a good reputation and sell it as an asset termed *good will*. Those department stores indulging regularly in questionable practices meet only with limited and temporary success because their eventual collapse is inevitable since patronage steadily declines with the public's detection of their irregularities. For any merchant to survive in business, not to mention succeed, it is both expedient and mandatory for him to commit himself completely to moral laws. The survival of the universe is contingent upon the fact that it is basically moral, whereas a fundamentally evil universe would commensally ravage its milieu before completely dissipating; hence, an absolutely evil world is an impossibility. *E. g.*, thieves who have robbed a bank are frequently motivated by greed to the point of destroying one another in order to increase their share of the spoils. The individual, nation, or business transgressing moral laws will discover its goals thwarted because the universe sustains only the endeavors of those acceding to them; "the intemperate man, for instance, returns to temperance for the sake of health; the liar to truth for the sake of reputation; the unjust man to common fairness for the sake of gain."[51] Although it would be wise to be moral for reasons of expedience, it would not suffice, since goodness on this plane does not exceed mere legality whereas man's moral impetus should stem from duty, *i. e.*, reverence for moral law.

16. Man's Nature as Basically Good

In spite of appearances to the contrary, man's essential nature is good inasmuch as the fundamental goodness of the universe implies the essential goodness of man. The evil that seems to becloud the issue originates from society's pernicious influences, *e. g.*, no one is born with prejudices, racial, religious, or otherwise; they are deeply instilled in a person early in childhood. Original sin is not an inheritance from Adam; sin is a noxious cultural legacy; "the vices that are grafted on this inclination may therefore be called vices of culture. . . ."[52] Cultural legacy or not, man is caught in sin and faces the obstacle of overcoming this wretched man within. Can one escape or possibly conquer this bent to sinning? "It must be possible to *overcome* it, since it is found in man as a freely acting being."[53] Man is an autonomous being; free to overcome evil within and that which lurks without; *man is free to do good!*[54] "When it is said that he is created good, and that can only mean that he is created for *good,* and the original *constitution* in man is good. . . . Now how is it possible that a man naturally bad should make himself a good man transcends all our conception; for how can a bad tree bring forth good fruit?"[55] The miracle that excels them all is man's capacity for goodness; to do evil is understandable, but to do good excites marvel. Kant was moved by two entities, both wondrous and awesome: the starry heavens above and the moral law within.

17. The Primacy of Practical Reason

Two great treatises of Kant are: *Critique of Pure Reason* (an epistemological work) and *Critique of Practical Reason* (an ethical treatise); *practical reason* is Kant's term for ethics, i. e., reason that is put into practice, viz., conduct. "One who is *acquainted with practical philosophy* is not, therefore, a *practical philosopher*. The latter is he who makes the *rational end* the principle of *his actions*. . . . The question is not only to know what it is a duty to do . . . but the chief point is the inner principle of the will, namely that the consciousness of this duty be also the *spring* of action, in order that we may be able to say of the man who joins to his knowledge this principle of wisdom, that he is a practical philosopher."[56]

It is not intimated that practical reason is not pure, in fact, a good translation or interpretation of the titles of these two books would be: *Critique of Pure Speculative Reason* and *Critique of Pure Practical Reason*; note that both forms are equally pure, the difference being that one is speculative and deals with scientific knowledge and the second is practical and treats the moral realm, viz., ethical knowledge. Critique merely means a critical estimate or evaluation, hence these books constitute a critical evaluation of theoretical knowledge, viz., science; and the second treats learning for practical purposes, viz., ethics. The ability to discriminate between practical and speculative reason is a necessary prerequisite to the understanding of the Kantian principle of the *primacy of pure practical reason, i. e.*, the priority of practical reason (ethics) over pure reason (science).[57] "By primacy between two or more things connected by reason, I understand the prerogative belonging to one, of being the first determining principle. . . . It means the prerogative of the interest of one in so far as the interest of the other is subordinated to it."[58] Practical reason (morals) has ascendancy over speculative reason (technology); scientific objectives must be prescribed by ethical considerations.

The import of this concept is of major significance; ethics is often defined as the study of the right and the good, viz., right conduct and the good life. It purports to resolve such questions as: Is life worth living? What is most worthwhile in life? How can one determine whether the act he is about to commit is moral or immoral? What are the true values in life? Ultimately, effort expended in science and technology has as its goal the task of enhancing man's lot, *i. e.*, the resolution of ethical problems. Major schools of technology and science have as their objective man's good; consequently, for man's welfare they create: airplanes, elevators, modern buildings, bridges, computers, automobiles, boats, television sets, radios, washing machines, etc. Oddly, the creation of atomic energy, including the bomb, is believed to be for the good of man; its peaceful uses are undebatable, but its destructive uses are questionable. Nevertheless, many Americans and others are convinced that the bomb serves as a weapon of defence for the maintenance of peace. "Thus, when pure speculative and pure practical reason are combined in one cognition, the latter has the *primacy* ... since all interest is ultimately practical, and even that of speculative reason is conditional, and it is only in the practical employment of reason that it is complete."[59] Inasmuch as science ministers to morality, obligation is *facile princips* over technology.

18. Metaphysic of Ethics

Kant's two outstanding books in the field of the ethics are: *Critique of Practical Reason* and *The Fundamental Principles of the Metaphysic of Ethics*: the explanation of *practical reason* has been given; *metaphysics* is the study of ultimate reality. The derivation of this term is from the Greek *meta,* which means beyond or after, and *physikos* (nature or physics), hence it is the study that treats the subject matter that goes beyond the physical, viz., ultimate reality. Some philosophers challenge this explanation by claiming the term comes from the Greek *meta ta physika* (after the physics); their contention is that in Aristotle's library, the arrangement of books were such that those on metaphysics appeared after the section on physics; not knowing precisely what to name the books treating this subject matter, he referred to them as "the books after the physics," hence metaphysics.[60] The latter explanation may be of interest, but is of little practical value since the term metaphysics is used today to mean the study of ultimate reality.

The groundwork has been laid for the transition of the meaning of the word metaphysics as it is generally employed in philosophy to its specific Kantian application to ethics. When Kant deals with pure morality as it is distinguished from applied morals (morals in practice), he uses the term metaphysics in the way one would use the term mathematics as a pure science in contradistinction to applied mathematics; hence the *metaphysic of ethics* is the study of morals treated independently of experience, *i. e.*, unhampered by temporal and spacial restrictions, in the same sense that the categorical imperative is free from qualifications. Let Kant speak for himself:

> Just as pure mathematics is distinguished from applied and pure from applied logic, so one may distinguish a pure philosophy of morals (metaphysic) from applied (that is, applied to human nature). This disintegration at once calls attention to the fact that moral principles are not founded upon the properties of human nature, but must subsist *a priori* of themselves, that from these principles, however, it must be possible to deduce practical rules for every rational nature, and therefore also for the nature of man.[61]

The metaphysic of ethics is the study of morals with a complete disregard of all possible application or utility; only principles are treated, independent of their practical use, similar to the study of symbolic logic divorced from its utilitarian value.

19. Kant's Social Ethics

The foregoing discussion of Kant's ethical theory has been restricted to personal or private ethics exclusively; the social ethics of Kant or what is often termed social or political philosophy (political theory) has been conspicuously absent. Persons interested in exploring this phase of Kant's thinking are referred to his book: *Eternal Peace* or *Perpetual Peace* depending on how the translator chooses to render the German text: *Zum ewigen Frieden.*

20. Evaluation of the Kantian Ethic

Some persons acclaim Kant the greatest philosopher of all time, such as Jean Paul Richter who writes: "For heaven's sake, buy two books: Kant's *Fundamental Principles of the Metaphysic of Morals,* and Kant's *Critical Examination of the Practical Reason.* Kant is not a light in the world, but a whole solar system at once."[62] On the other hand there are those such as the Logical Positivists[63] who find the Kantian system repugnant and repudiate it with vehemence. If Aristotle is correct about the middle road, and truth is to be found in the *via media,* then truth in respect to this system of thought falls somewhere between these two extreme opinions. To end on a positive note, the present evaluation of the Kantian ethic is divided dichotomously with the commendable comments following the adversely critical ones:

1. *Rigorous formalism.* The majority of the criticisms levied against Kant pertain to the fact that he is excessively formal and this formality creates an atmosphere of ethical coldness. He neglected to incorporate into his vast ethical network those warm and human feelings, rich in moral allusion, if not in ethical content, such as: love, kindness, sympathy, compassion.
2. John Stuart Mill criticized Kant on grounds that in order to employ the categorical imperative, one had to uncover the maxim of the act; this, in turn, necessitated resorting to *consequences* for its determination, a capi-

tulation which would render the Kantian ethic indefensible on a purely intuitive basis.

Mill adds a second criticism of the categorical imperative; he claims Kant "fails, almost grotesquely, to show that there would be any contradiction, any logical (not to say physical) impossibility, in the adoption by all rational beings of the most outrageously immoral, rules of conduct. All he shows is that the *consequences* of their universal adoption would be such as no one would choose to incur."[64]

3. Henry Sidgwick's[65] critical remarks are also addressed to the categorical imperative, claiming that it would render certain accepted practices as celibacy and bachelorhood immoral. Sidgwick's remarks may have intimations of an *ad hominem* argument inasmuch as Kant was a bachelor; not that Kant was opposed to marriage, actually he preferred matrimony for himself, however, being a perfectionist, he desisted because he failed to find the girl that represented his *beau ideal.*

4. Dr. Brand Blanshard contends that the categorical imperative does not work in every case for he maintains that there would be no contradiction in willing that all men lie. Why? If all men lied then it would be a relatively simple matter to determine the truth; it would be the opposite of what is said.

5. There is no guarantee of happiness to the disciple of Kantianism; the moral individual is entitled to happiness, but this does not mean that he will necessarily receive it. Other intuitionists, such as Butler, would consider this unfair to the moral individual who ought to and does receive it as his just desert.

6. Kant's adamant stand that promises cannot be rescinded for any reason even those that would prove deleterious, but if rescinded, beneficial, is not only an unnecessarily extreme stand, but a deterrent to making any promises whatever. It is interesting to compare this stand with that of Jesus who claims that since only God has control over future conditions and man has not, then man has no right to bind himself to a promise; "swear not at all;

neither by Jerusalem; for it is the city of the great king. Neither shalt thou swear by the head, because thou canst not make one hair white or black."[66]

7. Thomas Kingsmill Abbott claims that the categorical imperative does not furnish one with the essence of virtue, but with only a property of it. He maintains that the categorical imperative is negative and is not a clear test of moral actions, even when applied to the examples that Kant offered:

> For example, treating of Compassion, he supposes that if a man refuses aid to the distressed, it is out of selfishness, and then shows that if selfishness was the ruling principle, it would contradict itself. But why assume a motive for refusing help? What we want is a motive for giving help. There is nothing contradictory in willing that none should help others. So in the case of gratitude, there is no contradiction in that those who receive benefits should entertain no peculiar feeling toward their benefactor. It is true we should look for it ourselves; but this implies that such a feeling is natural to man, and that we approve it. Again, put the case of self-sacrifice, of a man giving his life to save his friend; it would seem as easy on Kant's principle to prove this a vice as a virtue.[67]

8. Hastings Rashdall objects that the Kantian system does not allow for foreseeable consequences; "the idea of 'right' is meaningless apart from a 'good' which right actions tend to promote."[68] In the absence of consequences, the categorical imperative would lack significance. This objection is a reiteration of one of Mill's.

9. In certain extraordinary cases, the categorical imperative is exposed to conflicts and contradictions, *e.g.*, to tell a falsehood is always wrong, but a person can be saved from his murderous pursuers only by the invention of

a lie, hence it would be immoral to save that individual's life.

Turning to the positive side of this evaluation, one will find that Kant's ethic has much to commend it:

1. The Kantian axiology places all mankind on an equal footing, *e. g., what is right for one is right for all* is the essence of democracy on the moral level; it is a philosophical "golden rule." The moral law is objective in that it is binding on all persons alike; it tolerates no partiality or special privilege.
2. The categorical imperative is readily and simply applicable by *anyone*; one need not have a thorough grounding in philosophy in order to utilize it. In fact, it is not necessary to have a complete knowledge of Kant's moral philosophy; even a child has the capacity of understanding and applying it; essentially it is the 'golden rule' in sophisticated form.
3. The categorical imperative is independent of particular circumstances which often becloud moral issues. Since it is a principle that is applicable to all situations, one escapes the problem encountered by complex conditions which tend to complicate the application of other codes of ethics.
4. The concept of *dignity* places all mankind on an equal footing; moreover, it commands self-respect as well as respect for others. This noble ethic has won even the esteem of those who subscribe to another school of thought, some of whom have incorporated elements of this system into their own.
5. This ethical system stimulates the nerve of moral endeavor by placing responsibility squarely upon the individual whose moral capability is assured by an autonomous will; each person wills for himself and is therefore answerable to no one but his own moral dictates. The good life is one of freedom as well as a self-governed life; no one has the power to enslave a person's will; each yields to his own rational understanding and conscience.

6. The Kantian system obligates one to do what is *rational* even though impulses would indicate a contrary course of action; moral problems created by feelings and impulses are avoided inasmuch as they do not fall under the direct control of the will, hence the individual is not morally accountable for them.
7. John Stuart Mill is persuaded that one who holds to a Kantian type of ethic will be more obedient to it than one who is committed to a subjectivistic ethic. Kant's is an ethic that commands obedience and encourages its practice.

21. Further Reading in the Philosophy of Kant

The works of Immanuel Kant consist of the following: *A General Theory of the Heavens* (1755), *On the Only Demonstrative Proof of the Existence of God* (1763), *Dreams of a Spirit Seer* (1766), *Inaugural Dissertation* (1770), *Critique of Pure Reason* (1781), *Prolegomena to Any Future Metaphysics* (1783), *The Fundamental Principles of the Metaphysic of Ethics* (1785), *Metaphysical Foundations of Natural Science* (1786), *Critique of Practical Reason* (1788), *Critique of Judgment* (1790), *Religion Within the Limits of Pure Reason* (1794), *Eternal Peace* (1795), *Metaphysical Elements of Morals* (1797), *Metaphysical Elements of Law* (1797), *Contest of the Faculties* (1797), *Metaphysical Elements of Ethics, On the Power of the Mind to Master the Feeling of Illness by Force of Resolution* (1794), *Education* (1803).

NOTES

IMMANUEL KANT

1. Let justice be done even though the heavens fall.
2. Immanuel Kant, *The Fundamental Principles of the Metaphysic of Ethics*, tr. by Otto Manthey-Zorn (New York: Appleton Century Crofts, 1938), 33.
3. Immanuel Kant, *Critique of Practical Reason*, tr. by Thomas Kingsmill Abbott (New York: Longmans, Green and Co., 1909), 151.
4. Immanuel Kant, *The Fundamental Principles of the Metaphysic of Ethics*, tr. by Otto Manthey-Zorn. *op. cit.,* 8.
5. *Ibid.*, 59.
6. *Ibid.*, 29.
7. Immanuel Kant, *The Metaphysic of Morality*, tr. by John Watson.
8. Kant, *The Fundamental Principles of the Metaphysic of Ethics*, op. cit., 11.
9. Immanuel Kant, *Education*, tr. by Annette Churton (Ann Arbor: The University of Michigan Press, 1960), 88.
10. *Ibid.*, 84.
11. Immanuel Kant, *Philosophical Theory of Religion* in *Kant's Critique of Practical Reason, And Other Works*, tr. by Thomas Kingsmill Abbott (New York: Longmans, Green and Co., 1909), 335.
12. Immanuel Kant. *Critique of Practical Reason*, tr. by Thomas Kingsmill Abbott, *op. cit.*, 227.
13. Kant, *The Fundamental Principles of the Metaphysic of Ethics*, op. cit., 33.
14. See James Martineau, *Types of Ethical Theory* (Oxford: Clarendon Press, 1898), vol. II, 485.
17. The Golden Rule is found in several of the great religions of the World. It is
15. Indebtedness is expressed to the late Dr. Edgar S. Brightman for this illustration.
16. Kant, *The Metaphysic of Morality. op. cit.* 543.
    referred to as the Silver Rule in its negative form as given by Confucius.
18. Kant, *op. cit.*, 551.
19. Kant, *The Fundamental Principles of The Metaphysic of Ethics*, *op. cit.*, 29.
20. Kant, *The Fundamental Principles of the Metaphysic of Ethics*, *op. cit.*, 19.
21. Immanuel Kant, *The Fundamental Principles of The Metaphysic of Morals*, in *Kant's Critique of Practical Reason and Other Works, op. cit.*, 43.
22. Kant, *The Fundamental Principles of the Metaphysic of Ethics*, tr. by Manthey-Zorn, *op. cit.*, 52.
23. Kant, *Philosophical Theory of Religion, op. cit.*, 346.
24. Kant, *The Fundamental Principles of the Metaphysic of Ethics, op. cit.*, 53.
25. This illustration is adapted from T. H. Green.

26. Kant, *The Fundamental Principles of the Metaphysic of Ethics*, op. cit., 46.
27. *Ibid.*, 54.
28. *Ibid.*, 52.
29. *Ibid.*, 45.
30. Note the similarity here with the position of Karl Marx: "These laborers, who must sell themselves piecemeal, are like a commodity, like every other article of commerce, and are consequently exposed to the vicissitudes of competition, to all the fluctuations of the market." Karl Marx, *The Communist Manifesto and Other Writings* (New York: Modern Library, 1932), 328. Cf. Karl Marx, *Capital* (New York: Modern Library, 1906), 186.
31. Kant, *The Fundamental Principles of the Metaphysic of Ethics*, op. cit., 47.
32. Kant, *Metaphysical Elements of Ethics*, in *Kant's Critique of Practical Reason and Other Works*, tr. by Thomas Kingsmill Abbott, op. cit., 285.
33. Kant, *The Fundamental Principles of the Metaphysic of Ethics*, op. cit., 22.
34. I Corinthians, 13:3.
35. Kant, *The Fundamental Principles of the Metaphysic of Ethics*, op. cit., 15.
36. *Ibid.*, 13.
37. Kant, *The Metaphysic of Morality*, op. cit. 542.
38. Kant, *The Fundamental Principles of the Metaphysic of Ethics*, op. cit., 58.
39. Kant, *Philosophical Theory of Religion*, op. cit., 353.
40. *Ibid.*, 358.
41. Aristotle, *Nicomachean Ethics*, 1140^a 32.
42. Kant, *Metaphysical Elements of Ethics*, op. cit., 290.
43. *Ibid.*, 316.
44. Kant, *Philosophical Theory of Religion*, op. cit., 355.
45. Kant, *Metaphysical Elements of Ethics*, op. cit., 305.
46. *Ibid.* 316.
47. *Ibid.*, 309.
48. Kant, *Critique of Practical Reason*, op. cit., 218.
49. *Ibid.*, 206.
50. *Ibid.*, 206.
51. Kant, *Philosophical Theory of Religion*, op. cit., 354.
52. *Ibid.*, 334.
53. *Ibid.*, 344.
54. Compare this to the position of St. Augustine who holds that only the good man is free; *he is free to do evil*.
55. *Ibid.*, 352, 353.
56. *Ibid.*, 216.
57. See Kant, *Critique of Practical Reason*, op. cit., 218.
58. *Ibid.*, 216.
59. *Ibid.*, 218.
60. See Edgar S. Brightman, *An Introduction To Philosophy* (New York: Henry Holt, 1925), 99.
61. Kant, *The Fundamental Principles of the Metaphysic of Ethics*, op. cit., 26.
62. Quoted in the rear of the title page of Kant's *Critique of Practical Reason*, op. cit.
63. See Alfred J. Ayer, *Language, Truth and Logic* (London: Victor Gollancz Ltd., 1936).

64. John Stuart Mill, *Utilitarianism* (Longmans, Green and Co., 1907), 6.
65. Henry Sidgwick, *The Methods of Ethics* (London: Macmillan and Co., Ltd., 1901).
66. Matthew 5:34-36.
67. Thomas Kingsmill Abbott, "Memoir of Kant," in *Kant's Critique of Practical Reason, op. cit.*, li.
68. Hastings Rashdall, *The Theory of Good and Evil* (London: Oxford University Press, 1924), 138.

JOSEPH BUTLER

Every man is naturally a law to himself ... every one may find within himself the rule of right, and obligations to follow it. ... Everything is what it is, and not another thing. (Butler)

1. Classical Intuitionism

Joseph Butler was one of the most outstanding, if not the foremost proponent of *Classical Intuitionism, i.e.*, the belief that moral questions are determined *a priori* without the necessity of considering their consequences. According to Butler, this is accomplished by the "moral faculty" of *conscience*, a human quality which is capable of making moral decisions. Although ethics is ultimately related to religion, or more accurately, God, Butler insists that his system is based on pure ethics, hence free from revealed theology. In other words, he employs the empirical approach in ethics basing it on the observed data of human experience.

Butler's intuitional ethic has drifted into an eclectic philosophy, *i.e.*, one which is composed of a patchwork of a number of other systems of ethics; at least, it has some overtones of this characteristic, *eg.*, he attempts to reconcile such divergent ethical philosophies as hedonism, Christianity, self-realization, and stoicism.

The highlights of Butler's ethical theory consist of the following: (1) the supremacy of *conscience* in determining right and wrong actions; (2) the derivation and composition of the ethical nature of man: (a) *benevolence,* (b) *self-love,* (c) *appetites, passions,* and *affections,* (d) *conscience* or the *principle of reflections,* (3) the concept of *man as a law to himself;* (4) the concept of society as a *moral* and *organic whole;* (5) the refutation of *psychological hedonism;* (6) *virtue* as following human nature.

2. The Nature of Virtue and Vice

Butler's definition of vice implies a "violation or breaking in upon our own nature," whereas virtue is the opposite course of action; hence, "virtue consists in following, and vice in deviating from it."[1] Inasmuch as virtue is obedience to one's own nature, it should come as a most effortless task; actually a "man is born to virtue . . . it consists in the following of nature . . . vice is more contrary to this nature than tortures or death."[2] Consequently, "nothing can possibly be more contrary to nature than vice."[3] A life of virtue should strike an individual with ease equivalent to eating, drinking, or any other natural act, while "injustice is moreover contrary to the whole constitution of the nature"[4] of man. The foregoing premises would indicate that vice is a perversion of human nature and virtue is the normal or natural state of the human being; furthermore, happiness accrues to the man of virtue, while misery follows in the wake of vice. "Virtue is naturally the interest or happiness, and vice the misery, of such a creature as man, placed in the circumstances which we are in this world."[5] It is a tragedy that the skeptic is "not convinced of this happy tendency of virtue."[6]

> Yet one may appeal even to interest and self-love, and ask, since from man's nature, condition, and the shortness of life, so little, so very little indeed, can possibly in any case be gained by vice; whether it be so prodigious a thing to sacrifice that little to the most intimate of all obligations; and which a man cannot transgress without being self-condemned, and, unless he has corrupted his nature, without real self-dislike.[7]

Vice is not in the best interests of any person including the individual committing the evil deed; its prospects must inevitably result in torment. Butler, satisfied that he has conclusively demonstrated his point writes: "This author has proved, that vice is naturally the misery of mankind in the world."[8] Inasmuch as virtue is a natural propensity in man, ensuing in happiness and the avoidance of misery, it would be logical to infer that "virtue is to be pursued as an end, eligible in and for itself."[9] Although man's nature would direct him in a virtuous path, nevertheless, he has the power to violate his nature and pursue vice, notwithstanding the fact that evil produces deleterious effects to everyone within its reach, including its author and instigator.

Virtue has been the subject of considerable controversial discussions, yet certain definite conclusions have been universally recognized.

> For, as much as it has been disputed wherein virtue consists, or whatever ground for doubt there may be about particulars, yet in general, there is in reality an universally acknowledged standard of it. It is that which all ages and all countries have made profession of in public; it is that which every man you meet puts on the show of it; it is that which the primary and fundamental laws of all civil constitutions over the face of the earth make it their business and endeavor to enforce the practice of upon mankind, namely, justice, veracity, and regard to common good.[10]

Virtue and happiness are not mutually dissident, on the contrary, they function harmoniously to augment the interests of each other for it was the intention of nature that they should converge. "The happiness of the world is the concern of him who is the Lord and the Proprietor of it.[11] The sum of the whole is plainly this. The nature of man considered in his single capacity, and with respect only to the present world, is adapted and leads him to attain the greatest happiness he can for himself in the present world. The nature of man considered in his public or social capacity leads him to a right behaviour in society, to that course of life which we call virtue."[12]

3. The Supremacy of Conscience in Adjudicating Moral Issues

There are a number of instincts that man has which are shared with animals, *e.g.*, appetite, yet there are some instincts that are exclusively in the human domain such as the ability to distinguish right and wrong actions, viz., *conscience*. "Mankind has various instincts and principles of action, as brute creatures have; some leading most directly and immediately to the good of the community, and some more directly to private good. Man has several which brutes have not; particularly reflection or conscience, an approbation of some principles or actions, and disapprobation of others."[13] One must bear in mind that whatever is natural is *ipso facto* moral, hence when one responds naturally to a situation, he is behaving morally, but the final criterion responsible for exercising decisive measures is conscience. The reason that other aspects of human nature, such as appetites cannot render definitive decisions is that they are only partial, and at best, permit of only partial truths, whereas the authority of conscience, which is the mental process of reflection, is integrative, that is, it considers the entire constitution of man in rendering moral decisions by giving due consideration to "the relations which these several parts have to each other." The component aspects of man's nature form an ascending graduated scale, "the chief of which is the authority of reflection or conscience."[14] Appetites and passions are to be found at the base of the scale and at the apex is "the supremacy of reflection or conscience" whose task it is to consider "the relations which the several appetites and passions in the inward frame have to each other . . . that we get the idea of the system or constitution of human nature. And from the idea itself it will as fully appear, that this our nature, *i.e.*, constitution, is adapted to virtue, as from the idea of a watch it appears, that its nature, *i.e.*, constitution or system, is adapted to measure time. . . . A machine is inanimate and passive: but we are agents. Our constitution is put in our power; we are charged with it, and therefore are accountable for any disorder or violation of it."[15]

By virtue of the fact that man possesses a *conscience,* rendering him capable of issuing moral decisions autonomously, *i.e.,* by self-legislation and not by the dictates of any other tribunal, he is said to be a *law to himself.* Man is a free moral agent subject not to any external law or force, but to the dictates of his *own conscience* which reigns supreme in every moral question, hence *"every man is naturally a law to himself, that every one may find within himself the rule of right, and obligations to follow it."*[16]

Animals are not moral agents because they do not possess the faculty of conscience; "it is by this faculty, natural to man, that he is a moral agent."[17] Conscience, by its *natural supremacy* holds the *prerogative* "of the faculty which surveys, approves or disapproves the several affections of our mind and actions of our lives, being that by which men *are a law to themselves,* their conformity or disobedience to which law of our nature renders their actions, in the highest and most proper sense, natural or unnatural."[18]

The eminent position of conscience is clearly seen when one realizes that in its absence man's moral life lacks judgment, direction, and superintendency. "Thus that principle, by which we survey, and either approve or disapprove our own heart, temper, and actions, is not only to be considered as what is in its turn to have some influence; which may be said of every passion, of the lowest appetites; but likewise as being superior; as from its very nature manifestly claiming superiority over all others: insomuch that you cannot form a notion of this faculty, conscience, without taking in judgment, direction, superintendency."[19] By virtue of the foregoing, conscience has a *natural right, office,* and *natural supremacy, i.e.,* "this faculty was placed within to be our proper governor; to direct and regulate all under principles, passions, and motives of action. This is its right and office: thus sacred is its authority."[20] The supremacy of conscience is indicated by the fact that it possesses the rule of right and wrong within and imposes this upon the whole nature of man. Conscience is not only its own authority, it is one's natural guide in moral matters enabling one to be consistent with himself eventuating in peace and tranquility of mind. Consequently, conscience may be designated *moral reason, moral sense,* or *divine reason* because it is capable of moral discernment in the same manner that speculative reason is productive of speculative truth and falsehood.

In conclusion, it may be said that conscience as a moral guide should not be overlooked as so many individuals have done, for "in reality the very constitution of our nature requires, that we bring our whole conduct before this superior faculty; wait its determination; enforce upon ourselves its authority, and make it the business of our lives, as it is absolutely the whole business of a moral agent, to conform ourselves to it. This is the true meaning of that ancient precept, Reverence thyself."[21]

4. Self-Love, Benevolence, and Appetite

Three major factors in the moral life of a person are (1) *self-love,* (2) *benevolence,* and (3) the realm of *appetites, passions,* and *affections.* Self-love is a moral necessity if one is to achieve self-respect or self-reverence and the happiness which accrues from them. "Self-love in its due degree is as just and morally good, as any affection whatever."[22] Self-love and benevolence are complementary and constitute important components of the moral life, hence are in harmony with virtue. Self-love attends the moral interests of the individual in regard to himself and his own needs, whereas benevolence constitutes the fulfillment of one's obligations to society or to another person. "There is a natural principle of *benevolence* in man; which is in some degree to *society,* what *self-love* is to the *individual.* And if there be in mankind any disposition to frienship; if there be any such thing as compassion, for compassion is momentary love; if there be any such thing as the paternal or filial affections; if there be any affection in human nature, the object and end of which is the good of another, this is itself benevolence, or the love of another. I must, however, remind you that though benevolence and self-love are different; though the former tends most directly to public good, and the latter to private: yet they are . . . perfectly coincident."[23] The primary function of self-love is the protection or security and the good of the individual, but although it fosters the good of the individual, one should not conclude that such practices would eventuate in detrimental consequences for others. On the contrary, when one properly exhibits self-love, he concomitantly is performing a service for society as well. The selfish person's injurious actions prove detrimental to himself as well as to others, *e.g.*, if one's ungoverned passions are allowed gratification, self-inflicted harm will result. This is due to the principle that self-interest or private interest is in natural harmony with society's interests. Furthermore, "there is no such thing as self-hatred, so neither is there any such thing as ill-will in one man towards another, emulation and resentment being away, whereas there is plainly benevolence or good-will; there is no such thing as love of injustice, oppression, treachery, ingratitude, but only eager desires after such and such external goods."[24]

It is necessary to draw a distinction between passion and cool self-love; the difference is not one of degree, but one of kind or nature, *e.g.*, "if passion prevails over self-love, the consequent action is unnatural; but if self-love prevails over passion, the action is natural: it is manifest that self-love is in human nature a superior principle to passion."[25] Consequently, when the two appear to be in conflict, one may determine the natural, *i.e.*, the moral course of affection by allowing reasonable self-love to govern. Discordant factors should be absent when each is naturally, that is, properly exercised.

"Happiness consists in the gratification of certain affections, appetites, passions"[26] provided they are expressed naturally rather than perversely. It is false that the promotion of another's happiness results in the diminution of one's own, inasmuch as there is no "peculiar rivalship or competition between self-love and benevolence."[27] However, since benevolence is the instrument of private enjoyment, it is, therefore, subservient to self-love; nevertheless benevolence is the "most excellent of all virtuous principles."[28]

5. The Social Nature of Man

Society is more than mere mechanical unity, such as the social contract philosophers taught, it is a moral and organic unity which nature designed. "It is as manifest that *we were made for society, and to promote the happiness of it, as that we were intended to take care of our own life, and health, and private good.*"[29] Man's nature bears out this fact, *e.g., benevolence* cannot be expressed except by societal relations; the same holds true for *public affections* and *passions* which, of necessity, must be directed towards another. Man, by nature, needs the companionship of others. "Men are so much one body, that in a peculiar manner they feel for each other shame, sudden danger, resentment, honour, prosperity, distress; one or another, or all of these, from the social nature in general."[30]

Butler provides a concise summary of his ethical theory:

> The nature of man is adapted to some course of action or other.... The correspondence of actions to the nature of the agent renders them natural.... An action is correspondent to the nature of the agent, does not arise from its being agreeable to the principle which happens to be the strongest. The correspondence therefore ... arises from ... a difference in nature and kind, altogether distinct from strength, between the inward principles. Some then are in nature and kind superior to others. And the correspondence arises from the action being conformable to the higher principle.... Reasonable self-love and conscience are the chief or superior principles in the nature of man.... Conscience and self-love, if we understand our true happiness, always lead us the same way. Duty and interest are perfectly coincident.... He who has given up all the advantages of the present world, rather than violate his conscience and the relations of life, has infinitely better provided himself, and secured his own interest and happiness.[31]

6. Evaluation of Butler's Intuitionism

The dominant theme in Butler's ethical theory is *conscience*; this is so emphatically the case that one may term this system: *the conscience theory of ethics*. It is undoubtedly the case that one of the most important characteristics of the moral life is conscience; it is totally absent in the animal kingdom together with any experience the animal possesses that can properly be interpreted as *moral*. Self-consciousness is a quality peculiar only to the human species, the "voice of conscience" is conspicuously lacking in the brute. For these reasons and others similar, it is readily comprehensible that conscience should be designated as the *criterion* of morality.

In spite of the fact that conscience is a major quality of moral experience, and perhaps its quintessence if not its *sine qua non*, it fails to meet the requirements of a good criterion of moral behavior. *E.g.*, many hardened criminals never suffer from the pangs of conscience when they rob, plunder, and murder innocent persons unjustly. Some criminals, after an episode of murder and larceny, often contemplate their heinous deeds with much satisfaction, inasmuch as they have been successful in conducting the crime without leaving a single clue behind. If conscience is a proper guide, then why is it not guiding such misled individuals? Perhaps their conscience is not in good working order, *i.e.*, such persons have perverted this aspect of their nature.

Many persons are afflicted with what could be called a "five-and-ten-cent" conscience, that is, they would be severely troubled by conscience if they went into a "five and ten cent store" and stole, for example, a tooth brush selling for ten cents and costing even less. Some persons could be so disturbed by conscience under such conditions that they would find it most difficult to be able to fall asleep at night, and succeed only in finding the pillow becoming tougher as the night draws on. Yet, the sleep of these same individuals remains undisturbed by the troublesome voice of conscience in a world of suffering humanity that is in dire need of help by way of medicine, food, etc. Actually, there is no excuse for not contributing to the alleviation of the hungry people the world over, since this can be simply arranged by a small donation to any number of fine world-wide organizations willing to expedite the matter on anyone's behalf, whether it be food, clothing, medicine, etc. If conscience were the brilliant criterion of duty or morality, then it would not lie dormant under such circumstances.

A number of persons have found themselves in the position of disagreeing with their conscience as though their very own conscience belonged to another, *i.e.*, functioning as *ego-alien*. Freud, as one of the many fruits of psychoanalysis, discovered this to be the case. Many persons suffer not as the result of their own conscience, but because of a parental conscience that has been buried deep into the subconscious mind; consequently, when the conscience speaks, it is not one's own, but that of the parent. *E.g.*, as the result of strict autocratic rearing during childhood, a person was taught that dancing was immoral and inspired by the devil. As a mature adult, this same person, convinced that dancing is not immoral behavior, still suffers from a disagreeable disturbance of conscience whenever he dances. The story[32] is told of an elderly lady whose patriotic spirit moved her to sew for service men during the war years; although she wanted to sew on Sunday because of the impending need, she found herself unable because of a poignant uneasiness and disturbance from conscience.

The ideal, mature, or wholesome conscience would be one that was not discordant with the rational aspects of one's personality, *i.e.*, one operating in perfect harmony with what one rationally concludes to be moral. Not many persons are fortunate enough to be in this position, consequently they must look to something other than conscience as a criterion of morality, but the beatific individual is the one whose legacy it has been to find himself in such a lofty and blessed state.

7. Further Reading in the Ethics of Butler

The important aspects of Butler's ethical philosophy are found in the following works: *Fifteen Sermons upon Human Nature*, London, 1726; 2nd ed., 1729; *The Analogy of Religion, Natural and Revealed, to the Constitution and Course of Nature*, London, 1736; *The Dissertation of the Nature of Virtue*, London, 1736.

NOTES

JOSEPH BUTLER

1. Joseph Butler, *Fifteen Sermons Upon Human Nature* (London: 1729, 2nd. ed.), preface.
2. *Idem.*
3. *Idem.*
4. *Idem.*
5. *Idem.*
6. *Idem.*
7. *Idem.*
8. *Idem.*
9. *Idem.*
10. Joseph Butler, *The Analogy of Religion* (London, 1736).
11. *Idem.*
12. Butler, *Sermons*, I.
13. *Ibid.*, preface.
14. *Idem.*
15. *Idem.*
16. *Ibid.*, II.
17. *Idem.*
18. *Idem.*
19. *Idem.*
20. *Idem.*
21. *Idem.*
22. *Idem.*
23. *Ibid.*, I.
24. *Idem.*
25. *Ibid.*, II.
26. *Ibid.*, XI.
27. *Idem.*
28. Butler, *The Analogy of Religion, op. cit.*
29. Butler, *Sermons*, I.
30. *Idem.*
31. *Ibid.*, III.
32. See Robert W. White, *The Abnormal Personality* (New York: The Ronald Press Co., 1956, 2nd. ed.), 193ff.

JAMES MARTINEAU

Self-evidently, it is persons exclusively, and not things, that we approve or condemn. . . . It follows, that what we judge is always the inner spring of an action . . . morality is internal.

(Martineau)

1. Idiopsychological Ethics

Idiopsychological Ethics is the foreboding term Martineau has chosen to label his intuitional ethic, a work which represents the efforts of over seventy years duration of an attempt to give philosophical formulation to the ethical teachings of Jesus. *Idiopsychological,* etymologically, is a composite of three Greek terms: *idios* (one's own or its own) prefixed to psychology; hence, *its own psychology.* Idiopsychological ethics is an attempt to "visit the moral consciousness in its own home, to look it full in the face, and take distinct notes of the story it tells of itself,"[1] *i.e.,* it is an endeavor to define with precision the inner facts of conscience itself.

The highlights of Martineau's ethics are: (a) *thirteen inner springs of moral action;* (b) *morality is inner* (intuitional ethic) (c) *duty has reference only to persons;* (d) the *criterion of moral conduct,* viz., "every action is right, which, in the presence of a lower principle, follows a higher."[2]

Martineau's ethical theory may be summarized as follows: The idiopsychological ethic is an intuitional ethic representing an attempt to systemize Christian ethics. Rightness or wrongness of moral conduct is solely a matter of motive, *i.e.,* impulses or emotions. Injurious results prompted from good motives are not immoral, *e.g.*, if a man's actions are inspired from love, then his conduct is right, regardless of the presence of any damaging consequences incurred. A noble *state of mind* constitutes morality of the highest magnitude. The criterion of right or moral behavior is the choice of the highest motive possible, *i.e.*, in the face of a lower motive, one selects a higher; on the other hand, immoral behavior consists in the choice of a lower motive in the presence of a higher one.

2. Duty

The essence of morality is *duty,* its *sine qua non, i.e.,* it transmutes an individual into a moral agent.

> Language is the great confessional of the human heart, and betrays, by its abiding record, many a natural feeling. . . . As a spectator of men on a theatre of character, I speak of their *Morals;* as an agent, uttering the corresponding consciousness secreted at my own centre, I speak of my *Duty.* The word I need not say, expresses that there is something *due* from me, — which I *owe,* — which I *ought* to do.[3]

One's duties or obligations become the rights of others; rights which another has every reason to expect will be fulfilled, *i.e.*, one's right to freedom of religion, becomes another's obligation to respect that right. "In any case, the word expresses the sense we have of a *debt* which others have *a right to demand* from us, and which we are *bound* to pay. And here we have another term, still more expressive of the inward feeling characteristic of a moral being: there is, it seems, something that *binds,* — in Latin, *obliges us,* — puts a restraint on the direction of our will, yet not an outward restraint upon its power, but an interior restraint from shame and reverence.[4]

Inner obligation, *i.e.*, duty is not an artifact of society, a social imposition, or an outer constraint, it is an inner personal authority independent of external forces, such as what the "world may say of us or do to us." Duty is an inner moral binding force which is expressed in outer restraint; it is one of the major factors responsible for the type and quality of nature one represents or develops.

Duty is a fundamental ethical fact without which there would be no morality whatever. Duty resides within a man solely; "self-evidently, it is *persons* exclusively, and not *things,* that we approve or condemn."[5] Physical objects cannot be said to be moral for they have no mind; they lack *intending thought;* they possess no prior and inner mind; they require an *outward observer and interpreter.* The Hebrew psalm: "The heavens declare the glory of God," is allegorical; as Comte noted, they declare the glory of Newton and Laplace, since they possess no glory until and unless they are brought into contact with *some mind.*

Inasmuch as physical objects, *i.e.,* the facts of nature, are not subjects of moral judgment, "it follows that what we judge is always the *inner spring* of an action, as distinguished from its outward operation."[6] It is not the action committed by an individual that renders the situation characteristically moral, but the quality of the internal spiritual nature of the person that may be adjudged moral or censored. "It may be briefly expressed in the phrase that *morality is internal.* The moral law, we may say, has to be expressed in the form, *'Be this,'* not in the form, *'Do this.' The possibility of expressing any rule in this form may be regarded as deciding whether it can or cannot* have a distinctly moral character.'"[7] Virtue presupposes an *ethics of motive* as distinguished from an *ethics of action.*

Martineau finds added support for his Ethical Intuitionism, viz., that morality is inner, in advocates such as F. H. Bradley and T. H. Green:

> Mr. F. H. Bradley, tells us: 'Morality has not to do immediately with the outer results of the Will:' 'acts, so far as they spring from the good will, are good:' 'what issues from a good character must likewise be morally good.' And with equal distinctness, Professor Green insists that

'it is not by the outward form that we know what moral action is. We know it, so to speak, on the inner side. We know what it is in relation to us, the agents; what it is as our expression. Only thus indeed do we know it at all.' And so 'it remains that *self-reflection* is the only possible method of learning what is the inner man or mind that our action expresses; in other words, what that action really is.[8]

Ethical Intuitionism of the present mode emphatically restricts moral duty to motive or intent, allowing no fact external to a person to be regarded as moral. The universe, *ab extra* to persons, is *amoral*. "Instead of measuring the worth of goodness by the scale of its external benefits, our rule requires that we attach no *moral value* to the benefits, except as signs and exponents of the goodness whence they spring; and graduate our approval by the purity of the source, not by the magnitude of the result.'"[9]

Duty is not to be equated to or confused with *wisdom;* duty refers to the intentions residing within a personality, whereas wisdom has reference to the prudent or sagacious manner in which an individual copes with or manipulates external circumstances with which he is confronted. By wisdom one may discover ethical goals, but by duty they are effected. "*Duty* consists in acting *from the right affection* . . . it is his wisdom *only* that consists in *pursuing the right end.*"[10] To select the wrong goal is not a *sinful* act, but may be a blundering or stupid one due to lack of experience or prudence. "Whoever lives out of the *universal order,* permitting the impulses that stir him to hold the rank which the voice of humanity assigns them, follows the *Moral* rule. Whoever lives out of his personal deflection from the universal order, and takes up with his egoistic forces of propensity, follows the Prudential rule.'"[11]

3. Criterion of Right Action: Moral Motives

Kant offered his categorical imperative as the criterion of right action; Martineau following Kant's initiative tenders one also: *"Every action is* RIGHT, *which, in presence of a lower principle, follows a higher*: *every action is* WRONG, *which, in presence of a higher principle, follows a lower.*"[12] The human being has a diversity and multiplicity of intentions, motives, predispositions residing within the human personality; if he allows a nobler motive to predominate over a lesser then by virtue of that fact, he has committed a moral action regardless of the ensuing consequences. The consequences in the case may prove disastrous, but as long as the motive (intent) from which the action sprung was the noblest of which the individual was capable, then *ipso facto,* it is morally right, even though the wisdom of such action is highly questionable or subject to being censored. *E.g.,* "the act of St. Peter in denying Christ was wrong, because the fear to which he yielded was lower than the personal affection and reverence for truth which he disobeyed. . . . The act of the manufacturer of adulterated or falsely-labelled goods is wrong, because done in compliance with an inferior incentive, the love of gain, against the protest of superiors, good faith and reverence for truth."[13]

One does not weigh the consequences of an action in order to determine its moral worth, one must assess the moral worth of the motive. Consider the case of a person who sacrifices $10,000 to pay his father's debts. "Motive, to do justice: additional intention, to endure privations, overbalanced by benefit to others: act good. Or, as we should state it: principle of action admitted, *sense of justice*: principle of action rejected, *love of riches and their enjoyment*: the former being higher than the other, the act is virtuous."[14]

In situations involving human conduct, a person's actions involve two important mental or psychological qualities: (1) his intelligence which detects the wisdom of the act, *i.e.,* whether or not the act is a prudent one in the light of the consequences or *end-in-view;* (2) his motives which indicate the deliberate intention of the act. "Thus, in the solution of all ethical problems, we have successive recourse to two distinct rules: viz., the *Canon of Principles,* which gives the true *Moral criterion* for determining the *right* of the case; and then, the *Canon of Consequences,* which gives the *Rational criterion* for determining its wisdom. The former suffices for the estimate of *Character;* but, for the estimate of *Conduct,* must be supplemented by the latter.[15] Nevertheless, virtue pertains to character, not to conduct. Although both canons are involved in ethical problems, only the Canon of Principles is morally significant, *i.e.*, determines whether a person's character is moral or base. "While the objects of *moral* preference are the *springs of action within us,* the objects of *prudential* preference are the effects of action upon us."[16]

4. Moral Springs of Action

Moral quality is found in *inner springs of action* solely; moral character is not apprehensible in overt action, but detectable internally by self-consciousness. The moral quality of an action is its mental antecedent, *i.e.*, the propensity or predisposition from which it was prompted, viz., motive or intent. In order to be moral, a person must respond from his better or higher impulses of moral worth which constitute his duty. "With this general conception of moral excellence, as *internal*, and consisting of rightly *ordered* springs of action . . . the whole ground of ethical procedure consists . . . we are sensible of a *grade-scale of excellence* among our natural principles, quite distinct from the order of their intensity, and irrespective of the range of their external effects."[17] Conscience is merely the sensitivity of the mind to the gradations of this scale of excellence. Conscience implies a degree of maturity, not only in the individual person, but in the history of the human race; facts of science, being explicit in nature are easier and earlier discerned; however, "for the *action of conscience, implicit knowledge* alone is needed, *a feeling, true to the real relations of duty*, that *this* is worthier than *that*."[18] Conscience is a moral factor, but the nature of intelligence is *unmoral*.

When one is motivated by loftier motives, he is said to be meritorious. *Merit* is *proved virtue, i.e.*, the *value* one places upon virtue or virtue's worth; merit differs from virtue as *price* differs from *utility in re* commodities. "According to this distinction, *merit is what you will give* for virtue . . .

it is *the virtue for which* you will give something . . . its amount is measured by its *marketable value,* and is dependent on the opinions and wants of others, not on conditions personal to the agent himself.'"[19] When it is said that a man has merit, it is implied that he has virtue possessing value to others, viz., to society, *i.e.,* he not only possesses *intrinsic value,* but value useful and helpful to others.

As has been previously stated, the criterion of moral behavior consists in choosing the higher motive when confronted with a lower; immoral conduct is the selection of a baser disposition when one could have responded from a higher motive. In the following table of *springs of action,* consisting of thirteen, it is to be noted that "springs of action do not naturally divide into *absolutely good and bad,* but only into better and worse . . . the 'malevolent affections,' *i.e.,* the tendency 'to inflict pain on others however aroused,' constitute a solitary exception and never quit the category of the bad."[20]

The scale is presented is ascending order; note that the highest moral motivation possible is *reverence,* whereas the lowest is passions of censoriousness, vindictiveness, and suspiciousness; consequently, these are invariably immoral and base, and reverence invariably moral. It would follow, therefore, that with the exception of the lowest and highest spring of action, each motive is relatively, not absolutely, moral or evil, hence censoriousness, vindictiveness, and suspiciousness are absolutely evil, and reverence is absolutely good.

5. Table of Springs of Action[21]

LOWEST

1. Secondary Passions; — Censoriousness, Vindictiveness, Suspiciousness.
2. Secondary Organic Propensions; — Love of Ease and Sensual Pleasure.
3. Primary Organic Propensions; — Appetites.
4. Primary Animal Propension; — Spontaneous Activity (unselective).
5. Love of Gain (reflective derivative from Appetite.)

6. Secondary Affections (sentimental indulgence of sympathetic feelings).
7. Primary Passions;— Antipathy, Fear, Resentment.
8. Causal Energy;— Love of Power, or Ambition; Love of Liberty.
9. Secondary Sentiments;— Love of Culture.
10. Primary Sentiments of Wonder and Admiration.
11. Primary Affections, Parental and Social;—with (approximately) Generosity and Gratitude.
12. Primary Affection of Compassion.
13. Primary Sentiment of Reverence.

HIGHEST

Note that there are two sets of impelling principles, viz., primary and secondary springs of action; the primary constitute an unreflecting instinct of one's natural expression and disposition, whereas the secondary emerge from self-knowledge and experience. "These names are the more appropriate, because serving to mark, not only an order of enumeration, but an order of derivation: the secondary feelings being not something entirely new, but the primary over again, metamorphosed by the operation of self-consciousness; and demanding a category to themselves, because their original features and their moral position are greatly changed by the process."[22]

6. Evaluation of Martineau's Intuitionism

Martineau's ethical theory is the product of extended research and industrious effort extending over a period of an average lifetime, including three revisions of a two volume book. He is a most effective voice of Classical Intuitionism and presents its case with remarkable cogency, establishing, with finality, the definite position of intent and motive as valid moral data.

Areas of weakness are to be found: (1) in his claims that one's psychological constitution is the essence of moral responsibility; (2) the springs of action are questionable both in number and degree, *i.e.,* quality and quantity; (3) one could challenge whether springs of action can be adjudged moral in the abstract, *i.e.,* whether it is possible to evaluate motives morally, independent of consequences.

Kant maintained that one could not be held morally responsible for the psychological aspects of his personality make-up, such as being obligated to love another with feeling, since this was beyond the power of human will; accordingly, love in the form of good will is the only quality one is morally incumbent to have towards his fellow man as a duty. Whatever is extraneous to will is extra obligatory, hence if one cannot by volition alter his personality and motivation, then he is not to be held ethically responsible.

The lowest motive possible that a person can display according to the table of thirteen springs of action is suspiciousness and vindictiveness. These can be challenged particularly in cases when one has reasonable grounds to be suspicious as in the case of habitually deceitful persons; certain nations have had long records of deceit and other questionable practices. As for vindictiveness, does not one have a right to damages suffered? Is this not the essence of justice? Otherwise the courts of law could not function. Cannot one then justly vindicate himself?

If it were not for the consequences resulting from motives, how would it be possible to designate one motive or intent as being good or noble and another immoral? Consequences, indeed, have moral value as G. E. Moore has effectively indicated, even if their moral value is instrumental at most, rather than intrinsic. "By their fruits ye shall know them" undoubtedly signifies that consequences illumine the nature and worth of the motive.

NOTES

JAMES MARTINEAU

1. James Martineau, *Types of Ethical Theory* (Oxford: Claredon Press, 1898, 3rd ed. 2 volts.), vol. II, 16.
2. *Ibid.*, 270.
3. *Ibid.*, 20.
4. *Ibid.*, 20.
5. *Ibid.*, 21.
6. *Ibid.*, 24.
7. *Idem.* Martineau has borrowed this quotation from Leslie Stephen, *Science of Ethics*, IV, PP. 16.
8. *Ibid.*, 25. Martineau's quotations cited from F. H. Bradley, *Ethical-Studies*, 207, 208; T. H. Green, *Prolegomena to Ethics*, bk. II, ch. 1.
9. *Ibid.*, 26.
10. *Ibid.*, 72.
11. *Ibid.*, 78.
12. *Ibid.*, 270.
13. *Ibid.*, 270, 271.
14. *Ibid.*, 274.
15. *Ibid.*, 275, 276.
16. *Ibid.*, 70.
17. *Ibid.*, 49.
18. *Ibid.*, 58.
19. *Ibid.*, 84.
20. *Ibid.*, 189.
21. *Ibid.*, 266.
22, *Ibid.*, 135.

HEDONISM AND UTILITARIANISM

JEREMY BENTHAM

Intense, long, certain, speedy, fruitful, pure—
Such marks in pleasures and in pains endure.
Such pleasures seek, if private be thy ends
If it be public, wide let them extend.
Such pains avoid, whichever be thy view;
If pains must come, let them extend to few.
                                            (Bentham)

1. Utilitarianism

Several appropriate terms are applicable and have been used in identifying Bentham's school of ethical thought: *Utilitarianism, Egoistic Hedonism, Psychological Hedonism, Quantitative Hedonism*; the classical work containing his chief ethical theories is: *An Introduction to the Principles of Morals and Legislation*. The rationale of writing a book which assimilates ethics with politics may be found in section one of Aristotle where it was explained that the subject matter of ethics and politics is logically correlated, *i.e.*, legislation is ethics on a social plane, viz., social ethics. Some philosophers defend with considerable cogency the position that extra-societal behavior is nonmoral, *e.g.*, one cannot cheat, steal, murder, commit adultery, lie, etc. without involving another person, hence individual ethics are essentially social. Bentham delineates the province of each: "private ethics teaches how each man may dispose of himself to pursue the course most conducive to his own happiness ... the art of legislation (which may be considered as one branch of the science of jurisprudence) teaches how a multitude of men, composing a community, may be disposed to pursue the course which upon the whole is the most conducive to the happiness of the whole community.'"[1]

(a) *Psychological Hedonism.* Bentham's fundamental thesis that "nature has placed mankind under the governance of two sovereign masters, pain and pleasure.'"[2] labels him a *psychological hedonist,* viz., one who believes that a person's natural constitution motivates him to pursue pleasure and avoid pain automatically, *i. e.,* independent of will and consciousness of motive. All hedonists, (*hedone* [pleasure] is the Greek word from which hedonism is derived), are not necessarily of the psychological type; hedonism is a philosophy of pleasure, hence a hedonist is a devotee of pleasure, viz., one whose prime goal in life is pleasure, but one who believes that he cannot do otherwise because of natural constitution, *i. e.,* human nature, is a psychological hedonist. On the other hand, an *ethical hedonist* is one who believes that he is *duty bound* to seek and enjoy pleasurable experiences and avoid painful ones. An important characteristic differentiating this group from the psychological is the belief that one ought to participate in moral pleasures, but only those to which he is rightfully entitled and refrain from whatever causes pain, except when morality dictates otherwise.

(b) *Quantitative Hedonism.* A quantitative hedonist, viz,. Bentham, restricts the meaning of pleasure to that which is subject to quantitative measurement. Since all pleasure is physical or sensual, differing only in amount, never in kind, the eventual outcome of one devoted to this philosophy is often a complete abandonment to the voluptuous gratification of appetite, viz., sensualism. Ethics defined from this philosophical standpoint is "the art of directing one's actions to the production of the greatest possible quantity of happiness on the part of those whose interest is in view.'"[3]

(c) *Egoistic Hedonism.* An egoistic hedonist is one who seeks pleasure primarily for self; such an ethic often implies complete indifference to the suffering of others. The egoistic hedonist assumes the prerogative of reaping his pleasure at another's expense when necessary, despite any deleterious consequences which may issue from his act, provided that any suffering does not ensue to him personally. He seizes the pleasures of the moment wherever they may be found, provided they are unadulterated by pain or punishment. Some philosophers have labeled Bentham's ethics *egoistic*, if this is an overstatement, at least there is a strong correlation prevalent between his system and egoistic hedonism.

Some persons doubt Bentham's sincerity, but his fidelity like most philosophers who are faithfully committed to their beliefs is beyond question. The risible story is told concerning Bentham's attempt to imbue as much pleasure in this life as possible and then to infuse posthumously whatever pleasure was attainable in that state; consequently he managed this vain feat by having his gaily clad corpse seated in a glass enclosed case in the University of London library for all who passed to admire. A visitor to England some years ago reported that the body still remained in that state unperturbed.

(d) *Qualitative Hedonism.* A qualitative hedonist is one who believes that pleasures differ in kind as well as in quantity; diminutive spiritual pleasures often outweigh enormous quantities of other pleasures, nothwithstanding their sizable amount, intensity, pleasantness, etc.; their inferior *quality,* by comparison, renders their worth negligible. John Stuart Mill, not Bentham, was a qualitative hedonist whose initial intention was to assume the position of chief expositor of Bentham's quantitative hedonism and defend it against the onslaught of hostile critics, but later he was driven by the dictate of probity to modify radically Bentham's crude and coarse ethical philosophy; the outcome of this refinement is termed qualitative hedonism and constitutes the subject matter of the succeeding chapter.

The proper groundwork having been laid, it is now in order to examine the fundamental idea underlying the utilitarian system of ethics. "By the principle of utility is meant that principle which approves or disapproves of every action whatsoever, according to the tendency which it appears to have to augment or diminish the happiness of the party whose interest is in question.'"⁴ The validity of this principle encompasses governments as well as individuals, *i.e.*, it is a social as well as a personal ethic. A fine distinction is drawn between the *principle* of utility and the *term* utility; by the *principle* of "utility is meant that property in any object, whereby it tends to produce benefit, advantage, pleasure, good, or happiness ... or ... to prevent the happening of mischief, pain, evil, or unhappiness;"⁵ no appreciable difference may be extracted from either of the following series of terms which are used synonymously: pleasure, good, or happiness; and mischief, pain, evil, or unhappiness. The word *utility*, claims Bentham in a revision of his book, is inexplicit in connoting pleasure and pain; consequently this situation necessitated the creation of a new term, hence the expression: *the greatest happiness principle* or *the greatest felicity principle,* which currently serves as the acceptable definition of Utilitarianism.

2. The Right and the Good

Philosophers often define ethics as *the study of right conduct and the good life;*⁶ a cursory glance at a shelf of books on ethics would support this explanation: *Things That Matter Most, The Definition of Good, Theory of Good and Evil, The Right and the Good, General Theory of Value, Ideals of Life.* The first portion of the definition emphasizes ethics as the study of right and wrong actions, moral and immoral intentions or motives; the latter part stresses the good in life or Life's values, *i.e.*, the life that is most worth living. Many of the classical moralists recognize ethics as either the study of the right *or* the study of the good, but not *both*; one is retained to the exclusion of the other. This discord has given birth to a perpetual debate as to whether fundamental ethical datum is the right or the good. One's particular conclusion has far reaching implications, *e.g.*, if good is given primacy, then good becomes the criterion of right conduct, on the other hand, if morality is basically a matter of right conduct (obligation), then good is merely right conduct, *i.e.*, whatever ensues from right conduct, viz., duty. If good supersedes right, then the right act is determined by that action which serves as the best possible means to the good; if right is in the ascendency, duty (the right act) dictates the good, regardless of whether the good is pleasurable, expedient, or in fact desired, *e. g.*, if lying is wrong, then one must tell the truth however disastrous the consequences, claim the *deontologists*; if *reverence for life* is the greatest good, then only those actions which have respect for life are moral, claim the *axiologists*.

Many philosophers refuse to accept the foregoing as a valid dichotomy because they recognize the necessity of each in its own right and claim that one is the complement of the other; right conduct inevitably leads one to the good (life), and the good defines right conduct.

Bentham, as is true of all hedonists, believes that the good determines right action and the *summum bonum* is defined as pleasure. Whatever action produces pleasure is *eo ipso* right, hence the good delineates one's duty, *e. g.*, "a man may be said to be a partisan of the principle of utility, (greatest happiness principle), when the approbation or disapprobation he annexes to any action, or to any measure, is determined by and proportioned to the tendency which he conceives it to have to augment or to diminish the happiness of the community."[7]

3. The Hedonistic Calculus

Bentham, the quantitative hedonist par excellence, went to great pains to cultivate safeguards and guarantees of the pleasures due one. Lest through ignorance one fail in securing his full complement of pleasure, he developed an ingenious pleasure measuring device called the *hedonistic calculus*. The calculus is effective in measuring pleasures *quantitatively* only, but this is all it need do, inasmuch as Bentham does not countenance qualitative differences in pleasures. All pleasures are of a single kind, viz., sensual (physical), hence one can speak of evaluating them only in terms of amount, *i. e., intensity, duration, purity, certainty, frequency,* etc. The object of the calculus is to unravel complex or multiple pleasures by sifting out impurities, quasi-pleasurable, or painful qualities thus simplifying the task of selecting the best pleasure out of a multiplicity of complex ones, the net result being the right course of action, viz., the most pleasurable.

Summarily, all pleasures are of equal worth, differing only in amount; the function of the calculus is to compute the specific value of a given pleasure in the light of its: *intensity, duration, certainty, propinquity, fecundity, purity, extent.*

(a) *The Intensity of the Pleasure.* Quantitatively, not all pleasures are of equal value, some excel in intensity. This rule recommends that when confronted with the choice of selecting one of two pleasures, all things being equal, except that one pleasure is more intense than the second, then the obligation incurred is to participate in the pleasure of greater intensity, *e. g.*, if dining in an attractive restaurant pervaded with an aesthetic atmosphere, partaking of a sumptuous dinner, is more intensely pleasing than attending the theatre, and a person is restricted from sharing in both, then it behooves him to indulge his appetite voluptuously and dine as sumptuously as possible.

(b) The Duration of the Pleasure. Inasmuch as some pleasures survive others, this rule requires the selection of the longest lasting pleasure, provided *ceteris paribus* one is faced with more than a single choice, *e. g.*, if one enjoys equally well an afternoon of golf and a favorite hour long television program, it would be incumbent upon him to participate in the pleasure that golf affords since it consumes the entire afternoon.

(c) *The Certainty of the Pleasure.* The hedonistic calculus calls for testing pleasures in the light of the certainty or uncertainty of their occurrence as well as their validity. Some pleasures are definitely within reach while others are highly tentative with dim prospects of realization. This rule makes it mandatory to accept the pleasure of which an individual is assured, in preference to one that is doubtful, *e. g.*, if one were extended the invitation of spending the weekend boating and also had the opportunity of spending the same weekend with friends visiting New York City, *ceteris paribus*, except the doubtful state of the weather, then this rule would direct one to enjoy the New York excursion.

(d) *The Propinquity of the Pleasure.* Propinquity, *i. e.*, the temporal nearness or remoteness of prospective pleasures, is of sufficient import to act as a deterrent to action. Some pleasures can be enjoyed immediately, while others must be reserved for the more or less distant and uncertain future. If two pleasures are alike in all respects, except for a temporal discrepancy, *i. e.*, the first necessitates a temporal delay, then one is obligated to gratify his desires with the more readily accessible pleasure, *e.g.*, if an employer grants one a paid vacation together with the option of taking it now or six months hence, then the proper course of action is to exercise the option by going on vacation forthwith. The probable rationale being that one does not know what the future holds in store; in six months the hazards of life may interfere with one's opportunity of taking the vacation, since by that date one could be ill, fired, or employed elsewhere.

(e) *The Fecundity of the Pleasure*. The fecundity or fruitfulness of the pleasure, *i.e.*, "the chance it has of being followed by sensations of the same kind"[8] must be considered when one is faced with the choice of two pleasures which are alike except that one is productive and will fructify into future pleasures. One ought to pursue the pleasure that has the fertility of producing subsequent pleasures, *e. g.*, if a man is pondering as to which girl he should invite to the country club dance, the only apparent difference involved being that the first girl lives in the locality, whereas, the second comes from out of state, briefly visiting in the vicinity, then it would be wiser to extend the invitation to the local girl in the prospects of its fecundating into subsequent engagements.

(f) *The Purity of the Pleasure* signifies "the chance it has of *not* being followed by the same sensations of the opposite kind: that is, pains, if it be a pleasure; pleasures, if it be pain."[9] This principle incorporates two features: the first is to select the pleasure that is unadulterated with any painful element; the second is to choose the pleasure unencumbered by any consequent misery, *e. g.*, if one enjoys a roast of beef and a lobster dinner equally well, except that the lobster has the tendency to cause bilious attacks, then the moral choice would be to indulge in the roast of beef dinner and avoid distress of indigestion. A second manner in which this principle is invoked pertains to two pleasures that are alike except that one is mingled with painful or annoying elements, e. g., if one has the choice of attending two theatres, both of which are equally rich in offering pleasure, except that one is in a traffic ridden area, then one should avoid driving through the congested traffic and enjoy the theatre free of such encumbrances.

(g) *The Extent of Pleasures.* "Its extent; that is, the number of persons to whom it extends, or (in other words) who are affected by it"[10] is the final rule of the calculus but it serves as an appendix to the preceding six inasmuch as it functions only when other persons are involved in the participation of the pleasures. If one is faced with the choice of two pleasures which are of equal value or strength, except that in the case of one, others have the opportunity of sharing in the pleasure, then the better act would be to select the pleasure in which others may partake, e. g., if one's pleasure is not diminished by allowing another to accompany him to a baseball game, then permission should be granted to allow one's guest the pleasure of one's company.

This final rule intimates altruism, which incidentally is an incongruous element in an egoistic ethic; it appears that Bentham reluctantly added it as an appendage, judging from the manner in which it is separated from the former six. Actually, an egoistic hedonist need not share his pleasure with others; furthermore on egoistic grounds he is justified in participating in any activity that while giving him pleasure concomitantly causes another pain. It seems incongruous for an egoistic hedonist even to consider another person's pleasures. Could Bentham, sensitive to the baseness of unadulterated egoism, be weakening? It was the undue disregard which this system had for others that contributed to this ethic's being branded the *pig philosophy.*

To help lodge effectively in the memory of his students the points of the hedonistic calculus and other tenets of his philosophy, Bentham inserted in the revised edition of his book the following mnemonic lines which summarize well the highlights of Utilitarianism:

Intense, long, certain, speedy, fruitful, pure —
Such marks in *pleasures* and in pains endure.
Such pleasures seek, if *private* be thy end;
If it be *public*, wide let them *extend*.
Such *pains* avoid, whichever be thy view;
If pains *must* come, let them *extend* to few.[11]

May one enjoy an immoral pleasure, *i. e.*, are pleasurable actions *ipso facto* moral? In the following section, Bentham addresses himself to the task of answering such questions.

4. The Four Sanctions

The meaning of the term sanction, for Bentham, conveys more than a principle which impels one to moral action or that which validates moral judgment; it encompasses the source of pain or pleasure. "A sanction, then, is a source of obligatory powers or *motives* . . . *sanctio*, in Latin, was used to signify the *act of binding*, and, by a common grammatical transition, anything which serves to bind a man;"[12] hence, a sanction is that which motivates one to obey that which is moral.

Apparently, Bentham was unperturbed concerning a person's deviating or wandering too far out of the moral line; the sanctions do more than permit an individual the liberty of enjoying pleasure, they function as an inhibiting force, *i. e.*, they keep him in check. Although in principle the sanctions permit the promiscuous person free course to his pleasure, they also function as an impediment, restricting him.

The four sanctions are: *physical, political, moral, religious*; so-called because they are "capable of giving a binding force to any law or rule of conduct."[13]

(a) *The Physical Sanction*. The physical sanction is nature at work, forcing her restrictions upon the individual by forbidding him excessive gratification of appetite. It is other than the dictates of society or the voice of one's personal conscience; it is nature's edict and manner of reprimanding those who disobey, *e.g.*, "a suffering which befalls a man in the natural and spontaneous course of things, shall be styled, for instance, a *calamity*; in which case, if it be supposed to befall him through any imprudence of his, it may be styled a punishment issuing from the physical sanction.'"[14]

Another example is that of over-indulgence of appetite in the matter of eating: one may enjoy a chocolate while viewing a favorite television program; the second may also prove delicious, and perhaps the third, fourth, and fifth; inevitably, the time arrives when one's appetite is completely *satisfied*, and should these confines be exceeded, he encounters the point of *satiation*; to violate this limit would result in the sensation of *nausea*; hence, the proof of the physical sanction's effectiveness. The *modus operandi* of the physical sanction is such that to exceed its circumscribed bounds would be to invite pain, illness, discomfort, etc.; this holds true for all sensual pleasures, *e. g.*, sex, thirst, sleep, play, hunger, etc.

(b) *The Political Sanction.* The political is a legal sanction, i. e., organized society with its representative, the judge, who levies various degrees of punishment for diverse types of misconduct. In other words, the law will see to it that one is punished for illicit pleasure, *e. g.*, a sadist, who derives pleasure in torturing others will have to curb his appetite or suffer weighty punishment meted by the authorities. Even as one encounters obstacles in exceeding the bounds of the physical sanction, he finds the legal or political sanctions also functioning as deterrents.

(c) *The Moral or Popular Sanction.* The moral or popular sanction pertains to *public opinion, i. e.*, the maintenance of a good reputation. Bentham's use of the term moral connotes *custom* or public opinion, *i. e.*, censorship or fear of ostracism; these function as effective devices in upholding morality and law; a desirable reputation, *i. e.*, winning the respect of others is a sufficient impetus to good behavior. There are persons who refrain from committing murder, not because of any legal deterrent but from social constraint, *i. e.*, the attitude of shocked friends, relatives, neighbors, associates, etc.

Many persons would prefer to violate certain minor laws than to transgress unwritten social codes with the consequence of facing severe adverse public opinion with the concomitant suffering of intense humiliation and embarrassment. Emotionally, it is less strenuous for some persons to drive through a traffic stop sign, which is a criminal offence, than it is for them to walk to their place of business in a bathing suit. The tenacity of public opinion has a much stronger hold on one than most persons concede.

(d) *The Religious Sanction.* Moral behavior prompted from fear of punishment "from the immediate hand of a superior invisible being, either in the present life or in a future, may be said to issue from the religious sanction."[15] Some persons refrain from trespassing morally circumscribed bounds because of religious scruples, *i. e.*, should they escape the law's punishment or society's sanction, then God will visit them with due retribution either in this life or with hell's torment in the next. Bentham aptly illustrates all four sanctions with a single illustration:

> A man's goods, or his person, are consumed by fire. If this happened to him by what is called an accident, it was a calamity; if by reason of his own imprudence (for instance, from his neglecting to put his candle out) it may be styled a punishment belonging to the political sanction — that is, what is commonly called a punishment; if for want of any assistance which his *neighbor* withheld from him out of some dislike to his moral character, a punishment of the *moral* sanction; if by an immediate act of *God's* displeasure, manifested on account of some *sin*, committed by him, or through any distraction of mind occasioned by the dread of such displeasure, a punishment of the *religious* sanction.[16]

Bentham appears to have left himself open to serious criticism: if pleasures are good, then by virtue of that fact they ought to be moral, and if moral, why should they be restricted by sanctions? If one sincerely believed in the ethics of egoistic hedonism and were persuaded that pleasures of whatever quantity are good, *i. e.*, moral, it would logically follow that he would seek to abolish the political sanction and to repeal other laws prohibiting pleasure. He would create an atmosphere of public opinion conducive to egoistic pleasure seekers, arguing that it was God's will that one indulge himself in selfish pleasure, inasmuch as it is good (moral). In other words, a sincere and serious adherent of this ethical system would discard every sanction as an invalid deterrent to rightful pleasure, egoistic as it may be, consequently unbridle his inhibitions, and wallow in unharnessed pleasure. Could this have been the major factor in labeling this system of ethics: the *pig philosophy*?

5. The Pig Philosophy

When one's primary goal and chief emphasis in life is solely the gratification of bodily pleasure then proper respect and appreciation for many of the great values of humanity suffer through neglect. The Benthamites were guilty of such complained John Stuart Mill, Bentham's successor of the Utilitarian school of thought. Mill bemoaned the deplorable depths to which Utilitarianism had fallen; he was disturbed with the fact that a Benthamite or Utilitarian became a term of opprobrium.[17] "From this neglect both in theory and in practice of the cultivation of feeling, naturally resulted, among other things, an undervaluing of poetry and of imagination generally, as an element of human nature. It is or was part of the popular notion of Benthamites, that they are the enemies of poetry; this was partly true of Bentham himself; he used to say that 'all poetry is misrepresentation.' "[18]

Bentham's hedonism, *a doctrine worthy only of swine*, as his contemporaries estimated it, apparently led to licentiousness for it moved Mill to write:

> Now such a theory of life excites in many minds ... inveterate dislike. To suppose that life has ... no higher end than pleasure — no better and nobler object of desire and pursuit — they designate it as utterly mean and groveling; as *a doctrine worthy only of swine* to whom the followers of Epicurus were ... contemptuously likened; and modern holders of the doctrine are occasionally made the subject of equally polite comparisons.[19]

Any system that assigns an unqualified goodness to pleasure runs the risk of regarding evil pleasures as good, narcissistic pleasures of equal value to noble ones, vile and depraved pleasures (deleterious or injurious to others), on a par with wholesome, desirable, and regenerate ones, yet Bentham's system condones such monstrous behavior. He argues: "Let a man's motive be ill-will; call it even malice, envy, cruelty; it is still a kind of pleasure that is his motive; the pleasure he takes at the thought of the pain which he sees, or expects to see, his adversary undergo. Now even *this wretched pleasure taken by itself is good*: it may be faint, it may be short, it must at any rate be impure; yet while it lasts, and before any bad consequences arrive, it is as good as any other that is not more intense."[20]

The pleasures, that are customarily considered base, are nevertheless good; to scoff at them is objectionable; lust, cruelty, avarice, etc. cannot be proved contemptible. Bentham fancies he has exposed the "emptiness of all those rhapsodies of commonplace morality, which consist in the taking of such names as lust, cruelty, and avarice and branding them with marks of reprobation. . . . Would you do real service to mankind, show them the cases in which sexual desire *merits* the name of lust; displeasure, that of cruelty; and pecuniary interest, that of avarice;"[21] lust and sexual desire stem from the same motive; if sexual desire is not evil, then lust is not either.

6. The Greatest Good of the Greatest Number

One of the more laudable features of the utilitarian ethic is its basic thesis: *the greatest happiness of the greatest number*, a phrase suggested to Bentham by Joseph Priestly. Later, when the amphibological characteristic of the phrase was detected, *i.e.*, whether to stress *happiness* or emphasize *number*, confusion and dissension mounted. If emphasis is placed on the *number* of people, then the majority is entitled to enjoy its pleasures at the expense and even misery of the minority; consequently minority groups will be sacrificed for the sake of the majority. This rendering was not Bentham's, he favored the interpretation that stressed *happiness;* hence a society ought to pursue the greatest amount of happiness, and if the greatest amount of happiness happens to favor the minority, then the majority, if it seeks the right course of action, ought to exercise its vote in favor of minority rights. In order to escape the confusion created by the ambiguous phrase, it was reduced to *the greatest happiness principle.*[22] The following is an example of its *modus operandi*: a town of one hundred persons would be justified in enacting a law that would make fifty-one citizens mildly happy and the remaining forty-nine miserable, provided stress was laid on *numbers* only; but if one favored stressing the *amount of happiness*, viz., the greatest happiness principle, then the town would defeat enacting such a law because when one subtracts the total amount of misery from the total quantity of happiness, the remainder would not warrant its enactment; consequently it would be encumbent upon the townspeople to provide a suitable substitute.

7. Everybody to Count for One, Nobody for More than One

Everybody to count for one, nobody for more than one, Mill termed *Bentham's dictum;* the dictum is the quintescence of a democratic philosophy for it gives everyone an equal claim to happiness, e.g., this principle places the happiness of a beggar on an equal plane with the happiness of a king. Bentham did little with the dictum, the reason probably being its involvement with the amphibological problems connected with the principle of *the greatest good for the greatest number.* Herbert Spencer noted a presupposition of the principle, viz., that everyone had an equal right to happiness, but John Stuart Mill was deeply impressed with the dictum and incorporated it in his own system of ethics. Further discussion of this topic is found in the succeeding chapter on the ethics of Mill.

8. The *Summum Bonum* and the Right Act

Happiness, in its greatest quantity, is the *summum bonum;* the *right act* is that which most effectively realizes the *summum bonum,* conversely "the general tendency of an act is more or less pernicious, according to the sum total of its consequences."[23] Consequences possessing value are only those that yield happiness or more accurately, sensual pleasure.

Intention or will is foreign to this philosophy, but at times these terms are used synonymously with act or consequences, *e. g.*, "a man's intention . . . may be styled good or bad with reference . . . to the consequence of the act."[24] Finally, after much deliberation, Bentham concludes: "It follows, therefore, immediately and incontestably, that *there is no such* thing as any sort of motive that is in itself a bad one."[25] The reason for this is that all motivation is pleasure and all pleasure is good, *e. g.*, the vilest pleasures of the most depraved individual are good as well as the noblest pleasures of the most refined and saintly person. Under certain circumstances, base pleasures are equal in value to the loftiest for the reason "that goodness or badness cannot with any propriety be predicated of motives."[26]

To epitomize: the right act is that course of action most conducive to the production of the greatest quantity of happiness. The responsibility for the promotion of happiness is the duty of the individual person and the function of the state; "the general object which all laws have, or ought to have, in common, is to *augment the total happiness of the community*; and therefore . . . to exclude, as far as may be, everything that tends to subtract from that happiness."[27] The matter can be catechistically summarized: What is good? Happiness (pleasure). What is morally right? That act which produces the greatest amount of happiness. What impetus is there for being moral? The doctrine of sanctions constitutes a system of rewards and penalties socializing the egoist by coercive measures.

9. Temptation

The degree of baseness of an act is calculable in terms of the tenacity of the temptation's impetus and the mode of its gratification. Weak stimuli or temptations intensify the viciousness of an action by unnecessarily creating detrimental consequences; "the less the strength of the temptation was, the more pernicious and depraved does it show his disposition to have been."[28] There are four rules dealing with the strength of the temptation by which one may judge the degree of depravity of a man's disposition.

Rule 1. *"The strength of the temptation being given, the mischievousness of the disposition manifested by the enterprise, is as the apparent mischievousness of the act."*[29] *E. g.*, it is more depraved to kill a man for a hundred dollars blood money that his enemy is willing to pay for the murder than to steal the same amount from the victim; or as Bentham put it: "it would show a more depraved disposition, to murder a man for the reward of a guinea, or falsely to charge him with a robbery for the same reward, than to obtain the same sum from him by simple theft."[30]

Rule 2. *The apparent mischievousness of the act being given, a man's disposition is the more depraved, the slighter the temptation is by which he has been overcome."*[31] *E. g.*, it is more depraved to kill a man out of sport than it is to kill him out of revenge; or as Bentham put it:

> It shows a more depraved and dangerous disposition, if a man kill another out of mere sport, as the Emperor of Morocco, Muley Mahomet, is said to have done great numbers, than out of revenge, as Sylla and Marius did thousands, or in the view of self-preservation, as Augustus killed many, or even for lucre, as the same Emperor is said to have killed some.[32]

Rule 3. *"The apparent mischievousness of the act being given, the evidence which it affords of the depravity of a man's disposition is the less conclusive, the stronger the temptation is by which he has been overcome."*[33] Temptation motivated by hunger is not as degenerate as temptation motivated by acquisitiveness, *e.g.*, it is less a sign of depravity for a poor man to steal the necessities of life than for a wealthy man.

Rule 4. *"Where the motive is of the dissocial kind, the apparent mischievousness of the act, and the strength of the temptation, being given, the depravity is as the degree of deliberation with which it is accompanied.*"[34] E. g., cold blooded premeditated murder is indicative of greater decadence than impulsive manslaughter incited by a sudden loss of temper. "Thus, it shows a worse disposition, where a man lays a deliberate plan for beating his antagonist, and beats accordingly, than if he were to beat him upon the spot, in consequence of a sudden quarrel: and worse again, if after having had him a long while together in his power, he beats him at intervals, and at his leisure."[35]

The four rules may be concisely reduced to one: *The stronger the temptation, the less monstrous the character or the weaker the temptation, the more atrocious the character,* i. e., "the weaker the temptation is, by which a man has been overcome, the more depraved and mischievous it shows his disposition to have been."[36] *The strength of a temptation depends upon a ratio between the force of the seducing motives and the forces that inhibit one from proceeding with the act.* A strong temptation is one which "the pleasure or advantage to be got from the crime is such as in the eyes of the offender must appear great in comparison of the trouble and danger that appear to him to accompany the enterprise."[37]

10. The Proof of Hedonism

Bentham contends that unlike other ethical systems, his does not require proof; its proof is self-contained. All other systems are in need of proof because ethical deliberations are debatable, *e. g.*, one can argue the morality of killing in time of war, the desirability of pacifism, the ethics of capital punishment, euthanasia, etc., but *happiness* or pleasure is the singular ethical fact not subject to debate. Why? Because any person experiencing happiness or pleasure must confess, "I like it," even if the particular pleasure is immoral, *i. e.*, a person may feel that he is not rightfully entitled to a particular pleasure, but he can never claim that the *experience* of pleasure does not "feel good," consequently, the only undebatable good is pleasure or happiness.

Furthermore, happiness is an ultimate term, hence does not require proof; proof is in terms of more basic concepts, but when one arrives at the ultimate, it requires no proof, it is axiomatic.[38] Bentham's query concerning Utilitarianism is: "Is it susceptible to any direct proof? It should seem not; for that which is used to prove everything else, cannot be proved; a chain of proofs must have its commencement somewhere. To give such proof is as impossible as it is needless."[39] Bentham continues his debate by taking refuge in psychological hedonism; by nature, *nolens volens*, this doctrine must be accepted; one's psychological constitution warrants it; the human creature automatically seeks pleasure and avoids pain; hence, "by the natural constitution of the human frame ... men in general embrace this principle, without thinking of it."[40]

11. Evaluation of Bentham's Ethic

Following precedents set earlier, the evaluation of Bentham's system of ethics opens with adverse critical comments:

1. Psychological hedonism is not pragmatically or empirically sound, *i.e.*, it fails to square away with the facts of experience, *e. g.*, Abraham Lincoln once feigned or fancied himself a psychological hedonist, if one may judge him from an isolated incident. Lincoln had the driver halt his coach, then alighted from the carriage for the purpose of freeing a pig caught in the roadway gutter mire. When Lincoln returned successfully from the task except for mud-laden clothing, the coachman complimented the president for his noble deed; whereupon, feeling unworthy of the coachman's expression of admiration, Lincoln declined its acceptance on the grounds that he was unworthy of it, inasmuch as, if he had done otherwise, he would have been utterly miserable worrying about the animal's survival.

Lincoln was mistaken in assuming that his deed lacked virtue; proceeding on the premise of the psychological hedonist who denies moral virtue, all that the president needed to do was to readjust his personality enabling him to become indifferent to or even amused by the animal's plight. This is easily accomplished as is evidenced by many individuals shouting and cheering at cock and bull fights. Lincoln could have remoulded his personality so that the next occurrence of the incident would have found him ordering the carriage stopped and offering to wager with the coachman regarding the pig's extricable abilities, with one of the men cheering in favor of the animal's success and the other clamoring for its downfall.

2. Hedonism, particularly egoistic, does not allow for what *consensus gentium* would designate a moral difference in pleasures, *e. g.*, the pleasures of a saint and sinner, a St. Paul and a Nero, an Albert Schweitzer and an Adolph Hitler. According to hedonism, whoever produces the greatest amount of pleasure is the most moral, but the pleasures of a Hitler or Nero are hardly those of a Jesus or Schweitzer; yet this philosophy would regard them of equivalent worth. G. E. Moore put it: "The state of mind of a drunkard, when he is intensely pleased with breaking pottery, is just as valuable, in itself — just as well worth having, as that of a man who is fully realizing all that is exquisite in the tragedy of King Lear, provided only mere quantity of pleasure in both cases is the same."[41]

3. Hedonism, with slight provocation, readily degenerates to the level of the *pig philosophy, i. e.*, "a doctrine worthy only of swine" as John Stuart Mill put it. This stricture, however, is not valid for all aspects of hedonism, nor all forms, *e. g.*, ethical hedonism escapes it.

4. Wilbar Marshall Urban's chief complaint against Utilitarianism is primarily the charge of *inadequacy*; pleasure divorced from value is immoral; "to find the locus of value in feeling is justified in so far that feeling is an element in or aspect of every experience of value. But feeling by itself affords . . . no adequate criterion of the good; feeling without reference to that which produces the feeling can not be equated with value."[42]

5. John Dewey and James H. Tufts object to the Utilitarian's claim that pleasure is quantitatively calculable:

"What practical sense is there in the notion that a pain may be found which is exactly equal to a pleasure, so that it may just offset it or reduce it to zero? How can one weigh the amount of pain in a jumping and long-continued toothache against, say, the pleasure of some charitable deed performed under conditions which may bring on the toothache? What relevancy has the quantitive comparison to a judgment of moral worth? How many units of pleasure are contained in the fulfillment of the intention of going to war for one's country? How many in the fulfillment of the intention to remain at home with one's family and secure profitable contracts from the government? How shall the pains involved in each act be detected and have their exact numerical force assigned them? How shall one set be measured over against the other?"[43]

6. Socrates has a potent case against hedonism; *consciousness of pleasure* is distinguishable from pleasure, *per se*; although animals undergo pleasurable experiences, having no knowledge of the experience, their pleasure is useless, or at least, unappreciable. This profound thought Plato ably records with lucidity possible only by the technique of dialogue; he places the following words in the mouth of Protarchus and Socrates:

> SOCRATES: Let there be no wisdom in the life of pleasure and no pleasure in the life of wisdom. For if either of them is the god, it cannot have need of anything else, and if either be found to need anything, we can no longer regard it as our true good.
> PROTARCHUS: No, of course not.
> SOCRATES: Shall we then undertake to test them through you?
> PROTARCHUS: By all means.
> SOCRATES: Then answer.
> PROTARCHUS: Ask.
> SOCRATES: Would you, Protarchus, be willing to live your whole life in the enjoyment of the greatest pleasures?
> PROTARCHUS: Of course I should.

SOCRATES: Would you think you needed anything further, if you were in complete possesion of that enjoyment?

PROTARCHUS: Certainly not.

SOCRATES: But consider whether you would not have some need of wisdom and intelligence and power of calculating your wants and the like.

PROTARCHUS: Why should I? If I have enjoyment, I have everything.

SOCRATES: Then living thus you would enjoy the greatest pleasures all your life?

PROTARCHUS: Yes, why not?

SOCRATES: But if you did not possess mind or memory or knowledge of true opinion, in the first place, you would not know whether you were enjoying your pleasures or not. That must be true, since you are utterly devoid of intellect, must it not?

PROTARCHUS: Yes, it must

SOCRATES: And likewise, if you had no memory you could not even remember that you ever did enjoy pleasure, and no recollection whatever of present pleasure could remain with you; if you had no true opinion you could not think you were enjoying pleasure at the time when you were enjoying it, and if you were without power of calculation you would not be able to calculate that you would enjoy it in the future; your life would not be that of a man, but of a mollusk or some other shellfish like the oyster. Is that true, or can we imagine any other result?

PROTARCHUS: We certainly cannot.

SOCRATES: And can we choose such a life?

PROTARCHUS: This argument, Socrates, has made me utterly speechless for the present.[44]

Bentham's system does have its laudable features to commend it:

1. Utilitarianism is a courageous departure from traditional systems of ethics, particularly for Bentham's time. He

has opened new vistas, some of which can be conveniently incorporated into one's personal ethical code with a fair degree of enhancement value.
2. Two doctrines, viz., *the greatest happiness principle* and *the greatest good for the greatest number*, are foundation stones of a democracy; they offer strong possibilities upon which to build a lofty democratic ethic.
3. Bentham's system places happiness and pleasure on an ethical foundation; a matter that had long been neglected. Many persons have frowned upon pleasure, *per se,* as being indecent, unclean, etc., particularly sexual pleasures, hence, such pleasures are usually condemned without a fair trial. The right of pleasure being enjoyed, *suo jure,* might be justified on an Augustinian basis, *i.e.,* pleasure is good, *per se,* its perverse use is evil.

12. Further Reading in the Philosophy of Bentham

The major works of Bentham are: *A Fragment on Government,* published anonymously (1776), *A Defence of Usury* (1787), *An Introduction to the Principles of Morals and Legislation* (1789), *Theory of Legislation* (1802), *A Table of the Springs of Action* (1817), *Codification Proposal* (1822), *The Book of Fallacies* (1824), *Rationale of Judicial Evidence* (1825), *Constitutional Code* (1830), The following were published posthumously: *Deontology* (1834), *The Works of Jeremy Bentham* (1843), *Anti-Senatica* (1926), *A Comment on the Commentaries* (1928), *Bentham's Theory of Fictions* (1932), *The Limits of Jurisprudence Defined* (1945).

NOTES

JEREMY BENTHAM

1. Jeremy Bentham, *An Introduction to the Principles of Morals and Legislation*, 17:20.
2. *Ibid.*, 1:1.
3. *Ibid.*, 17:2.
4. *Ibid.*, 1:2.
5. *Ibid.*, 1:3.
6. See A. C. Ewing, *The Definition of Good* (New York: Macmillan Co., 1947), Ch. IV.
7. *Ibid.*, 1:9.
8. *Ibid.*, 4:2.
9. *Idem.*
10. *Ibid.*, 4:4.
11. *Ibid.*, footnote to 4:2.
12. *Ibid.*, footnote to 3:2.
13. *Ibid.*, 3:2.
14. *Ibid.*, 3:8.
15. *Ibid.*, 3:6.
16. *Idem.*
17. John Stuart Mill, *Autobiography* (Oxford: University Press, 1873), 127.
18. *Ibid.*, 94.
19. John Stuart Mill, *Utilitarianism* (London: Longmans, Green and Co., 1907), 10.
20. Bentham, *op. cit.*, footnote to 10:10.
21. *Ibid.*, 10:30.
22. *Idem.*, see his footnote to 1:1.
23. *Ibid.*, 7:1.
24. *Ibid.*, 8:13.
25. *Ibid.*, 10:10.
26. *Ibid.*, 13:1.
27. *Ibid.*, 13:1
28. *Ibid.*, 11:41.
29. *Ibid.*, 11:42.
30. *Idem.*
31. *Idem.*
32. *Idem.*
33. *Idem.*
34. *Idem.*
35. *Idem.*

36. *Ibid.*, 11:41.
37. *Ibid.*, 11:40.
38. Cf. G. E. Moore, "The Indefinability of Good."
39. *Ibid.*, 1:11.
40. *Ibid.*, 1:12.
41. G. E. Moore, *Ethics* (Oxford: University Press, 1912), 238.
42. Wilbar Marshall Urban, *Fundamentals of Ethics* (New York: Henry Holt and Co., 1938), 92.
43. John Dewey and James H. Tufts, *Ethics* (New York: Henry Holt and Co., 1908), 276, 277.
44. Plato, *Philebus*, 21 a-d, tr. by Harold N. Fowler (Cambridge, Massachusetts: Harvard University Press, 1939).

JOHN STUART MILL

It is better to be a human being dissatisfied than a pig satisfied; better to be a Socrates dissatisfied than a fool satisfied. (Mill)

1. Utilitarianism

John Stuart Mill defines *Utilitarianism* as: "The creed which accepts as the foundation of morals *utility*, or the greatest happiness *principle*, holds that actions are right in proportion as they tend to promote happiness, wrong as they tend to produce the reverse of happiness. By 'happiness' is intended pleasure, and the absence of pain; by 'unhappiness,' pain, and the privation of pleasure.'"[1]

Both Bentham and Mill entertained utilitarian philosophies, but the Utilitarianism of Mill differed sharply on a fundamental point from that of Bentham resulting in a permanent rift, viz., quantitative *vs.* qualitative hedonism. Bentham's insistence that pleasures differ only in *quantity, i. e.*, their measurement is purely and solely quantitatively calculable, clashed with Mill's claim that there are levels of *qualitative* supersedure as well as quantitative gradations, *i.e.*, a difference in kind exists as well as amount. Mill vindicates his radical departure from Bentham's quantitative hedonism by claiming that "it is quite compatible with the principle of utility to recognize the fact, that some kinds of pleasure are more desirable and more valuable than others. It would be absurd that while, in estimating all other things, quality is considered as well as quantity, *the estimation* of pleasures should be supposed to depend on quantity alone.'"[2]

Mill maintained the thesis that diminutive pleasures existed which were enormously valuable because of their quality, *i. e.*, difference in kind; this qualitative difference is of sufficient import to render a minute pleasure of quality more desirable than a sizable pleasure of an inferior quality. "Pleasures derived from the higher faculties [are] to be preferable *in kind*, apart from the question of intensity, to those of which the animal nature . . . is susceptible."[3] Merely being human with rational capability is a value exceeding any and every quantitative pleasure, *e. g.*, the pleasures of a pig with its total amount of possible satisfaction, uninhibited by the customary human social restraints, unencumbered by anxieties and with complete freedom to gratify its pleasures to their utmost complement, is not preferable to the existence of a human being, miserable though he may be, ridden with mental conflicts, heartaches, anxieties, frettings, doubts, worries, etc. sufficiently severe to wish for death. The reason being that porcine pleasures, exotic or common, are inferior in value to human life and personality; merely *being* a man possesses greater worth than any pleasure or pleasures, and in any amount, afforded the pig.

Mill posed the dilemma: Is it better to be a pig happy or a man miserable? When Mill initially undertook the writing of his treatise, his primary intention was that of defending Bentham's quantitative hedonism against the onslaught of a myriad of opponents, and to take his stand in favor of porcine bliss, but at the climax of his writing of the book, he found himself incapable of preferring the pig's existence, for his hand refused to write the word, *pig*. In Mill's case, the foregoing incident is not to be construed as a sign of weakness since he was one of the most honest minds in all history, one of unimpeachable integrity, who was constantly constrained by probity to pursue truth wherever it led, consequently, he abandoned the Benthamite camp. Dissatisfaction of porcine pleasure, regardless of magnitude, was due to the fact that it failed to measure up to *human worth*; a pig in any state never approaches worth comparable to the value of *human existence*, even the wretched state of a man who longs for death. "A being of higher faculties requires more to make him happy, is capable probably of more acute suffering, and certainly accessible to it at more points, than one of an inferior type; but in spite of these liabilities, he can never really wish to sink into what he feels to be a lower grade of existence."[4]

The term *Utilitarianism* is used in reference to the ethical philosophy of Bentham and others who antedate Mill, but nevertheless Mill claims credit for originating the term, at least in its hedonistic context: Utilitarianism or "the theory of utility," means "not something to be contradistinguished from pleasure, but pleasure itself, together with exemption from pain; and instead of opposing the useful to the agreeable or the ornamental, [Utilitarians] have always declared that the useful means these, among other things."[5] The fact that Mill favors human values in preference to brute pleasure has alienated him from hedonism and Utilitarianism, *i. e.*, his ethic is not concerned with the *useful*, but the valuable, notwithstanding the fact that his book is entitled: *Utilitarianism*.

2. The *Summum Bonum* and the Right Act

"The utilitarian doctrine is that happiness ... is desirable, and the only thing desirable, as an end;" hence, happiness is the *summum bonum*, but only happiness that is qualitatively distinct, *i. e.*, peculiarly human modes of happiness are of greater worth proportionately to sensual pleasure. "Human beings have faculties more elevated than the animal appetites, and when once made conscious of them, do not regard anything as happiness which does not include their gratification."[6] The foregoing constitutes the rationale and *raison d'etre of* qualitative hedonism.

The determination of a right act stems from the characteristic nature of the *summum bonum*, viz., qualitative pleasure or happiness in its supernal form and magnitude; actions promoting the realization of the *summum bonum* are, by virtue of that fact, moral; by the same token, behavior deterrent to the realization of happiness is evil. "Happiness is the sole end of human action, and the promotion of it the test by which to judge of all human conduct; from whence it necessarily follows that it must be the criterion of morality, since a part is included in the whole."[7]

Although happiness is the test of moral good, it is only indirectly the criterion of right conduct. Bentham's hedonistic calculus, served as his criterion, but since its application was restricted to quantitative measurements, Mill had to develop another device suitable for calculating qualitative distinctions in pleasure. The *opinion of experts* served as Mill's computer. He contended that they were the only ones in a position to make a fitting decision due to their high I. Q., objectivity in making judgments, and actual hedonic experience. Mill aptly put it:

> If I am asked what I mean by a difference in quality in pleasures, or what makes one pleasure more valuable than another merely as a pleasure, except its being greater in amount, there is but one possible answer. Of two pleasures if there be one to which all or almost all who have experience of both give a decided preference, irrespective of any feeling of moral obligation to prefer it, that is the most desirable pleasure. If one of the two is, by those who are competently acquainted with both, placed so far above the other that they prefer it, even though knowing it to be attended with a greater amount of discontent, and would not resign it for any quantity of the other pleasure which their nature is capable of, we are justified in ascribing to the preferred enjoyment a superiority in quality, so far outweighing quantity as to render it, in comparison, of small account.[8]

Note that in the ethical philosophy of hedonism, obligation or duty is an extraneous consideration; hedonic experts are forbidden to use it as valid datum. Should an impasse occur as the result of a discrepancy arising among the experts by whom the judgment is to be issued, the problem is then resolved by allowing the majority of the hedonic senate who have had a first-hand experience of both pleasures decide, *i. e.*, a majority vote is taken on this aristocratic level, *e.g.*, "on a question which is best worth having of two pleasures ... apart from its moral attributes and from consequences, the judgment of those who are qualified by knowledge of both, or, if they differ, that of the majority among them, must be admitted as final.'"[9] To those disciples of Bentham and others dissatisfied with the lack of precision of Mill's system of hedonic computation, Mill replies: "There is no other tribunal to be referred to even on the question of quantity.'"[10]

Doubt arises concerning the qualifications of the hedonic experts in rendering valid decisions regarding pleasure they have not experienced, *e. g.*, pleasures of an animal or subnormal human being, such as the euphoric idiot. How can the experts claim the happiness of a fool to be inferior to their own, having never experienced it? The idiot, mentally abnormal, or ignorant individual may not seek to exchange his lot with the normal or intelligent person, if he fancies himself happier. With whom does the final decision rest? Mill favors the intelligentsia and he supports his stand with the argument that the enlightened man knows the worth of the experience of inferior beings by virtue of his greater understanding. The inverse does not hold true; the brute or the moron cannot appreciate the worth of wisdom and understanding; hence, only intelligent persons are in a position to make the proper value judgment.

> Now it is an unquestionable fact that those who are equally acquainted with, and equally capable of appreciating and enjoying, both, do give a most marked preference to the manner of existence which employs their higher faculties. Few human creatures would consent to be changed into any of the lower animals, for the allowance of the fullest pleasure of the beast's pleasures; no intelligent human being would consent to be a fool, no instructed person would be an ignoramus, no person of feeling and conscience would be selfish and base, even though they should be persuaded that the fool, the dunce, or the rascal is better satisfied with his lot than they are with theirs.[11]

In the final analysis, the *summum bonum*, viz., true happiness, would be a *human being*, both *intelligent* and *happy*, and in that order; however, if either one must be relinquished, then it is better to be a man wretched than an animal pleased, better to be an intelligent person miserable than a stupid one happy, *e. g.*, "it is better to be a human being dissatisfied than a pig satisfied; better to be a Socrates dissatisfied than a fool satisfied. And if the fool, or the pig, are of a different opinion, it is because they only know their own side of the question. The other party to the comparison knows both sides."[12]

3. Everybody to Count for One, Nobody for More Than One

"Everybody to count for one, nobody for more than one,"[13] Mill termed Bentham's dictum and incorporated it as an integral part of this ethic. The dictum, it must be admitted, is the quintescence of a democratic *Weltanschauung;* each person's happiness is as valuable as any other individual's; hence, the dictum repudiates *egoistic* hedonism. The utilitarian "standard is not the agent's own greatest happiness, but the greatest amount of happiness altogether;"[14] consequently one must sacrifice his own personal happiness and defer to the happiness of others when necessary, *i. e.,* provided others possess the *greatest* happiness. "It is involved in the very meaning of utility, or the greatest happiness principle ... one person's happiness, supposed equal in degree (with proper allowance made for kind), is counted for exactly as much as another's."[15] Each person's life is as important and as sweet to him as anyone else's is to that person; hence, every human being is equally entitled to the democratic claim of the *pursuit of happiness.* "The equal claim of everybody to happiness in the estimation of the moralist ... involves an equal claim to all the means of happiness..... All persons are deemed to have a *right* to equality of treatment."[16] *Justice* is the term that best designates this right to happiness and of equality; justice is a qualitative value worthy of being "guarded by a sentiment not only different in degree, but also in kind."[17] Its antithesis is *selfishness*, whose manifestations are prominent in the ethics of egoistic hedonism. Mill's opposition to egoistic hedonism is not limited to its reprehensibly immoral connotations, he contends that egoism is not even the road to pleasure, inasmuch as selfishness robs one of many of the pleasures in life. "Next to selfishness, the principle cause which makes life unsatisfactory is want of mental cultivation,"[18] viz., the development of one's mental and spiritual self. This qualification may echo the characteristics of a philosopher, however, most persons are not required to achieve that lofty goal, but everyone is expected to have an *inexhaustible interest* sufficiently potent to "retain as lively an interest in life on the eve of death as in the vigor of youth and health."[19]

4. The Two Sanctions

Bentham offered *sanctions* in order to validate his ethic; Mill follows suit, except that Mill has two compared to Bentham's four, viz., *internal* and *external*. To reiterate the connotation of sanction, it is the moral impetus or force which renders a moral principle sufficiently binding to command one's obedience; hence, it is a moral dictate or that which impels to moral action.

Mill confronts a crucial problem facing a utilitarian, viz., "Why am I bound to promote the general happiness?" He understands the seat of the difficulty to rest in the fact that the utilitarian principle is wanting the sanction other ethical codes enjoy such as the Ten Commandments; the reason being that Utilitarianism is not a principle in men's minds vested with sacredness, nor is it like those venerated customs which have been dignified by having a "halo" cast about them. Nevertheless, Utilitarianism does have two sanctions, viz., *external* and *internal*; the *external sanction* is "the hope of favor and the fear of displeasure, from our fellow-creatures or from the Ruler of the Universe."[20] There is little doubt that the external sanction is a composite of Bentham's moral and religious sanctions. He justifies the inclusion of the religious sanction in Utilitarianism on the grounds of God's approbation, *i. e.*, God wants his creatures to be happy and enjoy the pleasurable; this is a tribute to his providential concern. Furthermore,

Mill claims to have as much right as anyone else to invoke the religious sanction or motive in support of his ethic.

The *internal sanction* is a sense of obligation or duty summoning an individual's own sense of responsibility; "the internal sanction ... is a feeling in our own mind: a pain, more or less intense, attendant on volition of duty, which in properly cultivated moral natures rises, in the more serious cases, into shrinking from it as an impossibility. This feeling ... is the essence of conscience."[21] The internal is the ultimate sanction of all morality, its *raison d'etre*; since it is a subjective feeling in the mind, it is allied to the standard inherent in other moral systems, viz., the conscientious feelings of mankind, *i. e.*, conscience. Mill has reservations regarding the innateness of moral feelings, viz., conscience; his position is that they are acquired by self-cultivation or nurture, *i.e.*, socialization or social environmental influences. It is well within the range of possibility that moral feelings, viz., the moral faculty, are not part of human nature, but an epiphenomenon or by-product.

5. Justice

Justice is defined as "the animal desire to repel or retaliate a hurt or damage to oneself, or to those with whom one sympathizes, widened so as to include all persons, by the human capacity of enlarged sympathy and the human conception of intelligent self-interest."[22] Most persons will find this concept of justice familiar; they will recognize it as the *lex talionis* (law of retaliation), *e. g.*, "an eye for an eye and a tooth for a tooth," except that it is reduced to the level of a human sentiment.

Justice encompasses numerous characteristics: 1. It constitutes the legal rights of an individual regarding his personal liberty and property, *e. g.*, justice is respect for such rights and injustice their violation. 2. Justice is also composed of legal rights *due* an individual, *e. g.*, those of which he is temporarily deprived; hence, justice includes the rights one *ought* to have. 3. The third quality has an affinity to the second listed, viz., its service or dispensation, *e. g.*, each person ought to receive his just deserts, concomitant penalties for evil and accompanying rewards for deserving individuals. 4. Justice implies fidelity and integrity, *e.g.*, one must keep faith by making good his contractual promises. Justice connotes impartiality, its prime judicial virtue.

The essence of justice is equality, as an etymological analysis of the word indicates: the term is derived from the Latin *justum*, which is a form of *jussem*, i. e., that which has been ordered. The Greek derivative *dikaion*; comes from *dike*, a suit at law; *right* or *righteousness* stems from this term. The French, *la justice*, is the established term for judicature; hence, intimating justice to be conformity to law.

Justice and *duty* are inversely related, *e. g.*, a duty is an incurred debt which another has the right of exacting. Justice delineates the limits of *responsibility*, by restricting responsibility to volition, *i. e.*, that which is voluntarily executed. The scope of justice is not exhaustive, *i. e.*, certain anomalous cases emerge which escape the jurisdiction of justice and call for an overruling or overriding principle, *e.g.*, "to save a life, it may not only be allowable but a duty to steal or take by force the necessary food or medicine, or to kidnap and compel to officiate the only qualified medical practitioner. In such cases ... we usually say, not that justice must give way to some other moral principle, but that what is just in ordinary cases is, by reason of that other principle, not just in the particular case."[23] Mill furnishes no term or principle applicable to cases such as the foregoing; equity somewhat approximates it.

6. The Proof of Utilitarianism

"The only proof capable of being given that an object is visible, is that people actually see it. The only proof that a sound is audible, is that people hear it: and so of the other sources of our experience. In like manner, I apprehend, the sole evidence it is possible to produce that anything is desirable, is that people do actually desire it."[24] Mill offers the foregoing statement as the proof of the utilitarian doctrine. It seems ironic that Mill's proof of Utilitarianism should commit a glaring error in logic, inasmuch as he was a notable pioneer credited with formulating many of the current principles of logic and scientific method. His work in logic[25] is regarded as classic; it includes *five canons* for determining causation which are often quoted *verbatim ac litteratim* in many college textbooks.

The specific logical error committed is termed by logicians, the figure of speech fallacy:[26] in Mill's case, the error rests on the false assumption that a likeness in the suffixes of the words *visible, audible, desirable,* carries with it a similarity in meaning. The visibility of an object denotes its *ability* to be seen, *i. e.*, it *can* be seen, provided the object is in view; the significance of an object's audibility is its *ability* of being heard; the suffix *ible* is equivalent to the one affixed to visible; but an object's desirability does *not* convey ability as is true of the former two; the meaning of the suffix here is *ought* to be desired, in contradistinction to *is, can,* or *able* to be desired. Ought implies duty, obligation, and especially *choice, e. g.,* an object in full view must be seen, *nolens volens,* since it is visible, but that which is desirable need not be actually desired, such as the surgeon's admonition to his patient: "An appendectomy in your case is *highly desirable,*" does not mean that the patient will *in fact* desire or relish it; its import is, it *ought* to be desired, and one has a *choice* in abstaining and rejecting the desirability of good health.

Mill does have a formidable defence for the support of his ethic, viz., its *indisputability*; Utilitarians claim that other systems of ethics are subject to debate and argumentation, but pleasure and happiness are incontestable values, *e. g.*, even the redoubtable *Ten Commandments* are subject to controversy, *e.g.,* "Thou shalt not kill" is a debatable issue; some persons question its validity in times of war, self-defence, or capital punishment, but pleasure and happiness elude all such controversial discussion. The human being experiencing pleasure or happiness can never bring himself to say truthfully that he does not like it, *i. e.*, it is not good. "No general reason can be given why the general happiness is desirable except that each person . . . desires his own happiness. This, however, being a fact, we have not only all the proof which the case admits of, but all which it is possible to require, that happiness is a good: that each person's happiness is a good to that person."[27]

One's right to enjoy a pleasure is debatable, *e.g.*, eating delicious foods restricted by one's physician, seeking adulterous sex gratification, or stealing the irresistibly desirable; but their *de facto* pleasure is undeniable. It must be admitted that moments spent indulging in a delectable dinner are pleasant. One is forced to acknowledge that it is good in the sense that he likes it. Hence, "happiness has made out its title as *one* of the ends of conduct, and consequently one of the criteria of morality."[28]

Mill uses still another avenue to defend his position; he justifies his ethic on *theological grounds*. God is good, therefore wills pleasure for mankind; "God desires above all things, the happiness of his creatures, and that this was the purpose of their creation,"[29] hence God approves of men enjoying pleasures. "With regard to the religious motive, if men believe, as most profess to do, in the goodness of God, those who think that conduciveness to the general happiness is the essence, or even the criterion, of good, must necessarily believe that it is also that which God approves."[30] Furthermore, he contends that the ideal of the utilitarian morality when properly practiced is the *golden rule* in practice.

In his apologia of the utilitarian doctrine, Mill concedes that he is not employing proof in the ordinary or popular sense of the term, nevertheless, he is desirous of making a satisfactory contribution towards the understanding and appreciation of his mode of Utilitarianism, with the hope that it is sufficiently convincing to warrant its adoption. He rests his case with: "If this doctrine be true, the principle of utility is proved. Whether it is so or not, must now be left to the consideration of the thoughtful reader."[31]

7. Comparison of the Ethics of Bentham and Mill

Mill severed philosophical relations with Bentham on three major issues: (1) the repudiation of *psychological hedonism*; (2) the maintenance of *qualitative pleasures* and their *primacy* of value over quantitative pleasures; (3) the existence of *internal sanctions* as well as external ones.

(1) *Psychological hedonism*, the doctrine that an individual is constituted by nature in such a manner as to be deprived of all choice, except to seek pleasure and avoid the painful, was abandoned by Mill. His emphasis was on singularly human values; since men were of a higher species of being than animals, one should seek the pleasure most appropriate to this superior nature. Pleasures derived from purely human qualities provide value far surpassing any intensity possible on the animal level of existence.

(2) The supremacy of *qualitative pleasures* over quantitative is illustrated in the following example: It is conceivable that the vegetable, such as the cabbage is free from anxious care, escapes mental anguish caused by life's vexatious exigencies, is not plagued with doubts, mental turmoil, fret, etc.; it lives a simple existence of lying out in the field, basking in the sunshine, but *who wants to be a cabbage*? It is better to be a man vainly coping with all of one's worries, heartaches, problems, anxieties, than an animal with its full complement of pleasures and its mind free from care. The qualitative difference in enjoying human existence, regardless of the depth of wretchedness suffered, is not worth exchanging for the animal's lot. There is a value in merely being human that renders the greatest pleasure of the brute of negligible value.

(3) In contradistinction to the animal, man is endowed with internal sanctions, such as a conscience to guide him in his moral pursuits; furthermore, since he is a social being, he observes established moral rules of conduct, viz., laws, mores, etc. In this respect, a feeling of unity prevails over the human community; each person's happiness is shared according to the principle of justice, in an equitable manner, inasmuch as each man is the peer of every other; hence, the happiness of each man counts for one only, *i. e.*, each one to count for one, nobody for more than one. The internal sanction implies an innate goodness within the individual inducing him to do the right act, independent of external coercion, such as, fear of consequences, viz., punishment, hell, etc.

8. Evaluation of Mill's Ethic

The adverse critical comments will be treated first, following the pattern adopted previously:

1. One of the greatest problems confronting the student of the Utilitarian school of thought is that which arises from a transition from quantitative to qualitative hedonism. Mill differed from Bentham and Sidgwick in this respect, but it is precisely this issue which alienates him from the Utilitarian doctrine, *i.e.*, it would be a misnomer to refer to Mill as a Utilitarian. If pleasures of one kind are more desirable than those of another, not because of quantity, but because of quality, then it follows that pleasure, *per se*, cannot be the sole criterion of good, *value* has displaced pleasure as the definitive test, in other words, if it is better to be a dissatisfied Socrates than a pleasure filled pig, then Mill has modified Utilitarianism, if he has not completely surrendered it.

"If, indeed, we were to take the Utilitarian principle strictly, and to assume them to mean that the possession of pleasure by many persons was good in itself, the principle is not hedonistic: it includes as a necessary part of the ultimate end, the existence of a number of persons, and this will include very much more than mere pleasure."[32]

2. In matters of dispute concerning which is the more valuable of two pleasures, their respective values are determined by the tribunal of hedonic experts who are expected to execute their responsibilities "strictly impartially as a disinterested and benevolent spectator." This being the case, then the specific value of a given pleasure is more than mere sensation; it becomes a matter of *understanding discretion, judgment, evaluation,* or even *scientific inquiry.* Mill would have to yield to this point, since he insists that the more intelligent a being is, the greater his capability of rendering decisions, because by virtue of his superior intellect, he has an understanding of both pleasures, *i.e.*, his own and those of his inferiors, whereas the animal or fool has not.

3. One problem Mill created for himself in defending

his ethic, pertains to logic, viz., the *fallacy of composition,* *i.e.,* assuming that what is true of each part taken separately is necessarily true of the composite whole, *e.g.,* if a class of twenty school children were to stand in a line according to height and the smallest child's stature was increased by giving him a six inch box on which to stand, consequently elevating him to a position further up the line; it does not follow that the entire class would go further up the line if everyone were given a six inch box. They would revert to their original positions, if this were done.

Mill made the mistake of assuming that because each person's happiness is a good to that particular individual, then the general happiness is a good to the aggregate of all persons.

Mill fell prey to a second error in logic, viz., the *figure of speech fallacy.* Mere mention is made of this issue, inasmuch as it has been sufficiently treated in the section: *The Proof of Utilitarianism.*

4. There are times when a person ought to disapprove of conduct that results in the greatest happiness of the greatest number, in favor of doing that which is *just, equitable,* and right when it is called for, such as supporting the rights of minority groups.

5. Another objection to their system that Utilitarians have not resolved is the classic *hedonistic paradox,* viz., that one cannot find happiness by going in direct pursuit of it, inasmuch as happiness is a state of mind which issues as a by-product. A fuller treatment of this paradox may be found in the section on the evaluation of Aristotle.

6. Dr. Blanshard[33] observes that if the principles, "each one is to count for one and nobody for more than one" and the "greatest happiness principle" were put into operation, the majority would have the right to do whatever pleases them at the expense of the minority, even to the point of conducting cancer experiments on the minority, inasmuch as it would result in the greatest total of good for the greatest number, viz., the majority.

7. Mill, in resting the decision of identifying the more desirable pleasures to the hedonic senate, is appealing to majority rule on an aristocratic level as the criterion of truth. There is no logical guarantee that an aggregate of votes from such a body will furnish the truth; not to mention that they are expected to accomplish the feat invariably.

Many of the criticisms brought to bear against Hedonism in general are applicable here as well, but merely calling attention to this fact should suffice. The positive side of the evaluation warrants consideration:

1. Mill rescued Utilitarianism from degenerating to the depths of a *pig philosophy, i.e.,* "a doctrine worthy only of swine," and transformed it into a respectable ethic. This was achieved essentially through the introduction of qualitative hedonism which assigned moral status and value to man's higher faculties, consequently out of egoistic hedonism was born ethical hedonism.

2. Mill reclaimed Utilitarianism from psychological hedonism by ascribing autonomy to it, *e.g.,* an individual is both free to make a choice as to which pleasure he ought to select and he is in a position to select extra-sensual ones, *i.e.,* the qualitatively superior, namely the spiritual.

3. Whereas many ethical systems ignore the moral significance of pleasure and happiness, Mill has given them due consideration, *e.g.,* suffering and pain should be regarded as evils. One ought to accept as a moral responsibility any task that helps to banish or alleviate human pain and suffering. *Happiness* is an important human value well worth promoting.

4. Although *everybody to count for one, nobody for more than one,* is termed Bentham's dictum; it was Mill who named it and was responsible for the prominent position it enjoys in Utilitarianism; hence the credit should accrue to him. The dictum expresses the essence of human justice and serves as the basis upon which political democracies are built. The inalienable right to happiness and suffrage are some of its more important implications and consequences.

9. Further Reading in the Philosophy of Mill

The more important works of Mills are: *System of Logic* (1843), *Principles of Political Economy* (1848), *On Liberty* (1859), *Considerations on Representative Government* (1861), *Utilitarianism* (1863), *Examination of Sir William Hamilton's Philosophy* (1865), *Subjection of Women* (1869). The following were published posthumously: *Nature, The Utility of Religion, Theism* (1874), *Autobiography* (1873).

NOTES
JOHN STUART MILL

1. John Stuart Mill, *Utilitarianism* (Longmans, Green and Co., 1907), 9, 10.
2. *Ibid.*, 11, 12.
3. *Ibid.*, 16.
4. *Ibid.*, 13.
5. *Ibid.*, **8.**
6. *Ibid.*, 11.
7. *Ibid.*, **58.**
8. *Ibid.*, 12.
9. *Ibid.*, 15.
10. *Ibid.*
11. *Ibid.*, 12.
12. *Ibid.*, 14.
13. *Ibid.*, 93.
14. *Ibid.*, 16.
15. *Ibid.*, 93.
16. *Ibid.*, 94.
17. *Ibid.*, 96.
18. *Ibid.*, 20.
19. *Ibid.*
20. *Ibid.*, 40.
21. *Ibid.*, 41.
22. *Ibid.*, 79.
23. *Ibid.*, 95.
24. *Ibid.*, 52, 53.
25. John Stuart Mill, *A System of Logic* (New York: Harper and Brothers, 1846).
26. See Alburey Castell, *A College Logic* (New York: Macmillan Co., 1935), 17, 18 and W. H. Werkmeister, *An Introduction to Critical Thinking* (Lincoln, Nebraska: Johnsen Publishing Co., 1957), 35.
27. John Stuart Mill, *Utilitarianism, op. cit.*, 53.
28. *Ibid.*
29. ***Ibid.***
30. *Ibid.*, 41.
31. *Ibid.*, 61.
32. G. E. Moore, *Principia Ethica, op. cit.*, 107.
33. Brand Blanshard, *op. cit.*

EPICURUS

Let us eat and drink: for to-morrow we shall die.
(Isaiah 22:13)

1. Epicureanism

Epicurus, Aristotle's contemporary, unlike the other philosophers treated, did not write a systematic ethic; whatever semblance of a system is detectable in his *fragmental* writings, is left to the reader to piece together. Of major significance, richly supplementing the fragments, are his letters to diverse individuals and his biography written by Diogenes Laertius. Although Epicurus was a prolific writer, as intimated above, many of his writings are lost; nevertheless, a cursory summary of his philosophy is found in a letter writen to a young disciple.[1]

Epicureanism is a form of hedonism, closely resembling the hedonism of the Utilitarians, but one major modification being Epicurus' obsession with pain; his over-preoccupation with mental anguish and distress in this regard resembles psychological hedonism for he contends that "we avoid pain by instinct."[2] Much of his philosophy is negatively oriented, *i. e.*, his major emphasis is concerned with techniques of confronting pain to the almost complete indifference of the pursuit of pleasure. In this respect, Epicurus differed from other ancient hedonists such as Aristippus and the Cyrenaics whose prime objective was to seek and enjoy the pleasures of the moment before the opportunity slipped by. They lived by the code: "Eat, drink and be merry, for tomorrow we die." The Cyrenaics strongly advocated that one seize pleasures as quickly as possible, lest due to their elusive and fleeting quality, they slip away with no second opportunity offered; hence, one is urged to gratify whatever pleasure is within reach; to-morrow may be too late.

Epicurus repudiated the hedonism of Aristippus and the Cyrenaics on the grounds that *one may not die with the coming of the morrow*; rather, he may live to suffer and regret the lasting baneful consequences of momentary pleasures; "for this very reason we do not choose every pleasure, but sometimes we pass over many pleasures, when greater discomfort accrues to us as the result of them."[3] Sensual pleasures, particularly, leave great sums of misery and pain in their wake. "You tell me that the stimulus of the flesh makes you too prone to the pleasures of love. Provided you do not break the laws . . . you may indulge your inclination as you please. Yet it is not possible not to come up against one or other of these barriers; for the *pleasures of love never profited a man* and he is lucky if they do him no harm."[4]

As mentioned above, Epicurus stressed the avoidance of pain and gave minimal value to satisfactions of pleasure; furthermore, when discussing the enjoyment of pleasure, he expressed preference for the pleasures of the mind or soul, to the almost total exclusion of sensual pleasure, for spiritual pleasures would fructify without a deleterious aftermath. The following would qualify as genuine or legitimate pleasure: all pleasures of the mind, the avoidance of pain, mental tranquility, peace of soul. Pleasures are dichotomized into: *motion* (sensual) and *static pleasures* (spiritual), *e. g.,* "freedom from trouble in the mind and from pain in the body are static pleasures, but joy and exultation are considered as active pleasures involving motion."[5] Epicurus taught that pains of the soul are more oppresive than those of the body, *e.g.*, it is easier to endure a whip lashing upon the body than to suffer mental anguish.

Mental anxiety in its severest form is *fear of death*. Epicurus has a singular approach in confronting fear of death; its logic assumes the form of a dilemma: Fear of death is needlessly vain, inasmuch as when one is alive then death is nonexistent; and when one is in the state of death, there is no cause for fearing death if there is an immortality; but if death ends all, then one cannot worry anyway in that state. Epicurus expresses it, "death, the most terrifying of ills, is nothing to us, since so long as we exist death is not with us; but when death comes, then we do not exist. It does not then concern either the living or the dead, since for the former it is not, and the latter are no more."[6] It is not the pain which commonly accompanies death that is so dreadful, but the terrifying anticipation of it.

The wise man makes the most of life; it is not longevity, but the pleasant periods experienced, that are valuable. "The wise man neither seeks to escape life nor fears the cessation of life, for neither does life offend him nor does the absence of life seem to be any evil . . . it is the same training which teaches to live well and to die well."[7] The person who regrets being born is in an unenviable predicament from which there is no extrication; the most that he can hope to attain is partial alleviation through a proper attitude or psychological adjustment towards life. Since man has no control of his future, the wisest course of action is not to abandon hope on the forecast of an unpromising future, but to approach the future with anticipatory trust, a quality productive of happiness and tranquility; moreover, confident expectation, *i. e.*, an optimistic outlook on life will insure one's being alive when *la dolce vita* comes. All mental anguish in life is fundamentally fear of death; consequently, anxiety subsides by annihilating the craving for immortality; "there is nothing terrible in life for the man who has truly comprehended that there is nothing terrible in not living."[8] It is imperative that one become accustomed, *i. e.*, adjusted to the thought of death, and surrender to the recognition and acceptance of it as a reality, then death's sting will be rendered powerless and will prove no longer distressing. "All good and evil consists in sensation, but death is the deprivation of sensation. And therefore a right understanding that death is nothing to us makes mortality of life enjoyable, not because it adds to it an indefinite span of time, but because it takes away the craving for immortality."[9]

Man is by nature a pleasure seeking being, but it is folly for one to select every pleasure indiscriminately. Although all pleasures are good, not every pleasure is worthy of choice; some of them ought to be shunned, viz., those that subsequently accrue greater discomforts. On the other hand, all pain is evil but not all pain ought to be avoided; pains and pleasures must be weighed against each other; pains serving a good purpose are instrumental goods; consequently, ought to be accepted and endured. "The good on certain occasions we treat as bad, and conversely the bad as good."[10] Occasionally, it is better to forego pleasure and there are moments when it is advantageous to extinguish desires, inasmuch as sacrifice, continence, and temperance enhance pleasures, *i.e.*, heighten their enjoyment when partaken. "Bread and water produce the highest pleasure, when one who needs them puts them to his lips. To grow accustomed to simple and not luxurious diet gives us health to the full, and makes a man alert for the needful employments of life, and when after long intervals we approach luxuries, disposes us better towards them, and fits us to be fearless of fortune."[11] Although pleasure is life's ultimate goal, it is not the "pleasure of profligates and those that consist of sensuality" but a refined mode of pleasure that issues in "freedom from pain in the body and from trouble in the mind. For it is not continuous drinkings and revellings, not the satisfaction of lusts, not the employment of fish and other luxuries of the wealthy table, which produce a pleasant life, but sober reasoning."[12]

2. The Summum Bonum (Prudence)

Prudence, recognized by Epicurus as the *summun bonum*, is a necessary requisite in the attainment of the foregoing lofty goal. Prudence, the greatest good, even excels the preciousness of philosophy, because from it ensues every virtue, and the greatest pleasures, both of which are inseparably bound to the pleasant life. "The greatest good is prudence ... for from prudence are sprung all the other virtues, and it teaches us that it is not possible to live pleasantly without living prudently and honourably and justly, nor, again, to live a life of prudence, honour and justice without living pleasantly.

For all the virtues are bound up with the pleasant life, and the pleasant life is inseparable from them."[13] The prudent man can scoff at the mistress of all things, viz., *destiny*; inasmuch as he leaves nothing to fate "for he does not believe that good and evil are given by chance to man for the framing of a blessed life, but that opportunities for great good ... are afforded by it. ... It is better in a man's actions that what is well chosen should fail, rather than that what is ill chosen should be successful owing to chance."[14]

By way of epilogue, it is worth mentioning a final interesting feature in the philosophy of Epicurus, *i. e.*, the importance he attaches to *friendship*. His estimation of it is great enough to move him to offer the following encomiastic opinion: "of all the things which wisdom acquires to produce the blessedness of the complete life, far the greatest is the possession of friendship."[15]

3. Selected Proverbs of Epicurus

The following proverbs, maxims, exhortations, etc. are offered in the expectation that they will prove interesting as well as elucidative to the understanding of Epicurus' ethic.

a. FROM THE *PRINCIPLE DOCTRINES*

2. Death is nothing to us: for that which is dissolved is without sensation; and that which lacks sensation is nothing to us.

8. No pleasure is a bad thing in itself; but the means which produce some pleasures bring with them disturbances many times greater than the pleasures.

b. FROM THE *VATICAN COLLECTION*

38. He is a little man in all respects who has many good reasons for quitting life.

39. He is no friend who is continually asking for help, nor he who never associates help with friendship.

46. Our bad habits, like evil men who have long done us great harm, let us utterly drive from us.

48. We must try to make the end of the journey better than the beginning.

53. We must envy no one: for the good do not deserve envy and the bad, the more they prosper, the more they injure themselves.

61. Most beautiful too is the sight of those near and dear to us, when our original kinship makes us of one mind.

68. Nothing is sufficient for him to whom what is sufficient seems little.

77. The greatest fruit of self-sufficiency is freedom.

79. The man who is serene causes no disturbance to himself or to another.

c) FROM THE *SYMPOSIUM*

8. Sexual intercourse has never done a man good, and he is lucky if it has not harmed him.

d) FROM *ON THE END OF LIFE*

10. I know not how I can conceive the good, if I withdraw the pleasures of taste, and withdraw the pleasures of love, and withdraw the pleasures of hearing, and withdraw the pleasurable emotions caused to sight by beautiful form.

12. Beauty and virtue and the like are to be honoured, if they give pleasure; but if they do not give pleasure, we must bid them farewell.

e) FROM THE *LETTER TO ANAXARCHUS*

21. But I summon you to continuous pleasures and not to vain and empty virtues which have but disturbing hopes of results.

f) FROM THE *LETTER TO IDOMENEUS*

29. We think highly of frugality not that we may always keep to a cheap and simple diet, but that we may be free from desire regarding it.

g) FROM *LETTERS TO UNKNOWN RECIPIENTS*

37. I am thrilled with pleasure in the body, when I live on bread and water, and I spit on luxurious pleasures

not for their own sake, but for the inconveniences that follow them.

44. Think it not unnatural that when the flesh cries aloud, the soul cries too.

48. It is better for you to be free of fear lying upon a pallet, than to have a golden couch and a rich table and be full of trouble.

h) FROM *FRAGMENTS FROM UNCERTAIN SOURCES*

59. The beginning and the root of all good is pleasure of the stomach; even wisdom and culture must be referred to this.

74. Unhappiness comes either through fear or through vain and unbridled desire: but if a man curbs these, he can win for himself the blessedness of understanding.

79. I spit on the beautiful and those who vainly admire it, when it does not produce any pleasure.

80. The greatest fruit of justice is serenity.

4. Further Reading in the Philosophy of Epicurus

The extant writings of Epicurus consist of the following: Letters to *Herodotus, Pythocles, Menoeceus; Principle Doctrines;* the following *Fragments: Vatican Collection, Remains Assigned to Certain Books, Remains of Letters, Fragments from Uncertain Sources*; and finally *The Life of Epicurus by Diogenes Laertius.*

NOTES

EPICURUS

1. *Menoeceus.*
2. Diogenes Laertius, *The Life of Epicurus,* tr. by C. Bailey.
3. Epicurus, *Menoeceus.* Epicurus' extant writings are throughout this chapter translated by Cyril Bailey (Oxford: Clarendon Press, 1926).
4. Epicurus, *Fragments,* 51.
5. Diogenes Laertius, *op. cit.*
6. Epicurus, *Menoeceus.*
7. *Idem.*
8. *Idem.*
9. *Idem.*
10. *Idem.*
11. *Idem.*
12. *Idem.*
13. *Idem.*
14. *Idem.*
15. Epicurus, *Principle Doctrines,* 27.

STOICISM AND CYNICISM

EPICTETUS

Anytus and Meletus have power to put me to death, but not to harm me. (Socrates)

1. Stoicism

Epictetus, who lived in the first century after Jesus Christ, adhered to the *Stoic* school of philosophy; the school's founding was by Zeno in the fourth century B. C. The Stoical ideas emphasized by Epictetus are: (1) the importance of being *self-sufficient;* (2) the *universe as fundamentally good,* and the *absence of surd evil;*[1] (3) the *summum bonum as moral virtue;* (4) virtue defined as *living according to nature;* (5) man's provisional *resignation to and acceptance of whatever befalls i.e.,* accept whatever is not in one's power to alter, or else treat it with indifference; (6) *endurance* the supreme virtue; (7) the *properly disciplined will* as autonomous and unconquerable; (8) a *materialistic and mechanistic*[2] universe created by a pantheistic[3] God; (9) life's goal as eternal calm and tranquility; (10) the doctrine of the immanence of God, *i.e.,* the indwelling presence of God in man; (11) the function of logic and science as the instrument in achieving man's goal, viz., the good life; (12) stoical pessimism, viz., *taedium vitae, i.e.,* suicide or the doctrine that death's door is always open and one is at liberty to depart from this present life when weary of it.

2. Contentment

A decisive note in the teachings of Epictetus is the summons of being *content* with one's lot; it is not only unwise to complain about one's portion in life and covet another man's, but the practice is distressing to the soul; consequently robbing the mind of its tranquility. Epictetus elucidates upon one phase of mental serenity and reveals the technique of its achievement by the following incident which transpired in his personal life:

> If, then, you wish not to be choleric, do not feed the angry habit, do not add fuel to the fire. To begin with, keep quiet, and count the days when you were not angry. I used to be angry every day, then every other day, then every three days, then every four ... the habit is first weakened and then wholly destroyed ... I kept free from distress today, and again the next day, and for two or three months after; and when occasions arose to provoke it, I took pains to check it.[4]

Self-control plays a major role in Stoicism, its full fruition culminating in contentment. Self-mastery is imperative if peace of mind is sought. If one permits his mental equilibrium to become disturbed by another's provocations, then he is reduced to a slave existence, inasmuch as he has granted another the extravagant license and power of manipulating his spirit by a foreign will. If it is unthinkable to allow another to tamper perniciously with one's body, then why permit another to trifle with the mind's placidity, *e.g.,* "if anyone trusted your body to the first man he met, you would be indignant, but yet you trust your mind to the chance comer, and allow it to be disturbed and confounded if he revile you; are you not ashamed to do so?"[5]

Peace of mind is an achievement, but possible only to those who resign themselves to the inevitable, *i.e.,* what cannot be altered. Life's exigencies should be regarded as a test for the trial of men's souls; "difficulties are what show men's character. Therefore when a difficult crisis meets you, remember you are as the raw youth with whom God the trainer is wrestling."[6] One should accept, even welcome the vicissitudes of life as a vigorous exercise for the proper grooming, cultivation, and enhancement of the soul; in this manner one builds self-confidence and with it accrues tranquility of mind, freedom of soul, and the satisfaction and pride of being able to say, "no enemy is near, all is full of peace."[7]

Desire and want are often the cause of mental anguish; if mental turmoil is to be avoided, one must be content to accept life as it comes, *e.g.*, theft cannot hurt, if one is indifferent or lethargic to what is stolen, the cheat cannot injure one who cares little for what has been swindled. "Why then are we angry? Because we admire the material things of which they rob us. For only cease to admire your clothes, and you are not angry with him who steals them: cease to admire your wife's beauty, and you cease to be angry with the adulterer."[8]

Inability to *surrender* one's possessions looms as a constant threat to one's composure; it is mandatory that one learn to accept the hardships of life in the spirit of contentment, to enjoy the offerings of fortune, but to be resigned to its losses, if necessary.[9] This is accomplished through self-discipline, *i.e.*, apprising oneself of the true nature of the valued property, becoming cognizant that it is perishable or alterable, appreciating the fact that one does not bring anything into this world and retires from it in the same manner; hence, serenity is gained through surrender. Anxiety concerning life and daily bread is painfully distressing, therefore should be eradicated from the soul, "for it is better to die of hunger, so that you be free from pain and free from fear, than to live in plenty and be troubled in mind."[10] A mind at peace is prized more than life or death.

3. The Unconquerable Will

As long as a man's peace of mind is subject to externals, he is enslaved; even his own life must not be a source of disturbance, for it holds a destructive potential equivalent to external debilitating forces. Imprisonment does not consist in being jailed, but in being subjugated to extraneous forces. "What do you mean by prison? He is in prison already; for a man's prison is the place that he is in against his will, just as, conversely, Socrates was not in prison, for he chose to be there."[111] A man's will must be his sole directive to the good life guided by logical reason. Defeat emerges only when permitted, *e.g.*, a man may be the victim of a theft, whipping, physical injury inflicted by another or even put to death, but cannot be hurt, demoralized, or agitated unless he grants another the privilege or power to affect him in this manner. "I must die. But must I die groaning? I must be imprisoned. But must I whine as well? I must suffer exile. Can any one then hinder me from going with a smile, and a good courage, and at peace?"[12] No power foreign to one's will can break one's will, but it can be sold, surrendered, chained, etc., if allowed. "What say you, fellow? Chain me? My leg you will chain—yes, but my will—no, not even Zeus can conquer that."[113]

One must become acclimated to whatever circumstance befalls; furthermore, he must be content with his destiny regardless of the severity of the losses suffered. The task of self-discipline requires relentless determination from which one must never be dissuaded; this feat is achieved through training the will which successful attainment is recognized and rewarded when a man dies "as befits one who gives back what is not his own." One must acknowledge the fact that he entered the world naked and pauperized, therefore, he must learn to surrender his acquisitions, not only without a whimper, but graciously and undistraught. "It was in this spirit that Agrippinus used to say—do you know what? 'I will not stand in my own way!' News was brought to him, 'Your trial is on in the Senate!' 'Good luck to it, but the fifth hour is come'—this was the hour when he used to take his exercise and have a cold bath—'let us go and take exercise.' When he had taken his exercise they came and told him, 'You are condemned.' 'Exile or death?' he asked. 'Exile.' 'And my property?' 'It is not confiscated.' 'Well then, let us go to Aricia and dine',"[114] Not all things are within the power of one's will; when this is the case, then one must resign himself to fate.

4. Resignation

There are two approaches a man may take in facing the inevitable; one is to assume an attitude of indifference towards it and the other is to *accept it willingly, i.e., to go the second mile.*[15] Evil's sting[16] does not exist in the outer world, it dwells within the individual as a state of mind. "The essence of good and evil lies in an attitude of the will."[17] It is principally a condition of the soul, *e. g.*, as a body that is in good condition can endure the fluctuation of temperature, "so those whose souls are in good condition can bear anger and pain and exultation and the other emotions."[18] The avoidance of evil or its mastery issues as a concomitant of a well ordered house; it is the wholesome cultivation of the soul, *e. g.*, there is no sting to death, except what a man permits it, *i. e.*, only a vanquished soul suffers the pain of death. When death is imminent, its bitterness can be avoided through *resignation* in the same spirit of Socrates, "Well, Crito, if this be the gods' will, so be it."[19] The shame is not in undergoing suffering, but in succumbing to it. Again, Epictetus quotes Socrates, "Anytus and Meletus have the power to put me to death, but not to harm me." The evil endured at the hands of another cannot hurt unless one permits or indulges in self-pity.

It is imperative that one be unaffected by the exigencies of life and calmly accept them as they occur; *resignation* removes their irritating prick. Once more, Agrippinus is used to exemplify this principle: "It is right to praise Agrippinus for this reason, that having shown himself a man of the highest worth, he never praised himself, but blushed if anyone else praised him. His character was such that when any distress befell him he wrote a eulogy of it; if a fever was his portion he praised fever; if disrepute, he praised disrepute; and if exile, he praised exile. An the day when he was about to breakfast, a messenger interrupted him to say that Nero ordered him into exile. 'Well then,' said he, 'we will breakfast in Aricia.' "[20] This is illustratative of the *second mile* attitude that one is expected to assume toward evil. Another manner of achieving this objective is to have an individual meditate on death and other anxiety provoking situations so as to cushion their effect through the realization that ultimately it matters little what fate has in store. The sole course to freedom is "to despise what is not in our power."

What is beyond human power should be left in the hands of God; it is for this reason that one ought to avoid contracting promises; men are puppets on a string that is controlled by Another. Whatever the Author wants will be; "remember that you are an actor in a play, and the Playwright chooses the manner of it: if he wants it short, it is short; if long, it is long. If he wants you to act a poor man you must act the part with all your powers; and so if your part be cripple or a magistrate or a plain man. For your business is to act the character that is given you and act it well: the choice of the cast is Another's."[21] The road to contentment is a virtuous one that nature has prescribed for man; happiness ensues in trekking this road, *i. e.*, in living a life according to nature.

5. Virtue

Virtue is defined as *living according to nature*; an achievement culminating in a contentment of spirit. This objective is best attained by confronting certain basic facts of life such as man's mortality and living according to the natural laws by which one is governed. One must come to the realization that man is a mere mortal, subject to life's dangers and vicissitudes; at best, he is a little soul, "carrying a corpse."

Happily, man does not need much on which to subsist; furthermore, "the rarest pleasures give the most delight."[22] A superlative technique in achieving happiness is to remain within one's abilities; "we must not stretch our hopes too wide, any more than our stride."[23] Excess is unnatural; man's nature rebels when pushed to excess; "if man should go beyond the mean, the most joyous things would turn to utter joylessness."[24] All moral qualities are natural, *e. g.*, nature has endowed man with self-respect so that one blushes when uttering or committing shameful or ignominious deeds. God has endowed man with that which is "noblest and highest ... the power to deal with impressions. For this faculty when rightly exercised is freedom, peace, courage, steadfastness, and this too is justice and law and self-control and all virtue."[25] The best life to adopt is a simple one which abstains from self-indulgence, and restricts itself to the satisfactions that lie within one's power.

The virtuous person is resigned to nature by surrendering to all natural occurrences, *i. e.*, the demands of nature; such understanding and acceptance issues in a tranquil spirit. Epictetus admonishes, "remember always to say to yourself, 'What is nature?' If you are fond of a jug, say you are fond of a jug; then you will not be disturbed if it be broken. If you kiss your child or your wife, say to yourself that you are kissing a human being, for then if death strikes it you will not be disturbed. Moreover when death has taken a loved one from you, do not say that you lost him. Say that you have given him back. 'Has your child died? It was given back.'"[26]

6. Cynicism

Epictetus regards the Cynic as the ideal Stoic, *i.e.*, one who has distinguished himself from mediocrity by assuming for himself a rigorously austere and isolated life in "this great City of the Universe" where the "Master of the House" makes all of the assignments.

The Cynic's prime requirement is a complete change of conduct whereby all selfish ambition is displaced, and the desire for acquisition is banished, *e. g.*, he "must harbour no anger, wrath, envy, pity: a fair maid, a fair name, favourites, or sweet cakes,"[27] must hold no fascination for him. The Cynic's security is grounded in self-respect; he harbors no secrets, contrariwise, he enjoys a "free open-air spirit." As a true Cynic,[28] your prior requisite is to

> make your Governing Principle pure, and hold fast this rule of life, 'Henceforth my mind is the material I have to work on, as the carpenter has his timber and the shoemaker his leather: my business is to deal with my impressions aright.

My wretched body is nothing to me. Death? Let it come when it will, whether to my whole body or to a part of it. Exile? Can one be sent into exile beyond the Universe? One cannot. Wherever I go, there is the sun, there is the moon, there are the stars, dreams, auguries, conversation with the gods.[29]

Consequently, there emerges in the Cynic a growing realization that he is God's ambassador to men "concerning things good and evil, to show them that they have gone astray" and direct them to the true nature and locale of the good. He is a fearless prophet, devoted to the proclamation of the truth in an undisturbed and prophetic spirit, " and with a loud voice utter the words of Socrates: 'O race of men, wither are ye hurrying? What are you doing, miserable creatures? You wander up and down like blind folk: you have left the true path and go away on a vain errand, you seek peace and happiness elsewhere, where it is not to be found, and believe not when another shows the way.' "[30]

The Cynic submissively accepts whatever portion God has meted out to him, whether it is "greatness or many stripes," *i. e.*, fame or misfortune, *e. g.*, "he must suffer strokes like an ass and love the very men that strike him . . . for this too is a very fine strand woven into the Cynic's lot."[31] He counts his suffering a gain for "whatever pains he suffers are God's training of him;"[32] the world is the battlefield upon which the Cynic constantly wrestles in pancreations, entirely "devoted to the service of God." This he must do without whimpering or murmuring, for the Cynic "who excites pity is like a beggar."

The Cynic's goals cannot be achieved without wit or wisdom, for he is required to defend his position with a ready apologia, hence he must stand prepared to give a reason for the faith that is in him. The true Stoic flinches from no adversity in life's encounters, including its major obstacle to serenity, viz., death, toward which his attitude and response should be:

'When did I tell you that I was immortal? You will answer your part, and I mine. It is yours to kill, mine to die without quailing: yours to banish, mine to go into exile without groaning.'³³

In this manner one is able to "maintain the constant and tranquil mind, and therewith the careful spirit which is not random or hasty."³⁴

7. Sex

The Stoic repudiates *sexual cravings as undesirable*; he considers total abstinence and the avoidance of women as being the better part of valor. Sexual practices are regarded as a weakness, imprisonment, or slavery which ought to be avoided at all costs; sex addiction is comparable to the cruel sufferings of slavery, a deplorable existence eliciting bewailing; one is a "poor wretch, to be a slave to a paltry girl."³⁵

One must avoid feeding the sex habit, lest he fall prey to its many pitfalls and consequential sufferings. Sex is apparently an excessive exercise. Epictetus inquires, "When the girl was too much for you, did you get away unpunished?"³⁶ The implication here is that one may fancy he has eluded the normally recognized detrimental consequence of sex, but a treacherous and disastrous fate has escaped his notice, viz., slavery, "*A worthless girl has made a slave of me, Whom never foe subdued.*"³⁷ Epictetus prided himself on his ability to keep aloof from sex; he vaunts:

> To-day when I saw a handsome woman I did not say to myself, 'Would that she were mine!' and 'Blessed is her husband!' For he who says that will say, 'Blessed is the adulterer!' Nor do I picture the next scene: the woman present and disrobing and reclining by my side. I pat myself on the head and say, 'Bravo, Epictetus. . . . And if, though the woman herself, poor thing, is willing and beckons and sends to me, and even touches

and comes close to me, I still hold aloof and conquer. . . . This is a thing to be really proud of.[38]

There exists a correlation between one's spiritual tranquility and his sex continence; to the degree that he is liberated from sexual desires and practices, there is a corresponding or concomitant mental serenity.

8. Evaluation of Stoicism

Stoicism and, more particularly, Cynicism were seriously practiced philosophies to which their adherents were sincerely committed; in fact, they functioned as religions. Some of the goals of Stoicism are so idealistic, they do not permit achievement; at best, they can serve only as regulative values, indicating the proper direction by which to guide one's life, *e. g.*, the navigator heads his ship in the direction of the North Star, he never expects to reach it.

To become completely indifferent to any external circumstance, *e. g.*, torture, is to be completely divine or schizophrenic, *i. e.*, it is an impossibility. Nevertheless, as an ideal, Stoicism commends itself as a worthwhile philosophy, provided one does not veer into the disposition of the later Cynics, whose disgruntled spirits contained nothing but violent scorn and hate for mankind and its mores.

9. Further Reading in Epictetus

The following constitute the complete extant writings of Epictetus: *The Discourses of Epictetus, Fragments,* (which includes fragments from: *Arrian the Pupil of Epictetus, Rufus, The Memorabilia of Epictetus, Agrippinus, Epictetus*), *The Manuel of Epictetus.* Epictetus' major efforts are to be found in his *Discourses.*

NOTES

EPICTETUS

1. That is, *intrinsic* evil, that which is evil in and of itself as an end, without serving, even partially, as an instrumental good.
2. The belief that the universe is an enormous machine.
3. The belief that the universe is God and vice versa.
4. Epictetus, *Discourses*, Bk. 2, Ch. 18, tr. by P. E. Matheson, (Oxford University Press, 1916). P. E. Matheson is the translator of the works of Epictetus used throughout this chapter.
5. Epictetus, *Manual*, 28.
6. Epictetus, *Discourses*, Bk. 1, Ch. 24.
7. *Idem.*
8. *Ibid.*, 18.
9. Cf. St. Paul, Philippians 4:11, 12.
10. Epictetus, *Manual*, 12.
11. Epictetus, *Discourses*, Bk. 1, Ch. 12.
12. *Ibid.*, Ch. 1.
13. *Idem.* Cf. Kant on the "Autonomy of the Will."
14. *Idem.*
15. Cf. Matthew 5:38-42.
16. Cf. St. Paul, I. Corinthians 15:55-56.
17. Epictetus, *Discourses*, Bk. 1, Ch. 29.
18. Epictetus, *Fragments*, 20.
19. *Idem.* Cf. Matthew 26:39.
20. Epictetus, *Fragments*, 20.
21. Epictetus, *Manual*, 17.
22. Epictetus, *Discourses*, 33.
23. *Ibid.*, 31.
24. *Ibid.*, 34. Cf., Aristotle on virtue and happiness.
25. *Ibid.*, 4.
26. Epictetus, *Manual*, 3.
27. Epictetus, *Discourses*, Bk. 3, Ch. 22.
28. Epictetus would recognize Diogenes and Socrates as accomplished Cynics in the finest sense of the word; subsequent Cynics brought the name into disrepute by their severe and austere criticisms of social customs, etc., which earned them appellations, such as, misanthrope, captious critic, faultfinder, etc., hence, the reason for the world becoming a term of opprobrium.

29. Epictetus, *Discourses*, Bk. 3, Ch. 22.
30. *Idem.*
31. *Idem.*
32. *Idem.*
33. *Ibid.*, Bk. 1, Ch. 2.
34. *Ibid.*, Bk. 2, Ch. 5.
35. *Ibid.*, Bk. 4, Ch. 1.
36. *Ibid.*, Bk. 3, Ch. 25.
37. *Ibid.*, Bk. 4, Ch. 1, Epictetus is quoting Menander, *Fragment* 338, Koch.
38. *Ibid.*, Bk. 2, Ch. 18. Cf. Matthew 5:28, "I say unto you, that whosoever looketh on a woman to lust after her hath committed adultery with her already in his heart."

SOCRATES

The unexamined life is not worth living.
(Socrates)

1. Major Ethical Principles

Socrates, whose singularly brilliant moral life has often been compared to that of Jesus because of its many striking noble resemblances, emphasized the following major tenets of his ethical philosophy: 1. *knowledge is virtue* and virtue is happiness; 2. *know thyself*; 3. *nothing too much*; 4. elements of virtue, viz., wisdom, temperance, courage, justice, holiness; 5. *the unexamined life is not worth living*; 6. the will of God; 7. the Socratic method, viz., Socratic irony and dialectic.

2. The Socratic Method

The *Socratic method* has several important phases, the principle features of which are: *induction, dialectic,* and *irony*. Aristotle credits Socrates as the founder of the inductive method, *i. e.*, the technique whereby one gathers as many particular relevant facts as possible and then uncovers the form which is common to each, thereby obtaining the law or nature of the particular object. Although the *Socratic method* is the foundation of the scientific method, Socrates, displeased with the sterile results of natural science, viz., cosmology, turned its application to the study of the humanities, *i. e.*, the study of man, and in particular to the field of ethics.

Socratic irony is feigning ignorance in order to coerce one's opponent into answering leading questions and thereby exacting definitions from him. Many individuals base their arguments on presuppositions and take refuge in hiding behind words which they are incapable of or have neglected defining; Socrates would smoke them out, as it were, by pretending ignorance of the meaning of their terms, thereby forcing his opponents to give proper and precise definitions of the terms bandied about with a semblance of authority. Accurate definitions are difficult to formulate; nevertheless, they are necessary since for Socrates they constitute truth.

The *Socratic dialectic* (conversation) was the art of approaching a subject from every possible point of view, thereby uncovering its true nature and definition. The dialectic is a conversation of thought, by which a variety of points of view are contributed to a given problem from every conceivable viewpoint in order to ensure procuring the truth.

Socrates used all of the foregoing devices in his philosophical endeavors in combination with his ingenious technique of answering questions by posing other questions. Rarely did he make a declarative statement; even to questions directed at him, he responded interrogatively. All of the preceding techniques are magnificently utilized in the following discussion transpiring between Socrates and Euthydemus, an individual who prided himself on his outstanding philosophical acumen. The scene opens with Euthydemus claiming his right to be a statesman, inasmuch as he is adept in matters pertaining to justice:[1]

"Do you suppose," retorted Euthydemus, "that I am unable to rehearse the works of justice? Of course I can, — and the works of injustice too, since there are many opportunities of seeing and hearing of them every day."

SOCRATES: "I propose, then, that we write J in this column and I in that, and then proceed to place under these letters, J and I, what we take to be the works of justice and injustice respectively."

EUTHYDEMUS: "Do so, if you think it helps at all."

Note the use of the scientific method as it unfolds under the skillful manipulation of Socrates, who recommends drawing two columns in order to cope with the problem of the moral significance of justice. In the first column one list acts of immoral deception which are recognized as just and in the other, one lists acts of deception which are declared unjust.

DECEPTION

	J (Acts of justice)	I (Acts of injustice)	
Incidents of deception as just.	1....... 2....... 3....... 4....... 5....... 6.......	1....... 2....... 3....... 4....... 5....... 6.......	Incidents of deception as unjust.

The next step is to gather every factual experience or incident relating to deception and list in the appropriate column designated in the above blank. If every instance of deception can be proved to be immoral, *i.e.*, unjust, then one has inductively arrived at a universal moral law, viz., *lying is immoral* and the moral dictate of Moses found in the *Ten Commandments*, viz., *Thou shalt not bear false witness* is valid, but if cases emerge which justify deceit, then lying cannot be said to be universally valid, but would hold true for particular instances only. The conversation continues:

Having written down the letters as he proposed, Socrates went on:

SOCRATES: "Lying occurs among men, does it not?"
EUTHYDEMUS: "Yes, it does."
SOCRATES: "Under which heading are we to put that?"
EUTHYDEMUS: "Under the heading of injustice, clearly."
SOCRATES: "Deceit, too, is found, is it not?"
EUTHYDEMUS: "Certainly."
SOCRATES: "Under which heading will that go?"
EUTHYDEMUS: "Under injustice again, of course."
SOCRATES: "What about doing mischief?"
EUTHYDEMUS: "That too."
SOCRATES: "Selling into slavery?"

EUTHYDEMUS: "That too."
SOCRATES: "Then we shall assign none of these things to justice, Euthydemus?"
EUTHYDEMUS: "No, it would be monstrous to do so."
SOCRATES: "Now suppose a man who has been elected general enslaves an unjust and hostile city, shall we say that he acts unjustly?"
EUTHYDEMUS: "Oh, no!"
SOCRATES: "We shall say that his actions are just, shall we not?"
EUTHYDEMUS: "Certainly."
SOCRATES: "And what if he deceives the enemy when at war?"
EUTHYDEMUS: "That too is just."
SOCRATES: "And if he steals and plunders their goods, will not his actions be just?"
EUTHYDEMUS: "Certainly; but at first I assumed that your questions had reference only to friends."
SOCRATES: "Then everything that we assigned to injustice should be assigned to justice also?"
EUTHYDEMUS: "Apparently."

Note the Socratic technique of asking questions, never offering direct statements; note also the use of the dialetic, *i. e.*, the conversational method of approaching a subject from every conceivable point of view. The discussion contains some perceptive points worthy of comment, such as Socrates proving that deception is not necessarily unjust in all cases, hence one cannot make universal, the principle: *lying is wrong*. An appropriate suggestion one may offer Socrates is to request the insertion of the term *malicious* before deception and invariably the outcome will be an immoral act, *i. e.*, a universally valid moral law is possible, viz., *malicious lying is immoral*, categorically, *i. e.*, it is unjust to commit a malicious deception under any and all conditions.

Socrates continues the debate by offering the following proposal:

SOCRATES: "Then I propose to revive our classification, and to say: It is just to do such things to enemies, but it is unjust to do them to friends, towards whom one's conduct should be scrupulously honest!"

EUTHYDEMUS: "By all means."

SOCRATES: "Now suppose that a general, seeing that his army is downhearted, tells a lie and says that reinforcements are approaching, and by means of this lie checks discouragement among the men, under which heading shall we put this deception?"

EUTHYDEMUS: "Under justice, I think."

SOCRATES: "Suppose, again, that a man's son refuses to take a dose of medicine when he needs it, and the father induces him to take it by pretending that it is food, and cures him by means of this lie, where shall we put this deception?"

EUTHYDEMUS: "That too goes on the same side, I think."

SOCRATES: "And again, suppose one has a friend suffering from depression, and, for fear that he may make away with himself, one takes away his sword or something of the sort, under which heading shall we put that now?"

EUTHYDEMUS: "That too goes under justice, of course."

SOCRATES: "You mean, do you, that even with friends straightforward dealing is not invariably right?"

EUTHYDEMUS: "It isn't, indeed! I retract what I said before, if you will let me."

SOCRATES: "Why, I'm bound to let you; it's better than getting our lists wrong. But now, consider deception practised on friends to their detriment: we mustn't overlook that either. Which is the more unjust deception in that case, the intentional or unintentional?"

EUTHYDEMUS: "Nay, Socrates, I have lost all confidence in my answers; for all the opinions that I expressed before seem now to have taken an entirely different form. Still I venture to say that the intentional deception is more unjust than the unintentional."

By the mastery of his ingenious method, Socrates is able to maneuver his opponent circuitously to his own conclusions.

3. Virtue is Knowledge

Socrates equated virtue with knowledge; hence, *virtue is knowledge* and *knowledge is virtue, e. g.*, a man who knows what is good will automatically do what is right. The rationale is that it would be foolish for a person to do otherwise because it would prove detrimental to himself, *e. g.*, an individual would not distribute his money irrationally to strangers inasmuch as it is an asinine thing to do. The same holds true of all moral action, good is pursued because wisdom directs. "*He who knows the beautiful and good will never choose anything else,* he who is ignorant of them cannot do them, and even if he tries, will fail. Hence the wise do what is beautiful and good, the unwise cannot and fail if they try. Therefore since just actions and all other forms of beautiful and good activity are virtuous actions, it is clear that Justice and every other form of Virtue is Wisdom."[2]

Knowledge or wisdom is virtue also in the sense of being the dynamism capable of exerting the energy to drive or motivate an individual to the performance of right action; "knowledge is a noble and commanding thing, which can not be overcome, and will not allow a man, if he only knows the difference of good and evil, to do anything which is contrary to knowledge, but that wisdom will have the strength to help him."[3] It is not for the sake of reward, heavenly or earthly, that a man behaves morally; it is awareness of moral value dictated by wisdom; "consequently *those who know what is lawful concerning men do what is just.*"[4] From the foregoing implied premises, it would follow that no one knowingly would commit evil for it would strike him as a senseless act; "no wise man, as I believe, will allow that any human being errs voluntarily, or voluntarily does evil and dishonorable actions; but they are very well aware that all who do evil and dishonorable things do them against their will."[5] To say that a man will do what is evil knowingly is tantamount to admitting that he will futilely injure himself knowingly; "that a man does what is evil knowingly . . . does what is painful knowingly."[6] Conversely, the person who does what is good does what is pleasurable and therein finds his salvation, inasmuch as "the salvation of human life has been found to consist in the right choice of pleasures and pains."[7]

The impossibility of ignorance and virtue coexisting simultaneously within the same individual is bared by Socrates in the following encounter with Euthydemus:[8]

SOCRATES: "Next comes Courage, Euthydemus. Do you think it is a beautiful thing?"
EUTHYDEMUS: "I prefer to think it very beautiful."
SOCRATES: "So you think Courage useful for no mean purposes?"
EUTHYDEMUS: "Of course — or rather, for the greatest."
SOCRATES: "Then do you think that in the pressure of terrors and dangers it is useful to be ignorant of them?"
EUTHYDEMUS: "By no means."
SOCRATES: "So those who feel no fear of such things because they are ignorant of them are not courageous?"
EUTHYDEMUS: "Of course not, for in that case madmen and cowards would be courageous."
SOCRATES: "What of those who are afraid when there is no ground for fear?"
EUTHYDEMUS: "Still less, of course."
SOCRATES: "Then do you think that those who are good in the presence of terrors and dangers are courageous, and those who are bad are cowards?"
EUTHYDEMUS: "Certainly."
SOCRATES: "And do you think that any are good in the presence of such things, except those who can deal with them well?"
EUTHYDEMUS: "None but these."
SOCRATES: "And bad, except such as deal badly with them?"
EUTHYDEMUS: "These and none others."
SOCRATES: "Then do both classes behave as they think they must?"
EUTHYDEMUS: "How can they behave otherwise?"
SOCRATES: "Then do those who cannot behave well know they must behave?"
EUTHYDEMUS: "Surely not."
SOCRATES: "So those who know how they must behave are just those who can?"

EUTHYDEMUS: "Yes, only they."
SOCRATES: "Well now, do those who are not utterly mistaken deal badly with such things?"
EUTHYDEMUS: "I think not."
SOCRATES: "So those who behave badly are utterly mistaken?"
EUTHYDEMUS: "Presumably."
SOCRATES: *"It follows that those who know how to deal well with terrors and dangers are courageous,* and those who utterly mistake the way are cowards?"
EUTHYDEMUS: "That is my opinion."

4. Know Thyself

Virtue is knowledge,[9] but the most desirable knowledge is that of oneself. Self-knowledge results in self-mastery, and self-mastery fructifies into integrity and happiness; "for they live best ... who strive best to become as good as possible: and the pleasantest life is theirs who are conscious that they are growing in goodness."[10]

The Socratic dictum *gnothi sauton* (know thyself), an inscription Socrates obtained from the temple of Apollo at Delphi, was the ideal by which his life was governed. He was convinced that if an individual thoroughly understood himself, he would achieve self-mastery, *e.g.*, virtue, such as courage, is the by-product of self-understanding coupled with a knowledge of external facts and principles; "it follows that those who know how to deal well with terrors and dangers are courageous, and those who utterly mistake the way are cowards."[11]

Most persons fancy that they know themselves merely on the pretext that they are closer to their own spirits than anyone else, but they actually have only a superficial or nodding acquaintance with their real selves as Socrates ably uncovers in the following dialogue:[12]

Hereupon Socrates exclaimed:

SOCRATES: "Tell me, Euthydemus, have you ever been to Delphi?"
EUTHYDEMUS: "Yes, certainly; twice."
SOCRATES: "Then did you notice somewhere on the temple the inscription 'Know thyself?' "

EUTHYDEMUS: "I did."

SOCRATES: "And did you pay no heed to the inscription, or did you attend to it and try to consider who you were?"

EUTHYDEMUS: "Indeed I did not; because I felt sure that I knew that already; for I could hardly know anything else if I did not even know myself."

SOCRATES: "And what do you suppose a man must know to know himself, *his own name merely*? Or must he consider what sort of creature he is for human use and get to know his own powers; just as those who buy horses don't think they know the beast they want to know until they have considered whether he is docile or stubborn, strong or weak, fast or slow, and generally how he stands in all that makes a useful or a useless horse?"

EUTHYDEMUS: "That leads me to think that *he who does not know his own powers is ignorant of himself.*"

SOCRATES: "Is it not clear too that through self-knowledge men come to much good, and through self-deception to much harm? For those who know themselves, know what things are expedient for themselves and discern their own powers and limitations. And by doing what they understand, they get what they want and prosper: by refraining from attempting what they do not understand, they make no mistakes and avoid failure. . . . Those who do not know and are deceived in their estimate of their own powers are in the like condition with regard to other men and other human affairs. They know neither what they want, nor what they do, nor those with whom they have intercourse; but mistaken in all these respects, they miss the good and stumble into the bad. Furthermore, those who know what they do win fame and honour by attaining their ends. . . . But those who do not know what they do, choose amiss, fail in what they attempt and, besides incurring direct loss and punishment thereby, they earn contempt through their failures, make themselves ridiculous and live in dishonour and humiliation.

And the same is true of communities. You find that whenever a state, in ignorance of its own power, goes to war with a stronger people, it is exterminated or loses its liberty."

5. Virtue

Virtue is a prime value, "while gold and silver cannot make men better, the thoughts of the wise enrich their possessors with virtue;"[13] an unexamined life is fit only for animals. The Greek term *arete* (virtue) would be of truer significance if it were translated *excellence*, as this was the understanding of the term; virtue in its *ne plus ultra* form is moral insight, which was, for Socrates, the *summum bonum, i. e.*, the greatest thing in the world.

One could not speak of many virtues, for different virtues are merely "names of the same thing;" consequently, "wisdom and temperance and courage and justice[14] and holiness [are] five names of the same thing."[15] To speak of a diversity or kind of virtue is to err; fundamentally they are identical in essence and function and are not to be regarded as separate objects. Socrates was prepared to take Protagoras to task if he did not concede this point.

Another byword by which Socrates lived is a second inscription he found in the temple of Apollo at Delphi, viz., *maden agan* (nothing too much). The virtuous man, among other things, is temperate; he does not fall prey to the vice of incontinence which terminates in slavery. Slavery, in its lowest form of degradation, is to be victimized by the incontinent gratification of appetite as Socrates proves to Euthydemus:

SOCRATES: "Tell me, Euthydemus . . . do you think that freedom is a noble and splendid possession both for individuals and for communities?"
EUTHYDEMUS: "Yes, I think it is, in the highest degree."
SOCRATES: "Then do you think that the man is free who is ruled by bodily pleasures and is unable to do what is best because of them?"
EUTHYDEMUS: "By no means."
SOCRATES: "Possibly, in fact, to do what is best appears to

you to be freedom, and so you thing that to have masters who will prevent such activity is bondage?"

EUTHYDEMUS: "I am sure of it."

SOCRATES: "You feel sure then that the incontinent are bond slaves?"

EUTHYDEMUS: "Of course, naturally."

SOCRATES: "And do you think that the incontinent are merely prevented from doing what is most honourable, or are also forced to do what is most dishonourable?"

EUTHYDEMUS: "I think that they are forced to do that just as much as they are prevented from doing the other."

SOCRATES: "What sort of masters are they, in your opinion, who prevent the best and enforce the worst?"

EUTHYDEMUS: "The worst possible, of course."

SOCRATES: "And what sort of slavery do you believe to be the worst?"

EUTHYDEMUS: "Slavery to the worst matters, I think."

SOCRATES: "The worst slavery, therefore, is the slavery endured by the incontinent?"

EUTHYDEMUS: "I think so."

6. The Unexamined Life is Not Worth Living

Socrates was ever attendant to the voice of conscience which, to him, constituted a divine command;[16] his defence at his trial, which consummated in his execution by the drinking of a hemlock preparation, resounds of Martin Luther's apologia at Worms: "For I tell you that this would be a disobedience to a divine command, and therefore that I can not hold my tongue, you will not believe that I am serious; and if I say again that the greatest good of man is daily to converse about virtue, and all that concerning which you hear me examining myself and others, and that *the life which is unexamined is not worth living* — that you are still less likely to believe."[17]

Socrates was a very religious man in constant prayer, attempting to search out and follow the will of God; in planning future activities he would append them with "God willing."[18] Concerning his impeccable moral, spiritual, and religious life, Xenophon concludes his *Memorabilia of Socrates* with the following eulogy:

> For myself, I have described him as he was: so religious that he did nothing without counsel from the gods; so just that he did no injury, however small, to any man, but conferred the greatest benefits on all who dealt with him; so self-controlled that he never chose the pleasanter rather than the better course; so wise that he was unerring in his judgment of the better and the worse, and needed no counsellor, but relied on himself for his knowledge of them; masterly in expounding and defining such things; no less masterly in putting others to the test, and convincing them of error and exhorting them to follow virtue and gentleness. To me he seemed to be all that a truly good and happy man must be.

Plato adds his endorsement by concluding the *Phaedo*: "Such was the end, Echecrates, of our friend, whom I may truly call the wisest, and justest, and best of all men whom I have ever known."

7. Further Reading in Socrates

Socrates, himself, like Jesus, wrote nothing; the literary sources concerning his life and teaching come principally from Plato, Xenophon's *Memorabilia* and *Oeconomicus*. Rich sources from Plato are the *Protagoras, Phaedo, Apology, Crito, Symposium, Charmides, Lysis, Laches, Phaedrus*.

NOTES

SOCRATES

1. Xenophon, *Memorabilia*, Bk. IV, Ch. 2, Sec. 12 ff., tr. by E. C. Marchant, (Cambridge, Massachusetts: Harvard University Press, 1923).
2. *Ibid.*, Bk. III, Ch. 9, Sec. 5.
3. Plato, *Protagoras*, tr. by B. Jowett.
4. *Memorabilia*, Bk. IV, Ch. 6, Sec. 6.
5. Plato, *op. cit.*
6. *Ibid.*
7. *Ibid.*
8. *Memorabilia*, Bk. IV, Ch. 6, Sec. 10, 11.
9. Plato, *Protagoras*.
10. Xenophon, *op. cit.*, Bk. IV, Ch. 8, Sec. 6.
11. *Ibid.*, Bk. IV, Ch. 6, Sec. 9.
12. *Ibid.* Bk. IV, Ch. 2, Sec. 24-29.
13. *Ibid.*, IV, Ch. 6, Sec. 11.
14. Wisdom, courage, temperance, and justice are Plato's chief virtues; to these four, St. Thomas Aquinas added three from St. Paul, viz., faith, hope, and love; the combined seven are termed *the seven cardinal Christian virtues*.
15. Plato, *Protagoras*.
16. There are those who would interpret this inner voice as hallucinatory.
17. Plato, *Apology*, tr. by B. Jowett.
18. See the conclusion of Plato's *Laches*.

RELIGIOUS ETHICS

MOSES

Thou shalt love thy neighbor as thyself.... Thou shalt give life for life, eye for eye, tooth for tooth, hand for hand, foot for foot, burning for burning, wound for wound, stripe for stripe.
(Moses)
What doth the Lord require of thee, but to do justly, and to love mercy, and to walk humbly with thy God. (Micah)

1. The Decalogue

The *Ten Commandments,* as the *Decalogue* (The Ten Words) is commonly known, consist of ten brief phrases of only two words each in its primitive Hebrew form. These laws, which are found in both Exodus 20 and Deuteronomy 5, and attributed to Moses, were believed delivered theophanically to him by God at Mt. Sinai, hence they constitute a theocentric ethic of a theocratic nation. The Exodus version,[1] which has only minor differences from the Deuteronomic, is as follows:

1. Thou shalt have no other gods before me.[2]
2. Thou shalt not make unto thee any graven image, or any likeness of any thing that is in heaven above, or that is in the earth beneath, or that is in the water under the earth: Thou shalt not bow down thyself to them, nor serve them: for I the Lord thy God am a jealous God, visiting the iniquity of the fathers upon the children unto

the third and fourth generation of them that hate me; and showing mercy unto thousands of them that love me and keep my commandments.
3. Thou shalt not take the name of the Lord thy God in vain: for the Lord will not hold him guiltless that taketh his name in vain.
4. Remember the sabbath day, to keep it holy. Six days shalt thou labor, and do all thy work: But the seventh day is the sabbath of the Lord thy God: in it thou shalt not do any work, thou, nor thy son, nor thy daughter, thy manservant, nor thy maidservant, nor thy cattle, nor thy stranger that is within thy gates: For in six days the Lord made heaven and earth, the sea, and all that in them is, and rested the seventh day: wherefore the Lord blessed the sabbath day, and hallowed it.
5. Honor thy father and thy mother: that thy days may be long upon the land which the Lord thy God giveth thee.
6. Thou shalt not kill. (Jewish Bible reads murder).
7. Thou shalt not commit adultery.
8. Thou shalt not steal.
9. Thou shalt not bear false witness against thy neighbor.
10. Thou shalt not covet thy neighbor's house, thou shalt not covet thy neighbor's wife, nor his manservant, nor his maidservant, nor his ox, nor his ass, nor any thing that is thy neighbor's.

The Ten Commandments constitute for many persons the most famous summary of moral fundamentals; if it is not that, then at least, it is one of the most, and doubtless the most famous of its period. Some scholars believe that it was for mnemonic reasons that they were compressed into ten; it renders them easier to instruct and commit to memory, *e. g.,* enumerating each with the use of the ten fingers of one's hands.

Note the ethical division of The Decalogue: the first four pertain to *religious* duties, *i. e.,* obligations towards God; the fifth through the tenth treat *moral* obligations for which one is held responsible towards his fellow man. Occasionally these two divisions are referred to as the First Table and the Second Table respectively. The ethical duties, in turn, permit a sub-division: from the sixth to the eighth, immoral *actions* are treated; the ninth and tenth deal with immoral *thoughts*. The Decalogue is predominantly negative, only two are positive, viz., the fourth and fifth which command respect for parents and the sabbath. It is not known why these two commandments are in the affirmative, particularly when they too could have easily been rendered negatively.

The universal appeal of The Decalogue is so commanding that it has won status as a world document, and is without peer ethically in the Old Testament, with the possible exception of Micah's summons: "What doth the Lord require of thee, but to do justly, and to love mercy, and to walk humbly with thy God." (Micah 6:8).

The meaning which The Decalogue conveys today in the Judeo-Christian world is not the same as it meant to Israel in those early times, due to modification by the universalization of its tenets. When originally given, the commandments were binding only among co-religionists; the Israelite was not obligated to the foreigner unless he came within "the gates of the city." Furthermore, these moral laws were particularly for adults, not for minors, as is evidenced in the Seventh Commandment regarding adultery. The Ten Commandments have the impact of a "bill of rights" for the protection of the citizens of Israel.

The fifth law commands reverence for the aged, not for the particular purpose of young children respecting their parents, but for adults caring for their aged parents, financially and otherwise.

The ancient Hebrew world did not regard all killing as murder; this is similar to the attitude with which the contemporary world views the matter, but it is not to be construed that these philosophies are identical, for the ancient and venerable law did not recognize the killing of one's slave as murder. One could, however, avenge himself for the murder of his kin. The law regarding adultery extends not only to a man's wife, but to his betrothed; not only could a man claim damages for the adulterous behavior of his wife but also from her partner in the act. The law's objective was to protect a man's property rights in his wife (or concubine), since these women were regarded as chattel; moreover there existed the further consideration of guaranteeing the genuineness or legitimacy of one's children.

The rule prohibiting theft is based upon the high regard for a man's property and possessions; this is definitely the case in contemporary America. The laws pertaining to property, not only protected a citizen of Israel, but under certain circumstances, the foreigner as well.

The Ninth Commandment: "Thou shalt not bear false witness agains thy neighbor" is an injunction against *slander*; it was designed to protect one against defamation of character or character assassins; this is particularly of importance in a small and primitive community where a man's censorship could prove devastating and his opportunity for moving to another community doubtful or even out of the question.

The Tenth Commandment regarding covetousness was intended to control evil desire; the prohibition of jealous desire is a deterrent to immoral actions.

2. The *Lex Talionis* and the Concept of Justice

The *lex talionis* (law of retaliation) pervades the Mosaic ethic; it commands that justice be requited from the wrongdoer for any injury suffered; such reparations must be to the exact extent of the damages incurred. The Levitical phrasing of the *lex talionis* is:

> And he that killeth any man shall surely be put to death. And he that killeth beast shall make it good; beast for beast. And if a man cause a blemish in his neighbor; as he hath done, so shall it be done to him; breach for breach, eye for eye, tooth for tooth: as he hath caused a blemish in a man, so shall it be done to him again. And he that killeth a beast, he shall restore it: And he that killeth a man, he shall be put to death. Ye shall have one manner of law, as well as for the stranger, as for one of your own country.
> (Lev. 24:17-22).

It is interesting to compare this rendition of the *jus talionis* with the one found in Exodus: "Thou shalt give life for life, eye for eye, tooth for tooth, hand for hand, foot for foot, burning for burning, wound for wound, stripe for stripe." (Exodus 21:23-25). The law of retaliation of the early Hebrews should not be regarded as unbridled cruelty of a primitive tribal society, but a movement in the direction of humanizing acts of vengeance by prescribing the limits of revenge. Considering the early times of the history of civilization in which this moral law was spawned, it was a lofty principle and represented an advanced and refined code of ethics. This code sets a ceiling on acts of retribution by stipulating the appropriate legal extent of revenge. The sizable degree of progress from the time of Cain and Lamech in Genesis 4 to the days of Moses is noteworthy; Lamech was a murderer who could rejoice exultantly with a taunting tale in consequence of his depravity, viz., murderous indulgence. He triumphantly sings: "Adah and Zillah, hear my voice: ye wives of Lamech, hearken unto my speech: for I have slain a man to my wounding, and a young man to my hurt. If Cain be avenged sevenfold, truly Lamech seventy and sevenfold." (Genesis 4:23-24). Instead of being repaid on an equal and just basis, *i. e.*, "an eye for an eye," Lamech was repaid seventy-seven times greater than the damages incurred.

The *lex talionis* is not to be interpreted literally, but treated as a principle, *i. e.*, as a guide for just and equitable behavior; actually, the Rabbinical law did not encourage or even permit an individual to requite "an eye for an eye," but to accept money, property, or some other form of reparation in lieu of loss or damage to the eye.[3] Nevertheless, the fundamental *principle* of the *lex talionis* was never annulled, even as late as the Rabbinical days of the era of Jesus.[4]

3. The Great Commandment and the Golden Rule

The *Great Commandment* is the injunction to love God coupled to loving neighbor as oneself; it constitutes the *Shema*

(Hear) which is the first word of Deuteronomy 6:4-19 (essentially a confession of faith to be recited twice daily) in conjunction with Leviticus 19:18:

> Hear, O Israel: The Lord our God is one Lord: And thou shalt love the Lord thy God with all thine heart, and with all thy soul, and with all thy might. And these words which I command thee this day, shall be in thine heart: And thou shalt teach them diligently unto thy children, and shall talk of them when thou sittest in thine house, and when thou walkest by the way, and when thou liest down, and when thou risest up. And thou shalt bind them for a sign upon thine hand, and they shall be as frontlets between thine eyes. And thou shalt write them upon the posts of thy house, and on thy gates.
>
> **Thou shalt not avenge, nor bear any grudge** against the children of thy people, but thou shalt love thy neighbor as thyself.

It is designated the *Great Commandment* when the two are read together jointly: "Thou shalt love the Lord thy God with all thy heart, and with all thy soul, and with all thy might. And ... thou shalt love thy neighbor as thyself."[5] The Rabbis enumerated 613 different commandments in the law, but this one was recognized as the greatest. The Great Commandment is regarded both by Jews and Christians as God's paramount injunction and constitutes a summary of all commandments. The moral statute commanding one to love one's neighbor as self is considered one of the most noble precepts of all time, *i. e.*, when it is interpreted to include all mankind, the stranger as well as a co-religionist. The seeds of the *Golden Rule* are believed to be found in this teaching, but their first unmistakable appearance is found in the Apocryphal book of Tobit 4:15: "Do that to no man which thou hatest."

Tobit's phrasing of the Golden Rule is negatively stated; when negatively rendered, it is occasionally termed the *Silver Rule*. The Golden Rule in one of its two renditions is found in practically every major living religion; this phenomenon has led some scholars to speculate that it may be a fundamental ethical principle ingrained in all mankind, perhaps innately. *E. g.*, Confucius' Silver Rule reads: "What I do not wish men to do to me, I also wish not to do to them;" Hillel, an outstanding Jewish leader and contemporary of Jesus said: "What is hateful to thee, do not to thy neighbor;" Proverbs 24:29 reads: "Say not, I will do so to him as he hath done to me;" Aristotle enjoined men to behave towards their friends "as we would that they should act toward us;" in the Hindu sacred book, the *Mahabharata*, is found: "Do naught to others which if done to thee would cause thee pain;" Plato said: "May I do to others as I would that they should do to me;" In Buddhism is found: "Hurt not others with that which pains thyself;" in Zoroastrianism: "Do not do to others all that which is not well for oneself;" and finally from Jainism: "In happiness and suffering, in joy and grief, we should regard all creatures as we regard our own self, and should therefore refrain from inflicting upon others such injury as would appear undesirable to us if inflicted upon ourselves."[6]

4. Diverse and Sundry Ethical Principles

The following constitute a group of miscellaneous ethical practices and/or injunctions:

"And when ye reap the harvest of your land, thou shalt not wholly reap the corners of thy field, neither shalt thou gather the gleanings of thy harvest. And thou shalt not glean thy vineyard, neither shalt thou gather every grape of thy vineyard; thou shalt leave them for the poor and stranger." (Lev. 19:9-10). The Israelitish morality, strongly sympathetic with the unhappy plight of the poor and the occasional unfortunate predicament of the stranger or traveller, required those who had plenty to share with those less fortunate. If one gleaned his fields too closely then even the less desirable leftovers would be unavailable to the person in dire need, whereas a field that had a little edible matter left behind would at least prevent the poor from starving.

"Ye shall not steal, neither deal falsely, neither lie to one another." (Lev. 19:11). This constitutes a form of some of the commandments of the revered ten; however, here the emphasis on lying is *to* one another, rather than *about* another. This verse is followed with the injunction: "Thou shalt not defraud thy neighbor, neither rob him." Fraud and theft are closely related crimes; fraud might be conceived as a type of theft that utilizes lying. Lying and talebearing are not completely unrelated practices; accordingly verse 16 can be linked with the above: "Thou shalt not go up and down as a talebearer among thy people." The talebearer's intentions are never honorable, nor are rumors reliable, but forms of falsehood.

The following are self-explanatory: "In righteousness shalt thou judge thy neighbor. Thou shalt not hate thy brother in thine heart.... Thou shalt not avenge, nor bear any grudge against the children of thy people, but thou shalt love thy neighbor as thyself." (Lev. 19:15, 17, 18).

The practice of the injunction: "Love thy neighbor as thyself" was limited to co-religionists, *i. e.*, one was not obligated to the foreigner, unless he was "within the gates" of the city, then appropriate hospitality and obligations were due him. This command is emphasized in Leviticus 19:33, "And if a stranger sojourn with thee in your land, ye shall not vex him. But the stranger that dwelleth with you shall be unto you as one born among you, and thou shalt love him as thyself."

The Israelitish morality exercised strong strictures against incest, homosexuality, and bestiality, even more so than adultery:

> And the man that committeth adultery with another man's wife, even he that committeth adultery with his neighbor's wife, the adulterer and the adulteress shall surely be put to death. And the man that lieth with his father's wife hath uncovered his father's nakedness: both of them shall surely be put to death; their blood shall be upon them. And if a man lie with his daughter-in-

law, both of them shall surely be put to death: they have wrought confusion; their blood shall be upon them. If a man also lie with mankind, as he lieth with a woman, both of them have committed an abomination: they shall surely be put to death; their blood shall be upon them. And if a man take a wife and her mother, it is wickedness: they shall be burnt with fire, both he and they: that there be no wickedness among you. And if a man lie with a beast, he shall surely be put to death; and ye shall slay the beast. And if a woman approach unto any beast, and lie down thereto, thou shalt kill the woman, and the beast: they shall surely be put to death; their blood shall be upon them. And if a man shall take his sister, his father's daughter, or his mother's daughter, and see her nakedness, and she see his nakedness; it is a wicked thing; and they shall be cut off in the sight of their people: he hath uncovered his sister's nakedness; he shall bear his iniquity. And if a man shall lie with a woman having her sickness, and shall uncover her nakedness; he hath discovered her fountain, and she hath uncovered the fountain of her blood: and both of them shall be cut off from among their people. And thou shalt not uncover the nakedness of thy mother's sister, nor of thy father's sister: for he uncovereth his near kin: they shall bear their iniquity. And if a man lieth with his uncle's wife, he hath uncovered his uncle's nakedness: they shall bear their sin; they shall die childless. And if a man shall take his brother's wife, it is an unclean thing: he hath uncovered his brother's nakedness; they shall be childless. (Leviticus 20:10-21.)

NOTES

MOSES

1. Unless otherwise indicated, the King James version of the Bible is used throughout the entire section of "Religious Ethics."
2. Lutherans and Roman Catholics combine one and two together, regarding it as the First Commandment; the Jews do the same and treat it as the Second Commandment. The former two groups treat the tenth as two commandments; the Jews use as the first: "I am the Lord thy God, who brought thee out of the land of Egypt, out of the house of bondage." (Exodus 20:2.)
3. Some scholars consider this interpretation debatable; its possibility is conceded, but not its certainty.
4. See the chapter on Jesus; section 1 (a) "Sermon on the Mount" (Retaliation).
5. Cf. Matthew 22:36-40; Mark 12:29-34; Luke 10:27-28.
6. Cf. Dagobert D. Dunes, *A Pictorial History of Philosophy* (New York: Philosophical Library, Inc., 1955), 1.

JESUS

For what is a man profited, if he shall gain the whole world, and lose his own soul? or what shall a man give in exchange for his soul? (Jesus)

1. The Christian Ethic

The following are the highlights of the ethics of Jesus: (1) The *universal brotherhood* of man; (2) Human dignity, i. e., the belief in the *infinite intrinsic value of every human being*; (3) The *Golden Rule*; (4) The Great Commandment, viz., the *love of God and neighbor*; (5) the Sermon on the Mount; (6) *Agape* (Christian love); (7) the Christian utopia, viz., the kingdom of God on earth; (8) social ethics; (9) the Christian mandate to *love one another*; (10) The Beatitudes or true happiness; (11) ethics as internal, *i. e.*, moral promptings originate within the personality.

2. The Sermon on the Mount

The *Sermon on the Mount* has been regarded as the "Magna Charta of Christian Ethics;" it is found in the fifth through the seventh chapters of Matthew's Gospel, and opens with the majestic Beatitudes. There exists considerable discussion concerning the ethics of Jesus; scholarly debate centers on whether the Sermon on the Mount is an ideal which operates merely to point the direction to which moral behavior ought to be orientated, or is one expected to be completely committed to it as way of life, *i. e.*, to practice it regularly without a single deviation? Those who contend that it represents an ideal that cannot be attained in this life point to discrepant renditions by Matthew and Luke concerning the verse, "Be ye therefore perfect, even as your Father which is in heaven is perfect," as Matthew 5:48 records it compared to Luke 6:36 "Be ye therefore merciful, as your Father also is merciful." The reasoning is that one cannot be expected to be as *perfect* as God, but one can be expected to be as *merciful*; Jesus may have had in mind the Levitical injunction: "Ye shall be holy: for I the Lord your God am Holy." (Lev. 19:2).

(a) *The Beatitudes*:

Blessed are the poor in spirit: for theirs is the kingdom of heaven.
Blessed are they that mourn: for they shall be comforted.
Blessed are the meek: for they shall inherit the earth.
Blessed are they which do hunger and thirst after righteousness: for they shall be filled.
Blessed are the merciful: for they shall obtain mercy.
Blessed are the pure in heart: for they shall see God.
Blessed are the peacemakers: for they shall be called the children of God.
Blessed are they which are persecuted for righteousness' sake: for their is the kingdom of heaven.
Blessed are ye when men shall revile you, and persecute you, and shall say all manner of evil against you falsely. Rejoice, and be exceeding glad: for great is your reward in heaven.[1]

The word *beatitude* means blessed or consummate bliss; in Greek literary writings the same term denotes the highest stage of happiness; some translations of the New Testament render the original Greek work *makarioi*, happy. Matthew's account of the Beatitudes spiritualizes them in relation to the Lukean record, *e. g.*, Matthew states the *poor in spirit* are blessed, whereas Luke makes mention only of the poor, *i. e.*, the poverty-striken, the oppressed, the despised, the *Am Haaretz* (people of the land) as they were called. The New Testament is essentially a poor man's book, *i. e.*, it favors and supports the interests of the poor; rarely, if ever, does it have a favorable word for the rich: "Then said Jesus unto his disciples, verily I say unto you, that a rich man shall hardly enter into the kingdom of heaven. And again I say unto you, it is easier for a camel to go through the eye of a needle, than for a rich man to enter into the kingdom of God." (Mat. 19:23-24). "Go to now, ye rich men, weep and howl for your miseries that shall come upon you. Your riches are corrupted, and your garments are moth eaten. Your gold and silver is cankered; the rust of them shall be a witness against you. . . . Behold the hire of the labourers who have reaped down your fields, which is of you kept back by fraud, crieth: and the cries of them which have reaped are entered into the ears of the Lord of Sabaoth." (James 5:1-4).

The benediction regarding the meek who inherit the land finds its antecedent in Psalms 36:11; "The meek shall inherit the earth." Meekness as a virtue is a moot point among some scholars; some Christians do not consider meekness in the unfavorable sense of spiritlessness, *i.e.*, a meek little man, a virtue. They prefer to interpret the Greek *praeis* as gentle, in the sense of mild of temper, for it connotes good will; one French translation has it rendered *debonnaire*. Numbers 12:2 cites Moses as "very meek above all the men which were upon the face of the earth;" apparently, meekness here pertains to gentleness, rather than a timid soul.

The beatitude pertaining to the merciful is uniquely Christian since it is discordant with everything taught and practiced in the ancient world: the Romans abhorred pity, the Stoics rejected sympathy, and Jesus' religious contemporaries, the Pharisees, showed little mercy due to their self-righteous and supercilious attitude. The beatitude that insures the pure in heart a vision of God is unique and without precedent in the religion of Israel. The benediction upon the peacemakers received wide acceptance among all peoples of the Roman empire; Caesar Augustus was acclaimed for his talent as a peacemaker.

(b) *Murder and Anger.* "Ye have heard that it was said by them of old time, Thou shalt not kill, and whosoever shall kill shall be in danger of the judgment: But I say unto you, That whosoever is angry with his brother without a cause shall be in danger of the judgment: and whosoever shall say to his brother, Raca, shall be in danger of the council: but whosoever shall say, Thou fool, shall be in danger of hell fire." (Mat. 5:21-22). The injunction against murder came from the Deuteronomic law (The Ten Commandments); an alleged murderer would have to stand trial by the judgment, *i. e.*, the properly constituted authorities, viz., the supreme court, but Jesus claims that all one need do to be liable to the highest court of the land is to be angry with his fellow man, (*without a cause* is a gloss which is not found in some of the best manuscripts of the early church fathers, and almost critically weakens his point). The linking of murder and anger is quite understandable, since killing is often done in anger. Raca (good-for-nothing wretch) is an expression of contempt; its odiousness lies in the ill-spirit of which this expression is indicative, and to denounce a man contemptuously as a fool is probably indicative of a still lower level or spiritual degradation. Such persons are liable to the *Gehenna of fire* as the original Greek has it; Gehenna of fire is the dump which lies on the outskirts of the city, viz., the valley of Hinnom southwest of Jerusalem, where refuse was consumed by fire. The entire teaching is clear; anger and killing are equally heinous, the former spawns the latter.

(c) *Lust, Adultery and Divorce.*

Ye have heard that it was said by them of old time, Thou shalt not commit adultery: But I say to you, That whosoever looketh on a woman to lust after her hath committed adultery with her already in his heart. (Mat. 5:27-28.)

It hath been said, Whosoever shall put away

his wife, let him give her a writing of divorcement: But I say unto you, That whosoever shall put away his wife, saving for the cause of fornication, causeth her to commit adultery: and whosoever shall marry her that is divorced committeth adultery. (Mat. 5:31-32.)

The Jewish code restricted the meaning of adultery to cohabitation with the wife or betrothed of another Jew, but in the usage of Jesus it includes all forms of illicit coitus. The Deuteronomic code was excessively liberal in granting divorce to men who were so inclined, but the same privilege was withheld from women inasmuch as they were the property of men and must be so treated; accordingly when a man divorces his wife, he is in effect, disposing of his property. The Deuteronomic law states that "when a man hath taken a wife, and married her, and it come to pass that she find no favor in his eyes, because he hath found some uncleanness in her: then let him write her a bill of divorcement, and give it in her hand, and send her out of his house." (Deut. 24:1.) However, as late as Malachi, a stricter attitude toward divorce was beginnig to dawn: "Therefore take heed to your spirit, and let none deal treacherously against the wife of his youth. For the Lord, the God of Israel, saith that he hateth putting away." (Malachi 2:15-16.) Although a woman was dispossessed of any legal right to obtain a divorce against her husband, the law did make provision whereby she could sue under certain circumstances and the husband would be compelled to grant her a bill of divorcement.

The stricter injunction of Jesus against lustful desire appears sufficiently encompassing to implicate all men, *i. e.*, to look at a woman desirously is tantamount to adultery.[2] Here is another indication of the moral stress Jesus places upon one's *inner spirit*; morality is much more than what one actually does by way of an overt act, it constitutes what you are, *i. e.*, the quality or *character of the soul within*. From the soul within, all outward actions are born; "not that which goeth into the mouth defileth a man; but that which cometh out of the mouth, this defileth a man. . . . Those things which proceedeth out of the mouth come forth from the heart; and they defile the man. For out of the heart proceed evil thoughts, murders, adulteries, fornications, thefts, false witness, blasphemies: These are the things that defile a man.[3] A good man out of the good treasure of the heart bringeth forth good things: and an evil man out of the evil treasure bringeth forth evil things. But I say unto you That every idle word that men shall speak, they shall give account thereof. . . . For by thy words thou shalt be justified, and by thy words thou shalt be condemned.'' (Matthew 12:34-37.) Furthermore, he adds: ''Beware of false prophets which come to you in sheep's clothing, but inwardly they are ravening wolves. Ye shall know them by their fruits. Do men gather grapes of thorns, or figs of thistles? Even so every good tree bringeth forth good fruit; but a corrupt tree bringeth forth evil fruit. A good tree cannot bring forth evil fruit, neither can a corrupt tree bring forth good fruit. . . . Wherefore by their fruits ye shall know them.'' (Matthew 7:15-18, 20.)

Further insight into Jesus' moral attitude concerning the indissolubility of marriage is gained from a future discussion in which he emphatically repudiates divorce: ''For this cause shall a man leave father and mother, and shall cleave to his wife: and they twain shall be one flesh. Wherefore they are no more twain, but one flesh. What therefore God hath joined together, let no man put asunder.'' (Matthew 19:5-6.) Should a man divorce his wife and another man marry her, then the new husband is guilty of adultery; since a woman does not actively engage in marriage, but is given in marriage; the man's offence is against the first husband.

(d) *The Swearing of Oaths.* Jesus said:

> ''Ye have heard that it hath been said by them of old time, Thou shalt not forswear thyself, but shalt perform unto the Lord thine oaths: But I say unto you, Swear not at all; neither by heaven; for it is God's throne: Nor by the earth; for it is his footstool: neither by Jerusalem; for it is the city of the great King. Neither shalt thou swear by thy head, because thou canst not make one hair

white or black. But let your communication be, Yea, yea, Nay, nay: for whatsoever is more than these cometh of evil. (Mat. 5:33-37.)

Jesus repudiates the entire practice of oath-taking because the practice had fallen into disrepute. Persons would swear by everything under the sun, but had mental reservations which would render them immune to the oath taken; consequently oaths became meaningless, *e. g.*, to swear an oath in the name of Yahweh (God) was binding, but to take an oath in the name of heaven or earth held no validity. Jesus' contention is that heaven, earth, and Jerusalem relate to God, hence to swear by any of them is tantamount to swearing by God himself, consequently these oaths are valid. However, he sweeps aside all swearing as holding no guarantee that under it an individual will tell the truth, and maintains that the only assurance of truth is a man's own integrity which is sufficient bond for his telling the truth with a simple yes as his acknowledgment that he will.

One implication here is that a man should never bind himself to a promise since he has no control over circumstances, *e. g.*, he cannot naturally alter the color of his hair. Since God alone has power over future events, then only he can bind himself to a promise and redeem it whatever the circumstances.

(e) *Retaliation.* Matthew records Jesus as saying:

Ye have heard that it hath been said, An eye for an eye, and a tooth for a tooth: But I say unto you, That ye resist not evil: but whosoever shall smite thee on thy right cheek, turn to him the other also. And if any man will sue thee at the law, and take away thy coat, let him have thy cloak also. And whosoever shall compel thee to go a mile, go with him twain. Give to him that asketh thee, and from him that would borrow of thee turn not thou away. (5:38-42.)

It was on this very concept of turning the other cheek that Ghandi constructed his philosophy of non-violence or soul resistance, his philosophical attitude being that it was beneath the dignity of a man to strike back when smitten. This is not only a repudiation of the *lex talionis*,⁴ but an introduction of a new moral principle regarding revenge, which is an injunction against retaliation by violent means against the one who is evil or who has done one evil.

The principle of the *second mile* refers to forced labor which the Roman government levied upon the people of Palestine and other captive and subject nations. Certain individuals, such as soldiers, government men, etc., could enjoin subjects to assist them in their efforts, *e. g.*, carrying their sacks for them for one mile, but no further; such distances could be easily estimated by milestones. It requires little imagination to visualize how emotionally disturbed individuals would normally become who were drafted into forced labor, but if such draftees would accept their responsibilities willingly, which could be evidenced by aiding the soldier in his efforts a second mile, then the first mile would lose its sting.

(f) *Agape (Christian Love)*. Jesus said:

> Ye have hear that it hath been said, Thou shalt love thy neighbor, and hate thine enemy. But I say unto you, Love your enemies, bless them that curse you, do good to them that hate you, and pray for them which despitefully use you, and persecute you; That ye may be the children of your Father which is in heaven: for he maketh his sun to rise on the evil and on the good, and sendeth rain on the just and on the unjust. For if ye love them which love you, what reward have ye? do not even the publicans the same? And if ye salute your brethren only, what do ye more than others? do not even the publicans so? Be ye therefore perfect, even as your Father which is in heaven is perfect. (Mat. 5:43-48.)

The Deuteronomic injunction which enjoined one to the love of neighbor did not include the foreigner, and particularly one's enemies, but the commandment of Jesus obligates one to love his foes. A common thief or an infamous gangster loves and befriends those who love and are loyal to him;

consequently, an individual, whose moral code does not excel the principle which restricts love or good will to friends and co-religionists only, is on the moral level of the rogue. In God's moral code, love is extended to enemies, persecutors, etc.

The Semitic connotation of *hate* in this reference is merely lack of love, and the significance of love is to be hospitable, to welcome, to exercise a good will. Whereas in the Jewish community the principle of love of neighbor was limited to a fellow Israelite, to Jesus, "neighbor" signified any human being in need of assistance. The point is unequivocally stated and emphasized in his "parable of the Good Samaritan."[5]

(g) *Ostentation*. Jesus continues:

> Take heed that ye do not your alms before men, to be seen of them: otherwise ye have no reward of your Father which is in heaven. Therefore when thou doest thine alms, do not sound a trumpet before thee, as the hypocrites do in the synagogues and in the streets, that they may have glory of men. Verily I say unto you, They have their reward. But when thou doest alms, let not thy left hand know what thy right hand doeth: That thine alms may be in secret. (Mat. 6:1-3.)

A vulgar display of charity voids it of all virtue as Alexander Pope also aptly discerned:

> Who builds a church to God, and not to fame,
> Will never mark the marble with his name.[6]

The acceptance of recognition or reward for one's charitable endeavors is equivalent to payment in much the same manner that a person makes a purchase. One does not consider it virtuous when he gives $5,000 for a new automobile; in a similar manner, it is not virtuous to accept a reward as payment for one's noble efforts.

Jesus' reference to the sounding of trumpets was no mere idle expression for trumpets were actually sounded to call attention to the activities of generous benefactors as they made their contributions during special public services. The poor were supported by a graduated income tax, but this was insufficient to meet their needs, accordingly, they augmented welfare donations in this manner.

(h) *Anxiety.* Jesus proclaims:

> Behold the fowls of the air: for they sow not, neither do they reap, nor gather into barns; yet your heavenly Father feedeth them. Are ye not much better than they? Which of you by taking thought can add one cubit to his stature? And why take ye thought for raiment? Consider the lilies of the field, how they grow; they toil not, neither do they spin: And yet I say unto you, That even Solomon in all his glory was not arrayed like one of these. Wherefore, If God so clothe the grass of the field, which to-day is, and to-morrow is cast into the oven, shall he not much more clothe you, O ye of little faith? Therefore take no thought, saying, What shall we eat? or, What shall we drink? or Wherewithal shall we be clothed? . . . for your heavenly Father knoweth that ye have need of all these things. But seek ye first the kingdom of God and his righteousness; and all these things shall be added unto you. Take therefore no thought for the morrow: for the morrow shall take thought for the things of itself. Sufficient unto the day is the evil thereof.
> (Mat. 6:26-34.)

Anxiety, for Jesus is a moral issue; it robs one of a rich, wholesome, and healthy life, and cripples his moral and creative efforts. Rationally, worry is absurd for by it one cannot add a single step to his life's span; it may be possible to extend one's life with thoughtful living, but if anything, one's life will be reduced in measure both in length and breadth through anxious care.

Jesus employs an *a fortiori* argument to prove his case, viz., if God has provided for the existence of an insignificant, colorless, and almost worthless bird, then *a fortiori* he will be much more concerned about the highest form of his creative efforts, viz., man.

One is admonished to live just one day at a time, hence suspend anxiety concerning the future for to-morrow will take care of itself. There is little doubt that Jesus heeded his own counsels for he lived a life that afforded little security: "The foxes have holes, and the birds of the air have nests; but the Son of man hath not where to lay his head." (Mat. 8:20.) The anxious person is caught in the web of his own making; life is a paradox "for whosoever will save his life shall lose it: and whosoever will lose his life . . . shall find it," said Jesus. (Matthew 17:25.) "We seek pleasure first, and find nausea. We seek safety first, and find a cowardly and defenseless mind. We seek profits first, and find fratricide.'"[7]

(i) *Censoriousness.* The *Sermon on the Mount* continues:

> Judge not, that ye be not judged. For with what judgment ye judge, ye shall be judged: and with what measure ye mete, is shall be measured to you again. And why beholdest thou the mote that is in thy brother's eye, but considerest not the beam that is in thine own eye? Or how wilt thou say to thy brother, Let me pull out the mote out of thine eye; and behold, a beam is in thine own eye? Thou hypocrite, first cast out the beam out of thine own eye; and then shalt thou see clearly to cast out the mote out of thy brother's eye. (Matthew 7:1-5.)

Some scholars cite this passage as an indication of humor in the life and teachings of Jesus; the picture is indeed an amusing one when one imagines an individual with a beam, *i. e.*, a log of wood in his eye fancying that, in this state of distorted vision, he is capable of removing a speck of dust from a friend's eye. Jesus identifies this incident as hypocrisy, but contemporary psychologists refer to the practice as a typical case of *projection, i. e.*, seeing in another's personality one's own defects, or sensing in another in magnified form, one's own deeply repressed socially unacceptable characteristics. Since one sees through the glasses of his own personality, he condemns himself in the act of judging.

It is as if one were to say, "If I were committing that act, I would be doing it with an ill intent."

Further insight into the preceding may be gained from Luke's version:

> For if ye love them which love you, what thank have ye? for sinners also love those that love them. And if ye do good to them which do good to you, what thank have ye? for sinners also do even the same. And if ye lend to them of whom ye hope to receive, what thank have ye? for sinners also lend to sinners, to receive as much again. But love ye your enemies, and do good, and lend, hoping for nothing again; and your reward shall be great. . . . Be ye therefore merciful, as your Father also is merciful. Judge not, and ye shall not be judged; condemn not, and ye shall not be condemned: forgive, and ye shall be forgiven: Give, and it shall be given unto you. . . . For with the same measure that ye mete withal it shall be measured to you again. (Luke 6:32-38.)

(j) *The Golden Rule*:

> All things whatsoever ye would that men should do to you, do ye even so to them: for this is the law and the prophets. . . . Straight is the gate, and narrow is the way, which leadeth unto life, and few there be that find it. (Mat. 7:12, 14.)

The antecedents of the Golden Rule have been thoroughly treated in the chapter on Moses; the major difference in the presentation of Jesus is its positive rendition. A positive emphasis directs one to his obligations and summons him to action, while a negative stress merely dissuades one from evil without necessarily enjoining him to positive duties. George A. Buttrick[3] makes mention of an incident which transpired between two Rabbis and a Gentile approximately twenty years before the time of Jesus. The Rabbis were asked facetiously if the whole Rabbinical law could be taught while standing on one foot; Hillel's reply was: "Do not unto others what you would not have others do to you."

3. The Great Commandment

Jesus said..... Thou shalt love the Lord thy God with all thy heart, and with all thy soul, and with all thy mind. This is the first and great commandment. And the second is like unto it, Thou shalt love thy neighbor as thyself. On these two commandments hang all the law and the prophets.
(Mat. 22:37-40.)

These two injunctions in combination constitute the great commandment; they are found originally in Deuteronomy 6:5 and Leviticus 19:18 respectively. "The rabbis loved to make aphorisms summing up the heart of religion, as in Aboth 1:1-2; 2:9; and there was much discussion as to which were the 'weightiest' commandments. One Rabbi told how Moses gave 613 commandments, but David reduced them to eleven (Ps. 15:2-5), Isaiah to six (Isa. 33:15), Micah to three (Mic. 6:8), Amos to two (Amos 5:4), and Habakkuk to one (Hab. 2:4) ... and Jas 1:27 is another.'"[9] The Great Commandment is, of course, another. Of the 613 Commandments attributed to Moses, a majority of 365 are negative, only 248 affirmative.

Luke's version of the Great Commandment is identified with the parable of the Good Samaritan, and rightly so because the essential difference in the commandment to love one's neighbor rests in Jesus' broad concept of neighbor. The Jews interpreted it as signifying another Israelite, but Jesus broadens the concept to include all mankind, *i. e.*, any human being who is in need of assistance. The parable of the Good Samaritan makes it quite explicit that a person who is in dire circumstances has a claim to neighborly treatment, consequently a right to aid. The parable's implicit teaching is clear, viz., the *universal brotherhood* of all mankind includes even exercising good will towards one's hated enemies. This is the first appearance in the history of humanity that the belief in the universal brotherhood of man is offered; previous to this proclamation of Jesus, the belief expressed was in a brotherhood of co-believers such as was found in ancient Israel and in the religion of Islam (Mohammedanism).

4. The Christian Mandate

The *Christian mandate* is found only in St. John's record of the Gospel; it is the command which Jesus issued on the last Thursday of his life on earth. It is for this reason that Christians refer to the Thursday of Holy Week, *i.e.*, the Thursday before Easter as Maundy Thursday; *Maundy* is a corruption of the term *mandate*. Jesus' mandate is:

> A new commandment I give unto you, That ye love one another; as I have loved you, that ye also love one another. By this shall all men know that ye are my disciples, if ye have love one to another.
> (John 13:34-35.)

On occasion this has been referred to as the *Eleventh Commandment*, but this commandment is not stated negatively; furthermore it sums up the entire moral responsibility of man. Love is undoubtedly the greatest virtue in the estimation of Jesus; moreover the love of God would be the greatest good, but the love of God implies love of mankind, *i. e.*, love of one's neighbor. St. John bears this point out: "If a man say, I love God, and hateth his brother, he is a liar: for he that loveth not his brother whom he hath seen, how can he love God whom he hath not seen? And this commandment have we from him, That he who loveth God love his brother also." (I John 4:20-21.)

5. Human Dignity and the Brotherhood of Man

Jesus was the first person ever to proclaim the *universal* brotherhood of man as is evidenced in his parable of the Good Samaritan. Whereas others taught the brotherhood of co-believers, national or religious, such as is found in the religion of Israel and Islam, he taught that all human beings regardless of race, religion, status, or position are brothers, and as such are entitled to neighborly hospitality. This thought is implicitly contained in the doctrine of the universal Fatherhood of God.

A second, and equally important concept implicit in the doctrine of the Fatherhood of God, is the teaching which affirms that every human creature is of infinite intrinsic value, *i. e.*, priceless. This proceeds by virtue of the fact that every human being is a child of God, hence precious in God's sight and estimation. The philosophical concept of human dignity denotes infinite intrinsic worth, whereas all other objects on a subhuman level posses only exchange or instrumental value, *i. e.*, they have a price tag, a price for which they may be purchased, or their value is purely utilitarian, and their purpose expediential. But as for man, to sell himself at any price is to sell himself short; "for what is a man profited, if he shall gain the whole world, and lose his own soul? or what shall a man give in exchange for his soul?" (Mat. 16:26). Buttrick mentions that the Emperor Charlemagne was buried in a sleeping state, as it were, seated with the open Bible on his lap and his finger pointed to the words: *"For what is a man profited, if he shall gain the whole world, and lose his own soul?"* He perceptively notes: "What profit if a man gain $100,000 in the bank and lose his health? The minister says over his grave, 'Forasmuch as it hath pleased Almighty God of his great mercy to take unto himself . . .' but we can be reasonably sure that in one sense it did not please God. What profit if a man gain political preferment and salutations in the clubs, and lose his option in the enjoyment of nature or in the joy of great books or in genuine friendship? Poor exchange!"[10]

Jesus identified himself so completely with every single specimen of humanity that whatever was done to another individual he took personally as if imputed directly to him. He was one with humanity, and accepted every human reject as a brother, *e. g.*, the leper, the social outcast, the poor, unwanted children, etc. To harm any human being was to harm him; to aid any human being was an expression of kindness to him:

> He shall set the sheep on his right hand, but the goats on the left. Then shall the King say unto them on his right hand, Come, ye blessed of my Father, inherit the kingdom prepared for you. . . . For I was an hungred, and ye gave me meat: I was thirsty, and ye gave me drink: I was a stranger, and ye took me in: Naked and ye clothed me: I was sick, and ye visited me: I was in prison, and ye came unto me. Then shall the righteous answer him, saying, Lord, when saw we thee an hungred, and fed thee? or thirsty, and gave thee drink? When saw we thee a stranger, and took thee in? or naked, and clothed thee? Or when saw we thee sick, or in prison, and came unto thee? And the King shall answer and say unto them, Verily I say unto you, Inasmuch as ye have done it unto one of the least of these my brethren, ye have done it unto me. (Mat. 25:33-40.)

There is no finer thought in the entire New Testament; here morality has reached its pinnacle and is without peer. It is reminiscent of the moving and sacrifical offer of Moses to surrender his own life to God as a ransom for the sins of his people: "Yet now, if thou wilt forgive their sin —; and if not, blot me, I pray thee, out of thy book which thou hast written." (Exodus 32:32.)

The ethics of Jesus gives the first clear-cut case of elevating the status of women and children, and granting them rights which were heretofore reserved solely for the adult male. Women and children were regarded as property and treated as such; they could be given up, sold, or even put to death, but Jesus reverses this entire practice with an injunction against the abuse of them. The following incident is noteworthy.

> Jesus called a little child unto him, and set him in the midst of them, And said. . . . Whoso shall receive one such little child in my name receiveth me. But whoso shall offend one of these little ones which believe in me, it were better for him that a

millstone were hanged about his neck, and that he were drowned in the depth of the sea. . . . And whosoever shall give to drink unto one of these little ones a cup of cold water only in the name of a disciple, verily I say unto you, he shall in no wise lose his reward. (Mat. 18:2, 5, 6; 10:42.)

The pagan valuation of children was much lower than a person of contemporary western civilization would dare imagine. A now classic letter originally written on papyri has been discovered which dates back to the beginning of the Christian era in which an Egyptian writes most affectionately to his wife mentioning his love for her, a gift that he has for her, and instructions concerning their forthcoming child: if the child is born a boy, she is to care for its rearing, but if a girl, she is to allow her to die by exposure. In the ethics of Jesus, this would be unthinkable and the rankest form of murder.

It is needless to say that western civilization has been influenced by the ethical teachings of Jesus. The welfare of children, *e.g.*, child labor laws, and the Western respect for women emanated from Christian thought; New York State's ban on divorce except for adultery stems directly from this source; the high regard with which human life is respected is definitely Christian inspired; the respect for labor, and particularly the democratic way of life is definitely and directly traceable to the morality propounded by Jesus as well as many other notable endeavors, *e.g.*, institutions of higher learning, hospitals, charities, etc.

NOTES

JESUS

1. Matthew 5:3-12; Luke's version is found in 6:20-23, 11:28, 12:37.
2. Cf. Epictetus, Discourses II, 18, and in the present work, Section 7 in the chapter on Epictetus.
3. Matthew 15:11, 18-20.
4. See the section on the *lex talionis* in the chapter *on Moses*.
5. See the section on *The Great Commandment*.
6. Alexander Pope, *Moral Essays*, Epistle III, Line 285.
7. George A. Buttrick, *The Interpreter's Bible* (New York: Abingdon Press, 1951), Vol. VII, 325.
8. *Op. cit.*
9. Sherman E. Johnson, *The Interpreter's Bible, op. cit.*, 523.
10. George A. Buttrick, op. cit., 456; his quotation comes from the Church of Scotland, *Book of Common Prayer*.

ST. PAUL

Whatsoever things are true, whatsoever things are honest, whatsoever things are just, whatsoever things are pure, whatsoever things are lovely, whatsoever things are of good report; if there be any virtue, and if there be any praise, think on these things.

And now abideth faith, hope, love, these three; but the greatest of these is love. (St. Paul)

1. The Greatest Virtue (Love)

One of the greatest pieces of moral literature of any age is St. Paul's thirteenth chapter of the first epistle to the Corinthians. It is a most noble utterance which represents the climax of an extended reprimand to his Corinthian converts some of whom had descended to depths of immoral degeneracy. This passage is regarded as the pinnacle of St. Paul's talent; its poetic beauty is readily sensed, even if not written in meter; the mood and thought are lyrical. It is obviously a "Hymn to Love," which in the estimation of its author is the sublimest of human characteristics.

But covet earnestly the best gifts: and yet I show unto you a more excellent way.

Though I speak with the tongues of men and of angels, and have not charity, I am become as sounding brass, or a tinkling cymbal.

And though I have the gift of prophecy, and understand all mysteries, and all knowledge; and though I have all faith, so that I could remove mountains, and have not charity, I am nothing.

And though I bestow all my goods to feed the poor, and though I give my body to be burned, and have not charity, it profiteth me nothing.

Charity suffereth long, and is kind; charity envieth not; charity vaunteth not itself, is not puffed up, Doth not behave itself unseemly, seeketh not her own, is not easily provoked, thinketh no evil; Rejoiceth not in iniquity, but rejoiceth in the truth; Beareth all things, believeth all things, hopeth all things, endureth all things.

Charity never faileth: but whether there be prophesies, they shall fail; whether there be tongues, they shall cease; whether there be knowledge, it shall vanish away.

For we know in part, and we prophesy in part. But when that which is perfect is come, then that which is in part shall be done away.

When I was a child, I spake as a child, I understood as a child, I thought as a child; but when I became a man, I put away childish things.

For now we see through a glass, darkly; but then face to face: now I know in part; but then shall I know even as also I am known.

And now abideth faith, hope, charity, these three; but the greatest of these is charity.

The original Greek text which was rendered *charity* throughout is *agape*, which is the loftiest word in the Greek for *love*: There are three words translated from the Greek signifying love: *philia* connotes friendship or fondness, and *eros* suggests sexual love, but the word which conveys God's love or brotherly love is *agape*. The word charity denoting love has become archaic; today it implies almsgiving due to undergoing an evolutionary change of language.

St. Paul considered love an obligation; love is an innate and inalienable debt which one man owes to another by virtue of the fact that they are human beings, *i. e.*, brothers of a human family under the fatherhood of God: "Owe no man anything, but to love one another: for he that loveth another hath fulfilled the law. For this, Thou shalt not commit adultery, Thou shalt not kill, Thou shalt not steal, Thou shalt not bear false witness, Thou shalt not covet; and if there be any other commandment, it is briefly comprehended in this saying, namely, Thou shalt love thy neighbor as thyself. Love worketh no ill to his neighbor: therefore love is the fulfilling of the law."[1]

The love one has for God is not only an obligation, but an asset, for the one who loves God finds a wholesome harmony existing in his life. "We know that all things work together for good to them that love God."[2]

2. The Good Life

Another majestic passage of high ethical content is Romans twelve; here the various noble qualities of the good life are bared:

> I beseech you therefore, brethren, by the mercies of God, that ye present your bodies a living sacrifice, holy, acceptable unto God, which is your reasonable service.
>
> And be not conformed to this world: but be ye transformed by the renewing of your mind, that ye may prove what is that good, and acceptable, and perfect, will of God.
>
> For I say, through the grace given unto me, to every man that is among you, not to think of himself more highly than he ought to think; but to think soberly. . . .
>
> Let love be without dissimulation. Abhor that which is evil; cleave to that which is good. Be kindly affectioned one to another with brotherly love; in honour preferring one another; Not slothful in business; fervent in spirit; serving the Lord, Rejoicing in hope; patient in tribulation; continuing instant in prayer; Distributing to the necessity of saints; given to hospitality.
>
> Bless them which persecute you; bless, and curse not. Rejoice with them that do rejoice,

and weep with them that weep. Be of the same mind one toward another. Mind not high things, but condescend to men of low estate. Be not wise in your own conceits.

Recompense to no man evil for evil. Provide things honest in the sight of all men. If it be possible, as much as lieth in you, live peaceably with all men. Dearly beloved, avenge not yourselves, but rather give place unto wrath: for it is written, Vengeance is mine; I will repay, saith the Lord. Therefore if thine enemy hunger, feed him; if he thirst, give him drink: for in so doing thou shalt heap coals of fire on his head. Be not overcome of evil, but overcome evil with good.[3]

There exist a number of obstacles to the good life; one major deterrent is the flesh with its intense desires of lust and evil. The flesh, *i. e.*, one's sensual nature is the cause of considerable immoral action on the part of man "for the flesh lusteth against the Spirit, and the Spirit against the flesh: and these are contrary the one to the other: so that ye cannot do the things ye would. . . . Now the works of the flesh are manifest, which are these; adultery, fornication, uncleanness, lasciviousness, idolatry, witchcraft, hatred, variance, emulations, wrath, strife, seditions, heresies, envyings, murders, drunkenness, revellings, and such like. . . . But the fruit of the Spirit, is love, joy, peace, longsuffering, gentleness, goodness, faith, meekness, temperance: against such there is no law."[4]

Indications of spiritual maturity are perceptible when its chief characteristics are manifested as listed above; one inculcates them into the personality by constantly meditating upon them and similar qualities. St. Paul concludes his letter to the Philippians with the following admonition: "Finally, brethren, whatsoever things are true, whatsoever things are honest, whatsoever things are just, whatsoever things are pure, whatsoever things are lovely, whatsoever things are of good report; if there be any virtue, and if there be any praise, think on these things."[5] Spiritual exercise of this nature is edifying, rewarding, and inspiring: "Exercise thyself unto godliness: for bodily exercise is profitable for little; but godliness is profitable for all things."[6]

The good life consists of a multiplicity of virtues, but the one which excels them all is love: "Put on therefore . . . a heart of compassion, kindness, lowliness, meekness, longsuffering; forbearing one another, and forgiving each other . . . and above all these things put on love, which is the bond of perfectness."[7] The attainment of godliness is no mean achievement in St. Paul's estimation, particularly coupled with contentment, for "godliness with contentment is great gain."[8]

St. Paul was well versed in Stoical contentment, having achieved it for himself, but this did not deter him from enjoying wholesome and moral pleasures when offered. When he possessed pleasurable things, he enjoyed them, but when they had to be relinquished, he knew how to live content without them. He writes: "I have learned, in whatsoever state I am, therewith to be content. I know how to be abased, and how to abound: every where and in all things I am instructed both to be full and to be hungry, both to abound and to suffer need."[9] However, each person must live his own life and work things out for himself; you must "work out your own salvation"[10] in the light of your own conscience. St. Paul rhetorically queries: "Why is my liberty judged of another man's conscience?"[11]

3. The Moral Law of Compensation

A moral law of compensation is in effect in the universe whereby a man suffers for his ill behavior and is blessed for the good which he does "for the wages of sin is death."[12] The law of retribution is active in the nature of things and functions similarly to a system of rewards and punishments. "Be not deceived; God is not mocked: for whatsoever a man soweth, that shall he also reap. For he that soweth to his flesh shall of the flesh reap corruption; but he that soweth to the Spirit shall of the Spirit reap life everlasting. And let us not be weary in well doing: for in due season we shall reap, if we faint not. As we have therefore opportunity, let us do good unto all men."[13] Elsewhere, but in the same vein, he strongly advocates giving generously to charitable endeavors for the moral life has its compensations: "He which soweth sparingly shall reap also sparingly; and he which soweth bountifully shall reap also bountifully. Every man according as he purposeth in his heart, so let him give; not grudgingly, or of necessity; for God loveth a cheerful giver."[14] All things work together for good to the moral individual.

The moral law of compensation is seen most clearly in the matter of censoriousness, wherein one condemns himself in the act of judging others. He who forgives is forgiven, he who condemns is condemned. "O man, whosoever thou art that judgest: for wherein thou judgest another, thou condemnest; for thou that judgest doest the same things. . . . And thinkest thou this, O man, that judgest them which do such things, and doest the same, that thou shalt escape the judgment of God?"[15]

4. Interim Ethics

Some of the Pauline ethic is definitely eschatological, hence must be viewed as an interim ethic; this is particularly true of his social ethics regarding ideas on slavery, marriage, etc. *E.g.*, when the runaway slave, Onesimus, came to St. Paul for advice, he was told to return to his master and be a good slave; the reason being that the world was coming soon to a close, hence there was no great call for disturbing the *status quo*. What was needed was an ethic for the interim period, *i. e.*, the last few days, months or so before the end of the world; such being the case, there was no necessity for extensive social reforms of any great magnitude. St. Paul had his converts so convinced that the end of the age was imminent, that many of them went into retirement with the understanding that it was futile to till the soil since they would not be around to reap the harvest. To counteract this display of loitering, he issued a statement to the effect "that if any would not work, neither should he eat."[16]

Marriage under these uncertain conditions was inadvisable, consequently his advice was "to the unmarried and widows, it is good for them if they abide even as I, But if they cannot contain, let them marry: for it is better to marry than to burn."[17] It is assumed that St. Paul was unmarried; his advice to others who were unmarried was to remain in that state, but if they could not contain themselves, it would be better for them to marry even though it would be of brief duration due to the impending close of this present era, than to be aflame with passion, not to burn in hell fire as many mistakenly read into the record eisegetically.

5. Miscellaneous Moral Teachings

1. *Money.* "The love of money is the root of all evil." (I Timothy 6:10.)
2. *Living life well to the end.* "I have fought a good fight, I have finished my course, I have kept the faith." (II Timothy 4:7.)
3. *Hypocrisy.* "Thou therefore which teachest another, teachest thou not thyself? thou that preachest a man should not steal, dost thou steal? Thou that sayest a man should not commit adultery, dost thou commit adultery?" (Romans 2:21-22.)
4. *The moral paradox.* "For the good I would I do not: but the evil which I would not, that I do." (Romans 7:19.)
5. *The higher retaliatory ethic.* "Being reviled, we bless; being persecuted, we suffer it: being defamed, we intreat." (I Corinthians 4:12-13.)

    "We exhort you, brethren, admonish the disorderly, encourage the fainthearted, support the weak, be long-suffering toward all. See that none render unto anyone evil for evil; but always follow after that which is good, one toward another, and toward all." (I Thessalonians 5:14-15; Revised Standard.)
6. *The relation of immortality to morality.* "If the dead are not raised, let us eat and drink, for to-morrow we die." (I Corinthians 15:32; Revised Standard.)
7. *Evil companions.* "Be not deceived, evil companionships corrupt good morals." (I Corinthians 15:33; Revised Standard.)

8. *Love.* "Let all that ye do be done in love" (I Corinthians 16:14; Revised Standard.)
9. *Courage.* "We are troubled on every side, yet not distressed; we are perplexed, but not in despair; persecuted, but not forsaken; cast down, but not destroyed." (I Corinthians 4:8-9.)
10. *Conceit.* "For if a man think himself to be something, when he is nothing, he deceiveth himself." (Galatians 6:3.)
11. *Aid to others.* "Bear ye one another's burdens ... and let us not be weary in well doing." (Galatians 6:2, 9.)
12. *Wrath.* "Be ye angry, and sin not: let not the sun go down upon your wrath." (Ephesians 4:26.)
13. *Vile language.* "Let no corrupt communication proceed out of your mouth, but that which is good to the use of edifying.... Let all bitterness, and wrath, and anger, and clamour and evil speaking, be put away from you, with all malice: and be ye kind one to another, tenderhearted, forgiving one another." (Ephesians 4:29, 31, 32.)
14. *Purity of heart.* "The end of the commandment is charity (love) out of a pure heart, and of a good conscience, and of a faith unfeigned." (I Timothy 1:5.)
15. *Prejudice and partiality.* "Observe these things without prejudice, doing nothing by partiality." (I Timothy 5:21; Revised Standard.)
16. *Stoicism.* "For we brought nothing into this world, and it is certain we can carry nothing out." (I Timothy 6:7.)
17. *Fear as alien to man.* "For God hath not given us the spirit of fear; but of power, and of Love, and of a sound mind." (II Timothy 1:7.)

NOTES

ST. PAUL

1. Romans 13:8-10.
2. Romans 9:28.
3. Romans 12:1-3, 9-21.
4. Galatians 5:17, 19-23.
5. Philippians 4:8.
6. I Timothy 4:7-8; Revised Standard.
7. Colossians 3:12-14; Revised Standard.
8. I Timothy 6:6.
9. Philippians 2:12.
9. Philippians 4:11-12.
10. Philippians 2:12.
11. I Corinthians 10:29.
12. Romans 6:23.
13. Galatians 6:7-10.
14. II Corinthians 9:6-7.
15. Romans 2:1, 3.
16. II Thessalonians 3:10.
17. II Corinthians 7:8-9.

SAINT AUGUSTINE

Thou hast made us for thyself, and our heart is restless until it repose in thee. (St. Augustine)

1. Natural Goodness of All Things

Inasmuch as God is the creator of all things, it must follow that all things were created essentially good, in proper perspective and in their normal state, they are completely good:

> By the Trinity, thus supremely and equally good, all things were created; and these are not supremely and equally and unchangeably good, but yet they are good, even taken separately. Taken as a whole, however, they are very good, because their *ensemble* constitutes the universe in all its wonderful order and beauty.[1]

When evil is controlled and order restored, all things, including evil, contribute to the enhancement of the good; "and in the universe, even that which is called evil, when it is regulated and put in its own place, only enhances our admiration of the good; for we enjoy and value the good more when we compare it with the evil."[2]

Since God is the originator of all that exists, then *ipso facto*, every existing being must be good. "All things that exist, therefore, seeing that the Creator of them all is supremely good, are themselves good."[3] Evil would consist in the corruption of good, by consuming or deteriorating it. When good "is corrupted, however, its corruption is an evil, because it is deprived of some sort of good. For if it be deprived of no good, it receives no injury; but it does receive injury, therefore it is deprived of good. Therefore, so long as a being is in process of corruption, there is in it some good of which it is being deprived. . . . Wherefore corruption can consume the good only by consuming the being. Every being, therefore, is a good; a great good, if it can not be corrupted; a little good, if it can."[4]

Vice is contrary to the nature of God and men, hence evil, "solely because it corrupts their good nature. It is not their nature but their vice that is contrary to God; evil only being contrary to good. And who denies that God is the best good? So then vice is contrary unto God, as evil is unto good."[5] Nature, including man, is good because it was made with inherent order and harmony, it becomes vitiated when perverted and distorted. However, in their natural unadulterated form, "all natures are good, because they have their form, kind, and a certain harmony withal in themselves."[6]

Man is good by nature: "he is good because he is a man."[7] One cannot condemn man without, at the same time, condemning the work of God, inasmuch as God is responsible for man's creation. "Therefore every being, even if it be a defective one, in so far it is a being is good, and in so far as it is defective is evil."[8] Whatever debilitates nature is evil "and all sin is against nature and hurtful thereunto."[9]

2. Evil as the Privation of Good

"For what is that which we call evil but the absence of good? In the bodies of animals, disease and wounds mean nothing but the absence of health; for when a cure is effected, that does not mean that the evils which were present — namely the diseases and wounds — go away from the body elsewhere: they altogether cease to exist; for the wound is not a substance, but a defect in the fleshly substance — the flesh itself being a substance and therefore something good, of which those evils — that is, privations of the good which we call health — are accidents. Just in the same way we call vices in the soul are nothing but privation of natural good. And when they are cured, they are not transferred elsewhere; when they cease to exist in a healthy soul, they cannot exist anywhere else."[10]

Inasmuch as evil is the privation of good, it follows that evil cannot exist without the presence of good, hence evil's nature is parasitic. On these premises, evil could not have sprung into existence without good; "from what is good, then, evils arose, and except in what is good they do not exist."[11] If human nature were incorruptible, evil would be an impossibility. Evil has no source, it does not come from anywhere; it is goodness decaying, it is order degenerating to chaos, it is harmony succumbing to discord, but without good, order, and harmony, evil cannot survive. "Evil cannot exist without good, or in anything that is not good. Good, however, can exist without evil."[12] Only men or angels are subject to wickedness, but as long as these beings are true to their natures, they are good, but to the extent one perverts his nature, he is evil. God does not create evil, he merely tolerates it; "nor can we doubt that God does well even in the permission of what is evil."[13]

3. Freedom of the Will

Nothing is the result of fate, but every human action is directly attributable to the will which is autonomous. "So when we say that if we will anything, we must of necessity will it with a freedom of will, that is true: and we do not put our will under any such necessity as deprives it of its freedom. So our wills are ours willing what we will; and if we will it not, neither do they will it: and if any man suffer anything by the will of another against his own will, his will has its own power still, and his sufferance comes from the power of God."[14]

Evil stems from an evil will, but nothing causes an evil will. The evil will is a state, viz., the privation of good. "For the will turning from the superior to the inferior, becomes bad, not because the thing whereunto it turns is bad, but because the turning is bad and perverse."[15] St. Augustine illustrates the foregoing by citing the case of two men viewing a beautiful woman; one's mind remains chaste, but the other is seething with lustful desire. The objective beautiful sight, viz., the body, is not the cause for each man responded differently to the same sight; nor is the mind of the men the cause or root of the evil, because each man is alike in that respect. The cause is the man's consenting to succumb — "this consent therefore — the cause of this assent of the will to vicious desire"[16] is the root of evil. "The evil will therefore causes evil works, but nothing causes the evil will."[17] For the will to become evil, it falls from a loftier position, it has no efficient cause; "for it is not efficient but deficient, nor is there any effect but defect, namely falling from that highest essence unto a lower, this is to have an evil will."[18]

A man who covets gold is sinful, not because there is any vice in gold *per se*, but the perversity that exists in loving gold, "nor is lust the fault of sweet beauteous bodies, but the soul's that runs perversely to bodily delights. . . . Vainglory is not a vice proper to human praise, but the soul's that perversely desires praise of men. . . . Nor is pride his vice that gives the power, but the soul's perversely loving that power. . . . It is not the thing to which we fall, but our fall that is evil; that is, we fall to no evil natures, but against nature's order, from the highest to the lower. Herein is evil."[19]

A captive woman ravished by the violent lusts of soldiers is morally pure provided she does not consent willingly, *i.e.*, enjoy it desirously, for "the sanctity of body is no more lost, if the sanctity of mind remain (though the body be ravished), then it is kept, if the mind's holiness be polluted, though the body itself be untouched. . . . Tush, another's lust cannot pollute thee; if it do, it is not another's but thine own. . . . Chastity being a virtue of the mind . . . it learns rather to endure all evils, than consent to any."[20]

Consequently, a maiden who has been raped has no right to commit suicide to redeem her shame. *A fortiori* it would follow that no one has the moral right to take his life for any reason whatever. "Wherefore if there be no reason, that a woman that hath already suffered another's villainy against her own will should destroy herself by voluntary death, how much less ought this course to be followed before there be any cause?"[21] Augustine vehemently repudiates the stoical doctrine that one may escape the problems and vicissitudes of the present life by taking refuge in suicide because "there is no authority which allows Christians to be their own deaths in whatsoever cause...either for attaining of immortality, or avoiding of calamity."[22] A wise man is indeed to endure death with patience, but that must come *ab externo*, "from another man's hand and not from his own."[23]

The human will is the *sine qua non* of all morality; if it is good, then the soul and its activities are good. "What is desire, and joy, but a will consenting to that which we affect? And what is fear, and sorrow, but a will contrary unto what we like?"[24] *Consenting* to desire renders the will evil or good, not the object of one's desires. Man in his normal state loves good and hates evil, "and because none is evil by nature, but all by vice, he that lives after God's love owes his full hate unto the evil; not to hate the man for his vice, nor to love the vice for the man, but hate the vice and love the man: for the vice being cured, he shall find no object of his hate, but all for his love."[25]

4. The *Summum Bonum* (God)

Man's chief good cannot merely be the greatest good of the body only, it must also be the soul's primary good, hence it cannot be bodily pleasure such as the hedonists teach nor can it be the absence of pain, neither strength, beauty, or anything else reckoned as one of the goods of the body. The soul also is not the greatest good of man for that implies that man's essence is physical and the soul is its greatest good. An object's greatest good is that which perfects it; since virtue perfects the soul and the soul obtains virtue by following God; the pursuit of God is not only the greatest virtue, but issues in happiness. "The supreme good is that which is possessed of supreme existence,"[26] viz., *God*, "whom we are to seek after with supreme affection,"[27] viz., *love*.

"God is the one object of love; therefore he is man's chief good. Nothing is better than God."[28]

The attainment of God is not achieved in becoming like him, but in drawing close to him, *i.e.*, approaching his presence via "immaterial contact with him, and in being inwardly illuminated and occupied by his truth and holiness."[29] All creatures receive their goodness as a consequence of God; such good is obtained *from* him, not *of* him. "The highest good, than which there is no higher, is God, and consequently He is unchangeable good, hence truly eternal and truly immortal."[30]

God is the creator of nature, therefore all nature is good; evil is nature corrupted, either in measure, form or order. "When accordingly it is inquired, whence is evil, it must first be inquired, what is evil, which is nothing else than corruption . . . Nature therefore which has been corrupted, is called evil."[31] Nature, even human nature, when corrupted is in some degree good, unless its corruption is complete, *i.e.*, entirely chaotic and totally lacking in order; but "nature which cannot be corrupted is the highest good."[32] From this highest good, come all other good things, great and small, viz., God who alone is the supremely good. "For if God is man's chief good . . . it clearly follows, since to seek the chief good is to live well, that to live well is nothing else but to love God."[33]

5. The Greatest Virtue (Love of God)

"I hold virtue to be nothing else than perfect love of God."[34] Augustine employs and interprets the four virtues of Plato, viz., temperance, courage, wisdom, justice, in a Christian light, *i.e.*, as four forms of love: "temperance is love giving itself entirely to that which is loved; fortitude (courage) is love readily bearing all things for the sake of the loved object; justice is love serving only the loved object, and therefore ruling tightly; prudence is love distinguishing with sagacity between what hinders it and what helps it. The object of this love is not anything, but only God, the chief good, the highest wisdom, the perfect harmony."[35] The four may be compactly summarized in the following definition: "temperance is love keeping itself entire and incorrupt for God; fortitude is love bearing everything readily for the sake of God; justice is love serving God only, and therefore ruling well all else, as subject to man; prudence is love making a right distinction between what helps it towards God and what might hinder it."[36]

The four virtues are in a sense, four aspects of one and the same virtue, viz., *love;* when the virtues are faithfully practiced they issue in a reward, viz., eternal life and the knowledge of the truth. Each of these four moral duties has a distinct and separate office in the exercising of the love of God:

Temperance enables one to pursue a life of happiness by avoiding being seduced by those impediments to the blessed life, viz., incontinence, covetousness, and other sins of the soul which flourish through want of self-control. "The office of temperance is in restraining and quieting the passions which make us pant for those things which turn us away from the laws of God and from the enjoyment of His goodness, that is, in a word, from the happy life."[37] The intemperate man succumbs to the gratification of bodily delights and loves sensuous objects, hence the usurpation of love that rightfully belongs to God. "God then alone is to be loved; and all this world, that is, all sensible things, are to be despised, — while, however, they are to be used as this life requires."[38] The moral function of temperance is love "which ought with all sanctity to burn in desire for God . . . in not seeking for earthly things."[39]

Love expressed in the form of fortitude or courage enables one to stand steadfast in pain or great struggles; "there is nothing, though of iron hardness, which the fire of love cannot subdue. And when the mind is carried up to God in this love, it will soar above all torture free and glorious, with wings beauteous and unhurt, on which chaste love rises to the embrace of God. Otherwise God must allow the lovers of gold, the lovers of praise, the lovers of women, to have more fortitude than the lovers of himself, though love in those cases is rather to be called passion or lust."[40] Courage is the result of the love of God; if a person's love for God were sufficiently intense, then he would be able to endure any plight, regardless of the extent of the tragedy.

The discussion on justice is quickly dismissed but not without a striking comment by way of conclusion: "The lover, then, whom we are describing, will get from justice this rule of life, that he must with perfect readiness serve the God whom he loves, the highest good, the highest wisdom, the highest peace."[41]

With equal brevity prudence or wisdom is discussed, but its importance is indicated by the fact that the foregoing discussion of virtue would be impossible without it. "It is the part of prudence to keep watch with most anxious vigilance, lest any evil influence should stealthily creep in upon us," and create "this mental somnolence, which makes us insensible to destruction advancing on us step by step."[42]

A concomitant of the love of God is love of self and the love of one's neighbor; love of neighbor implies benevolence or good will, "that is, that we cherish no malice and no evil design against another. For man is the nearest neighbor of man."[43] Love of neighbor is "a sort of cradle of our love to God" so that "there is a sense in which these either rise together to fullness and perfection, or, while the love of God is first in beginning, the love of neighbor is first in coming to perfection."[44] The reason for this is that one reaches perfection easier and earlier in lower things. Furthermore, an indispensable prerequisite to one's own happiness is the love of neighbor; "no one should think that while he despises his neighbor he will come to happiness and to the God whom he loves. . . . These things require more than mere good-will, and can be done only by a high degree of thoughtfulness and prudence."[45]

6. Confessions of St. Augustine

Some significant moral ideas and concepts can be extracted from the confessions and life of St. Augustine: Man is created by God in such a manner that unless man orientates his life in the light of God and his will, frustration will inevitably result. Man must for the sake of his own happiness pursue the moral road initiated by God or as Augustine worded it: "Thou madest us for thyself, and our heart is restless, until it repose in thee."[46]

Man's need of God is of great moment; spiritual starvation is more serious and acute than physical hunger: "For within me was a famine of that inward food, Thyself, my God."[47] Not only does the soul experience a sense of constriction ("narrow is the mansion of my soul; enlarge thou it, that thou mayest enter in")[48] in the absence of God, but in the concomitance of his presence is spiritual wealth and happiness: "Oh! that thou wouldst enter into my heart, and inebriate it, that I may forget my ill, and embrace thee, my sole good."[49]

Augustine's internal moral struggle in pursuit of the moral life indicated two discordant forces relentlessly tearing his spirit asunder as though the personality were irreconcilably split, for in despair he sighs: "Thus did my two wills, one new, and the other old, one carnal, the other spiritual, struggle within me; and by their discord, undid my soul."[50] The struggle within reached its climax in the complete abandonment to the gratification of appetite when he prayed haltingly and doubtfully for chastity by petitioning God with the words: "Give me chastity and continency, only not yet."[51]

The culmination of the internal moral battle resulted in triumphant victory, when after a period of despondency, "I sent up these sorrowful words; How long? how long, 'to-morrow, and to-morrow?' Why not now? why not is there this hour an end to my uncleanness?"[52] He was answered with the chanting words: "Take up and read; Take up and read" which he did; the Biblical passage his eyes fell upon was a critical one for it resulted in a complete and definite conversion of his moral life. He relates his own story: "I seized, opened, and in silence read that section, on which my eyes first fell: *Not in rioting and drunknness, not in cham-*

bering and wantonness, not in strife and envying; but put ye on the Lord Jesus Christ, and make not provision for the flesh, in concupiscence. No further would I read: nor need I: for instantly at the end of this sentence, by a light as it were of serenity infused into my heart, all the darkness of doubt vanished away,''[53] forever.

7. Further Reading in St. Augustine

St. Augustine was a most prolific writer whose works encompass many volumes; some of them are as follows: *The City of God, Confessions, On the Morals of the Catholic Church, On the Morals of the Manichaeans, Enchiridion, The Trinity, The Spirit and the Letter, Ten Homilies on the First Epistle General of St. John, On the Spirit and the Letter, On Nature and Grace, On Man's Perfection and Righteousness, On Grace and Free Will, Retraction, On Christian Doctrine, On the Merits and Remission of Sins, On the Proceedings of Pelagius, On the Grace of Christ, On Marriage and Concupiscence, On the Soul and Its Origin, Against Two Letters of the Pelagians, On Rebuke and Grace, On the Predestination of the Saints, On the Gift of Perseverance, On Two Souls, Against the Manichaeans, Acts or Disputation against Fortunatus the Manichaean, Against the Epistle of Manichaeus Called Fundamental, Reply to Faustus the Manichaean, Concerning the Nature of Good, Against the Manichaeans, On Baptism, Against the Donatists, Answer to Letters of Petilian,—Bishop of Cirta, The Correction of the Donatists, The Soliloquies, The Teacher, On True Religion, The Usefulness of Belief, Faith and the Creed, On Various Questions, Of Continence, On the Good of Marriage, Of Holy Virginity, On the Good of Widowhood, On Lying, Of the Work of Monks, On Patience, On Care to be Had for the Dead, On the Catechising of the Uninstructed.*

NOTES

ST. AUGUSTINE

1. St. Augustine, *The Enchiridion* (tr. by J. F. Shaw, Edinburgh, 1892), ch. X.
2. *Ibid.*, XI.
3. *Ibid.*, XII.
4. *Idem.*
5. St. Augustine, *The City of God* (tr. by John Healey, Griffith Farran and Co., 1890), XII, 3.
6. *Ibid.*, 5.
7. *The Enchiridion*, XIII.
8. *Idem.*
9. *The City of God*, XII, 1.
10. *The Enchiridion*, XI.
11. *Ibid.*, XIV.
12. *Idem.*
13. *Ibid.*, XCVI.
14. *The City of God*, V, 10.
15. *Ibid.*, XII, 6.
16. *Idem.*
17. *Idem.*
18. *Ibid.*, 7.
19. *Ibid.*, 8.
20. *Ibid.*, I, 17.
21. *Idem.*
22. *Ibid.*, 19.
23. *Ibid.*, XIX 4.
24. *Ibid.*, XIV, 6.
25. *Idem.*
26. St. Augustine, *On The Morals of the Manicheans* (tr. by Richard Stothert, T. and T. Clark, Edinburgh, 1872), I.
27. St. Augustine, *On the Morals of The Catholic Church* (tr. by Richard Stothert, T. and T. Clark, Edinburgh, 1872), VIII.
28. *Ibid.*, XI.
29. *Idem.*
30. St. Augustine, *Concerning the Nature of the Good* (tr. by Albert H. Newman, 1887), I.
31. *Ibid.*, IV.
32. *Ibid.*, VI.
33. *On the Morals of the Catholic Church*, XXV.
34. *Ibid.*, XV.
35. *Idem.*
36. *Idem.*

37. *Ibid.*, XIX.
38. *Ibid.*, XX.
39. *Ibid.*, XXII.
40. *Idem.*
41. *Ibid.*, XXIV.
42. *Idem.*
43. *Ibid.*, XXVI.
44. *Idem.*
45. *Idem.*
46. St. Augustine, *Confessions* tr. by E. B. Pusey, (London: J. M. Dent and Sons, Ltd., 1907), I, 1.
47. *Ibid.*, III, 1.
48. *Ibid.*, I, 5.
49. *Idem.*
50. *Ibid.*, VIII, 5.
51. *Ibid.*, 7.
52. *Ibid.*, 12.
53. *Idem.*

ST. THOMAS AQUINAS

The last end of any intellectual substance is called happiness or beatitude, for it is this that every intellectual substance desires as its last end, and for its own sake alone. Therefore the last beatitude or happiness of any intellectual substance is to know God. (St. Thomas)

1. Synopsis of the Thomistic Ethic

The following constitute the highlights of the ethics of St. Thomas: (1) the *self-realization* of one's human and supernatural nature; (2) *happiness,* human and divine, as the *summum bonum;* (3) the supremacy of the intellectual faculty over the will; (4) ultimate happiness as the contemplation of God; (5) mortal and venial sins; (6) seven cardinal Christian *virtues*: temperance, fortitude, wisdom, justice, faith, hope, charity; (7) natural law as God's will; (8) the dual road to truth, viz., revelation and reason.

2. Self-Realizationism

St. Thomas, taking his cue from Aristotle, developed a religious ethic based on the thought of Aristotle whose moral philosophy was particularly well adapted for such an enterprise. Aristotle's philosophy lent itself to modification for religious purposes; what St. Thomas did with it for the Christian world, Averroes accomplished for the Arabian community.

In his work: *Summa contra Gentiles,* he develops most ably the self-realization principle found in the ethical philosophy of Aristotle; the beauty of its logical unfolding is graceful, and each point is treated with meticulous care.

A fundamental premise of self-realizationism is that every object is created with a purpose and it tends to develop accordingly; in the case of a rational being, viz., man who possesses a will, he is expected to exercise this prerogative by *will*, since only man is endowed with a free will. "Every agent, by its action, intends an end. For those things which clearly act for an end we declare the end to be that towards which the movement of the agent tends. . . . This may be seen in the physician who aims at health, and in a man who runs towards an appointed goal."[1] An agent acts either by nature or intellect, since only man is endued with intellect, he alone can be motivated to act intelligently.

(a) *Good, Evil, and the Summum Bonum.* Utimately every person acts in his own best interest, *i.e.*, for the sake of his own good and welfare; he does not seek to do himself any harm or injury. Even one's appetite seeks this end, *e.g.*, an animal seeks its own good when it desires food. "*The good is the object of every appetite.* . . . It is the very notion of good to be the term of appetite, since *good is the object of every appetite.* Therefore all action and movement is for a good."[2] Conversely, evil is incidental, accidental, or unintentional; evil occurs fortuitously and comparatively infrequently. "What is evil absolutely is utterly without intention in the operations of nature, for example, the birth of monstrosities; but which is evil, not absolutely, but relatively, is intended by nature, not directly, but accidentally."[3] Consequently, evil is not essential to the nature of things; evil "is nothing else but *the privation of what is connatural and due to anyone;* for the term *evil* is used in this sense by all. Now privation is not an essence, but is *the non-existence of something in a substance.* Therefore evil is not a real essence."[4] To inquire as to the cause of evil would logically indicate it to be a good; "since evil does not act save by virtue of a good . . . it follows that good itself is the primary cause of evil,"[5] but it is caused only accidentally by a good. Since evil is incapable of an independent existence, it must reside in some good for evil is ultimately a privation or corruption of good, but such does not imply that evil is capable of completely destroying good. Furthermore, "it follows from this that there cannot be a highest evil, that is the principle of all evils. For a highest evil must needs exclude the association of all good, just as the highest good is that which is wholly disconnected from all evil. Now there cannot be an evil entirely apart from good, for it has been proved that all evil resides in some good. Therefore nothing is supremely evil. Again. If anything be supremely evil, it must be essentially evil, even as the supreme good is that which is essentially good. But this is impossible, since evil has no essence. . . . Therefore it is impossible to suppose a supreme evil that is the principle of evils."[6] Moreover, evil cannot be considered a first principle, since a first principle is uncaused, and evil is caused accidentally by good.

It was noted above that things are created with a purpose, a goal, an end for which they were made, and the end of all things is evidently a good since every creature seeks its own good and "every agent acts for some good." The ultimate end, or good towards which all things are directed is God; this follows obviously from the fact that all things tend toward what is good for themselves; since God is the greatest good, then all things tend toward God. "For if nothing tends to something as its end, except in so far as this is good, it follows that good, as such, is an end. Consequently that which is the supreme good is supremely the end of all. Now there is but one supreme good, namely God. . . . Therefore all things are directed to the highest good, namely God, as their end."[7] God, being the highest good, must therefore be the source, *i.e.*, cause of everything in that genus, viz., all other good. Accordingly, God is the cause of goodness, the greatest good, and also the end toward which all things tend; hence the purpose for which all things were made. This being the case, all things would naturally tend to be like God; moreover they were made like him. Each person in his own manner imitates the divine nature, *i.e.*, divine goodness. "For the divine being contains the whole fullness of perfection, as we proved. . . . Therefore, since a thing is good so far as it is perfect, God's being in His perfect goodness; for in God, to be, to live, to be wise, to be happy, and whatever else is seen to pertain to perfection and goodness, are one and the same in God, as though the sum total of His goodness were God's very being."[8]

Every rational being is oriented in such a manner that the supreme object of his knowledge is to know God. "Now, seeing that all creatures, even those that are devoid of reason, are directed to God as their last end, and that all reach this end in so far as they have some share of a likeness to Him, the intellectual creature attains to Him in a special way, namely, through its proper operation, by understanding Him. Consequently this must be the end of the intellectual creature, namely, to understand God."[9] All rational human beings tend towards God as their ultimate end; they are adapted by nature to pursue this end. The attainment of God via the intellect is accomplished through a thorough knowledge and understanding of him. "Further. Everything tends to a divine likeness as its own end. Therefore a thing's last end is that whereby it is most of all like God. . . . God is always actually understanding. . . . Furthermore, in understanding actually, the intellectual creature is especially like God in understanding God; for by understanding Himself God understands all other things. . . . Therefore the last end of every intellectual substance is to understand God."[10] It should now be apparent that the goal of the intellectual life is the supreme end of all human action, viz., to seek what is good and what is true, *i.e., God*. "Therefore the last end of the whole man, and of all his deeds is to know the first truth, namely, God."[11] Man, by nature, desires as his ultimate achievement to know his first cause, viz., God who is the object of all his intellectual desires and pursuits. "Now the last end of man and of any intelligent substance is called *happiness* or *beatitude,* for it is this that every intellectual substance desires as its last end, and for its own sake alone. Therefore the last beautitude or happiness of any intellectual substance is to know God."[12]

(b) *Will vs. Intellect.* A major theological controversy arose regarding the character of God, the central figures of which were the Scholastics, St. Thomas and John Duns Scotus. The central issue concerned the nature of God's personality; the specific question raised was: Does God's intellect precede the will, or does his will have primacy over the intellect? The implications of either position are of major import; if God's will has the ascendency, as John Duns Scotus contended, then whatever God wills is automatically good by virtue of the fact that it is God who is willing it. *e.g.*, if God should will evil, such as the senseless murder of a child, then it would be good or moral for it is God who is willing it. St. Thomas objected to this position, and maintained that God is good because he invariably wills the good; since he determines the good by his intellect, then it follows that his intellect is in the ascendency over the will, *i.e.*, God's will selects only what the intellect understands to be good or moral.

> That the will is a higher power than the intellect, as being the latter's motive power, is clearly untrue. Because the intellect moves the will first and *per se*, for the will, as such, is moved by its object, which is the apprehended good; whereas the will moves the intellect accidentally as it were, in so far, namely, as the act of understanding is itself apprehended as a good, and on that account is desired by the will, with the result that the intellect understands actually. Even in this, the intellect preceded the will, for the will would never desire understanding, did not the intellect first apprehend its understanding as a good. — And again, the will moves the intellect to actual operation in the same way as an agent is said to move; whereas the intellect moves the will in the same way as the end moves, for the good understood is the end of the will. Now the agent in moving presupposes the end,

for the agent does not move except for the sake of the end. It is therefore clear that the intellect is higher than the will absolutely, while the will is higher than the intellect accidentally and in a restricted sense.[13]

The will is a rational appetite, and in the earthly sphere, is exclusively found in man; purely human actions are voluntary. Animals, that is, irrational animals, not man, are said to be incapable of performing voluntary deeds since this requires both a will and knowledge of the end of one's action. All volition proceeds from will which is both autonomous and free from any external force. "It is contrary to the nature of the will's own act that it should be subject to compulsion or violence; just as it is also contrary to the nature of the natural inclination or the movement of a stone to be moved upwards. For a stone may have an upward movement from violence, but that this violent movement be from its natural inclination is impossible. In like manner, a man may be dragged by force, but it is contrary to the very notion of violence that he be thus dragged of his own will."[14] Several things have an influence or bearing on the will: it is moved by the intellect towards the direction of the good, it is moved by the appetite, *i.e.*, a particular feeling which one believes fitting and proper, but the will also moves itself through its own volition in the light of the end, *i.e.*, it moves itself to will the means. Enjoyment is an act of the appetitive power, *i.e.*, will; hence rational creatures alone, not brute animals, can experience enjoyment since this necessitates telic powers. "Therefore, it is clear that things devoid of knowledge . . . have no enjoyment of the end; but this is for those only that are endowed with knowledge."[15] Although non-human objects attain ends, they do so without knowledge, will, or intention, which is itself an act of will, and all three are necessitated in enjoyment. Furthermore, irrational animals are not endowed with choice, whereas man not only chooses, but does so with freedom.

(c) *Happiness*. Genuine happiness does not consist of carnal pleasures, namely the pleasures of the table and sex, which constitute the primary pleasures of the body; the objective of carnal intercourse is to obtain offspring and eating is for the preservation of the body. Pleasures of appetite are sensual, shared with animals, consequently cannot be regarded as happiness since true happiness is a quality peculiar to man alone. Although animals experience pleasure, they cannot be said to enjoy happiness. Man's greatest happiness must be identified with the highest element in his nature, viz., intelligence. "The aforementioned pleasures do not befit man according to what is most noble in him, namely, the intellect, but according to the sense. Therefore happiness is not to be located in such pleasures. Besides. The highest perfection of man cannot consist in his being united to things lower than himself, but consists in being united to something above him; for the end is better than that which tends to the end. . . . Further. That which is not good unless it be moderate is not good in itself, but receives its goodness from its moderator. . . . The last end of everything is God. . . . We must posit as man's last end that by which especially man approaches to God. Now man is hindered by the aforementioned pleasures from his chief approach to God, which is effected by contemplation.''[16] Genuine happiness comes as the reward of virtue, *i.e.*, from a knowledge of or contemplation of God.

There are a number of things which have been confused with happiness: honor, glory, wealth, worldly power, goods of the body, sensuality, acts of virtue, prudence, and art, but none of these qualify. Each for some specific reason fails to meet the necessary qualifications: It is possible for an evil person to be the recipient of high honors, but the highest good is perfect, hence incompatible with any evil. Glory, *i.e.*, fame is subject to the whims and fancies of public opinion and as such is an inconsistent and unreliable criterion. Wealth, at best, is merely an instrumental good. Worldly power is not subject to a man's will, but is the result of chance and good fortune. The goods of the body, *i.e.*, health, beauty, strength are not within a man's will, nor are they stable; furthermore they are shared by good and evil persons alike, *i.e.*, one need not be good to possess them. The supreme good cannot consist of sensual pleasures, *i.e.*, those of the table and sex, for these are held in common with the animal kingdom; true happiness is restricted to the human kingdom, accordingly must be related to the intellect since this is singularly man's. "Since man is man through the possession of reason, his proper good, which is happiness, must needs be in accordance with that which is proper to reason. . . . The last end of all things is to become like God. Therefore that in which man chiefly becomes like God will be his happiness."[17] "Man's ultimate happiness consists in man's most excellent operation,"[18] viz., intelligence. Prudence does not qualify because it is solely concerned with acts of moral virtue, and in turn acts of moral virtue fail since they merely function as a mean in the guidance or moderation of one's passions.[19]

Ultimate happiness consists in contemplating God. Man's supernal nature consists of the intellect whose highest function is the meditation of the supreme being; such activity issues in the greatest measure and quality of happiness. "Man's ultimate happiness consists in wisdom, based on the consideration of divine things."[20]

3. The Seven Cardinal Christian Virtues

The *seven cardinal Christian virtues* find their basis in the ethical thought of St. Thomas; four of them termed cardinal virtues, viz., *temperance, fortitude, prudence, justice* are from Plato, and three which he designates theological virtues, viz., *faith, hope, charity* (love), come from St. Paul. Essentially, human virtues are *good habits,* and an act of virtue is the good use of free choice, hence it is important that virtues be active operative habits for the sake of subsistance or survival. Reference to virtue as being a good habit implies that it is productive of good deeds. The term is adequately defined by Peter Lombard: "*Virtue is a good quality of the mind, by which we live righteously, of which no one can make a bad use, which God works in us without us;*"[21] but St. Thomas feels that the definition can be improved upon by substituting *habit* for the word *quality.*

(a) *The Intellectual Virtues.* Three classes of virtues exist: (1) the intellectual virtues, viz., *wisdom, science, understanding;* (2) the moral virtues, *e.g., temperance, fortitude, magnanimity,* and *meekness* in respect to passions, and *justice* in regard to operations; (3) the theological virtues; *faith, hope, charity* (love).

Intellectual virtues are termed such because they are habits of the speculative intellect which perfect it "for the consideration of truth; for this is its good work."[22] Beyond this point, St. Thomas has very little to say regarding the intellectual virtues.

(b) *The Moral Virtues.* Moral virtue is not a passion because passion is a movement of the sensitive appetite; moral virtue is not the impetus of the appetite, *per se,* but its principle of movement, *i.e.,* its *habitual* manner of behaving. Furthermore, good or evil cannot be predicated of passions *per se,* but only in rational terms, *i.e.,* their orderly behavior in the light of reason. Not all moral virtues pertain to passions, for there is one respecting operations which may be considered perfect because it is free from inordinate affections, viz., justice.

Moral virtues are habits of the soul's appetitive aspect; such are dichotomously divided into *irascible* powers or passions and *concupiscible* powers or passions. "There are different virtues about . . . passions; *e.g.,* temperance, about the concupiscible passions; fortitude, about fear and daring; magnanimity, about hope and despair; meekness, about anger."[23] One fundamental distinction between moral virtue and passion is that "the perfection of virtue depends on the reason, whereas the perfection of passion depends on the sensitive appetite."[24]

(c) *The Cardinal Virtues.* The cardinal or principal virtues are selected from the moral virtues because they are perfect virtues, *i.e.,* they fulfill *every* function of a virtue, viz., the rectitude of appetite, the ability to do well, and fructification in good deeds. Imperfect virtues, *e.g.,* modesty, liberality, etc., merely rectify the appetite, without conferring any ability to excellence nor resulting in good works. The entire foundation of good rests on the four cardinal virtues, which may be classified according to their formal principles or subject matter:

> For the formal principle of the virtue of which we speak now is the good as defined by reason. This good can be considered in two ways. First, as existing in the consideration itself of reason, and thus we have one principal virtue called *prudence*. — Secondly, according as the reason puts its order into something else, and this either into operations, and then we have *justice*, or into passions, and then we need two virtues. For the need of putting the order of reason into the passions is due to their thwarting reason; and this occurs in two ways. First, when the passions incite to something against reason, and then we need a curb, which we thus call *temperance;* secondly, when the passions withdraw us from following the dictate of reason, *e.g.*, through fear of danger or toil, and then man needs to be strengthened for that which reason dictates, lest he turn back, and to this end there is *fortitude*.
>
> In like manner, we find the same number if we consider the subjects of virtue. For there are four subjects of the virtue of which we now speak, viz., the power which is rational in its essence, and this is perfected by *prudence*; and that which is rational by participation, and is threefold, the will, subject of *justice*, the concupiscible power, subject of *temperance*, and the irascible power, subject of *fortitude*.[25]

All virtues are reducible to one of the cardinal four, both in respect to subject matter and to formal principles, but prudence is the absolute principal of all virtue, each of the others is principal in its own genus or class. Other virtues may be principal in some other way, but not in the manner described above.

(d) *The Theological Virtues*. Virtue perfects a man and leads him to happiness, a happiness that is twofold: one that is natural and the other supernal; the former is obtained from obeying principles which govern one's nature, the latter surpasses man's striving and nature for it issues from God. Supernatural happiness is obtained with divine assistance, *i.e.*, by following the will or laws of God., viz., the *theological virtues*. "They are so called, first, because their object is God, inasmuch as they direct us rightly to God; secondly, because they are infused in us by God alone; thirdly, because these virtues are not made known to us, save by divine revelation, contained in the Holy Scripture."[26]

The theological virtues surpass human nature and by participating in them, man becomes partaker of the divine nature. The exercise of these virtues leads one directly to God where they issue in supernal happiness. The theological virtues are distinguished from both the intellectual and moral virtues by having as their objective, God himself, who is the ultimate goal of all, and the fullness of whose knowledge surpasses man's reason. He is directly known by revelation and the joy and happiness which proceed from him are attained by the practice of the theological virtues. By way of contrast, the intellectual and moral virtues are comprehensible to human reason; they serve to direct man to the perfection of his intellect and appetite according to the dictates of human reason and human nature, whereas the theological virtues accomplish the same supernaturally, hence culminate in supernatural happiness. "In relation to both intellect and will, man needed to receive in addition something supernatural to direct him to a supernatural end. First, as regards the intellect, man receives certain supernatural principles, which are held by means of a divine light; and these are the things which are to be believed, about which is *faith*. — Secondly, the will is directed to this end, both as to movement of intention, which tends to that end as something attainable,—this pertains to *hope*—and to a certain spiritual union, whereby the will is, in a way, transformed into that end—and this belongs to *charity*. For the appetite of a thing is naturally moved and tends towards its connatural end and this movement is due to a certain conformity of the thing with its end."[27]

As to precedence or degree of ascendency among the theological virtues, there exists a twofold order: (1) generation, such as matter precedes form or the imperfect precedes the perfect, in which case faith precedes hope, and hope, charity; (2) order of perfection, in which case charity precedes faith and hope, "because both faith and hope are quickened by charity, and receive from charity their full complement as virtues. For thus charity is the mother and the root of all the virtues, inasmuch as it is the form of them all."[28]

All virtues, intellectual and moral, are acquired through faithful practice until they become imbedded habits; this is possible due to natural principles pre-existing in man, but the theological virtues are bestowed on one by God for the purpose of directing man to Himself. All virtues, without exception, direct man to good, but "the good of moral virtue consists in conformity with the rule of reason. Now it is clear that between excess and deficiency the mean is equality or conformity. Therefore it is evident that moral virtue consists in a mean."[29] "As was stated above, the mean of virtue depends on conformity with its rule or measure, in so far as one may exceed or fall short of that rule," but this does not apply to the theological virtues. "For our faith is ruled according to divine truth; charity, according to His goodness; hope, according to the immensity of His omnipotence and loving kindness. This measure surpasses all human power, so that never can we love God as much as He ought to be loved, nor believe and hope in Him as much as we should. Much less, therefore, can there be excess in such things. Accordingly the good of such virtues does not consist in a mean, but increases the more we approach to the summit."[30]

Ultimately, all moral virtues are contingent upon charity, accordingly are interfused. Without charity, other virtues are imperfectible, but perfect charity is possible alone, hence is in the ascendency. Charity signifies a friendship with God as well as the love of him, *i.e.*, a mutual communion with a certain reciprocity of love. As to the moral virtues, justice excels them all; regarding the intellectual virtues, wisdom surpasses the rest for it is architectonic among them all by directing and exercising judgment over them.

e) OUTLINE OF THE THOMISTIC VIRTUES

I. The three classes of virtues:
   1. The intellectual virtues:
      a. Wisdom
      b. Science
      c. Understanding
   2. The moral virtues:
     (i) pertaining to passions, *e.g.*
        a. Temperance
        b. Fortitude
        c. Magnanimity
        d. Meekness
     (ii) pertaining to operations, *e.g.*
        a. Justice
   3. The theological virtues:
      a. Faith
      b. Hope
      c. Charity (Love)

II. The cardinal virtues:
      a. Temperance
      b. Fortitude
      c. Wisdom
      d. Justice

III. The seven cardinal Christian virtues:
      a. Temperance
      b. Courage
      c. Wisdom

d. Justice
e. Faith
f. Hope
g. Love

4. Venial and Mortal Sin

The major distinction between a *venial* and *mortal* sin is the *debt* of punishment; mortal sins cause *irreparable damage,* whereas for venial sins one may make amends or restitution. Sin, by definition, is a sickness of the soul, and is comparable to disease, *e.g.,* one who is mortally ill perishes, his condition is beyond redress; the same holds true in the spiritual realm, for mortal sins there is no indemnity, but restoration is possible for venial sins.

> For sin, being a sickness of the soul ... is said to be mortal by comparison with a disease, which is said to be mortal through causing an irreparable defect consisting in the loss of a principle ... Now the principle of the spiritual life, which is a life in accord with virtue, is the order to the last end. ... And if this order be lost, it cannot be restored by any intrinsic principle, but only by the power of God. ... For disorders in things referred to the end are restored through the end, even as an error about conclusions can be corrected through the truth of the principles. Hence the defect of order to the last end cannot be restored through something else as a higher principle, as neither can an error about principles. Therefore such sins are called mortal, as being irreparable. On the other hand, sins which imply a disorder in things referred to the end, but under the condition that the order to the end itself is preserved, are reparable. These sins are called venial, because a sin receives its acquittal (*veniam*) when the debt of punishment is taken

away, and this ceases when the sin ceases. ... Accordingly, mortal and venial are mutually opposed as reparable and irreparable. ... Therefore, venial sin is fittingly co-divided against mortal sin.[31]

One of the technical implications of sinning venially is to behave wrongfully, not by explicitly breaking a law, but by not observing that which the law intends. Venial sins are pardonable, as is obvious from the term *venia* (pardon); such sins are unencumbered with obstacles which would prevent atoning for them. Venial sins are never worthy of everlasting punishment, but at most temporal. The extent of guilt is a factor in determining cases of venial sins, *e.g.*, sins committed out of weakness or ignorance are invariably venial.

Sins may be venial or mortal in genus or species of an act judged in the light of its objective, *e.g.*, all actions contrary to charity are mortal because they prevent a man from achieving his supreme and ultimate goal, viz., God and his love from which one derives supernal happiness. "Consequently, it is a mortal sin in genus, whether it be contrary to the love of God, *e.g.*, blasphemy, perjury and the like, or against the love of one's neighbor, *e.g.*, murder, adultery, and the like. Sometimes, however, the sinner's will is directed to a thing containing a certain inordinateness, but which is not contrary to the love of God and one's neighbor, *e.g.*, an idle word, excessive laughter, and so forth; and such sins are venial by reason of their genus."[32]

Sins are judged in the light of both the intention and nature of the action committed; an act undeliberated by reason will reduce a sin in genus mortal to one of venial status. The disposition of the agent is significant in determining the goodness or malice of moral action, for in the light of such, a venial sin may be regarded as mortal in character. Although motive may affect the moral quality of an act, circumstances cannot reduce venial sins to the level of mortal since circumstances are merely accidental, not essential. "Yet a circumstance may happen to be taken as the specific difference of a moral act, and then it loses its nature of circumstance, and constitutes the species of the moral act. This happens in sins when a circumstance adds the deformity of another genus. Thus when a man has knowledge of another woman than his wife, the deformity of his act is opposed to chastity; but if this other be another man's wife, there is an additional deformity opposed to justice which forbids one to take what belongs to another. Accordingly, this circumstance constitutes a new species of sin known as adultery."[33]

Although venial sins are immoral, they do not carry the gravity of evil that accompanies mortal sins, nor do they stain the soul, *i.e.*, cause the soul to lose its splendor. "Now venial sin is a hindrance to actual splendor, but not to habitual splendor, because it neither destroys nor diminishes the habit of charity, and of the other virtues . . . but only hinders their acts. On the other hand, a stain denotes something permanent in the things stained, and therefore it seems in the nature of a loss of habitual rather than of actual splendor. Therefore, properly speaking, venial sin does not cause a stain in the soul."[34] Unlike venial sins, the mortal destroy the habit of virtue and alienate one from God by severing the bond of charity, hence divorce him from the highest form of happiness attainable.

5. Further Reading in the Philosophy of St. Thomas

St. Thomas wrote numerous books in the field of philosophy, his most famous being the *Summa Theologica;* second to this is the *Summa contra Gentiles;* among the other important works in philosophy are: a commentary on Peter Lombard's *Sentences;* commentaries on Aristotle's physics, astronomy, ethics, politics, metaphysics, and psychology; *Being and Essence.*

NOTES

ST. THOMAS AQUINAS

1. St. Thomas Aquinas, *The Summa contra Gentiles* from the *Basic Writings of Saint Thomas Aquinas* tr. by Laurence Shapcote, edited and annotated by Anton C. Pegis (New York: Random House, Inc., 1945), Bk. III, Ch. 2. This translation is used throughout.
2. *Ibid.*, Bk. III, Ch. 3.
3. *Ibid.*, Bk. III, Ch. 6.
4. *Ibid.*, Bk. III, Ch. 7.
5. *Ibid.*, Bk. III, Ch. 10.
6. *Ibid.*, Bk. III, Ch. 15.
7. *Ibid.*, Bk. III, Ch. 17.
8. *Ibid.*, Bk. III, Ch. 20.
9. *Ibid.*, Bk. III, Ch. 25.
10. *Idem.*
11. *Idem.*
12. *Idem.*
13. *Ibid.*, Bk. III, Ch. 26.
14. *The Summa Theologica*, Q. 6., Art. 4.
15. *Ibid.*, Q. 11, Art. 2.
16. *The Summa contra Gentiles*, Bk. III, Ch. 27.
17. *Ibid.*, Bk. III, Ch. 34.
18. *Ibid.*, Bk. III, Ch. 35.
19. This must be understood in the light of the Aristotelian ethics.
20. *The Summa contra Gentiles*, Bk. III, Ch. 37.
21. *The Summa Theologica*, Q. 55, Art. 4 Cf. Peter Lombard, *Sentences*, II, XXVII, 5.
22. *Ibid.*, Q. 57, Art. 2.
23. *Ibid.*, Q. 60, Art. 4.
24. *Ibid.*, Q. 60, Art. 5.
25. *Ibid.*, Q. 61, Art. 2.
26. *Ibid.*, Q. 62, Art. 1.
27. *Ibid.*, Q. 62, Art. 3.
28. *Ibid.*, Q. 62, Art. 4.
29. *Ibid.*, Q. 64, Art. 1.
30. *Ibid.*, Q. 64, Art. 4.
31. *Ibid.*, Q. 88, Art. 1.
32. *Ibid.*, Q. 88, Art. 2.
33. *Ibid.*, Q. 88, Art. 5.
34. *Ibid.*, Q. 89, Art. 1.

EVOLUTIONARY NATURALISM

FRIEDRICH NIETZSCHE

The annihilator of morals, the good and the just call me: my story is immoral.

The whole of history is the refutation by experiment of the principle of the so-called "moral world order."

If we have our own why of life, we shall get along with almost any how. Man does not strive for pleasure; only the Englishman does. (Nietzsche)

1. Outline of Nietzsche's Evolutionary Naturalism

The major tenets of Nietzsche's ethical naturalism may be summarized under the following heads: (1) The transvaluation of all values, or the *revaluation of all values;* (2) The genealogy of morals; (3) *Master-morality* vs. *slave-morality;* (4) Critique of the ethics of Christianity; (5) The *overman* or *superman;* (6) The *will for power,* or the ethics of power; (7) *Philosophizing with a hammer* (iconoclasm); (8) The doctrine of *eternal recurrence;* (9) Moral evil as fundamentally *resentment.*

2. The Genealogy of Morals

The genealogy of morals, *i.e.*, Nietzsche's treatment of it, purports to be an expose of the Judeo-Christian moral culture of contemporary western civilization, which he claims is directly attributable to the Christianity of St. Paul who is the key figure responsible for society's perversion of every natural and pure moral impulse. Christian morality which is the dominant morality of the present day is the precise inversion of every wholesome natural instinct in the "human animal."

The problem facing modern man is: "Why is he a stranger to himself?" and "From whence did moral prejudices originate?" The latter question constitutes a problem which has impregnated every book written by Nietzsche, in fact, one of his major works is entitled: *The Genealogy of Morals*.[1]

The epitome of the inversion of the pure morals of nature is exemplified in the Schopenhauerian *ethics of pity*, which is a capitulation to the *decadent* morals of Christianity. Nietzsche addresses his book: *Human, All Too Human* to Schopenhauer, his great teacher, as though he were still alive; Schopenhauer's ethics which constitute essentially the heart of Christian ethics in disguised form, robs an individual of every self-assertive impulse conducive to mental health and wholesome living. Schopenhauer's ethic has supplanted nature's ethic with a desexualized neurotic's ethic which is void of every wholesome instinctual expression. "The point at issue was the value of the non-egotistical instincts, the instincts of compassion, self-denial, and self-sacrifice, which Schopenhauer above all others had constantly guilded, glorified, 'transcendentalized' until he came to see them as *absolute* values allowing him to deny life and even himself."[2] However, this ethic, which is indicative of a decadent society is basically "the danger of dangers."[3]

The time has come to consider the "gay science" of morality even though "the Darwinian brute and the ultramodern moral milksop who no longer bites walk hand in hand, the latter wearing an expression of bonhomie and refined indolence"[4] does not consider the problems of morality worthwhile. Nietzsche admonishes: "Let's get on with the comedy! These antiquated morals are part of it too!"[5] Objection is made to the prejudicial reduction of all moral valuations to the terms *moral, altruistic,* and *disinterested* investing them with the "obsessive force of an *idée fixe*."

1. *The distinction between "good and evil" and "good and bad."* The dichotomous distinction of *good and evil* (*böse*) in moral values can be traced to the slaves of antiquity; the aristocracy or masters (*Herron*) differentiated only between *good and bad* (*schlecht*). *Evil* and *bad* carried different connotations by their respective employers, *e.g.*, masters spoke of bad as signifying cowardice, inferiority, the simple, the untruthful, the resentful, *i.e.*, the "dark, especially blackhaired (*hic niger est*), as the pre-Aryan settler of the Italian soil, notably distinguished from the new blond conqueror race by his color . . . the characteristic term for nobility, eventually the good, noble, pure, originally the fair-haired as opposed to the dark, black-haired native population."[6] Evil is the term employed by the priests of the slave races because of their impotency and hatred of the masters; evil is a "Jewish inversion of values . . . it was the Jews who started the slave revolt in morals. It was the Jew who, with frightening consistency, dared to invert the aristocratic value equations good / noble / powerful / beautiful / happy / favored-of-the-gods and maintain, with the furious hatred of the underprivileged and impotent, that 'only the poor, the powerless, are good; only the suffering, sick and ugly, truly blessed. But you noble and mighty ones of the earth will be, to all eternity, the evil, the cruel, the avaricious, the godless, and thus the cursed and damned!' "[7] Religion is effeminate and its virtues consist of an "old ladies morality."

2. *The ethics of the aristocracy., i.e.,* those who constitute the master race, is one in which the concept of *good* embraces nobility of mind, and bad denotes *common, plebeian, base*, viz., the simple folk. Nietzsche notes: "The most eloquent proof of this is the etymological relationship between the German words *schlecht* (bad) and *schlicht* (simple). For a long time the first term was used interchangeably with the second, without any contemptuous connotation as yet, merely to designate the commoner as opposed to the nobleman."[8] The ushering in of *anarchal democracy* prompted the inversion of ethics of the noble with that of the ignoble, *i.e.*, the weak's technique in subduing the strong. "Who knows whether modern democracy, the even more fashionable anarchism, and

especially that preference for the *commune*, the most primitive of all social forms, which is now shared by all European socialists — whether all these do not represent a throwback, and whether, even physiologically, the Aryan race of conquerors is not doomed?'"[9] Democratic ethics presupposes a society composed of weak, sickly, feeble individuals seeking power for themselves that naturally belongs to the chivalrous and aristocratic whose valuations presuppose physical strength, exuberant health, and the safeguards of its preservation, viz., combat, adventure, war games, etc. Present culture is an indication of the triumph of the masses, viz., the slaves, the mob, the herd, *i.e.*, the successful culmination of a slave revolt in morals. Slave-morality is a denial of all that is normal or natural; it is the inhibition of human instincts issuing in misery or "what is called happiness among the impotent and oppressed, who are full of bottled-up aggressions. Their happiness is purely passive and takes the form of drugged tranquility, stretching and yawning, peace, 'sabbath,' emotional slackness . . . the rancorous person is neither truthful nor ingenious nor honest and forthright with himself. His soul squints; his mind loves hideouts, secret paths, and back doors . . . he is an expert . . . in self-depreciation, and self-humiliation. A race of such men will, in the end, inevitably be cleverer than a race of aristocrats.'"[10]

In contrast to the slave ethic is the true or noble morality which emanates from triumphant self-affirmation; it is the valuation of the aristocrat, the Hyperborean with a "positive, intense and passionate credo, 'We noble, good, beautiful, happy ones,' . . . [*e.g.*,] Mirabeau, who lacked all memory for insults and meannesses done him, and who was unable to forgive because he had forgotten. Such a man simply shakes off vermin which would get beneath another's skin — and only here, if anywhere on earth, is it possible to speak of 'loving one's enemy.' The noble person will respect his enemy, and respect is already a bridge to love. . . . Imagine, on the other hand, the 'enemy' as conceived by the rancorous man! For this is his true creative achievement: he has conceived the 'evil enemy,' the Evil One, as a fundamental idea, and then as a pendant he had conceived a Good One — himself.'"[11]

The slave ethic is the product of the poisonous eye of resentment; it constitutes a reversion to the innocence of wild animals who are capable of returning from orgies of murder, arson, rape, and torture with the inner jubilance and peace of one who had committed a fraternity prank. These pseudo-moralists, who brand good enemies evil, "amongst themselves, are so strictly constrained by custom, worship, ritual, gratitude, and by mutual surveillance and jealousy, who are resourceful in consideration, tenderness, loyalty, pride and friendship, when once they step outside their circle become little better than uncaged beasts of prey. Once abroad in the wilderness, they revel in the freedom from social constraint and compensate for their long confinement in the quietude of their own community."[12] Such behavior is the upshot of a slave ethic, which is the product of a people who have been crushed, despoiled, brutalized, and sold into slavery; accordingly, culture for these persons signifies the domestication of man's savage instincts; their behavior represents a flagrant human retrogression resulting in Europe's predicament, viz., with the fear of man, perishes also "the love of man, reverence for man, confidence in man, indeed the *will to man*. . . . I, especially, find intolerable; that I am unable to cope with; that asphyxiates me . . . a bad smell. The smell of failure, of a soul that has gone stale."[13]

Ethical codes emerging from conditions of slavery transmute weakness into merit, *e.g.*, "the inoffensivenes of the weak, his cowardice, his ineluctable standing and waiting at doors, are being given honorific titles such as patience," or "impotence, which cannot retaliate, into kindness, pusillanimity into humility; submission before those one hates into obedience."[14] Slaves fancy that they will be rewarded for such behavior, not in gold, but in happiness, as though such behavior can be termed bliss. Nietzsche replies: "But I've had all that I can stand. The smell is too much for me. This shop where they manufacture ideals seems to me to stink of lies' . . . these black magicians, who precipitate the white milk of loving-kindness out of every kind of blackness. . . . 'And what do they call that which comforts them in all their sufferings — their phantasmagoria of future bliss?' 'Do

I hear correctly? They call it Judgment Day, the coming of *their* kingdom, the 'Kingdom of God.' Meanwhile they live in 'faith,' in 'love,' in 'hope.' 'Stop! I've heard enough.'"[15] Such morals thrive where man has grown tame, *e.g.*, the Jews "were the priestly, rancorous nation *par excellence*," while the Romans, whose every vestige is a sheer delight, were the strongest and most noble of all.

Man, that being bred with the right to make promises, has been victimized by the weak, the religious, the priests, who seek to gain power over him by creating an unnatural phenomenon, viz., consciousness of guilt, *i.e.*, a bad conscience, which requires of a person who pursues successfully his natural right, retribution, punishment, *i.e.*, *compensation*. One indication of this is that the word *Schuld* (guilt) originates from the term *Schulden* (to be indebted). Guilt is a concept created by the weak to keep the strong from a life that affirms itself, *i.e.*, a life that satisfies its natural instincts. "To speak of right and wrong *per se* makes no sense at all. No act of violence, rape, exploitation, is intrinsically 'unjust,' since life itself is violent, rapacious, exploitative, and destructive and cannot be conceived otherwise. . . . Legal conditions . . . limit the radical life-will bent on power and must finally subserve, as means, life's collective purpose, which is to create greater power constellations. To accept any legal system . . . is an anti-vital principle which can only bring about man's utter demoralization and, indirectly, a reign of nothingness.'"[16] Christian morality, which is responsible for contemporary culture and legal conditions, is nothing but a will to deny life; its assertion that nothing counts but moral values is a most dangerous and sinister form of the will to destruction; it is a sign of "profound sickness, moroseness, exhaustion, biological etiolation.'"[17] which smothers one under a load of contempt and constant negation; consequently, it is worthless in itself, and unworthy of desire.

3. "Master-Morality" *vs.* "Slave-Morality"

One of Nietzsche's books is entitled: *Beyond Good and Evil;* by *good and evil*, he specifically does not mean *good and bad.*[18] Bad connotes weakness, inferiority, etc., whereas evil denotes a conscience striken sense of immorality. Nietzsche rejects the latter as the creation of weak and destitute slaves as a means of gaining power over their masters; masters speak of the *bad*, not of evil. Nietzsche's contention is that the moral distinction of good and evil disappears in a superior society where the strong live according to nature in all its purity; such will be the case in the society and culture of the superman who does not recognize evil as a reality, hence lives beyond good and evil. The *master race* is free of such distinctions, whereas the culture which stems from those whose moral code was cultivated in slavery speak of evil and use it as a means of exerting a will to power.

From a master race, an aristocratic society can be developed wherein each person gains a *self-mastery,* and whose power is primarily psychic rather than physical. The aristocrat, who is the product of a master race, cultivates a *master-morality, i.e.,* an ethical code orientated from the point of view of the victor who possesses the power to do what he chooses; such an "one has duties only toward one's equals; toward beings of a lower rank, toward everything foreign to one, one may act as one sees fit, 'as one's heart dictates' — in any event, 'beyond good and evil.' "[19] Toward one's equals, the master-morality would obligate one to gratitude and vengefulness, as a requital and retaliation; actually, he has a need of enemies as an outlet for his passions of envy, quarrelsomeness and wantonness. The aristocrat morality regards the coward, timid man, as despicable; "likewise the suspicious man with his cowed look, the one who humiliates himself, the dog-type who lets himself be mistreated, the begging flatterer, and above all the liar: it is the basic faith of all aristocrats that the common people are liars. 'We truthful ones' the noble called themselves."[20] The aristocrat creates his own values; moreover, they are not subject to another's ratification; he judges that what is harmful to himself, is harmful *per se*; consequently, his morality is self-glorification. Those born of a master-morality maintain power over themselves and take delight in being "rigorous and hard with themselves" and respect those who are rigorous and hard. Such an individual is free from compassion and pity, either for himself or others; his distinction and courageousness frees him from the need of helping others. The weak need to help others so that they too will be helped. "Belief in oneself, pride in oneself, basic hostility and irony against 'selflessness' is as sure a part of distinguished morality as an easy disdain and cautious attitude toward the fellow-feelings and the 'warm heart'."[21] The aristocrat is *beyond* good and evil; for him there are *no moral facts*; "morality is mere sign language, mere symptomatology. ... My demand upon the philosopher is known, that he take his stand *beyond* good and evil and leave the illusion of moral judgment *beneath* himself. This demand follows from an insight which I was the first to formulate: that *there are altogether no moral facts.*"[22] Occasionally, the aristocrat is hunted, cornered, and tamed like the beast by the priest under the guise of improvement, *e.g.*, "in the early Middle Ages, when the church was indeed, above all, a menagerie, the most beautiful specimens of the 'blond beast' were hunted down everywhere; and ... 'improved.' But how did such an 'improved' Teuton who had been seduced into a monastery look afterward? Like a caricature of man, like a miscarriage: he had become a 'sinner,' he was stuck in a cage. ... And there he lay, sick, miserable, malevolent against himself: full of hatred against the springs of life, full of suspicion against all that was still strong and happy. In short, a 'Christian.' "[23] The slave's technique in making the strong weak, in order that he may be subdued, is to make him sick, resulting in his ruin.

Slave-morality is essentially one of utility, it has created the concept of evil to further its feeble ends; consequently, the slave looks unfavorably upon the moral values of the powerful, and condemns them as evil, *e.g.*, a slave-morality would designate the *evil* man as inspiring fear, but a master-morality would state the *good* man does and wants to engender fear.

The ethics of Christianity and democracy with its emphasis on equality is a pseudo-morality which neglects to consider differences existing among men. "The demand of one morality for all means an encroachment upon precisely a superior type of man. There is, in short, an order of rank between men and hence also between moralities."[24] Equality is a revaluation of naturalistic ethics; it is **an inversion of** the hierarchal differences present in nature. "The *inequality* of rights is the first condition for the existence of any rights at all."[25] Rights are privileges and must be earned. Equal rights is a myth emanating from socialist rabble, chandala apostles, anarchists, democrats, Christians, etc.; "the source of wrong is never unequal rights but the claim of 'equal' rights."[26]

It would constitute a blunder to represent a Cesare Borgia type as indicative of the superman as some of Nietzsche's contemporaries have done, but "on the other hand, let us not doubt that we moderns, with our thickly padded humanity, which at all costs wants to avoid bumping into a stone, would have provided Cesare Borgia's contemporaries with a comedy at which they could have laughed themselves to death. Indeed, we are unwittingly funny beyond all measure with modern 'virtues.' "[27] A slave ethic issues from a subjugated people who are physically and mentally sick to the point of weakness and destitution, "hence everyone is to a certain extent sick, and everyone is a nurse for the sick. And that is called 'virtue.' Among men who knew differently — fuller, more squandering, more overflowing — it would have been called by another name: 'cowardice' perhaps, 'wretchedness,' 'old ladies' morality.' "[28] The freeman is a warrior who is not in need of democratic principles since he is superior to the *hoi polloi*. In a society dominated by a slave-morality, the virtuous of a master-morality are ostracized by society; "it is society, our tame, mediocre, emasculated society, in which a natural human being, who comes from the mountains or from the adventures of the sea necessarily degenerates into a criminal."[29] unless, like Napoleon, he is able to prove stronger than society and transform it.

4. Critique of the Ethics of Christianity

Accuracy in reporting the ethics of Nietzsche is extremely difficult because of the many apparent discrepancies that appear self-contradictory; this is especially true in his treatment of Jesus and the Christian ethic. The conflict is partially resolved in the Nietzschean system by severing Jesus from Christianity; in praise of Jesus he writes: "The very word 'Christianity' is a misunderstanding; in truth, there was only *one* Christian, and he died on the cross. The 'evangel' *died* on the cross. What has been called 'evangel' from that moment was actually the opposite of that which *he* had lived: *'ill* tidings,' a dysangel."[30] In fact, Nietzsche's superman may be thought of as one possessing the characteristics of Jesus, Caesar, and possibly Socrates; but as for Christianity, which he attributes to St. Paul, he repudiates vehemently: "I condemn Christianity. . . . The Christian church has left nothing untouched by its corruption; it has turned every value into an un-value, every truth into a lie, every integrity into a vileness of the soul."[31]

The Christian goal, *i.e.*, ethic, is not achieved through faith, but only through practicing "a life such as he *lived* who died on the cross."[32] The life and ethics of Jesus is not only a possibility today, but a necessity; genuine or original Christianity is always possible. Faith is "only a cloak, a pretext, a screen behind which the instincts played their game. . . it is the characteristic Christian *shrewdness* — one always *spoke* of faith, but always *acted* from instinct alone."[33] Jesus stands in marked contrast to the Christian:

> This "bringer of glad tidings" died as he had lived, as he had taught — *not* to "redeem men" but to show how one must live. This practice is his legacy to mankind: his behavior before the judges, before the catchpoles, before the accusers and all kinds of slander and scorn — his behavior on the *cross*. He does not resist, he does not defend his right, he takes no step which might ward off the worst; on the contrary, he *provokes* it. And he begs, he suffers, he loves *with* those, *in* those, who do him evil. *Not* to resist, *not* to be angry, *not* to hold responsible — but to resist not even the evil one — to *love* him.[34]

Christianity does not consist in credos or faith, at least not a genuine or true Christianity; "To reduce being a Christian, Christianism, to a matter of considering something true, to a mere phenomenon of consciousness, is to negate Christianism. *In fact, there have been no Christians at all.*"[35]

Modern Christianity, which is not the Christianity of Jesus, but of St. Paul, is a slave-morality characterized by *resentment*; it has created "the values in which mankind now sums up its supreme desiderata are decadence-values."[36] Christianity is essentially an *ethics of pity*; pity has depressing effects and stands as the direct antithesis to the "tonic emotions" which give zest and vitality to life. Judeo-Christian morality opposes the life-giving morals by denaturing all natural values, *e.g.*, the Christian "notion of the *immaculata conceptio* christianizes, that is, *dirties,* the origin of man;"[37] it has reduced the values of sex to a state of degeneracy. The superior view declared in the law of Manu concerning women is both tender and gracious, *e.g.*, "the 'mouth of a woman' — 'the bosom of a girl . . . are always pure.' Another passage: 'There is nothing purer than the . . . breath of a girl. . . . Only in the girl is the whole body pure.'"[38] Christianity has injured life-affirmation values by "poisoning, slander, negation of life, contempt for the body, the degradation and self-violation of man through the concept of sin."[39]

The Judeo-Christian ethic, which is diametrically antonymous to "noble-morality," found its chief expositor in St. Paul who constructed his slave-morality on a foundation of resentment which repudiated beauty and self-affirmation by reducing good to evil, true to false, consequently making mankind *sick*. It has made the valuable, valueless or "*antivaluable*" by the "parasitism" of the priest who "devalues, *desecrates* nature." The concept of sin is indispensable to organized religion: "The priest *lives* on sins, it is essential for him that people 'sin.' Supreme principle: 'God forgives those who repent'— in plain language: those who submit to the priest."[40] Jesus, himself, rebelled against such tactics of the priests; his was a "rebellion against 'the good and the just,' against 'the saints of Israel,' against the hierarchy of society — *not* against its corruption, but against caste, privilege, order and formula; it was *disbelief* in the 'higher man,' the No to all that was priest or theologian. . . . This brought him to the cross. He died for *his* guilt. All evidence is lacking, however often it has been claimed, that he died for the guilt of others."[41] Jesus was a *free spirit*, exemplary of the superman of the master-morality; his doctrine of the kindgdom of heaven is a state of the heart realizable here and now. St. Paul is the contradictory of the "evangel" of Jesus, a "dysangelist" who "sacrificed to hatred" and *"invented his own history of earliest Christianity* . . . in the *lie* of the 'resurrected' Jesus. At bottom, he had no use at all for the life of the Redeemer — he needed the death on the cross[42] . . . the impertinent doctrine of personal immortality . . . Paul . . . taught it as a reward."[43] Theology is a weapon the slaves, *i.e.*, subject persons use to subdue the strong, *i.e.*, masters and superior persons. Christianity "attains its ultimate mastery as the art of lying in a holy manner. The Christian, this *ultima ratio* of the lie, is the Jew once more — even three times more. . . . One must not be led astray: 'judge not,' they say, but they consign to hell everything that stands in their way. By letting God judge, they themselves judge . . . by demanding virtues of which they happen to be capable — even more, which they require in order to stay on top."[44]

A *revaluation of all values* (*Umwerthung aller Werthe*) is essentially a repudiation of the Christian ethic which has dominated Western civilization for almost two thousand years; the task ahead is to transform this *ethics of pity* and *resentment* which had denied life instincts into one of self-affirmation of a master morality. "I call Christianity the one great curse, the one great innermost corruption, the one great instinct of revenge, for which no means is poisonous, stealthy, subterranean, *small* enough — I call it the one immortal blemish of mankind. And time is reckoned from the *dies nefastus* with which this calamity began — after the *first* day of Christianity! *Why not after its last day? After today?* Revaluation of all values!"[45]

Nietzsche refers to Christianity as the "most corrupt kind of corruption" and continues his haranguing with a prolonged diatribe:

> This stealthy vermin which sneaked up to every single one in the night, in fog and ambiguity, and sucked out of each single one the seriousness for *true* things and any instinct for *realities* — this cowardly, effeminate, and saccharine pack alienated "souls" step by step from that tremendous structure — those valuable, those virile, noble natures who found their own cause, their own seriousness, their own pride in the cause of Rome. The sneakiness of prigs, the conventicle secrecy, gloomy concepts like hell, like sacrifices of the guiltless, like unto *mystica* in drinking blood; above all, the slowly fanned fire of revenge, of chandala revenge . . . the same kind of religion against which, in its pre-existent form, Epicurus already had waged war.[46]

The fundamental defect of Christianity is that it proclaims a philosophy of denial which negates man's instincts, viz., *sex, the lust to rule,* and *selfishness*: three values that "have so far been best cursed and worst reputed and lied about."[47] "Man has felt too little joy: that alone, my brothers, is our original sin."[48]

5. The Superman

The Nietzschean *superman* or *overman* (*Uebermensch*) stands in majestic contrast to the obsequious member of the *hoi polloi*. "What is the ape to man? A laughing-stock or a painful embarrassment. And man shall be just that for the overman."[49] The superman is a spiritual giant who will usher in the moral transvaluation. Citing the fact that Jesus' *kingdom of heaven* is not that which is to appear after death or a state above the earth, but a state of the heart;[50] The same holds true for the superman, *i.e.*, the courageous man within who seeks expression. Zarathustra speaks: "*I teach you the overman.* Man is something that shall be overcome. What have you done to overcome him. All beings so far have created something beyond themselves; and do you want to be the ebb of this great flood and even go back to the beasts rather than overcome man?"[51]

The average man is a link between the ape and superman; he is a "rope, tied between beast and overman — a rope over an abyss. . . . What is great in man is that he is a bridge and not an end: what can be loved in man is that he is an *overture* and a *going under.*"[52] The superman is the prototype of life affirmation; he is a soul who *squanders itself* and *makes his virtue his addiction;* for the sake of virtue he wants to live on and to live no longer than virtue's reign, since he loves virtue dearly.

The antithesis of the superman is found in the individual who despises life by decaying and poisoning himself spiritually; his soul looks contemptuously upon the body and seeks to render the body meager, ghastly, and starved; such a soul is impoverished, polluted with a stream of filth and wretched contentment. This person's soul is ridden with revenge; he is like the tarantula, Wherever he bites, black scabs grow; his poison makes the soul *whirl with revenge;* his spirit is laden with aggrieved conceit, repressed envy and revenge; "mistrust all in whom the impulse to punish is powerful. . . . Mistrust all who talk much of their justice! Verily, their souls lack more than honey . . . do not forget that they would be pharisees, if only they had — power."[53] These persons are of a low sort and stock, "inverse cripples I call them" with a spirit of ill will and revenge, whose lives are hypocritical lies that create "good" consciences to justify their actions. These are small people who need small virtues; they are *modest in virtue,* since only a *modest virtue* makes contentment possible. The small man lives by the letter of the law, adhering to an insipid "cut and dried" morality, whereas superman is a "law unto himself" who lives by love; "what is done out of love always occurs beyond good and evil.[54] Jesus said to his Jews: 'The law was for servants; love God as I love him, as his son. What are morals to us sons of God?' "[55] Good and evil are man's creations: "There are no moral phenomena, only a moral interpretation of phenomena.''[56]

The superman is despicable because he does not despise himself; he is creative, *inventing happiness*, is productive of love and warmth. He is a free spirit and a free heart whose soul is so overfull that he forgets self; such an one justifies the future and redeems the past. The superman gives meaning to one's existence; he is " the lightening out of the dark cloud of man," but to men he is the "mean between a fool and a corpse."[57] The superman is an *annihilator of morals* in the eyes of the ordinary member of the common herd; he does not requite evil with good for this creates shame in his enemy, rather he proves that his enemy provided him with some good; "and if you have been done a great wrong, then quickly add five little ones: a gruesome sight is a person single-mindedly obsessed by a wrong."[58] The love of the superior person finds uncommon modes of expression, *e.g.*, "if a friend does you evil, then say: 'I forgive you what you did to me; but you have done it to *yourself* — how could I forgive that?' Thus speaks all great love: it overcomes even forgiveness and pity."[59] Pity is a folly for it is the greatest cause of suffering. "God too has his hell: that is his love of man. . . . God is dead; God died of his pity for man.''[60] Great love transcends pity. Actually, there never has been a superman for the greatest and the smallest man are still *all-too-similar* to each other; furthermore, the greatest is *all-too-human*.

The superman cherishes virtue; as a mother does not wish to be repaid for her love for her child, superman does not seek to be paid for his virtue, his dearest of all possessions. The vengeful designate virtue, *vices grown lazy;* "thus they call their evil eye virtue," but virtue to them requires a police force to maintain. The rabble seek to master others, but the superman pursues self-mastery, "I am *that which must always* overcome itself.''[61] The highest type of freemen are found where the highest resistance is constantly overcome; danger is useful in acquainting one with his own resources, virtues, spirit, and forces one to be strong. Julius Caesar most beautifully exemplifies this type; such a *free spirit* "spits on the contemptible type of well-being dreamed of by shopkeepers, Christians, cows, females, Englishmen, and other democrats. The free man is a warrior.'"[62]

Jesus, too, is a *free spirit*: He resists any kind of dogma, formula, law, word, etc., because the word or dogma strangles and kills; only the innermost being is life, truth, light. Christianity betrayed Jesus by reversing all for which he stood: he does not negate life or the world; in him, dialectic is lacking, "his proofs are inner 'lights,' inner feelings of pleasure and self-affirmations, all of them 'proofs of strength.' "[63] The doctrines of Jesus are incapable of contradiction for they do not permit antithetical judgments. In the psychology of Jesus, guilt, punishment, reward are absent; the significance of the *gospel* is precisely the abolition of any distance that separates God and man; the blessed state is not reserved for the future it is a present existent reality. The sequel of such a state results in a genuine evangelical practice:

> He no longer required any formulas, any rites for his intercourse with God — not even prayer. He broke with the whole Jewish doctrine of repentance and reconciliation; he knows that it is only in the *practice* of life that one feels "divine," "blessed," "evangelical," at all times a "child of God." Not "repentance," not "prayer for forgiveness," are the ways to God: *only the evangelical practice* leads to God, indeed, it *is* "God!" What was disposed of with the evangel was the Judaism of the concepts of "sin," "forgiveness of sin," "faith," "redemption through faith"— the whole Jewish *ecclesiastical* doctrine was negated in the "glad tidings."
>
> The deep instinct for how one must *live*, in order to feel oneself "in heaven," to feel "eternal," while in all other behavior one decidedly does *not* feel oneself "in heaven"— this alone is the psychological reality of "redemption." A new way of life, *not* a new faith.[64]

Although the Nietzschean superman may be visualized as a

cross between a Caesar and a Jesus, in the final analysis superman has never appeared on the human scene: "Never yet has there been an overman. Naked I saw both the greatest and the smallest man: they are still all-too-similar to each other. Verily, even the greatest I found all-too-human. Thus spoke Zarathustra."[65]

6. The Will for Power

Power is the *criterion* of moral value:
What is good? Everything that heightens the feeling of power in man, the will to power, power itself.
What is bad? Everything that is born of weakness.
What is happiness? The feeling that power is growing, that resistance is overcome.
Not contentedness but more power; not peace, but war; not virtue but fitness (Renaissance virtue, *virtu*, virtue that is moraline-free).
The weak and the failures shall perish: first principle of *our* love of man. . . .
What is more harmful than any vice? Active pity for all the failures and all the weak: Christianity.[66]

The preceding epitomizes to a fair degree the ethical position of Nietzsche. Essentially this is a naturalistic ethic, characterized by an ethics of power; the enhancement of power is by virtue of that fact deemed good, its distraction is adjudged evil. Inasmuch as pity is the greatest deterrent to power, it is pronounced a major vice; it appears that Nietzsche has succumbed to a bias regarding this pronouncement, not only for the reason that Christianity emphasizes compassion, but particularly because of the cardinal position it occupies in the ethical theory of Schopenhauer, a philosopher Nietzsche once held in high veneration, but long since has repudiated with uncontrollable disdain. Nietzsche contends that Christianity has always sided with all that is weak and base; *base* signifying that which is baneful to the undermining of power. This conclusion is inferred from the basic premise that whatever inhibits instinct is *ipso facto* evil; "Christianity has sided with all that is weak and base, with all failures; it has made an ideal of whatever *contradicts* the instinct of the strong life to preserve itself; it has corrupted the reason even of those strongest in spirit by teaching men to consider the supreme values of the spirit as something sinful, as something that leads into error — as temptations.''[67]

Life affirmation, power, instinct are common terms that flow freely in the writings of Nietzsche, in many instances they may be used interchangeably; power is basic to life, it stagnates or degenerates without it. The frustration of instincts results in the corruption of the personality; the adopted values of contemporary society inhibit instinctual urges, run counter to any progressive will for power, and are symptomatic of decadence and regression. "Life itself is to my mind the instinct for growth, for durability, for an accumulation of forces, for *power*: where the will to power is lacking there is decline. It is my contention that all the supreme values of mankind *lack* this will.''[68] Societies that impede the free expression of the will for power are retrogressive, often they build up a tremendous degree of inward tension that eventually is discharged in terrible and ruthless hostility to individuals within the society and to the world without. All lasting and progressive institutions must be based on instinct or the will for power; "never, absolutely never, can an institution be founded on an idiosyncrasy; one cannot, as I have said, found marriage on 'love' — it can be founded on the sex drive, on the property drive (wife and child as property), on the drive to dominate, which continually organizes for itself the smallest structure of domination, the family, and which needs children and heirs to hold fast . . . to an attained measure of power.''[69]

Existing societies and those of the past may be categorized into two fundamental types: *Dionysian* and *Apollonian*, each is mutually antithetical; the former is characterized by the voluntarism of the Schopenhauerian *will* and the latter by the intellectualism of the Hegelian concept of *idea*. Both forms are Hellenic; that of Apollo has, as its prototype, Socrates, the great exemplar of *theoretical man*, whose strength and power lay in intellectual pursuits. Socrates believed that thought "guided by the thread of causation, might plumb the farthest abysses of being and even *correct* it . . . Socrates . . . was able not only to live under the guidance of that instinctive scientific certainty but to die by it. . . . For this reason the image of the dying Socrates — mortal man freed by knowledge and argument from the fear of death — is the emblem which, hanging above the portal of every science, reminds the adept that his mission is to make existence appear intelligible and thereby justified."[70] Socrates is representative of the archetype of the *theoretical man,* strong in the optimistic belief that nature is fathomable and knowledge is a genuine panacea of human ill and evil. The conquest of life is a gnostic endeavor distinguished by an insatiable zest for knowledge among those predisposed towards Apollo's *Weltanschauung,* whereas the Dionysian seeks instinctive expression in the *will to life.* An orgiastic psychology dominated by a zest for life and strength typifies the ethical philosophy of the Dionysians with its will to live even amidst life's strangest and hardest problems, rejoicing in its inexhaustibility for making sacrifices of the highest type to the demands of life.

> For the Greeks the *sexual* symbol was therefore the venerable symbol par excellence, the real profundity in the whole of ancient piety. Every single element in the act of procreation, of pregnancy, and of birth aroused the highest and most solemn feelings. . . . *Pain* is pronounced holy: the pangs of woman giving birth hallow all pain; all becoming and growing — all that guarantees a future — involves pain. That there may be eternal joy of creating, that the will to life may eternally affirm itself, the agony of the woman giving birth *must* also be there eternally.
>
> All this is meant by the word Dionysus. . . . Here the most profound instinct of life, that directed toward the future of life, the eternity of life, is experienced religiously. . . .

And herewith I again touch that point from which I once went forth: *The Birth of Tragedy* was my first revaluation of all values. Herewith I again stand on the soil out of which my intention, my *ability* grows — I, the last disciple of the philosopher Dionysus — I, the teacher of eternal recurrence.[71]

7. Evaluation of Nietzschean Value Theory

The late Prof. Edgar S. Brightman remarked that Charles Darwin hurt religion chiefly because of his indifference to it; had he promoted religion, he would have enhanced it, had he attacked it, he would have rejuvenated it. Nietzsche can hardly be accused of this; for on a social and ethical plane, he has been Christianity's severest critic, not to mention Judaism's and Democracy's. It is desirable to have a critic play the devil's disciple to keep one mentally alert and one's philosophy tested by the severest blows possible, hence preventing one's succumbing to lethargy and resting content with a worthless and indefensible position. Nietzsche has rendered this service par excellence; if he has done nothing else, he has certainly awakened Judeo-Christian philosophers from their dogmatic slumbers. Some philosophers summarize Nietzsche's importance solely on the basis of the service he has rendered by way of caustic criticisms lodged against contemporary morality and culture.

Nietzsche probably fancied himself an iconoclast, this is indicated by the title and contents of his work: *Twilight of the Idols* with the subtitle: *How One Philosophizes With a Hammer.* The suggestion is that there are idols that must be smashed or at least hit with a hammer, plus the hint that the idols are in the twilight of their existence; the use of the concept idols was probably inspired by Bacon together with the employment of the aphoristic technique. One is justified in suspecting that Nietzsche derived a measure of pleasure in playing the part of the devil's disciple and iconoclast, which was partially responsible for his continued bellicosity.

A psychologist would find an intriguing subject in Nietzsche, for the man's life and personality presented a forthright antithesis to his writings. Alfred Adler would pronounce this psychological phenomenon a clear case of *overcompensation*, viz., Nietzsche's philosophy is the outward manifetation of the inward weakness he sought to erase from his personality. He propounded a Renaissance virtue that was moraline-free, yet his personal habits were meticulous and morally demanding for he neither smoked nor drank — even coffee.

He proudly states his elevated standards: "First: I attack only causes which are victorious.... Second: I attack only causes against which I cannot expect to find allies.... Third: I never attack persons.... Fourth: I attack only causes in which any personal difference is out of the question ... to attack is with me a proof of good will, and sometimes of gratitude."[72] Alas, these lofty principles were not adhered to, for the older he became, and the closer he drew to insanity, the more numerous were the violations and the greater the breach of principle. Socrates, Jesus, Wagner, Schopenhauer, and others to whom he was indebted and had earlier paid homage, he later degenerated to the abuse of attacking with *ad hominem* arguments characterized with expressions of contempt: In 1895 he wrote an entire book attacking Wagner, entitled: *Nietzsche Contra Wagner* in which he portrays him as a "decaying and despairing decadent;" in *The Antichrist*, he refers to Jesus as *idiot*;[73] by way of contrast, he assesses himself in the book *Ecco Homo*, a treatise consisting of four chapters entitled respectively: "Why I Am So Wise," "Why I Am So Clever," "Why I Write Such Good Books," and "Why I Am A Destiny."

Nietzsche's greatest shibboleth lay in his obsession and extravagant enjoyment of hyperbole, viz., abstracting extreme minutiae from persons and philosophical sources, over-simplifying them, and building an enormous and unwarranted system on such meager foundations. *E.g.*, he believes in instincts and maintains their essential goodness, but he isolates egoistic instincts and denies the reality of social urges; one may have the will for power and sex, but an individual also has the need for friendship, the need to be wanted and loved. Durant aptly expresses it: "The essential function of Christianity has been to moderate, by the inculcation of an extreme ideal of gentleness, the natural barbarity of men; and any thinker who fears that men have been corrupted out of egoism into an excess of Christian virtue needs only to look about him to be comforted and reassured."[74]

Among the characteristic features of the slave-morality, Nietzsche lists equality and contemns it: "You preachers of equality, the tyrannomania of impotence clamors thus out of you for equality: your most secret ambitions to be tyrants thus shroud themselves in words of virtue. Aggrieved conceit, repressed envy ... erupt from you as a flame and as the frenzy of revenge."[75] The equality of rights has been championed by the free as well as by the enslaved; Hobbes noted that men in numbers are equal; contemporary sociologists claim that any group, regardless of their level of civilization or savagery can be elevated to the advanced state and power of any other nation when properly cultivated, furthermore once enjoying the values of a superior culture, they desist from returning to the antiquated and obsolete culture.

The thought of carrying out the Nietzschean philosophy on a grand scale would cause any thoughtful person to shudder with deep concern. Hitler attempted it, when fancying himself to be the superman, he indoctrinated the Third Reich with this philosophy which resulted in a collective nightmare that humanity would prefer to believe never blotted its records — a thought reminiscent of an aphorism of Nietzsche: " 'I did this,' says my memory. 'I cannot have done this,' says my pride, remaining inexorable. Eventually, my memory yields."[76] There is no justification for confusing courage and bravery with cruelty and sadism, nor is there any in mistaking pity, sympathy, and compassion with weakness or cowardice; to so do would indicate irrationality or a perverted personality — in fact, only the truly strong can afford to be sympathetic.

Mencken summarizes the strictures of Nietzsche's critics as follows:

(a) He was a decadent and a lunatic, and in consequence his philosophy is not worthy of attention.[77]
(b) His writings are chaotic and contradictory and it is impossible to find in them any connected philosophical system.
(c) His argument that self-sacrifice costs more than it yields, and that it thus reduces the average fitness of a race practising it, is contradicted by human experience.
(d) The scheme of things proposed by him is opposed by ideas inherent in all civilized men.
(e) Even admitting that his criticism of Christian morality is well-founded, he offers nothing in place of it that would work as well.[78]

Nietzsche's ethics is essentially a naturalistic *ethics of power* which promotes the naturalistic *law of the jungle*, namely the *law of tooth and claw* which may prove satisfactory for non-moral animals, but for rational human beings capable of exercising moral agency ought to prove repugnant. There is no evidence that indicates the strong are in the right nor any warrant for justifying abusive actions, such as cruelty, on the part of the powerful. Furthermore, a man of keen intellect could wield more power than one of sheer brute strength endowed by nature, but brilliant minds are not in the habit of utilizing their power for their own selfish ends with a complete disregard of the rights and needs of others. Even the strong need the respect, friendship, and other values that cannot be arrogated by power, but must be won by noble techniques.

An ethics of power may have a temporary measure of success in a radically individualistic or anarchistic society akin to the animal kingdom, but in a contemporary collectivistic society composed of a sizable number of experts in a multiplicity of fields, each making his own contribution to the common good, and completely dependent and relying on others for the making of theirs, a process of equalization emerges rendering persons comparatively proportional and necessary. *E.g.*, what medic could perform his duties competently without the engineer, mechanic, scientist, or even farmer, shopkeeper, etc.? In modern society with the ever present threat of nuclear bombs hanging ominously overhead, one is reminded of his relative ease of extinction by the simple and feeble individual who is capable of exercising the power of their demolition; in the light of the contemporary scene, it approaches close to meaninglessness to speak of the strong and the weak. Nietzsche criticized the Christian ethic as the ethics of the weak, but the world's salvation at the present time is contingent upon the common acceptance and exercise of the ethics of Jesus. Gilbert Keith Chesterton aptly discerns: Christianity has not been tried and found wanting, it has not yet been tried. The Hindu Gandhi, employing the ethics of Jesus successfully as the guide of his personal life and as the basis of his moral rule of non-violence, eventually won victory and freedom for his followers and his nation.

NOTES

FRIEDRICH NIETZSCHE

1. In order to facilitate the expeditious handling of documentation, Walter Kaufmann's system of bibliographical abbreviation will be utilized as follows: *The Antichrist*, A; *Birth of a Tragedy*, GT; *Untimely meditations*, U; *Human, All-too-Human*, MA; *The Wanderer and his Shadow*, S; *The Dawn*, M; *The Gay Science*, FW; *Thus Spoke Zarathustra*, Z; *Beyond Good and Evil*, J; *Toward a Genealogy of Morals*, GM; *The Wagner Case*, W; *The Twilight of the Idols*, G; *Ecce Homo*, EH; *Nietzsche Contra Wagner*, NCW; prefaces are abbreviated V, *e.g.*, GM-V signifies the preface of *The Genealogy of Morals*. The derivation of the key is from the German text and not the English translation, *e.g.*, V is the initial letter of *Vorrenden*.

    The translators used for this chapter are: Marianne Cowan for *Beyond Good and Evil* (Chicago: Henry Regenery Co., 1955); Francis Golffing for *The Birth of a Tragedy* and *The Genealogy of Morals* (New York: Doubleday & Co., 1956); the remainder is by Walter Kaufmann, (New York: Princeton University Press, 1954).

    The numbers following the key will refer in each case to respective sections rather than the publisher's page number.

    To avoid reduplication, the books of Nietzsche listed in this footnote will substitute for the section that would have been entitled: "Further Reading in the Philosophy of Nietzsche."

2. GM-V, 5.
3. GM-V, 7.
4. GM-V, 7.
5. GM, 2.
6. GM, 5.
7. GM, 7. Nietzsche considered Christianity merely a continuation of Judaism.
8. GM-footnote, 4.
9. GM, 5.
10. GM, 10.
11. GM, 10.
12. GM, 11.
13. GM, 12.
14. GM, 14.
15. GM, 14.
16. GM, 11.
17. GT, 5.
18. Cf. GM, 17.
19. J, 260.
20. J, 260.
21. *Idem.*

22. G, "The Improvers of Mankind," 1.
23. *Ibid.*, 2.
24. J, 228. See also Z, "On The Tarantulas."
25. A, 57.
26. A, 57.
27. G, "Skirmishes of an Untimely Man," 37.
28. *Idem.*
29. *Ibid.*, 45.
30. A, 39.
31. A, 62.
32. A, 39.
33. A, 39.
34. A, 35.
35. A. 39.
36. A, 26.
37. A, 27.
38. A, 42.
39. A, 41.
40. A, 6.
41. A, 56.
42. A, 56.
43. A, 56.
44. A, 44.
45. A, 62.
46. A, 58.
47. Z, "On The Three Evils," 1.
48. Z, "On The Pitying."
49. Z-V, 3.
50. A, 34.
51. Z-V, 3.
52. Z-V, 4.
53. Z, "On the Tarantulas."
54. J. 153.
55. J, 164.
56. J, 108, Cf. Z, "On Old and New Tablets."
57. Z-V, 7.
58. Z, "On the Adder's Bite."
59. Z, "On the Pitying."
60. *Idem.*
61. Z, "On Self-Overcoming."
62. G, *op. cit.*, 38.
63. A, 32.
64. A, 33.
65. Z, "On Priests."
66. A, 2.
67. A, 6.
68. *Idem.*
69. G, *op. cit.*, 39.
70. GT, 15.
71. G, "What I Owe to the Ancients," 4, 5. Nietzsche's doctrine of *eternal recurrence* presupposes the infinity of time, but the limited number of possible combinations of matter results in the intermittent cyclical recurrence of events

and persons; forces responsible for past circumstances will be constantly recurring to recreate them. It constitutes a spurious form of personal immortality.
72. EH.
73. A, 29.
74. Will Durant, *The Story Of Philosophy* (New York: Garden City Publishing Co., 1938, Rev. Ed.), 481.
75. Z, "On The Tarantulas."
76. J. 68. Note this and the many other precursory ideas that Sigmund Freud and the psychoanalysts assume as their own distinct discoveries. Freud does indirectly mete a measure of credit to Nietzsche in his *History of the Psychoanalytic Movement* (New York: Random House, Inc.), 1938, page 939: "In later years I denied myself the great pleasure of reading Nietzsche's works, with the conscious motive of not wishing to be hindered in the working out of my psychoanalytic impressions by any preconceived ideas. I have, therefore, to be prepared—and am so gladly— to renounce all claim to priority in those many cases in which the laborious psychoanalytic investigation can only confirm the insights intuitively won by the philosophers."
77. Nietzsche died insane.
78. H. L. Mencken, *The Philosophy of Friedrich Nietzsche* (Boston: Luce and Co., 1913), 269.

HERBERT SPENCER

The conduct to which we apply the name good is the realatively more evolved conduct; and that bad is the name we apply to conduct which is relatively less evolved. (Spencer's dictum)

We regard as good the conduct furthering self-preservation, and as bad the conduct tending to self-destruction. (Spencer)

1. Ethics of Survival

Spencer, the precursor of Charles Darwin, became the foremost spokesman of his time for the philosophical expression of the theory of evolution; in fact, often a person will quote Spencer, believing that he is quoting Darwin. Spencer's ethics is essentially an ethics of survival; all life is directed towards this end, viz., the survival of the individual and society. All nature, both human and non-human works towards this end: "If we observe how the lungs aerate the blood which the heart sends to them; how heart and lungs together supply aerated blood to the stomach, and so enable it to do its work; how these cooperate with sundry secreting and excreting glands to further digestion and to remove waste matter; and how all of them join to keep the brain in a fit condition for carrying on those actions which indirictly conduce to maintenance of life at large; we are dealing with functions,"[1] and such functions imply teleology (purpose).

Moral behavior and moral laws are developed as a consequence of evolution; not only do they survive because of their utilitarian value, but moral values in their contemporary refined form emerged by gradual steps in consequence of needed adjustments to life. Actually life is defined as "the continuous adjustment of internal relations to external relations."[2] Adjustments to life can be most complex even though they may have arisen from humble and simple adjustments to a physical environment; now the situation has become complicated with the emergence of moral values. Life is "joined with what we call conduct by insensible gradations. Suppose the weapon seized is to ward off a blow. Suppose a counterblow is given. Suppose the aggressor runs and is chased. Suppose there comes a struggle and a handing him over to the police. Suppose there follow the many and varied acts constituting a prosecution. Obviously the initial adjustment of an act to an end, inseparable from the rest must be included with them under the same general head; and obviously from this initial simple adjustment, having intrinsically no moral character, we pass by degrees to the most complex adjustments and to those on which moral judgments are passed."[3] Nevertheless, the better the adjustment, the happier is life and the greater the chances of survival.

Activity, *per se*, is not conduct, *e.g.*, physical activity on the level of the protozoa must not be construed as conduct; one must pass to creatures far superior before conduct can be alleged. The more advanced species, not only exercise conduct for self-survival, but they behave in behalf of the survival of the race. "Mankind exhibits a great progress of like nature. Compared with brutes, the savage, higher in his self-maintaining conduct, is higher too in his race-maintaining conduct,"[4] *e.g.*, provision is made for the wants of their offspring. However, this does not entitle one to conclude "that on reaching a perfect adjustment of acts to ends subserving individual life and the rearing of offspring, the evolution of conduct becomes complete"[5] unless the highest form of conduct known to man is achieved, viz., social co-operation which constitutes the highest phase of evolution. Co-operation is necessary for both individual and social adjustment of acts to ends which are components of that "struggle for existence." One must be sufficiently competent to live up to his ideal of conduct, lest one confront "death by starvation from inability to catch prey," hence showing "a falling short of conduct from its ideal."[6] Modern man is a being whose conduct, both moral and otherwise has undergone a process of long evolutionary development; he has now arrived at the realization that he cannot survive personally without assuring others of their survival. "For beyond so behaving that each achieves his ends without preventing others from achieving their ends, the members of society may give mutual help in the achievement of ends. And if, either indirectly by industrial cooperation, or directly by volunteered aid, fellow-citizens can make easier for one another the adjustments of acts to ends, then their conduct assumes a still higher phase of evolution; since whatever facilitates the making of adjustments by each, increases the totality of the adjustments made, and serves to render the lives of all more complete."[7]

2. The Evolution of Conduct

Ethics as it is known today is the result of an evolutionary process which has permitted survival only to those codes of ethics, *i.e.*, patterns of conduct which enhanced individual and social adaptation, viz., survival. Moral laws make their first appearance in the latter stages of evolution, but were formulated gradually as the result of practices which were most conducive to adjustment or survival. "Ethics has for its subject matter that form which universal conduct assumes during the last stages of its evolution."[8] Universal moral conduct, *i.e.*, virtues are explicable as implications of the "Evolution Hypothesis," *e.g., courage* is universally regarded as a virtue because it is a necessary quality that the men of any society possess if that society is to survive against the onslaught of enemies, human or animal, and the hardships or catastrophies of nature. If men were cowardly, then their enemies would overtake them, terminating the existence of that society, but if the nation's men were courageous, then they would resist and combat their enemies even in the face of death. Consequently, for the sake of the survival of society, courage must be promoted as a virtue and cowardice denounced as a vice. It is noteworthy that women are not expected to be courageous for in the evolutionary process they were not utilized in warfare for the defence of society, consequently timidity in women is not condemned as a vice, but often praised and enjoyed as quaint.

The Lamarckian theory of inherited acquired characteristics is also used to explain moral law and its mode of appearance in modern civilization, *e.g.*, *justice* is a principle which has all of the appearances of being innate in contemporary civilization and in human individuals. This is explained in terms of primitive man's realization that the best practice for the sake of adaptation and survival, both individual and social is justice. Primitive man practiced justice since it was the best means of social adjustment, consequently made it an internal habit as well as a social amenity, *i.e.*, a hard and fast practice in society. In the course of time as one generation passed on its useful and successful practice of justice to another, a generation of human beings eventually appeared who no longer needed to be taught the principle of justice for it was imbedded in them innately, *i.e.*, they were born with the principle of justice as part of human nature.

All this holds true of moral science. As by early and rude experiences there were inductively reached, vague but partially true notions respecting the overbalancing of bodies, the motions of missiles, the action of levers; so by early and rude experiences there were inductively reached, vague but partially true notions respecting the effects of men's behavior on themselves, on one another, and on society; to a certain extent serving in the last case as in the first, for the guidance of conduct. Moreover, as this rudimentary mechanical knowledge, though still remaining empirical, becomes during early stages of civilization at once more definite and more extensive; so during early stages of civilization these ethical ideas, still retaining their empirical character, increase in precision and multiplicity. But just as we have seen that mechanical knowledge of the empirical sort can evolve into science only by first omitting all qualifying circumstances, and generalizing in absolute ways the fundamental law of forces; so here we have to see that empirical ethics can evolve into rational ethics only by first neglecting all complicating incidents, and formulating the laws of right action apart from the obscuring effects of special conditions. And the final implication is that just as the system of mechanical truths, conceived in ideal separation as absolute, becomes applicable to real mechanical problems in such way that making allowance for all incidental circumstances there can be reached conclusions far nearer to the truth than could otherwise be reached; so a system of ideal ethical truths, expressing the absolute right, will be applicable to the questions of our transitional state.

In the first place, given the laws of life as they are, and a man of ideal nature cannot be produced in a society consisting of men having natures remote from the ideal. As well might we expect a child of English type to be borne among Negroes, as expect that among the organically immoral, one who is organically moral will arise. Unless it be denied that character results from inherited structure, it must be admitted that since, in any society, each individual descends from a stock which, traced back a few generations, ramifies everywhere through the society, and participates in its average nature, there must, notwithstanding marked individual diversities, be preserved such community as prevents any one from reaching an ideal form while the rest remain far below it.[9]

It is worth noting that the Lamarckian theory of inherited acquired characteristics has fallen into disrepute; the evolutionary psychologist, William McDougall, conducted experiments in the hope of substantiating the claims of the doctrine, but the experiments conclusively indicated its falsity.

3. Psychological Hedonism and Optimism

Psychological hedonism is the belief that man by human nature seeks pleasure and avoids pain, whether or not he is aware of such activity; this is the contention of Spencer. Intrinsic good, that is something good in and of itself, does not exist; all goods are utilitarian, *i.e.*, good for a practical purpose. "In which cases do we distinguish as good, a knife, a gun, a house? And what trait leads us to speak of a bad umbrella or a bad pair of boots? The characters here predicated by the words good and bad, are not intrinsic characters; for apart from human wants, such things have neither merits nor demerits, We call these articles good or bad according as they are well or ill adapted to achieve prescribed ends."[10] *E.g.*, a good knife is one that cuts well, a good home is one that shelters well; conversely, a bad umbrella is one that fails to keep rain from falling upon me, and "we call a day bad in which storms prevent us from satisfying certain of our desires."

Good and *right* must be defined in terms of adjustment, adaptation, and survival; take, for example, "the primary set of adjustments — those subserving individual life. Apart from approval or disapproval of his ulterior aims, a man who fights is said to make a good defense, if his defense is well adapted for self-preservation."[11] Implicit in the foregoing statement is the belief that moral values develop as a result of an object's worth, *i.e.*, usefulness in aiding one's adaptation to life, *e.g.*, a home, food, clothing are good because they aid in survival. "All such approving and disapproving utterances make the tacit assertion that, other things equal, conduct is right or wrong according as its special acts, well or ill adjusted to special ends, do or do not further the general end of self-preservation."[12] One need not force a person to do what is right or moral when it is for the sake of his own good because strong desires furnish sufficient drive, but often he must be prompted or even forced to do what is right when another person's welfare it at stake. Egoistic hedonism has no place in an ethics of evolutionary naturalism which maintains that an individual's survival or adjustment depends upon the support of society in his behalf, hence the enhancement of society becomes a moral obligation on the part of every individual, ultimately for his own good, *i.e.*, welfare.

The way has now been paved for an understanding of Spencer's dictum, *i.e.*, his criterion of morality: "The conduct to which we apply the name good, is the relatively more evolved conduct; and that bad is the name we apply to conduct which is relatively less evolved."[13] The ground for this thesis is that evolution tends one ever toward self-preservation; preservation in its highest stage is civilized behavior; consequently the criterion of right and wrong action must be defined in the following manner: "We regard as good the conduct furthering self-preservation, and as bad the conduct tending to self-destruction."[14] Evolution, or what amounts to the same, morality "becomes the highest possible when the conduct simultaneously achieves the greatest totality of life in self, in offspring, and in fellow men; so here we see that the conduct called good rises to the conduct conceived as best, when it fulfills all three classes of ends at the same time."[15] The following constitute three classes of ends to which the terms good and bad are applicable: (1) those which are conducive to self-preservation; (2) those which are beneficial to one's offspring; (3) those deeds which aid another's welfare, *i.e.*, the good of society.

This entire ethical philosophy is based on one primary and indispensable premise: "Life *is* worth living." Otherwise one cannot predicate good to actions which are conducive to life; the case would have to be reversed and one would be compelled to say that an act which destroys life is good, and those actions are evil which keep it alive; consequently euthanasia would then be an acceptable and laudatory moral philosophy. The ethical pessimist would accept this negative outlook and proceed accordingly; he would proceed to argue that evolution has been a drastic mistake, particularly that "evolution which improves the adjustment of acts to ends in ascending stages of organization." Such pessimists would believe that "life is not a benefit but a misfortune, conduct which prolongs it is to be blamed rather than praised; the ending of an undesirable existence being the thing to be wished, that which causes the ending of it must be applauded; while action furthering its continuance, either in self or others, must be reprobated. Those who, on the other hand, take an optimistic view, or who, if not pure optimists, yet hold that in life the good exceeds the evil, are committed to opposite estimates; and must regard as conduct to be approved that which fosters life in self and others, and as conduct to be disapproved that which injures or endangers life in self or others."[16] The moral implications of pessimism are rather ridiculous, *e.g.*, it would be praiseworthy to commit murder since this would save a man from the miseries and sufferings of life. The pessimist's condemnation of life is based on his contention that it results in more pain than pleasure, whereas the optimist takes the converse position and believes that life's pleasures predominate over pain. A Spencerian evolutionist takes the stand of the optimist and accepts the belief that life is a blessing with pleasures exceeding its pains. "Thus there is no escape from the admission that in calling good the conduct which subserves life, and bad the conduct which hinders or destroys it, and in so implying that life is a blessing and not a curse, we are inevitably asserting that conduct is good or bad as its total effects are pleasurable or painful."[17]

A definition of morality and right conduct have been given, it remains now to identify the *good* which for Spencer is defined as *pleasure*. Not only is that which normally preserves life or makes for its effective adaptation pleasurable, but pain or displeasure usually accompanies those things that are detrimental to life. *Intrinsic* good is pleasure and is universally so. "If we call good the enjoyable state itself, as a good laugh — if we call good the proximate cause of an enjoyable state, as good music — if we call good any agent which conduces immediately or remotely to an enjoyable state, as a good shop, a good teacher — if we call good considered intrinsically, each act so adjusted to its end as to further self-preservation and that surplus of enjoyment which makes self-preservation desirable — if we call every kind of conduct which aids the lives of others, and do this under the belief that life brings more happiness than misery; then it becomes undeniable that, taking into account immediate and remote effects on all persons, the good is universally the pleasurable."[18] As a consequence of this mankind has regarded as preferable conduct that which is conducive to happiness, not merely because it is instrumentally preferable to adaptation or survival, but because it is intrinsically preferable, hence it serves as an ultimate end. A good object or experience must always be defined in the light of its pleasure producing effects; an object which produces pain cannot be said by anyone to be good; "so the moralist who thinks this conduct intrinsically good and that intrinsically bad, if pushed home, has no choice but to fall back on their pleasure-giving and pain-giving effects. To prove this it needs but to observe how impossible it would be to think of them as we do, if their effects were reversed."[19] Spencer is sympathetic with the ethical theory of the Utilitarian philosophers and objects to those ascetics who designated it by the contemptuous title of "pig philosophy."[20] By implication, it would follow that those who repudiate pleasure would regard blessedness a kind of happiness, but blessedness must be one of three qualities: painful, indifferent, pleasurable; since it is neither painful nor indifferent, it must be pleasurable.

Spencer summarizes his ethical theory: "That which ... we find to be highly evolved conduct, is that which ... we find to be what is called good conduct; and the ideal goal to the natural evolution of conduct ... we ... recognize as the ideal standard of conduct ethically considered. . . . Other things equal, well-adjusted, self-conserving acts we call good; other things equal, we call good the acts that are well adjusted for bringing up progeny capable of complete living; and other things equal, we ascribe goodness to acts which further the complete living of others. This judging as good, conduct which conduces to life in each and all, we found to involve the assumption that animate existence is desirable. . . . Whence it follows that if we call good the conduct conducive to life, we can do so only with the implication that it is conducive to a surplus of pleasures over pains."[21]

4. Evaluation of the Spencerian Ethic

The warrant or basis of the Spencerian ethic rests heavily upon the Lamarckian theory of inherited acquired characteristics which has been repudiated by most biologists and psychologists. Of recent years, only the psychiatrist Carl Jung held to the doctrine; since his death in 1961, there has not been a single psychologist of note who subscribes to the belief. The noted psychologist William McDougall who was eager to prove the existence of instincts on the Lamarckian theory, met with dismal failure in his experimental efforts with rats.

The theory of inherited acquired characteristics implies that laws of logic, moral laws, and mathematical axioms are merely subjective habits which have proved conducive to social or political enhancement, consequently survived by becoming habits in early man but in a subsequent generation have appeared as hereditary racial traits, *e.g.*, if justice is impressed upon the mind generation after generation then it becomes innate. Spencer argues that these habits, *i.e.*, logical, mathematical, and ethical principles have survived because they possessed utilitarian value: self-evident truths are associations of observation which have become habitual and eventually *inherited* because of the human race's exposure to them; furthermore they have become so uniform that mankind has lost the insight and ability to conceive of the opposite, *e.g.*, the laws of causation are merely matters of habit. Such conclusions seem highly unreasonable for if the laws of logic are merely subjective habits then how is it possible that they retain any validity? How can they reveal objective truths, or any truths whatever? It appears that Spencer has permitted himself to become involved in a contradictory predicament for if the laws of logic are merely habits and Spencer derives all of his truths from such laws, it would follow that all of his reasoning must be false; at least, there is no ground for their validity.

5. Further Reading in the Philosophy of Spencer

For those interested in pursuing the thought of Herbert Spencer further, they may do so by reading any of the following works: *Social Statics* (1850), *The Theory of Population* (1852), *Progress, Its Law and Cause* (1857), *Essays* (1858), *Education: Intellectual, Moral, Physical* (1861), *First Principles* (1867, 6th ed., 1900), *Principles of Biology* (1864-1867), *Principles of Psychology* (1872), *The Study of Sociology* (1873), *The Principles of Sociology* (1876-1896), *Man versus the State* (1884), *Factors of Organic Evolution* (1886), *Inadequacy of Natural Selection* (1893), *Fragments* (1897), *Facts and Comments* (1902), *Autobiography* (posthumously in 1904).

NOTES

HERBERT SPENCER

1. Herbert Spencer, *The Data of Ethics* (1879), Ch. 2, "The Evolution of Conduct."
2. *Idem.*
3. *Idem.*
4. *Idem.*
5. *Idem.*
6. *Idem.*
7. *Idem.*
8. *Idem.*
9. *Ibid.*, Ch. 15, "Absolute and Relative Ethics."
10. *Ibid.*, Ch. 3, "Good and Bad Conduct."
11. *Idem.*
12. *Idem.*
13. *Idem.*
14. *Idem.*
15. *Idem.*
16. *Idem.*
17. *Idem.*
18. *Idem.*
19. *Idem.*
20. The psychological hedonism of Bentham was nick-named the "pig philosophy."
21. *Ibid.*

ETHICAL PESSIMISM AND EXISTENTIALISM

ARTHUR SCHOPENHAUER

For the greatest crime of man is that he ever was born. (Calderon)

Human life must be some kind of mistake.

Our present problem has to deal with that natural compassion, which in every man is innate and indestructible, and which has been shown to be the sole source of non-egoistic conduct, this kind alone being of real moral worth. (Schopenhauer)

1. The Ethics of Pessimism

"All *willing* arises from want, therefore from deficiency, and therefore from suffering. The satisfaction of a wish ends it; yet for one wish that is satisfied there remain at least ten which are denied. Further, the desire lasts long, the demands are infinite; the satisfaction is short and scantily measured out. But even the final satisfaction is itself only apparent; every satisfied wish at once makes room for a new one; both are illusions.... No attained object of desire can give lasting satisfaction, but merely a fleeting gratification; it is like the alms thrown to the beggar, that keeps him alive today that his misery may be prolonged till the morrow.'"[1] As long as consciousness is filled with striving, desires, wishes, needs, with their concomitant fears, frustration, and feelings of insecurity, lasting happiness or peace is an impossibility, and without peace, no true well-being is possible. "The subject of willing is thus constantly stretched on the revolving wheel of Ixion, pours water into the sieve of the Danaids, is the ever-longing Tantalus."[2] Man is caught in an endless stream of will which enslaves him to itself; to escape its claws is to find peace, *i.e.*, the painless state which Epicurus prized as the highest good, but, alas, "we keep the Sabbath of the penal servitude of willing . . . and the unquiet frame of mind, disturbed by vehement willing."[3]

One's insecurity is heightened by the constant threat of annihilation by a superior power from which there is no escape. "If we lose ourselves in the contemplation of the infinite greatness of the universe in space and time, meditate on the thousands of years that are past or to come, or if the heavens at night actually bring before our eyes innumerable worlds and so force upon our consciousness the immensity of the universe, we feel ourselves dwindle to nothing; as individuals . . . as transient phenomena of will, we feel ourselves pass away and vanish into nothing like drops in the ocean."[4] However, the vastness of the world need not disquiet one provided he become one with the world; in this manner, oppression ceases and one becomes exalted with its immensity. As the universe is sublime, an individual also may ethically become a sublime character.

Man is caught in a web from which he vainly tries to extricate himself for he is a victim of his own nature which is the source of his troubles. "Now the nature of man consists in this, that his will strives, is satisfied and strives anew, and so on for ever. Indeed, his happiness and well-being consist simply in the quick transition from wish to satisfaction, and from satisfaction to a new wish. For the absence of satisfaction is suffering, the empty longing for a new wish, languor, *ennui*."[5] The unrelenting will is responsible for this state of affairs, and as long as life exists, the will is present for life is indissolubly attached to the will as one's shadow accompanies the body. All nature manifests this phenomenon, viz., the fulfillment of the will to live, but the loss of an individual does not appreciably affect the whole of nature. Consequently, "it is not the individual, but only the species that Nature cares for, and for the preservation of which she so earnestly strives, providing for it with the utmost prodigality through the vast surplus of the seed and the great strength of the fructifying impulse. The individual, on the contrary, neither has nor can have any value for Nature."[6] Nature is interested in preserving the race, not the individual, consequently she takes great pains in making the drive of reproduction intensely forceful so that a man vainly curbs his sex desires by practicing continence; furthermore the spermatozoa is extravagantly lavished far beyond necessity during a single act of copulation to insure the successful realization of its objective. "Man is at once impetuous and blind striving of will (whose pole or focus lies in the genital organs)."[7] The tenacity of the drive and desire of sex is blind because one's partner in sex is not rationally chosen; furthermore one's partner may be detested or the two may experience mutual enmity between each other for sex often irrationally "flings itself upon persons who, apart from the sexual relation, would be hateful, contemptible, and even abhorrent to the lover. But so much more powerful is the will of the species than that of the individual that the lover shuts his eyes to all those qualities which are repellent to him, overlooks all, and blinds himself for ever to the object of his passion — so entirely is he blinded by that illusion, which vanishes as soon as the will of the species is satisfied, and leaves behind a detested companion for life.... Finally, sexual love is compatible even with the extremest hatred towards its object: therefore Plato has compared it to the love of the wolf for the sheep.... For he is under the influence of an impulse which, akin to the instincts of insects, compels him, in spite of all grounds of reason, to pursue his end unconditionally, and to undervalue everything else: he cannot give it up."[8]

The attainment of lasting satisfaction is an impossible achievement which is evidenced by the abortive attempts of the many who have attempted to pursue this end. It is due to the *negative* nature of happiness, which instead of providing lasting satisfaction and gratification, merely delivers one from pain and want, and if carried to any extent, *i.e.*, if one avoids happiness to any degree then his existence culminates in some new pain, languor, empty longing, or ennui. "Every epic and dramatic poem can only represent a struggle, an effort, and a fight for happiness, never enduring and complete happiness."[9] The hero of any drama is conducted through numerous difficulties and dangers before it is possible for him to embrace his goal, and at this moment the curtain falls posthaste, otherwise the expected happiness from the glittering goal would be quickly followed up with problems, if the happiness itself did not turn out to be another disappointment.

Enduring happiness is not possible because *the will* of which human life is the objectification and phenomenon is a "striving without aim or end." The average person does not reach the extremes of human life and striving: (1) the powerful will, *i.e.*, the strong passions which influence the will; (2) pure knowing, *i.e.*, the comprehension of Ideas (Platonic ideals) which is capable of freeing one from the service of the will; (3) the greatest lethargy of the will, viz., empty longing, life-benumbing languor. Most individuals do not become permanently fixed in any one of these extremes, but do oscillate from one to the others, from desiring trifling objects to escaping ennui. "It is really incredible how meaningless and void of significance when looked at from without, how dull and unenlightened by intellect when felt from within, is the course of life of the great majority of men. It is a weary longing and complaining, a dreamlike staggering through the four ages of life to death, accompanied by a series of trivial thoughts. Such men are like clockwork, which is wound up, and goes it knows not why; and every time a man is begotten and born, the clock of human life is wound up anew, to repeat the same old piece it has played innumerable times before, passage after passage, measure after measure, with insignificant variations. Every individual, every human being and course of life, is but another short dream of the endless spirit of nature, of the persistent will to live; is only another fleeting form, which it carelessly sketches on its infinite page, space and time; allows to remain for a time so short that it vanishes into nothing in comparison with these, and then obliterates to make new room."[10] Furthermore, the obligation is preceded by many and deep sufferings before the bitter and long feared death comes at last; it is for this reason that the sight of a corpse shocks and staggers one into seriousness. "But the never satisfied wishes, the frustrated efforts, the hopes unmercifully crushed by fate, the unfortunate errors of the whole life, with increasing suffering and death at the end, are always a tragedy."[11] To escape from this tumultuous world of care and anxiety, the human mind creates for itself a pleasant imaginary world or a thousand different superstitions designed to cope with the torment which this world affords in the form of want, wretchedness, affliction, misery, and death.

To escape misery, the uncultured individual beclouds himself with the veil of Maya (illusion) so that he cannot see the *thing-in-itself* (reality, objective will), but only the phenomenon (body) in time and space, the *principium individuationis* (principle of individuation), and the principle of sufficient reason (the logic of Leibniz). Such an individual places pleasure and pain in two different categories, when they are in reality one. "He sees one man live in joy, abundance, and pleasure, and even at his door another die miserable of want and cold. Then he asks, Where is retribution? And he himself, in the vehement pressure of will which is his origin and nature, siezes upon the pleasures and enjoyments of life, firmly embraces them, and knows not that by this very act of his will he seizes and hugs all those pains and sorrows at the sight of which he shudders. He sees the ills and he sees the wickedness in the world, but far from knowing that both of these are but different sides of the manifestation of the one will to live.... For the knowledge that sees through the principle of individuation, a happy life in time, the gifts of chance or won by prudence, amid the sorrows of innumerable others, is only the dream of a beggar in which he is a king, but from which he must awake and learn from experience only a fleeting illusion had separated him from the suffering of his life."[12] His condition is further aggravated by witnessing evil individuals committing misdeeds and cruelties of every type and description, yet live a life of happiness and escape the world unpunished; in contrast to this the oppressed endure a life of suffering, and drag out an unendurable existence without an avenger or requiter coming to the rescue.

Actually the afflicter and the sufferer differ only in respect to being a different phenomenon, but reality which is the thing-in-itself, *i.e.*, the *will*, dwells in both individuals, and the deception which is created is due to the ignorance that one is bound to its service, and the will, seeking to increase the happiness in one of its phenomena, *i.e.*, in one individual, effects it by producing great suffering in another. Ultimately, "the inflicter of suffering and the sufferer are one. . . . If the eyes of both were opened, the inflicter of suffering would see that he lives in all that suffers pain in the wide world, and which, if endowed with reason, in vain asks why it was called into existence for such great suffering, its desert of which it does not understand. And the sufferer would see that all the wickedness which is or ever was committed in the world proceeds from that will which constitutes *his* own nature also. . . . 'For the greatest crime of man is that he ever was born'."[13] This expresses the significance of the Christian *doctrine of original sin*.

2. Evil as Positive

In direct contradiction to many philosophers, Schopenhauer repudiates the concept that evil is negative[14] in character, *i.e.*, it is the privation of good; he argues that evil is positive, it is good which is negative, *i.e.*, the absence of evil. "Every feeling of satisfaction, is negative in character; that is to say, it consists in freedom from pain, which is the positive element of existence."[15] One proof of this is that one never finds that the actually experienced pleasure lives up to one's expectations, but conversely pain is greater than anticipated, *e.g.*, two animals engaged in devouring each other experience greater pain in having their bodies torn asunder and eaten than the pleasure which is found in devouring the other's flesh. "We are like lambs in a field, disporting themselves under the eye of the butcher, who chooses out first one and then another for his prey. So it is that in our good days we are all unconscious of the evil Fate may have presently in store for us — sickness, poverty, mutilation, loss of sight or reason.'"[116]

Life proves constantly to be an unprofitable enterprise; it is an episode which disturbs the blessed calm of non-existence. Even when life proceeds with tolerable calm, the longer one lives the more clearly he discovers that on the whole, "life is *a disappointment, nay, a cheat*. . . . It is a blessing that we do not know what is really going to happen. Could we foresee it there are times when children might seem like innocent prisoners, condemned, not to death, but to life, and as yet all unconscious of what their sentence means. Nevertheless every man desires to reach old age; in other words, a state of life of which it may be said: 'It is bad to-day, and it will be worse to-morrow; and so on till the worst of all'."[117] Life is so miserable that if children were to be brought into this universe by an act of pure reason alone, instead of overwhelming desire, the human race would cease to exist for man; sympathy and pity for the future generation would spare it the misery of existence. At least, man does not usher in the coming generation in cold blood, but by hot passion and desire which he is incapable of subduing. If this philosophy is comfortless, it is that way merely because it is true, but people like to be deceived into believing that everything which is created is good.

Happiness in any given life is to be measured by the extent to which it has been sufficiently fortunate to escape suffering, not by the pleasures enjoyed. Emotional desire gives rise to pain, hence ought to be eschewed. Man's rational nature, rather than assisting in aiding his escape from the plight in which he is caught, "develops his susceptibility to happiness and misery to such a degree that, at one moment the man is brought in an instant to a state of delight that may prove fatal, at another to the depths of despair and suicide."[118] To alleviate the mean predicament in which he is trapped, man seeks luxury in all of its forms: delectable food, tobacco, opium, intoxicating beverages, attractive clothes, and a thousand other things. Man's suffering exceeds that of the brute for his mental torture is absent in the animal; furthermore the boredom man suffers is a downright scourge. Even wealth becomes a punishment since it leads to inactivity and ennui, and to escape it, one races frantically in all directions at once. "No sooner do they arrive in a place than they are anxious to know what amusements it affords; just as though they were beggars asking where they could receive a dole! Of a truth, need and boredom are the two poles of human life. . . . Finally . . . passionate love . . . is the source of little pleasure and much suffering."[19]

3. The Vanity of Existence, Suicide and Death

"Human life must be some kind of mistake" for its every goal is sought in vain. "How insatiable a creature is man. Every satisfaction he attains lays the seeds of some new desire, so that there is no end to the wishes of each individual will."[20] Man is a slave to *Will* (desire, instinct, force) which is the lord of all worlds, and this will is insatiable and endless. Life is a burden; its two fundamental tasks are: vainly satisfying desires (instincts) and warding off boredom, which sets in as soon as an individual has coped with his desires with any measure of success. Life's vanity is indicated by the abrupt disappearance of sensual pleasure the moment its aim is attained and by the lack of delight in living except when one is struggling for something; both courses inevitably lead to boredom, hence the proof of the worthlessness of life.

Suicide is no solution for it is incapable of annihilating the *will* which is eternal; moreover there is no assurance that the individual does not survive death as Hamlet's monologue intimates: "He merely declares that if we had any certainty of being annihilated by it, death would be infinitely preferable to the world as it is. But *there lies the rub!*"[21] Suicide is wrong because it thwarts attainment of man's highest ethical aim, viz., *moral freedom,* and it vainly seeks to accomplish relief from this world of misery by substituting a solution that is merely apparent, not real. "Suicide may also be regarded as an experiment — a question which man puts to nature, trying to force her to an answer. The question is this: What change will death produce in a man's existence and in his insight into the nature of things? It is a clumsy experiment to make; for it involves the destruction of the very consciousness which puts the question and awaits the answer."[22]

Fear of death is not the terrifying or disturbing factor in man, but it is the craving and desire for life that is troublesome. If a man could bring himself to relinquish life willingly, then death would lose its torment. "Whoever is oppressed with the burden of life, whoever desires life and affirms it, but abhors its torments, and especially can no longer endure the hard lot that has fallen to himself, such a man has no deliverance to hope from death, and cannot right himself by suicide."[23] The relentless drive of Will continues beyond the portals of death. Man is the only creature who has knowledge of the fact that he will die some day: "man alone, carries about with him, in abstract conceptions, the certainty of his death . . . but no man is observably disturbed by the thought of certain and never-distant death, but lives as if he would live for ever."[24] Actually no one really carries with him a vivid image or lively conviction of the certainty of his death; if he did then no great difference would exist between the frame of mind of an ordinary individual and that of a condemned criminal. The particular phenomenon of the will, *i.e.*, an individual person has a temporal beginning and end, but the *Will* itself as thing-in-itself is not affected by it, nor is its correlative, viz., "the knowing but never known subject, and that life is always assured to the will to live." The will and its pure subject of knowing lie outside of time. It is "only as phenomenon that an individual is distinguished from the other things of the world; as thing-in-itself he is the will which appears in all, and death destroys the illusion which separates his consciousness from that of the rest: this is immortality."[25]

The love of life, *i.e.*, the strong urge or desire to live operates in a dual capacity, it forces one to shun death and enables him to carry on the business of life with an ease that seems to ignore death, at least he is not conscious or sensitive to it, but the love of life is not sufficiently successful in aiding the individual's escape from being seized by the fear of death since one constantly employs devices to prevent death. The sting in fear of death is not pain that one may suffer in post existence for such pain obviously lies on this side of death, that is, pain is experienced only by the living; furthermore some persons take refuge from pain or relief from pain by embracing death and in the same vein some people endure the most fearful forms of suffering just to escape death; hence pain and death should be regarded as two distinct evils. What is feared in death is the end of the individual; the individual who is a particular objectification of the *Will* to live, consequently rebels against death with every fiber of his being active in the struggle. "A man who had thoroughly assimilated the truths we have already advanced, but had not come to know, either from his own experience or from a deeper insight, that constant suffering is essential to life, who found calmly and deliberately desire that his life, as he had hitherto known it, should endure for ever or repeat itself ever anew, and whose love of life was so great that he willingly and gladly accepted all the hardships and miseries to which it is exposed for the sake of its pleasures, — such a man would stand 'with firm-knit bones on the well-rounded, enduring earth,' and would have nothing to fear. Armed with the knowledge we have given him, he would await with indifference the death that hastens towards him on the wings of time. He would regard it a false illusion, an impotent spectre, which frightens the weak. . . . He could not be terrified by an endless past or future in which he would not be, for this he would regard as the empty delusion of the web of Maya [illusion]. Thus he would no more fear death than the sun fears the night.'"[26]

4. Ethical Salvation

Man is confronted with a dilemma: both death and life are disagreeable thoughts and experiences, and some method of release is necessary. "Life itself is a sea, full of rocks and whirlpools, which man avoids with the greatest care and solicitude, although he knows that even if he succeeds in getting through with all his efforts and skill, he yet by doing so comes nearer at every step to the greatest, the total, inevitable, and irremediable shipwreck, death . . . this is the final goal of the laborious voyage, and worse for him than all the rocks from which he has escaped."[27] Although life is a miserable existence, one still holds on, driven by a relentless striving after existence which is inherent in all living things in the hope of attaining the *summum bonum*, viz., "a final satisfaction of the will, after which no new desire could arise."[28]

Since death provides no freedom from the driving force of will, therefore suicide affords no means of escape, consequently if a person would free himself from the will and its concomitants, viz., fears and desires so that "nothing can trouble him more, nothing can move him, for he has cut all the thousand cords of will which hold us bound to the world, and, as desire, fear, envy, anger, drag us hither and thither in constant pain."[29]

Salvation may be effected in two ways: the first mode of achievement results in only partial success, it is attained through *art, i.e.,* through aesthetics or the contemplation of the Platonic ideals; the second manner is accomplished through a *denial of the will to live, i.e.,* to reject the *desire* to live, not life, *per se*. Aesthetic relief "consists in great measure in the fact that in entering the state of pure contemplation we are lifted for the moment above all willing, *i.e.,* all wishes and cares; we become, as it were, freed from ourselves."[30] In this state, one no longer subordinates himself to the service of constant willing, but has his mind stayed on eternal Platonic ideals which are purified and free from will. This blessed state affords enjoyment of the beautiful with the drive of desire extinguished.

Some persons attempt to destroy the will by its complete denial, viz., asceticism, *i.e.,* by enforced renunciation of every kind, such as penance or the deliberate choice of embracing whatever is disagreeable in order to suppress the will. By the term asceticism, "I mean in its narrower sense this *intentional* breaking of the will by the refusal of what is agreeable and the selection of what is disagreeable, the voluntary chosen life of penance and self-chastisement for the continual mortification of the will."[31]

Other persons win a denial of the will through a universal love of humanity whereby they regard the sufferings of the world as their own by sympathy, but only a few ever succeed with this technique. It is noteworthy that the world's great tragedies end by breaking the will of the strong-willed heroes to the point of complete resignation, and finally the will to live ceases.[32]

The most effective means of salvation constitutes the climax of Schopenhauer's monumental work: *The World as Will and Idea*. Permanent salvation is found in Nirvana, *i.e.*, the abolition of will by being caught up into empty nothingness via the extinguishing of all desires. Perfect holiness is "the denial and surrender of all volition, and thus the deliverance from a world whose whole existence we have found to be suffering, this appears to us as a passing away into empty nothingness."[33] But the great obstacle which prevents one achieving this goal is his own nature with its unquenchable will to live; "that we abhor annihilation so greatly, is simply another expression of the fact that we so strenuously will life."[34] Nevertheless there are those who through perfect self-knowledge have overcome the world, have found themselves, have freely denied the will, "and who merely wait to see the last trace of it vanish with the body which it animates; then instead of the restless striving and effort, instead of the constant transition from wish to fruition, and from joy to sorrow, instead of the never-satisfied and never-dying hope which constitutes the life of the man who wills, we shall see that peace which is above all reason, that perfect calm of the spirit, that deep rest, that inviolable confidence and serenity . . . only knowledge remains, the will has vanished. We look with deep and painful longing upon this state. . . . Yet this is the only consideration which can afford us lasting consolation, when, on the one hand we have recognized incurable suffering and endless misery as essential to the manifestation of will, the world; and, on the other hand, see the world pass away with the abolition of will, and retain before us only empty nothingness. Thus in this way, by contemplation of the life and conduct of saints ... who are brought before our eyes by their written history, and, with the stamp of inner truth, by art, we must banish the dark impression of that nothingness which we discern behind all virtue and holiness as their final goal, and which we fear as children fear the dark, we must not even evade it like the Indians, through myths and meaningless words, such as reabsorption in Brahma or the Nirvana of the Buddhists. Rather do we freely acknowledge that what remains after the entire abolition of will is for all those who are still full of will certainly nothing; but, conversely, to those in whom the will has turned and has denied itself, this our world, which is so real, with all its suns and milky-ways — nothing.''[35]

5. Ethics of Pity

The only fount of true morality is *pity* or *compassion* because it is the sole non-egoistic source or spring of action and the only thoroughly effective impetus of moral conduct; conversely cruelty which is the depth of deficiency of compassion is, *ipso facto,* the depth of depravity. Compassion, a quality which extends to the kingdom of all living things, is the foundation of loving-kindness and the antidote to egoism and a most soothing balm for the inevitable suffering that prevails in the world. There is little value in condemning others, since all alike are co-sufferers; the best course of action is pity, *i.e.*, compassion. "It is this Compassion alone which is the real basis of all *voluntary* justice and all *genuine* loving-kindness. Only so far as an action springs therefrom, has it moral value; and all conduct that proceeds from any other motive whatever has none. When once compassion is stirred within me by another's pain, then his weal and woe go straight to my heart, exactly in the same way, if not always to the same degree, as otherwise I feel only my own.

Consequently the difference between myself and him is no longer an absolute one."[36]

Only three fundamental springs of human conduct exist: *egoism, malice, compassion*. Egoism, with its limitless desires is restricted to the self; malice seeks the ill of others and can reach the extent of cruelty; compassion is interested solely in the welfare of others and may reach to a degree of nobleness or magnanimity. Sympathy lies dormant and is not quickened except by the sufferings of another; the well being of another never incites one's compassion. This is due to the fact that pain, suffering, want, privation, need, and every wish is positive, hence affects one's consciousness directly, but satisfaction, enjoyment, happiness, etc. consist "solely in the fact that a hardship is done away with, a pain lulled: whence their effect is *negative*. . . . Pain, then, is positive, and makes itself known by itself: satisfaction or pleasure is negative — simply the removal of the former."[37]

Compassion as a moral incentive is the only adequate ground for unselfish justice and genuine loving-kindness, and these two cardinal virtues lay the basis on which all other virtues depend. *E.g.*, compassion is responsible for one's desisting from inflicting physical injury or mental suffering on another; compassion inhibits one's gratification of desires at another's expense. One's ethical stature, and also, the assurance that he is on the direct road to his ethical salvation, reaches its height when he is able to say with sincerity on contact with every human being "Tat twam asi!" (This thou art), *i.e.*, when he can sympathetically put himself in another's position of hardship and be moved in his behalf. "Love, the origin and nature of which we recognised as the penetration of the principle of individuation leads to salvation, to the entire surrender of the will to live, *i.e.*, of all volition, and also how another path, less soft but more frequented, leads men to the same goal, a paradoxical proposition must first be stated and explained; not because it is paradoxical, but because it is true, and is necessary to the completeness of the thought I have present. It is this: 'All love (*agape, caritas*) is sympathy'."[38]

Schopenhauer concludes his treatise on ethics with reiterated emphasis that "natural Compassion, which in every man is innate and indestructible, and which has been shown to be the sole source of *non-egoistic* conduct, this kind alone being of real moral worth"[39] is the true basis of morality.

6. Evaluation of the Schopenhauerian Ethic

Schopenhauer has sired many pregnant and provoking ideas. The philosophers of evolution, Lloyd Morgan, Roy Wood Sellars, and S. Alexander who advanced the concept of emergent evolution were inspired by Schopenhauer's doctrine of being and causality. Much of Psychoanalysis finds Schopenhauerian concepts as its forerunner; in fact, many passages from the writings of Freud would lead one to believe that they were taken directly from the writings of Schopenhauer. Henri Bergson's concept of *élan vital* (vital impulse), intuition, teleology, and the intellect was most likely influenced by Schopenhauer. Unquestionably, much of the philosophical thinking of Nietzsche is Schopenhauerian inspired, as well as Eduard von Hartmann and Hans Vaihinger's *Philosophy of As If*.

Schopenhauer suffered a number of unfortunate experiences which affected his personality; for some of them he was directly responsible, other unhappy and tragic occurrences were in no way due to him. His neurotic personality rendered him incapable of loving nor was he himself a lovable personality; unmarried, he had a dog as his one true friend. He referred to himself as not having a "milk and water" nature; his disposition was egotistical, suspicious, childish, passionate, and lacking generosity and magnanimity. The story is told of his mother's ejecting him down a flight of stairs so that she could be alone with her lover; another is told of his scheduling his lectures at Heidelberg, where the popular Hegel taught philosophy, during the same hours when Hegel held his own classes. He fancied that if anyone could come under his tutelege he would never consider studying with Hegel, but as it turned out he was forced to resign his first semester since no one signed up for his courses. Being a *Privatdocent*, his salary was gained from the fees of students registered for his classes, but Hegel needed none as he assumed the coveted chair of professor. His rivalry with Hegel had other facets; as a direct slur against Hegel, he proclaimed that there were no great philosophers since the time of Kant except himself. When his classic work: *The World as Will and Idea* was neither read not purchased due to famine and poverty that had gripped Europe, Schopenhauer claimed that the indifference paid his book was attributable to a conspiracy of silence led by the professors of philosophy whom he derogatorily called "philosophers by trade." However, two years before his death, his efforts as an able philosopher were vindicated, the famine had ended, the world atmosphere was optimistic and could afford the reading of pessimistic literature, and his books became bestsellers.

There are several complications in the philosophy of pessimism which Schopenhauer left unresolved. Two pertain to desire: (a) If reality is desire, as Schopenhauer claims it is, then there can be no escape or salvation from its clutches for who can escape from reality, except by psychoses. (b) The annihilation of desire is an inescapable paradox, which leads to one's being caught in a condition of desiring to escape desire.

DeWitt H. Parker perceptibly notes: "Schopenhauer saw more clearly than any one before him the intimate connection between art and pain, and art's liberating function. But Schopenhauer was wrong in thinking that art liberates by ridding us of desire; for it is rather by giving a new, imaginative form to desire that art frees us, not from desire, itself, but from its burdensomeness."[40]

The most serious objection is Schopenhauer's pessimistic conclusions which are drawn from premises which would permit non-pessimistic ones. He condemns desire as misery, but desire is often pleasurable; in fact, desirable anticipation of a new occupation, vacation, new home, etc., is often more enjoyable than its realization. Striving often is not only pleasurable, but it is a most effective drive in making progress, both individual and social; furthermore, the satisfaction that ensues from such efforts is most rewarding and pleasing.

7. Further Reading in the Philosophy of Schopenhauer

The following list of Schopenhauer's works are listed in chronological order: *On the Fourfold Root of the Principle of Sufficient Reason* (1788) *On Vision and Colors* (1813), *The World as Will and Idea* (1818), *On the Will in Nature* (1836), *The Basis of Morality* (1840) *The Two Main Problems of Ethics* (1841), *Parerga and Paralipomena* (1851).

NOTES

ARTHUR SCHOPENHAUER

1. Arthur Schopenhauer, *The World as Will and Idea*, tr. by R. B. Haldane and J. Kemp (London: Trubner and Co., 1883), Bk. III, Ch. 38.
2. *Idem.*
3. *Idem.*
4. *Idem.*
5. *Ibid.*, Bk. III, Ch. 52.
6. *Ibid.*, Bk. IV, Ch. 54.
7. *Ibid.*, Bk. III, Ch. 38.
8. *Ibid.*, Supplement, 44, "The Metaphysics of Love and the Sexes."
9. *Ibid.*, Bk. IV, Ch. 58.
10. *Idem.*
11. *Idem.*
12. *Ibid.*, Bk. IV., Ch. 63.
13. *Idem.*
14. Cf. St. Augustine and St. Thomas who maintain that evil is the privation of good.
15. Arthur Schopenhauer, "On the Sufferings of the World" from *Studies in Pessimism*, tr. by T. Bailey Saunders (London: George Allen and Unwin Ltd., 1890).
16. *Idem.*
17. *Idem.*
18. *Idem.*
19. *Idem.*
20. Arthur Schopenhauer, "The Vanity of Existence," *ibid.*
21. *Idem.*
22. *Idem.*
23. Op. cit., *The World as Will and Idea*, Bk. IV, Ch. 54.
24. *Idem.*
25. *Idem.*
26. *Idem.*
27. *Ibid.*, Bk. IV, Ch. 57.
28. *Ibid.*, Bk. IV, Ch. 65.
29. *Ibid.*, Bk. IV, Ch. 68.
30. *Idem.*
31. *Idem.*
32. Cf. Goethe's *Faust.*
33. *Ibid.*, Bk. IV, Ch. 71.
34. *Idem.*
35. *Idem.*
36. Arthur Schopenhauer, *The Basis of Morality*, tr. By Arthur Brodrick Bullock (London: Swan Sonnenschein and Co., Ltd., 1903), 170.
37. *Ibid.*, 172, 173.
38. Op. cit., *The World as Will and Idea*, Bk. IV, Ch. 66.
39. Op. cit., *The Basis of Morality*, 264.
40. DeWitt H. Parker, ed., *Schopenhauer Selections* (New York: Charles Scribner's Sons, 1928), XXV.

SOREN KIERKEGAARD

I am Janus bifrons; I laugh with one face, I weep with the other.

My sorrow is my castle.

Had I to crave an inscription on my grave I would ask for none other than "the individual."   (Kierkegaard)

1. Dialectical Ethics

Soren Kierkegaard,[1] "the great parentheses" and "the father of existentialism," propounded the following ideas: (1) an ethics of *pessimism;* (2) *eternity* supercedes time in importance; (3) the preference of *suffering over sin;* (4) man, an egoist by nature, is regenerated through *despair;* (5) reason results in paradox; truth is found in *paradox;* (6) *three* stages of the ethical *dialectic*: (a) aesthetic, (b) ethical, (c) religious; (7) only the subjective *individual* exists; (8) truth is *subjectivity;* (9) God is beyond man and his rational power; (10) the Christian ethic is realizable only in eternity; (11) *purity of heart* is to will one thing, viz., the good in truth; (12) *self-realizationism, i.e.,* the transformation of potentialities into actualities; (13) life confronts one with an either/or *choice* from which there is no escape or evasion.

The individual matures ethically through a dialectical process of moral growth which begins with the *aesthetic stage,* moves upward to the *ethical stage,* and comes to full fruition in the *religious stage.* Each stage superceded its predecessor, in temporal priority and apparently in ascendency. The first stage of life represents the aesthetic, a life abandoned to hedonistic pursuits or intellectual exercise; the second stage is marked by ethical concern, *i.e.*, self-realization and the relinquishment of pleasure; it is dominated by remorse; the third stage, a transformation of the previous two is the religious and represents the goal of all human striving.

S. K., as Kierkegaard is traditionally known, was a prolific writer of many pseudonymous books, the first of which was *Either/Or,* a verbose work and difficult to read, but whose title became the name by which he was known to the man on the street. The book's provocative title suggests an existential relationship or dialectical situation which maintains between an individual's aesthetic and ethical natures. It was intended to be a polemic against the speculative philosophy of Hegel who taught that the nature of the dialectic is a dynamic movement effected by the principle of negativity proceeding from thesis to antithesis, culminating in a synthesis which represents a reconciliation and combined product of the two plus a new quality or reality which has emerged from the violent clash or conflict of thesis with antithesis. S. K. repudiated the Hegelian synthesis, for to him it represented a *both/and* concept; his contention was that life confronts one with *aut-aut* (either/or) situations only. "What is either/or? — if it is I who must say it who surely must know. Either/or is the word at which the folding doors fly open and the ideals appear — O blessed sight! Either/or is the pass which admits to the absolute — God be praised! Yea, either/or is the key to heaven... Both-and is the way to hell."[2]

Life invariably confronts one with either/or choices, never with both-and; life is fundamentally pessimistic forasmuch as one inevitably chooses wrongly regardless of which horn of the *either/or* disjunction is selected. "Yes, I perceive perfectly that there are two possibilities, one can either do this or that. My sincere opinion and my friendly counsel is as follows: Do it/ or don't do it — you will regret both. . . . Life is a masquerade . . . your occupation consists in preserving your hiding-place . . . your mask is the most enigmatic of all. . . . You yourself are nothing, an enigmatic figure on whose brow is inscribed Either/or — 'For this,' you say, 'is my motto, and these words are not, as the grammarians believe, disjunctive conjunctions; no they belong inseparably together and therefore ought to be written as one word, inasmuch as in their union they constitute an interjection which I shout at mankind'."[3]

A moral decision, *i.e.*, achieving right results, is an impossibility for truth is subjectivity or *inwardness;* its sole value is one of decisive edification for the subject. Truth is essentially different from all "objective knowledge," but this does not mean that truth is subjective, *i.e.*, a matter of opinion, it means that *subjectivity is true,* i.e., the subject is true; the individual subject together with all of his feelings, pathos, inner experiences is true. "Ask yourself, and continue to ask until you find the answer. For one may have known a thing many times and acknowledged it, and yet it is only by the deep inward movements, only by the indescribable emotions of the heart, that for the first time you are convinced that what you have known belongs to you, that no power can take it from you; for only the truth which edifies is truth for you.'"[4]

Inasmuch as subjectivity or existence is reality, one must take his existential possibilities and make them genuinely exist, *posse* must become *esse, i.e.,* existential possibility must break through to existence, not merely tend toward existence; melancholy is its essential characteristic quality. The aestheticist who is a superior thinker and dialectician "endowed with all the seductive gifts of soul and understanding" is occupied with objective systems of thought or the fulfillment of pleasure and seeks existence via these means. The ethicist who differs from the aestheticist in his belief that "it is every man's duty to reveal himself" attains an ethical victory over concealment, melancholy, illusory passion, and despair through truth, viz., *existential inwardness.* The either/or decision is reducible to two diverse philosophies of life: (a) the aesthetic which teaches that the better way of life is one of intellectual endeavor, *i.e.*, understanding the world and life by intellectual systems, viz., science and philosophy, or the pursuit of pleasure and enjoyment; (b) the ethical which consists in self-realization. S. K. is noncommittal as to the preferred choice; each individual is confronted with choice and must choose for himself. Although S. K. declines to make a choice for the reader, he does comment on the merits of each and their common values. He notes that the merit of the book consists essentially "in not giving any result, but in transforming everything into inwardness: in the first part [aesthetic], an imaginative inwardness which evokes the possibilities with intensified passion, with sufficient dialectical power to transform into nothing in despair; in the second part, an ethical pathos, which with a quiet, incorruptible, and yet infinite passion of resolve embraces the modest ethical task, and edified thereby stands self-revealed before God and man."[5] The ethicist effects his salvation through despair by "abolishing concealment in self-realization," *i.e.*, by psychoanalyzing himself. The ethical self is found in despair, "so that the individual by persisting in his despair at last wins himself. He has indeed used a determination of freedom: to choose himself.[6] . . . When I despair, I use myself to despair, and therefore I can indeed by myself despair of everything; but when I do this, I cannot by myself come back. In this moment of decision it is that the individual needs divine assistance, while it is quite right to say that one must first have understood the existential relationship between the aesthetic and the ethical in order to be at this point; that is to say, by being there in passion and inwardness one will doubtless become aware of the religious — and of the *leap*. . . . The ethicist had with the passion of the infinite in the moment of despair chosen himself out of the fearful plight of having his self, his life, his reality, in aesthetic dreams, in melancholy, in concealment.'"[7]

Edification of the truth as *inwardness* is produced by the "necessary adequate *fear,* otherwise the edification is reduced to an illusion. . . . Whoever has had the inwardness enough to lay hold of the ethical with infinite passion, and to understand the eternal validity of duty and the universal, for him there can neither in heaven or on earth or in hell be found so fearful a plight, as when he faces a collision where the ethical becomes the temptation,"[8] *i.e.*, becomes a hindrance rather than an aid to the individual's revelation, by advancing one's own cause without at the same time advancing the ethical welfare of others. There are no compass directions to inwardness, but tension is a measure of the intensity of inwardness; there in the inner abyss of inwardness, fear and trembling are most fearsome.

2. Either/Or

"My friend, What I have so often said to you I say now once again, or rather I shout it: Either/or, *aut/aut.*"[9] Life confronts one with a choice: either live *ethically* or *aesthetically;* either choice that is made will be regretted. To himself man is enigmatic, his nature is essentially one of anxiety, but the paradox or irony is that he finds delight in the dread of others. Either/or is not a complete dilemma since the object of one's choice is always the same, viz., *good*. The either/or that is posited is not a choice between good and evil for one always chooses the good; it constitutes a choice between the manner in which the good is pursued, *i.e.*, whether the mode of approach is aesthetical or ethical. "People are not so completely depraved as really to desire evil, but they are blinded and do not really know what they are doing."[10] And on the other hand, people have not sufficient moral fiber to practice Christian ethics. "Most people really believe that the Christian commandments (*e.g.*, to love one's neighbor as oneself) are intentionally a little too severe—like putting the clock on half an hour to make sure of not being late in the morning."[11] In contradistinction to the aesthetical, frugality is characteristic of the ethical whose maxim is *nil ad ostentationem, omnia ad conscientiam* (nothing for appearance, everything for conscience).

By choice the finite personality is made infinite, and by freedom he "infinitely chooses himself." Objective distinctions between good and evil do not exist; one cannot think under the rubric of good and evil because it exists as subject only. "The good *is* for the fact that I will it, and apart from my willing it, it has no existence. This is the expression for freedom. It is so also with evil, it is only when I will it. . . . The good is the *an-und-fur-sich-Seiende* when I will it. . . . The good is the *an-und-für-sich-Seiende* posited by the *an-und-für-sich-Seiende* (being in and of itself), both good and evil. That man is essentially evil is evidenced by the fact he needs to express repentance. Although man is both good and evil, and some men may find themselves more evil than good, this does not mean that they must be resigned to evil and allow it to take its course, but rather one should repress the evil and allow the good to pour forth. There remains much good in every man and he is deserving of commendation for the fact that in spite of his many qualifications for becoming bad, nevertheless he became good. "Everyone can be a good man who wills it, but it always requires talent to be bad, *e.g.*, to be evil requires a fair or good measure of intelligence, but to be virtuous such as being humble, one need only will it."

The ethical person has a formula for conquering the temptations of passion: *"This instant I will not do it, in an hour I will;"* the inference is that in an hour one will have escaped the temptation, and should its force still linger the formula may be repeated.

He who lives ethically does not annihilate mood, he takes it for an instant into consideration, but this instant saves him from living the moment, this instant gives him mastery over the lust for pleasure, for the art of mastering lust consists not so much in annihilating it, or entirely renouncing it, as in determining the instant. Take whatever lust you will, the secret of it, the power in it consists in the fact that it is absolutely in the moment. One often hears people say that the only remedy is for one to abstain from it entirely. This is a very wrong method, which also can be successful only for a short time. Imagine a man who is addicted to gambling. Lust awakens

> with all its passion, it is as if his life were in jeopardy if the lust were not satisfied. If he is capable of saying to himself, "*This instant I will not do it, in an hour I will,*" he is cured. This hour is the continuity which saves him.... When a man lives ethically his mood is centralized, he is not moody, he is not in a mood, but he has mood and he has mood in himself. What he labors for is continuity, and this is always master over mood. His life does not lack mood, yea, it has total mood; but this is acquired, it is what one might call *equale temperamentum* (equable temperament), but this is not aesthetic mood, and no one has it by nature or immediately.[13]

The man who through a measure of success and self-control has been sufficiently blessed in achieving the foregoing must not revel in the thought lest such pride prove his downfall. He should choose himself with *freedom,* not aesthetically, *i.e.,* out of necessity, or else he will discover that "like Narcissus he has fallen in love with himself." One must by choice divest himself of the hero's dress, *i.e.,* like a tragic hero take delight in his pain and suffering; he must not be proud of his sufferings, but should feelingly confess: "I am the humbled man, conscious of my guilt, I have only one expression for my pain . . . repentance one hope before my eyes . . . forgiveness, and if I find this difficult, ah, I have only one prayer, I would cast myself upon the ground and implore and . . . repent."[14] In this manner one gives sorrow an ethical expression and masters sorrow ethically, *i.e.,* sorrow is neither rejected nor forgotten, it is repented, eventuating in the loss of its beguiling power. Aesthetic tears alone, *i.e.,* to sorrow with feeling, but ignoring the ethical steps necessary is of little avail inasmuch as one has failed to choose himself. "Choosing oneself is identical with repenting oneself; for repentance puts the individual in the most intimate connection and the most exact cohesion with a surrounding world."[15]

Mysticism is a practice that ought to be eschewed for numerous reasons: (1) very little of the mystic's life is ethically determined; (2) mystical experiences render one dead to the world; (3) he develops a disdain for reality which God created for him; (4) the mystic's life is a deceit against the world and an evasion of obligations; (5) he has chosen without right the solitary life and divorces himself from mankind; (6) he repents metaphysically, not ethically (metaphysical repentance is ill-timed superfluity). Mysticism is a subset of aestheticism.

The aesthete is confronted with the dilemma: "to be/or not to be," and his condition is aggravated by the fact that his mounting needs and desires remain unfulfilled, consequently he is as good as dead. "Suicide is the negative form of infinite freedom. It is a form of the infinite freedom, but the negative form. Hail to him who finds the positive form."[16] However the man who lives ethically can endure the broodings of the darkest storms because he is anchored fast to "his self," but should the ethicist indulge in mere gymnastic experimentation in the realm of knowledge then he ceases to live ethically and is reduced to sophistry.

The ethical individual's success is attributable to his willingness to be *transparent, i.e.,* "know thyself" as Socrates taught, be thoroughly acquainted with one's motives, both conscious and subconscious, know every area of one's personality including the most secret resources of the mind. To be transparent is to be psychologically naked before oneself, one's God, and others; "one becomes the normal man by becoming utterly stark naked." The principal difference and decisive factor in distinguishing the ethical individual from the aesthetic is that of transparency and the fact that the ethicist does not live *ins Blaue hinein;* the ethicist has undergone a thorough psychological self-analysis. "He who lives ethically has seen himself, knows himself, penetrates with his consciousness his whole concretion, does not allow indefinite thoughts to potter about within him, nor tempting possibilities to distract him with their jugglery; he is not like a witch's letter from which one sense can be got now and then another, depending upon how one turns it. He knows himself. The expression *gnothi seauton* (know thyself) has been repeated often enough and in it has been seen the goal of all human endeavor. The ethical individual knows himself ... it is a reflection upon himself which itself is an action, and therefore I have deliberately preferred to use the expression 'choose oneself' instead of know oneself. ... This self which the individual knows is at once the actual self and the ideal self. ... Only within him has the individual the goal after which he has to strive.'"[17]

The ethical person recognizes duties as residing within the personality; he is clad in duty since it is the expression of his inmost nature. One who has oriented himself to this concept of duty will possess infinite security; otherwise one can encounter an unhappy and agonizing existence in his attempt to cope with or fulfill duties that lie outside himself since this is an impossibility. One must be capable of making fine distinctions between what is essentially and what is accidentally his duty, *i.e.*, distinguish between his true and superficial nature.

The ethical consists in the individual's consciousness of seeking to do good, but if duty were external to the person rather than within then no distinction between good and evil would exist "for in the ethical realm there is never any question about the external but only about the internal. But however much the external may change, the moral content of action may nevertheless remain the same. ... When with all his energy a person has felt the intensity of duty he is then ethically mature.''[18] The multifarious duties with which one is confronted is not of major import, but the total impression of duty, hence one does not have many duties, but only one, viz., duty in earnest. When a man lives ethically, his life acquires beauty, truth, significance, security, and his doubts are set at rest. It is everyone's duty to have a calling, and when one finds his calling, existence becomes beautiful; one's task in life is to do what he is capable of accomplishing, viz., actualize his talents. "It is very dangerous to go into eternity with possibilities which one has oneself prevented from becoming realities. A possibility is a hint from God. One must follow it.'"[119] Furthermore it becomes one's duty to be a friend and to acquire friends; finally it is a duty to become *revealed*.

3. Purity of Heart

Purity of heart is to will one thing, viz., the willing of the good in truth, i.e., one's choice must be in simplicity, with singlemindedness and without dissimulation of spirit. Purity of heart is assisted by "eternity's emissaries to man," viz., *remorse, repentance,* and *confession,* but one may encounter deterrents such as *double-mindedness,* enticement, *e.g., reward,* discouragement provoked by *illness,* intimidation, *e.g., punishment,* and other ulterior motives. The manifold cost of willing one thing is complete commitment and loyalty to the service of the good, sacrificial suffering without evasiveness. The task of him who would will only one thing is attentiveness to duty, living as an individual, the search and pursuit of one's occupation or calling, and assuming a right relationship with God.

Kierkegaard dedicates his book: *Purity of Heart* to "that solitary individual" (*hiin Enkelte*) who alone can achieve purity of heart by *willing one thing,* viz., the good in truth. Man has been alienated from God by sin, consequently he is unable to *will one thing* until through grief and anxiety, a reconciliation is effected. The resulting atonement will give the "victory in the day of need so that what neither a man's burning wish nor his determined resolution may attain to, may be granted unto him in the sorrowing of repentance: to will only one thing."[20] Man's efforts will prove futile in the attempt to *will one thing* unless accompanied by remorse, repentance, confession, these "three emissaries of eternity;" repentance and remorse with their concomitants fear and trembling should be exercised regularly as proper guides to willing of one thing.

One impediment to willing one thing is boredom or more precisely the craving of variety; such persons are hopelessly entangled with pleasures which are incapable of satisfaction. "For such a man wills first one thing and then immediately wills the opposite, because the oneness of pleasure is a snare and a delusion. It is the diversity of pleasures that he wills. So when the man of whom we are speaking had gratified himself up to the point of disgust, he became weary and sated. Even if he still desired one thing — what was it that he desired? He desired new pleasures; his enfeebled soul raged so that no ingenuity was sufficient to discover something new — something new! It was change he cried out for as pleasure served him, change! change! And it was change he cried out for as he came to pleasure's limit, as his servants were worn out — change! change!"[21]

If a man is to *will one thing* then he must will the good in truth, not for reward since this stems from double-mindedness; the good is one thing, but reward is another, hence the man who wills for the sake of reward wills two things, viz., the good and reward. *"Therefore, if it be possible for a man to will one thing, then he must will the Good, for only the Good is one. Thus if it becomes a fact that he wills one thing, he must will the Good in truth,"*[22] and not for an ulterior motive.

There exists a number of barriers to *willing one thing*; fear of punishment is accounted one, inasmuch as good is one thing and fear of punishment is a second, resulting in double-mindedness. It is proper that one should fear to do wrong, but this is not to be confused with fear of punishment which is a slavish state of mind. "Therefore — if there were no punishment! In that 'if' lurks double-mindedness. If there were no punishment! In that 'if' hisses double-mindedness. ... Only one thing can help a man to will the Good in truth: the Good itself."[23]

Another obstacle to *willing one thing* is the "desire to score a victory" which is motivated out of willfulness or self-centeredness, hence double-mindedness. "The double-minded man stands at a parting of the ways, and sees there two apparitions: the Good, and the Good in its victory, or even in its victory through him. ... In eternity they are the same, but not in time. And they must be kept apart."[24] Another barrier is committing oneself to the good only up to a certain degree, *e.g.*, hesitancy and reluctancy imply doublemindedness, hence disturb the unity within the individual. One must have complete commitment to truth, not a conviction that is subject to vacillation from one moment to another.

Commitment, loyalty, readiness to suffer all, exposure to evasions, and assent to suffering is the price involved in *willing one thing;* this calls for sincerity, devotion, and a willingness to sacrifice and suffer in its behalf, otherwise one will be distracted, dissuaded, irresolute, and indecisive in willing one thing. "Not in that commitment by which he is exempted from suffering, but that by which he remains intimately bound to God, in which he wills only one thing; namely, to suffer all, to be and to remain loyally committed to the Good."[25] One must willingly accept forced suffering, for herein is freedom found; he must display that courage which voluntarily accepts inescapable suffering. The imprisoned individual must be capable of saying: "Of my own free will I accept my imprisonment." "When a man dares declare, 'I am eternity's free citizen,' necessity cannot imprison him, except in voluntary confinement."[26] Purity of heart is comparable to the purity of the sea; the purity of each depends on its constancy in depth and transparency; in this state a pure heart can weather life's vicissitudes and yearns for the good, hence wills but one thing. As the pure sea reflects the heavens, so does the pure heart.

Willing one thing requires that a person live as an *individual, i.e.*, be himself for each man is accountable for himself alone. The person of high station, *e.g.*, a king, or a person of low estate, *e.g.*, a beggar, each will be judged as an individual; each must render to eternity an accounting through the voice of conscience as to what he has done of good or evil. A complete accounting will include the use of one's talents, *i.e.*, the fulfillment of his calling because "at each man's birth there comes into being an eternal vocation for him, expressly for him. To be true to himself in relation to this eternal vocation is the highest thing a man can practice, and, as that most profound poet has said: 'Self-love is not so vile a sin as self-neglecting.' Then there is but one fault, one offense: disloyalty to his own self or the denial of his own better self."[27]

One must find his calling, *i.e.*, his life's occupation; it is irrelevant to question whether it is majestic or prosaic, of great prestige or menial, or the nature of the financial remunerations since these are trivial considerations and must be discarded; the major issue is: "*In your occupation, what is your attitude of mind? And how do you carry out your occupation?*" The means too are accounted as important as the end, otherwise it would be impossible to *will one thing*. "Eternally speaking there is only one means and there is only one end: the means and the end are one and the same thing. There is only one end: the genuine Good; and only one means: this, to be willing only to use those means which genuinely are good — but the genuine Good is precisely the end."[28] One is eternally responsible for the nature of the means he employs and must select the only proper one, viz., that which is genuinely good, lest he stand under the judgment of eternity. The means and goal are both important and the relationship of one to the other may be depicted as a target and the aim taken; in the simile, the goal is like hitting the bull's-eye and the means analogous to taking aim. Furthermore in respect to conscience, the means invariably is of equal importance to the end.

In the final judgment, each is accountable as an individual, not as a member of a society or group. "For in eternity there is not the remotest thought of any common plight. In eternity, the individual, yes, you, my listener, and I as individuals will each be asked solely about himself as an individual and about the individual details in his life."[29] The reason being that only the individual can will the good and only the individual is capable of evil, hence purity of heart by willing only one thing belongs to an individual's existence. Accordingly, one's prayer should be: "give to the intellect, wisdom to comprehend that one thing; to the heart, sincerity to receive this understanding; to the will, purity that wills only one thing."[30]

4. The Individual

No concept in the philosophy of Kierkegaard is more prominently emphasized than *the individual,* in fact he goes to the extent of saying: "Had I to crave an inscription on my grave I would ask for none other than 'the individual'."[31] All truth, all morality (good and evil), all existence resides in *the individual;* although heretofore neglected by scholars it is a category through which the history of civilization must pass.

The Kierkegaardian concept of *the individual* is an antithetical reaction to the Hegelian thesis: *die Wahrheit ist die Ganze* (the truth is the whole), *i.e.,* the more complete the reality, the greater the truth, *e.g.,* the individual finds his reality in the social, and in turn society finds its reality in the absolute. In Hegelian thought the individual loses his reality when isolated from society; the individual can perform no nobler deed than to sacrifice his life in the interests of society's survival. S. K. emphatically repudiates the Hegelian thesis, supplanting it with the antithesis that the true or the real is the individual; the social is false, deceptive, misleading. His disdain for the crowd, *i.e.,* society breaks forth with unfailing regularity with hostile words such as: "For many fools do not make a wise man, and the crowd is doubtful recommendation for a cause."[32]

In the light of eternity one is not judged in a group, but individually; furthermore eternity does not consider the crowd important, only the individual. "Eternity . . . never counts. The individual is always one and conscience in its meticulous ways concerns itself with the individual. In eternity you will look in vain for the crowd. . . . In eternity you will be forsaken by the crowd. And this is terrifying."[33] The individual is not morally responsible for the actions of society, but only for his own, hence he must be eternally vigilant lest he be seduced by the crowd; "you will be asked only whether you may not have ruined the best within you by joining the crowd."[34] The individual must alienate himself from the group so that he may act decisively; decisive action is imperative if moral regeneration is to be effected. "Once a man acts in a decisive sense and comes out into reality, existence can get a grip on him and providence educate him."³⁵ The "university of providence" will school a man who is *decisive* and virile, but is at enmity with those who are of an effeminate disposition, they must remain content at being autodidact. On this point S. K. complains that he has not been understood since the bias of the times was completely under the unyielding dominance of the Hegelian influence, viz., the identification of evil with "isolated subjectivity," and its concomitant condemnation as pure negativity. But *isolated individuality* is not to be shunted aside, truth is found by piercing subjectivity through to *the individual,* a technique employed by all great heroes. "Take Socrates for instance! In those days one sophist after another came forward and showed that the misfortune was the lack of sufficient knowledge, more and more research was necessary, the evil was ignorance — and then along came old father Socrates saying: no, it is precisely ignorance which is our salvation. . . . He was looked upon as representing evil; for, in the eyes of the age, ignorance was evil. . . . It is perfectly true, isolated subjectivity is, in the opinion of the age, evil; but 'objectivity' as a cure is not one whit better. The only salvation is subjectivity."³⁶ Hence it is necessary for a man "a la Socrates," to be taught by historical fact, if he would have recourse to eternal happiness. Scientific inquiry and research would be the wrong technique since one cannot be helped directly, "and so I say to myself: I choose; that historical fact means so much to me that I decide to stake my whole life upon that if. Then he lives; lives entirely full of the idea, risking his life for it: and his life is the proof that he believes. . . . That is called risking. . . . *To be related to spirit means to undergo a test.*"³⁷ Cowardly and effeminate natured persons cannot comprehend this because they do not want to understand it; they prefer to permit someone else to undergo the risk, then follow when assured of its safety.

Hegel, completely ignoring *the individual* by subordinating him to the race has produced "a race of animals gifted with reason," but *the individual,* not society, is created in the image of God, hence in Hegelian thought the individual has been pre-empted from his rightful position.

The individual, as an individual, not as a member of society is responsible for making his own choices; furthermore, it is imperative that he make his choice with the freedom granted him by virtue of the fact that he is an individual. In a sense he has no choice for he is morally compelled to choose one thing; "consequently, the very fact that in this case there is no choice expresses the tremendous passion or intensity with which it must be chosen. ... You shall choose the one essential thing but in such a way that there is no question of a choice — if you drivel any longer then you do not in fact choose the one essential thing. ... However astonishing it may seem, one is therefore obliged to say that only 'fear and trembling,' only constraint, can help a man to freedom. Because 'fear and trembling' and compulsion can master him in such a way that there is no longer any question of choice — and then one chooses the right thing. At the hour of death most people choose the right thing."[38]

The greatest gift bequeathed to man is *freedom, i.e.,* choice, and the only manner of its preservation is to return it to its Author together with oneself. Freedom is lost once it is imbued with egoistic desire and temptation, and the punishment meted for such is a form of confusion emanating from the *pride* of possessing the power of freedom; once terminated, *e.g.,* by loss, it may be redeemed only through intense grief. "Freedom really only *exists* because the same instant it (freedom of choice) exists it rushes with infinite speed to bind itself unconditionally by choosing resignation, the choice of which it is true that in it there is no question of a choice."[39] If one is overly preoccupied with the power of his freedom of choice so that it becomes an *idée fixe*, instead of making choices he forfeits both freedom and freedom of choice, both of which are redeemable only through deep "fear and trembling." The best cure for *idée fixe* is to treat it as one does "a cramp in the foot — stamp on it."

The majority of persons has never found true existence, never discovered genuine subjectivity; they are "curtailed 'I's'; what was planned by nature as a possibility capable of being sharpened into an I is soon dulled into a third person. It is a very different thing to have an objective relation to one's own subjectivity."⁴⁰ Socrates attained the technique of assuming a proper objective attitude towards himself when facing dangers, *e.g.*, when he was condemned to die he related his condemnation as though he were a third person. "The majority of men are subjective towards themselves and objective towards all others, terribly objective sometimes — but the real task is in fact to be objective towards oneself and subjective towards all others."⁴¹ Like Socrates, S. K.'s earnest petition was to bring people to their senses so they neither squander nor dissipate their lives. The aristocrats have abandoned the masses as a lost hope "but I do not want that. I wish to make men aware of their own ruin. And if they will not listen to good then I will compel them through evil ... I do not mean that I am going to strike them ... I mean to make them strike me. And in that way I all the same compel them through evil ... I shall have won an absolute victory. In that respect I am completely dialectical. ... People are not so completely depraved as really to desire evil, but they are blinded and do not really know what they are doing."⁴²

Individualism vs. pantheism; these two are diametrically opposed rival concepts, "but 'the individual' is and remains the anchor in the confusion of Pantheism, the hellebore which can sober people ... I bind myself to make every man whom I can include in the category 'the individual.' ... As 'that individual' he is alone, alone in the whole world, alone — before God."⁴³ Pantheism is an "optical illusion" whose accidental birth is produced by a random temporal existence: it is a view that cannot be taught and its practice is dangerous, but "the individual," a concept first introduced by Socrates in a dialectical and decisive manner, is effective in producing inward changes and disintegrating paganism.

5. The Self, Freedom, and Will

The self is a synthesis composed of infinity and finiteness; this synthetic relationship signifies freedom, *i.e.*, it relates itself to itself dialectically in terms of possibility and necessity. Awareness of despair makes consciousness decisive, *i.e.*, "consciousness of self, is the decisive criterion of the self. The more consciousness, the more will, and the more will the more self. A man who has no will at all is no self; the more will he has, the more consciousness of self he has also."[44] Consequently, the self is a conscious synthesis and whose objective it is to "become itself;" an accomplishment that is possible only through relating oneself to God. However, to reach selfhood necessitates concretion, not finiteness nor infinitude, but a synthesis. The self must realize itself or face despair. "A self, every instant it exists, is in process of becoming, for the self potentially does not actually exist, it is only that which it is to become. In so far as the self does not become itself, it is not its own self; but not to be one's own self is despair."[45]

That the self as a synthesis of two factors is an inherent dialectical fact for despair cannot be defined undialectically, *i.e.*, directly, but only in terms of its antithesis. Consequently, the will to become infinite issues in despair. "The self is in sound health and free from despair only when, precisely by having been in despair, it is founded transparently in God,"[46] *i.e.*, a thorough psychoanalysis of self by self.

One projects into infinity or engages in the process of infinitizing through the medium of the imagination which is the faculty for all faculties. "The self is reflection, and imagination is reflection, it is the counterfeit presentment of the self, which is the possibility of the self. Imagination is the possibility of all reflection, and the intensity of this medium is the possibility of the intensity of the self."[47] One may exist without noticing that he has or is a self, *i.e.*, he can occupy himself with routine and mundane tasks, work, marry, rear a family and never become aware that in a deep and significant sense, he lacks a self. "The greatest danger, that of losing one's own self, may pass off as quietly as if it were nothing; every other loss, that of an arm, a leg, five dollars, a wife, etc., is sure to be noticed.... 'That a sparrow can live is comprehensible; it does not know anything about existing before God. But to know that one exists before God — and then not to go crazy or be brought to naught!'"[48]

There is a type of despair related to finitude which is due to the lack of infinitude, *i.e.*, becoming completely socialized by falling into the customs and manners of society so that one has "deprived oneself of one's primitiveness; it consists of having emasculated oneself, in a spiritual sense."[49] One may become so excessively socialized that he loses all individuality, he is reduced to an amorphous being with "no understanding of the narrowness and meanness of mind which is exemplified in having lost one's self — not by evaporation in the infinite, but by being entirely finitized, by having become, instead of a self, a number, just one man more, one more repetition of this everlasting *Einerlei*."[50] Although it is one's birthright to become a self, some have given it up entirely by becoming lost in the currents of society eventuating in despair. "But while one sort of despair plunges wildly into the infinite and loses itself, a second sort permits itself as it were to be defrauded by 'the others.' By seeing the multitude of men about it, by getting engaged in all sorts of worldly affairs, by becoming wise about how things go in this world, such a man forgets himself, forgets what his name is, does not dare to believe in himself, finds it too venturesome a thing to be himself, far easier and safer to be like the others, to become an imitation, a number, a cipher in the crowd."[51] Although a victim of the foregoing circumstances suffers despair, it usually passes unnoticed, *i.e.*, the individual is not conscious of his plight, *e.g.*, a successful business man goes through life unperturbed and ignorant of his precarious condition. "Here there is no hindrance, no difficulty, occasioned by his self and his infinitization, he is ground smooth as a pebble, *courant* as a well-used coin."[52] As is evidenced here the average man lives his life out without any inkling of what is truly dreadful; such persons undergo despair, but suffer no embarrassment or discomfort for this mode of despair is not countenanced as such by society. "But he who knows what the dreadful is, must for this very reason be most fearful of every fault, of every sin, which takes an inward direction and leaves no outward trace. So it is too that in the eyes of the world it is dangerous to venture. And why? Because one may lose. But not to venture is shrewd. And yet, by not venturing, it is so dreadfully easy to lose that which it would be difficult to lose in even the most venturesome venture, and in any case never so easily, so completely as if it were nothing . . . one's self."[53] To follow the ways of the world, to become lost anonymously in the crowd is to pawn oneself to the world, but all this must be done at the sacrificial cost of going without a self — "however *selfish* they may be for all that."

6. Evaluation of the Ethics of Kierkegaard

This is unquestionably the most difficult philosopher the reader has encountered; it is due to a complexity of factors: (1) Kierkegaard's style of writing and grammar leave much to be desired; some of his translators have been thrown into a quandary ruminating as to whether to translate his grammar as written or to give it the polish it desperately needs. (2) The dialectical method entails antithetical concepts, antinomies, and paradoxes that are seemingly incompatible logically, consequently are difficult to manipulate intellectually. (3) It is difficult to cope with the dynamic approach which delves into the depths of the subconscious and the irrational regions of the personality.

Not only is his form laden with difficulties but the content also has its coarse features; the three major being: his *pessimistic* emphasis, his undue *depreciation of society*, his extreme emphasis on the *irrational*. Granted that Hegel overemphasized the role of society in his philosophy, this in no way serves as a call for S. K. to veer to the other extreme with an attitude of total indifference and even hostility towards the social. Interpersonal relations unquestionably account for some measure of moral significance, such as Dewey and a number of the other philosophers aptly discerned. Even if the individual stands alone before God, as S. K. contends, even in this relationship he must explain his involvements, *i.e.*, his activities which had to take place in a society — not in a vacuum.

His weighty emphasis on pessimistic qualities of life, such as dread, sorrow, despair, anxiety, fear, trembling, remorse, guilt, etc., is to overplay realism to the extent of evidencing a neurotic and sick mind; that S. K. was neurotic has been long conceded by Kierkegaardian scholars. It may be true that these pessimistic experiences are found in life, and in everyone's life, but they do not characterize the average and normal life to the extent that S. K. and other existentialists have carried the matter. It may be the case temporarily in one's life, but as a permanent trait it is found only with the sufferer of mental, emotional, or nervous illnesses.

Irrationalism is a self-defeating philosophy subject to a *reductio ad absurdum* argument: The irrationalist's attempt to displace reason as the criterion of truth obligates him to employ an *irrational* criterion to attack and defeat reason as a proper test of truth and at the same time utilize this irrational rule to evaluate all other truth. If a person argues that reason cannot uncover truth, but that an irrational rule can, he finds himself in the logically uncomfortable position of either using reason to prove the validity of his irrational rule or principle (which is tantamount to accepting reason as the criterion of truth) or he must attack reason's claim as a valid test of truth by employing irrational methods, *i.e.,* absurdity. DeWolf aptly demonstrates the dilemma confronting the rebel of reason: "Shall he try to be true to his revolutionary profession or not? At every moment when he willingly deviates from it, preferring to abide by the norms of reason in preference to mystery and insoluble paradox, he pays willing tribute to reason and denies his profession. But at every moment when he wills to be faithful to his principle, rejecting logical norms and preferring his paradoxes instead, he is willingly even with stern determination, paying tribute to that very norm which he despises most of all, the norm of logical consistency as guide. . . . Ironically, the rebels who would deny the validity of reason as arbiter . . . are doomed to spend their lives paying voluntary . . . tribute to that selfsame reason."[54] To paraphrase Hobbes: He who puts away reason to make room for anything else, puts out the light of both.

7. Further Reading in the Philosophy of Kierkegaard

The following are Kierkegaard's works which have been translated into English: *The Journals* (1939), *The Concept of Irony, Either/Or* (1944), *Eighteen Edifying Discourses* (1943-44), *Repetition* (1941), *Fear and Trembling* (1939), *Philosophical Fragments* (1936), *The Concept of Dread* (1944), *Three Discourses on Imagined Occasions* (1941), *Stages on Life's Way* (1940), *Concluding Unscientific Postscript to the Philosophical Fragments* (1941), *Edifying Discourses in Various Spirits;* the discourses translated are: *Purity of Heart* (1938), *The Lilies and the Birds* (1941), *The Gospel of Suffering* (1942), *The Present Age* from *A Literary Review* (1940), *The Wars of Love, Christian Discourses* (1939), *Two Minor Ethico-Religious Treatises* included in *The Present Age* (1940), *The Sickness unto Death* (1941), *The High Priest — The Publican — The Woman that Was a Sinner* in *Christian Discourses,* (1940), *The Point of View for My Work as an Author* (1939), *The Individual* (1939), *About My Work as an Author* (1939), *Training in Christianity* (1941), *An Edifying Discourse* (1941), *Two Discourses at the Communion* (1941), *For Self-Examination* (1941), *Judge for Yourself* (1941), *God's Unchangeableness* (1941), *The Attack on "Christendom"* (1944), *On Authority and Revelation* (1955), *Farce is Far More Serious* (1955), *The Gospel of Suffering* (1948), *Johannes Climacus* (1958), *A Personal Confession* (1934), *The Prayers of Kierkegaard* (1956).

NOTES

SOREN KIERKEGAARD

1. The Danish name Kierkegaard is pronounced Su'ren Kir'kegor. "Parentheses" is an expression commonly found in the writings of Kierkegaard.
2. Journals of S. Kierkegaard; quoted in Walter Lowrie, *A Short Life of Kierkegaard* (Princeton: Princeton University Press, 1942), 125.
3. S. Kierkegaard, *Either/Or*, tr. by Walter Lowrie (Princeton: Princeton University Press, 1944, 2 vols.), vol. II, 163, 164.
4. *Ibid.*, 356.
5. S. Kierkegaard, *Concluding Unscientific Postscript*, tr. by David Swenson and Walter Lowrie (Princeton: Princeton University Press, 1944), 227, 228.
6. "To choose oneself" is the Socratic injunction, "know thyself."
7. *Ibid.*, 230, 231.
8. *Ibid.*, 231.
9. *Either/Or*, vol. II, 161.
10. S. Kierkegaard, *Journal*, tr. by Alexander Dru (Oxford: University Press, 1939), 1847 entry.
11. *Ibid.*, 1848 entry.
12. *Either/Or*, vol. II, 228.
13. *Ibid.*, 234, 235.
14. *Ibid.*, 242.
15. *Ibid.*, 245.
16. *Ibid.*, 251.
17. *Ibid.*, 263.
18. *Ibid.*, 269, 270.
19. *Journals*, 1848 entry.
20. S. Kierkegaard, *Purity of Heart is to Will One Thing*, tr. by Douglas V. Steere (New York: Harper and Brothers, 1938), 32.
21. *Ibid.*, 57.
22. *Ibid.*, 68.
23. *Ibid.*, 83, 84.
24. *Ibid.*, 103.
25. *Ibid.*, 159.
26. *Ibid.*, 175.
27. *Ibid.*, 140, the poet Kierkegaard quoted is William Shakespeare (Henry V, Act 2, Scene 4).
28. *Ibid.*, 202.
29. *Ibid.*, 212.
30. *Ibid.*, 218.
31. *Journals*, 1847 entry. He also writes: " 'The individual,' the category which is so wedded to my name that I wish that on my grave might be put 'the individual.' "
32. *Purity of Heart*, 191.

33. *Idem.*
34. *Ibid.*, 190.
35. *Journals*, 1850 entry.
36. *Idem.*
37. *Idem.*
38. *Idem.*
39. *Idem.*
40. *Ibid.*, 1954 entry.
41. *Ibid.*, 1847 entry.
42. *Idem.*
43. *Idem.*
44. S. Kierkegaard, *The Sickness Unto Death*, tr. by Walter Lowrie (Princeton: Princeton University Press, 1941), III.
45. *Ibid.*, III, a.
46. *Ibid.*, III, 1.
47. *Idem.*
48. *Idem.*
49. *Ibid.*, III, 2.
50. *Idem.*
51. *Idem.*
52. *Idem.*
53. *Idem.*
54. L. Harold DeWolf, *The Religious Revolt Against Reason* (New York: Harper and Brothers, 1949), 139, 130.

ETHICAL PRAGMATISM

JOHN DEWEY

The bad man is the man who no matter how good he has been is beginning to deteriorate, to grow less good. The good man is the man who no matter how morally unworthy he has been is moving to become better. Growth itself is the only moral "end."

(Dewey)

1. Ethical Inquiry

Every particular moral situation calls for inquiry in order to determine the right course of action. Mere activity cannot be regarded as morally significant unless deliberation and choice have been exercised prior to carrying out the decision. "A moral situation is one in which judgment and choice are required antecedently to overt action. . . . Hence, inquiry is exacted: observation of the detailed makeup of the situation; analysis into its diverse factors; clarification of what is obscure; discounting the more insistent and vivid traits; tracing the consequences of the various modes of action that suggest themselves; regarding the decision reached as hypothetical and tentative until the anticipated or supposed consequences which led to its adoption have been squared with actual consequences. This inquiry is intelligence."[1]

Inquiry must be brought into play in every moral situation; each situation must be treated in the light of its own peculiar problems, "hence every moral situation is a unique situation having its own irreplaceable good."[2] Consequently, there is no fixed principle or rule applicable to every particular case.

The only good alternative to determine morality in the absence of moral law then is to "follow the pragmatic rule, and in order to discover the meaning of the idea ask for its consequences."[3] This task is accomplished through the use of intelligence "which does not destroy responsibility; it only locates it."[4] Rather than appeal to principle in the deliberation of moral issues, one should place "the initial and final weight upon the individual case, stimulated painstaking inquiry into facts and examination of principles"[5] is needed.

Traditional ethicists have formulated rules or moral principles for resolving complex moral questions or they have suggested "pursuing fixed ends," *i.e.*, the good, but the procedure that should be followed is the "detection of the ills that need remedy in a special case and the formation of plans and methods for dealing with them;"[6] this technique eliminates the causes of controversy in moral theory, and is helpful in bringing moral theory in "contact with exigencies of practice." Moral theory with its stress on values in *general* is of little utility since "action is always specific, concrete, individualized, unique. And consequently judgments as to acts to be performed must be similarly specific."[7] *E.g.*, A person does not seek justice or the ideal of good health in the abstract, but rather in the concrete, *i.e.*, he seeks to live healthily or justly. "These things, like truth, are adverbial. They are modifiers of action in special cases."[8] One is not confronted with moral problems in general, but with specific situations; "not man in general but a particular man suffering" is the nature of human experience. Not health in the abstract, but health in actual human existence is what one seeks.

There are many aims in life, not merely one; the person who pursues but a single goal is a fanatic. There are certain times when one may devote himself to a single aim, and other times when he is cultivating a second, but actively seeking and developing morally such as acquiring health, justice, and artistic culture should never terminate.

Moral science is any science that contributes to uprooting the problems that plague mankind and to alleviating his condition. It is improper to speak of natural and moral science as separate entities; "when physics, chemistry, biology, medicine, contribute to the detection of concrete human woes and to the development of plans for remedying them and relieving the human estate, they become moral; they become part of the apparatus of moral inquiry or science."[9] Natural science becomes humanistic in quality when it does not divorce itself from humanity. Science becomes intellectually indispensable, not when it pursues truth for its own sake, but when it does so with a sense of its "social bearing." "It is technical only in the sense that it provides the technique of social and moral engineering. When the consciousness of science is fully impregnated with the consciousness of human value . . . the split between the material, the mechanical, the scientific and the moral and ideal will be destroyed."[10] The mind must not be content with abstractions. Ends must be related to specific needs and opportunities, and the natural sciences put to social and moral use, if things intellectual are to be moralized and the "vexatious and wasteful conflict between naturalism and humanism" is to be terminated.

"Inquiry, discovery take the same place in morals that they have come to occupy in sciences of nature. Validation, demonstration become experimental, a matter of consequences. Reason, always an honorific term in ethics, becomes actualized in the methods by which the needs and conditions . . . are worked out."[11] Reasoning by way of abstract generalities anticipates nature, *i.e.*, jumps to unwarranted conclusions, whereas the issue should be shifted to the analysis of a specific situation where inquiry becomes "obligatory and alert observation of consequences imperative." Former decisions and old principles become antiquated, hence are unreliable for the determination of a proper course of action. "No amount of pains taken in forming a purpose in a definite case is final; the consequences of its adoption must be carefully noted, and a purpose held only as a working hypothesis until results confirm its rightness. Mistakes are no longer either mere unavoidable accidents to be mourned or moral sins to be expiated and forgiven."[12] Such should be accepted as lessons learned from experience enabling one to know better in a future course of action. They should be recognized as obligations and opportunities for learning and developing; even the finest and the most advanced standards and ideals require revision and improvement. This protects the moral life from stagnation or from falling into formalism and rigid repetition; it is kept "flexible, vital, growing." Accept moral flaws as "indications of the need of revision, development, readjustment;" in this way "ends grow, standards of judgment are improved."[13]

Moral experience lacks logical continuity, *i.e.*, the nature of moral judgments are such that "nothing can be systematically extracted from one of them which is of use in facilitating and guaranteeing the formation of others."[14] Scientific judgments are based upon causation, but logic as used in ethical inquiry is unique in that "to endeavor to control the construction and affirmation of any content of moral judgment by reference to antecedent propositions is to destroy its peculiar moral quality."[15] The reason for this is that ethical inquiry is involved with norms, values and ideals, rather than with facts; the subject matter of ethics is concerned with what *ought* to be, not with what actually *is* the case. Scientific judgments stem from observation and state a set of conditions upon which predictions are possible; moral judgments state purposes of categorical value. "The scientific judgment states a connection of conditions; the moral judgment states the unconditioned claim of an idea to be made real."[16] Although moral judgments are completely individual experiences and must be so treated, this does not in any way diminish their distinctly ethical value. The sharp dichotomy drawn between ethical and scientific judgments is not a valid one for scientific judgments have all of the logical characteristics of the ethical in that they apply to unique and individual cases.

2. Reconstruction of Moral Conceptions

Moral reconstruction must begin with proper forms of ethical inquiry which are capable of coping with specific individual cases, *i.e.*, it provides the necessary tools of inquiry and methods of dealing with specific cases for there are never two exactly alike. The greatest need in ethics is for specific methods of inquiry, *i.e.*, techniques that are capable of locating evils; evils are deficiencies, *i.e.*, ills that call for action so that goods and moral ends can exist. "Experimental logic when carried into morals makes every quality that is judged to be good according as it contributes to amelioration of existing ills."[17]

Reconstruction in morals calls for the abolition of traditional distinctions between moral goods and natural goods, *i.e.*, between virtues, and goods such as health, art, science, etc. Economic goods, for example, should be regarded as intrinsically valuable as other goods for only in this way will social progress prevail over the "brutality of our economic life."

As far as the greatest good is concerned, where the need is greatest, the remedy of it is the greatest good; if two needs are equally great, then both are of equal importance. "Every case where moral action is required becomes of equal importance and urgency with every other. If the need and deficiencies of a specific situation indicate improvement of health as the end and good, then for that situation health is the ultimate and supreme good."[18] The same holds true of the other facets of life, such as one's economic and family welfare, which in traditional ethics were given instrumental status value only. "Anything that in a given situation is an end and good at all is of equal worth, rank and dignity with every other good of any other situation, and deserves the same intelligent attention."[19]

One of the moral concepts that has undergone reconstruction is the problem of evil; it loses its metaphysical significance and acquires practical meaning for it is essentially the very practical problem of alleviating human ills, *i.e.*, reducing or eradicating social and physical evils that plague mankind, viz., "discovering the causes of humanity's ills." Pessimism is an undesirable philosophy for its paralyzing effects render human effort futile, hence "destroys at the root every attempt to make the world better and happier."[20] Wholesale optimism is equally vain since it explains away evil, rather than obliterating it.

Meliorism is the most felicitous attitude one can assume towards the problem of evil for it "encourages intelligence to study the positive means of goods and the obstructions to their realization, and to put forth endeavor for the improvement of conditions."[121] Meliorism inspires the confidence needed to better conditions regardless of their comparative good or bad state at any given moment.

Metaphysics with its emphasis on good as ultimately real has a tendency to treat lightly or ignore everyday evils by which the common man is confronted. It lends itself most readily as a creed to the wealthy and others who are successful to the complete neglect of those who must wrestle with concrete problems, *i.e.*, evils.

Happiness is another moral concept that must undergo reconstruction. "Happiness is not . . . a bare posession; it is not a fixed attainment . . . happiness is found only in success; but success means succeeding, getting forward, moving in advance. It is an active process, not a passive outcome."[122] Moralists have expressed contempt for happiness, but have often replaced it with the idea by another name, *e.g.*, bliss. Goodness without happiness, virtue without satisfaction, and ends without conscious enjoyment are impractical, self-contradictory and intolerable conceptions. Pure happiness as a fixed object of attainment is likewise unsatisfactory, except for the most delicate of "molly-coddles." Such a happiness is selfish, unworthy, and merits only condemnation, but a happiness that is worthwhile is rich in aesthetic sensitiveness and enjoyment.

Nevertheless, Utilitarianism has made the best contribution by way of transition from the classic theories of value to the present for it taught that "institutions are made for man and not man for the institutions;" as well as promoting social reforms, making moral good humane, keeping in touch with life by opposing an other-wordly morality, but it fell short in accepting the idea of a fixed, final, and supreme end. Consequently, Utilitarianism must be reconstructed so that it will be emancipated from its non-instrumentalism.

Moral reconstruction is necessary in education also in that "the educative process is all one with the moral process, since the latter is a continuous passage of experience from worse to better . . . consequently growing, or the continuous reconstruction of experience, is the only end.'"[23] Antiquated modes of education furnished the student with facts for later use, *i.e.*, for adult life; it stressed the acquisition of knowledge for future use, but a person is in a process of growth regardless of his age, hence education is only a by-product of something that is to come late. "Getting from the present the degree and kind of growth there is in it is education. This is a constant function. . . . The heart of the sociality of man is in education. . . . Moral independence for the adult means arrest of growth, isolation means induration.'"[24] The moral responsibility of democracy is to contribute to the complete growth of each member of society.

3. Moral Growth

Moral responsibility is calculated in terms of a person's intellectual ability and learning, hence each person is responsible only to the extent of the light that is within him. The moral responsibility of each person must be judged as a separate case, insmuch as no two people are identical in nature or circumstance. "When one factor of the situation is a person of trained mind and large resources more will be expected than with a person of backward mind and uncultured experience. No individual or group will be judged by whether they come up to or fall short of some fixed result, but by the direction in which they are moving. The bad man is the man who no matter how good he *has* been is beginning to deteriorate, to grow less good. The good man is the man who no matter how morally unworthy he *has* been is moving to become better.'"[25] This method of judging is considerably more humane in respect to others although it may be severe in reference to oneself, at least it diminishes arrogance which stems from censoring others by using the measure of fixed standards.

Moral reconstruction lays heavy stress upon the *process of growth, improvement,* and *progress* in contradistinction to other ethical systems which emphasize the static result of one's efforts only. *E.g.,* health *per se* as a fixed goal is not as significant as the needed improvement in health; "health — a continual process — is the end and good." The important factor is not the ideal, but the "active process of transforming the existent situation. Not perfection as a final goal, but the ever-enduring process of perfecting, maturing, refining is the aim in living."[26] Morality and its values are essentially "*directions of change* in the quality of experience. *Growth itself is the only moral 'end.'* "[27]

4. Value Theory

"*Judgments about values are judgments about the conditions and the results of experienced objects; judgments about that which should regulate the formation of our desires, affections and enjoyments.*"[28] If intelligent judgment does not accompany value decisions, then they will be accepted on the basis of prejudice, self-interest, class-interest, customs, the circumstances of the moment, or any other inadequate means which will serve to fill the gap left by the lack of intellectual assistance in framing ideas and beliefs about values. One's course of conduct, both personal and social is decided on the basis of that which is responsible for the framing of value judgments for this determines one's main course of action.

Values are inextricably related with judgment for they are "connected inherently with liking, and yet not with *every* liking but only with those that judgment has approved, after examination of the relation upon which the object liked depends."[29] Although all values are enjoyable, not all enjoyments are values; the former are accidental, the latter have a "claim upon our attitude and conduct." Distinction must also be made between what is actually enjoyed and what is enjoyable, what is in fact desired and what is desirable, and in like manner is the satis*fying* compared to the satis*factory*. To state that an object is actually enjoyed is to make a statement of fact of that which is in existence and is comparable to saying "snow is white;" it is not a judgment of value. The same is true of desired and satisfying, "but to call an object a value is to assert that it satisfies or fulfills certain conditions. . . . To say that something satisfies is to report something as an isolated finality. To assert that it is satis*factory* is to define it in its connections and interactions. The fact that it pleases . . . poses a problem to judgment. How shall the satisfaction be rated? Is it a value or is it not? Is it something to be prized and cherished, *to be* enjoyed? . . . To declare something satis*factory* is to assert that it meets specific conditions. It is, in effect, a judgment that the thing 'will do.' . . . It asserts a consequence the thing will actively institute. . . . That it is satisfying is the content of a proposition of fact; that it is satisfactory is a judgment, an estimate, an appraisal.''[30] To say that something is satisfying is to recognize its *de facto* value only, but to exercise a value judgment regarding an object as satisfactory is to claim that it posseses *de jure* as well as *de facto* value.

Values have infiltrated every phase of human activity; all deliberately planned conduct, personal and social, has been influenced, "if not controlled, by estimates of value or worth of ends to be attained,"[31] even good sense has been equated with a good perspective of relative values. "All conduct that is not simply either blindly impulsive or mechanically routine seems to involve valuations."[32] Any natural object takes on value once it becomes the aim of certain human activities, *e.g.*, a diamond becomes an object of value when it becomes the desired end of an individual person's activity. The words *valuing* and *valuation* when used as verbs signify *prizing, i.e.*, connote preciousness, dear, while appraising denotes "putting a value upon, assigning value to." Such an activity is one of rating, concerned with an intellectual *estimate*, and not with subjective or emotive *esteem*; hence valuation is connected with *prizing, appraising, enjoying,* etc. An adequate theory of valuation implicitly contains good with its connotation of useful, serviceable, helpful, and bad signifying harmful, detrimental.

Dewey is adamantly opposed to Ayer's position, viz., that value judgments are unverifiable, hence do not exist. Ayer errs in claiming that moral disputes are merely arguments about attitudes, and that what one is actually seeking is a change in his opponent's attitude only. Ayer's stand fails to explain "why the attitude is called 'moral' rather than 'magical,' 'belligerent,' or any one of thousands of objectives that might be selected at random."³³ Even in the case of a crying infant Ayer's explanation proves inadequate; the original cries of a baby may be purely ejaculatory, but then appears the cry made on purpose, one intended to evoke response with its ensuing consequences; this "cry exists in the medium of language; it is a linguistic sign that not only says something but is intended to say, to convey, to tell."³⁴

An acceptable criterion of norms suitable for exercising value judgments in regard to proposed types of behavior must not restrict itself to statements of general propositions about factual data, but it must be "capable of stating relations between things as means and other things as consequences," and to distinguish these from mere custom, convention, tradition, etc. Proper value judgments are based upon empirical data and tested by their cause and effect relations in order to determine their existential relations. *E.g.*, the physician evaluates the better course of action for him to take in regard to his patient's welfare, not on the basis of whims, but upon acknowledged physical laws, *i.e.*, on experimentally ascertained principles of chemistry and physics. Techniques and devices used in medicine and other fields have been greatly improved, *i.e.*, *bettered* since they were first invented, and "that betterment in the relation of means to consequences is due to more adequate scientific knowledge of underlying physical principles."³⁵ Medical quackery requires little examination to expose it and distinguish it from the *good* or *better* methods employed by competent physicians. "Appraisals of courses of action as better and worse, more and less serviceable, are as experimentally justified as are nonvaluative propositions about impersonal subject matter. . . . Propositions which lay down rules for procedures as being fit and good, as distinct from those that are inept and bad, are different in form from the scientific propositions upon which they rest. For they are rules for the use, in and by human activity, of scientific generalizations as means for accomplishing certain desired and intended ends."³⁶ These evaluations are based upon their relation of *means to ends or consequences, i.e.,* their serviceability or needfulness; the criterion of value is invoked wherever better or needed action is called for or a desired end to be reached, *e.g.*, in medical practice the materials and techniques are valued for their fitness in achieving the desired end or result. Then one's outcome differs from that which was intended, it lays the basis for a better judgment in the future both as to the means used and the desired end. If the objection is raised, as some persons have done, that the present view of valuation applies only to means, whereas genuine value judgments apply to ends, then "it may be noted here that ends are appraised in the same evaluations in which things as means are weighed."[37] *E.g.*, ends are evaluated in the light of the means, if the means are unacceptable, then they render the end prohibitive, *i.e.*, the end is appraised and rejected as bad. The foregoing may be summarized as:

> (1) There are propositions which are not merely about valuations that have actually occurred (about, *i.e.*, prizings, desires, and interests that have taken place in the past) but which define and describe certain things as good, fit, or proper in a definitive existential relation: these propositions, moreover, are *generalizations*, since they form rules for the proper use of materials. (2) The existential relation in question is that of means-ends or means-consequences. (3) These propositions in their generalized form may rest upon scientifically warranted empirical propositions and are themselves capable of being tested by observation of results actually attained as compared with those intended.[38]

One objection levied against the view here is its failure to distinguish between instrumental and intrinsic goods, *i.e.*, between those goods that serve as a means to an end and those goods that are an end in themselves, viz., good in its own right. According to this criticism, *appraising* pertains to means only, while *prizing* is applicable to ends. The practice of separating ends and means is deeply ingrained in one as the result of long philosophical tradition, but means are inextricably tied to ends. The empirical fact is that if one regards the end as precious, then he will value the means by which it is obtained; devotion and loving care is invariably bestowed on the instruments and agencies productive of any prized end. Furthermore, isolated from the means, end appraisals become impossible. In the last analysis, "valuation of desire and interest, as means correlated with other means, is the sole condition for valid appraisal of objects as ends."[39] A definite ratio exists between failure in achieving one's desired ends and the formation of desire or interest. "Wherever there is an *end-in-view* of any sort whatever, there is affective-*ideational*-motor activity; or, in terms of the dual meaning of valuation, there is union of prizing and appraising."[40]

The error of divorcing prizing and appraisal, ends and means stems from the failure of making an accurate empirical investigation of conditions as they actually exist in which desires and interests arise and function, and in which the end-objects or the ends-in-view acquire their actual contents. "*Propositions in which things (acts and materials) are appraised as means enter necessarily into desires and interests that determine end-values.*"[41] The consideration of means is an indispensable factor in the appraisal of ends.

Valuation is a "*relation* between a personal attitude and extra-personal things;"[42] this definition of value does not permit the end to be separated from the means. Furthermore it emphasizes the subjective aspect of value as being a feeling; not a feeling of something, but a feeling with value *suo jure*. If it were said that it is a feeling *of* something then the value might be interpreted as the object of feeling, not feeling *per se*. "To pass from immediacy of enjoyment to something called 'intrinsic value' is a leap for which there is no ground. The *value* of enjoyment of an object *as* an end, an outcome, stands in relation to the means of which it is the consequence. Hence if the object in question is prized *as* an end or 'final' value it is valued *in this relation* or as mediated."[43] To speak of something as being *an end-in-itself* is to utter a self-contradictory term inasmuch as ends without means do not exist, i.e., *ends* cannot be "valued apart from the appraisal of the things used in attaining them."

It is a sign of immaturity to believe in absolute ends;

for all ends are moving conditions with consequences which in turn become new ends. To treat the end as final in the sense of coming to a complete stop is acceptable, however these are limited periods of arrests and not absolute terminal points, "but to treat them as models for forming a theory of ends is to substitute a manipulation of ideas, abstracted from the contexts in which they arise and function for the conclusions of observation of concrete facts. It is a sign either of insanity, immaturity, indurated routine, or of a fanaticism that is a mixture of all three."[44] Ideas as absolute ends exist as expressions of habit or as uncritical and invalid ideas; they are abstractions in that they are disconnected with any particular case, hence absolute values do not exist. Desires confer value on objects as ends; the only sense in which a value is final is that it is the conclusion of an appraisal of particular conditions which involves both desires and conditions, hence values that are final, are final for particular cases only. They are applicable only to a "specific temporal *means-end relation* and not to something which is an end per se. . . . There is no end which is not in turn a means."[45] *E.g.*, A physician who is to restore his patient to health has no idea of absolute health as an end-in-itself, *i.e.*, "an absolute good by which to determine what to do." Abstract conceptions of absolute health develop eventually from dealing constantly with health as a desired end and good in a particular case by the techniques of medical knowledge available at the time.

The worth of an end-in-view is concomitantly related to its ability to resolve the problem under investigation; this must be accomplished on the basis of empirical data as there are no a priori standards for determining values; each solution must be wrought in a particular concrete case. The end-in-view must be distinguished from the actual end or outcome as it did in fact take place; the end-in-view is an expected goal, a purpose, a predicted outcome, whereas the actual goal is a *de facto* situation. Although there are not a priori standards of good health, one can from past experience derive certain criteria which can be operatively applied to present cases or new ones as they arise. "Ends-in-view are appraised or valued as *good* or *bad* on the ground of their serviceability. . . . They are appraised as fit or unfit, proper or improper, *right* or *wrong*, on the ground of their *requiredness* in accomplishing this end."[46] Any content that the end-in-view possesses comes from the means, not from abstract ideals or absolute standards. "The content of the end as an object *held in view* is intellectual or methodological; the content of the attained outcome or the end *as consequence* is existential."[47] No physical object may be considered a means unless it is used in some human activity to accomplish some end.

Dewey summarizes his theory of valuation:
The net outcome is (i) that the problem of valuation in general as well as in particular cases concerns things that sustain to one another the relation of means-ends; that (ii) ends are determinable only on the ground of the means that are involved in bringing them about; and that (iii) desires and interests must themselves be evaluated as means in their interaction with external or environing conditions. Ends-in-view as distinct from ends as accomplished results, themselves function as directive means or, in ordinary language as *plans*. Desires, interests, and environing conditions as means are modes of action, and hence are to be conceived in terms of energies.... Co-ordination or organization of energies, proceeding from the two sources of the organism and the environment, are thus both means and attained result or "end" in all cases of valuation.[48]

5. Rights, Duties, and Moral Standards

Moral conduct is defined as *"activity called forth and directed by ideas of value or worth, where the values concerned are so mutually incompatible as to require consideration and selection before an overt action is entered upon."*[49] Moral experience is activity involving conflicting goals or ends which must be resolved by deliberation and choice; it differs from other forms of experience in that it involves the consideration of values. Nevertheless, "every act is *potential* subject-matter of moral judgment, for it strengthens or weakens some habit which influences whole classes of judgments."[50]

Rights are abilities to act in particular ways, and include an intimate unity of the individual with society.[51] Although a right is individual, it is social in both origin and intent; absolute rights do not exist, if by absolute is meant not related to any social order and free from social restrictions. Rights do not entitle one to wholesale indefinite activity, but are limited by obligations; although the individual is free, he is free to exercise his obligations which are his social duties, *i.e.*, imposed by society, *e.g.*, his right to own property implies the obligation to pay taxes, his right to use public highways implies the obligation to restrict his speed, etc. Hence, rights and obligations are correlative terms. Even the so-called *natural rights*, life, liberty, limb, etc., are social; one fancies them natural because they are so basic and "fundamental to the existence of personality that their insecurity or infringement is a direct menace to the social welfare." [52]

As far as the *good* is concerned, "the better is the good; the best is not better than the good but is simply the discovered good. Comparative and superlative degrees are only paths to the positive degree of action. The worse or evil is a rejected good. In deliberation and before choice presents itself as evil. Until it is rejected, it is a competing good. After rejection, it figures not as a lesser good, but as the bad of that situation."[53]

Morality implies deliberate action or reflective choice, hence wherever such is found, the situation or question is a moral one, resulting in consequences making it better or worse. Potentially, every act is within the domain of morals, since at any time there is the possibility of it becoming a candidate for judgment involving decisions which are productive of better or worse consequences. Furthermore, every moral decision is a tentative one since "all moral judgment is experimental and subject to revision by its issue."[54]

Ethical theories, such as Intuitionism, which identify ethics with motives or duty have ill effects by diverting one's thoughts into unimportant side issues, and declare a "moral moratorium" for everyday affairs. Morality is found in everyday situations where better and worse are considerations; it is a "continuing process not a fixed achievement." Morality implies growth of conduct, actually, it is identical with *growing*; in a broader sense "morals is education." "The good satisfaction, 'end,' of growth of present action in shades and scope of meaning is the only good within our control, and the only one, accordingly, for which responsibility exists."[55] Anything more than this must be considered *luck*.

Present activity is morally significant for progress is present reconstruction, whereas the slipping away of the present is retrogression. Present evils should act as a stimulant to remedial action, viz., converting regression into progression, strife into harmony, limitation into expansion, and monotony into variegated scene. The foregoing is progress; its need is recurrent and constant. "If it is better to travel than to arrive, it is because traveling is a constant arriving while arrival that precludes further traveling is most easily attained by going to sleep or dying."[56] Dewey's version of the categorical imperative is: "So act as to increase the meaning of present experience."[57] The doctrine of evolution is of ethical import because it preaches or at least implies the "gospel of present growth." It removes the "fixed and eternal ends" and absolutes of the old tradition, replacing them with concepts of continuity and change in terms of growth. "The doctrine of progress is not yet bankrupt. . . . Adherents of the idea that betterment, growth in goodness, consists in approximation to an exhaustive, stable, immutable end or good, have been compelled to recognize the truth that in fact we envisage the good in specific terms that are relative to existing needs, and that the attainment of every specific good merges insensibly into a new condition of maladjustment with its need of a new end and a renewed effort."[58]

6. Morality as Social

Morality is social, not that it *ought* to be social; it is in fact social, *i.e.*, it is social due to facts. Moral judgment and moral responsibility stem from one's social milieu; the response of others to one's actions, *i.e.*, social or public opinion affect the meaning and decisions of a person. Social environment is as significant as physical environment, in fact with the advancement of civilization, physical environment becomes humanized.

"All morality is social. . . . Our conduct is socially conditioned whether we perceive the fact or not."[59] However, this should not be interpreted as meaning that only social action is right conduct and individualistic behavior is evil, for social behavior does not guarantee the rightness or goodness of an act; in fact, self-interest is as much social conditioning as is altruistic or benevolent behavior. Self-seeking and self-interest endeavors such as seeking money and economic power are socially rooted, for money, property, and economic opportunities are social, legal, and financial institutions. If money making is evil, it is due to the way the social facts are dealt with, rather than the rugged individualist's tactics; an extreme individualist such as the hermit would have no use for money; its use is social. The egoistic tycoon and his actions are both facts due to society; they are social phenomena. "He pursues his unjust advantage as a social asset. . . . Morals is as much a matter of interaction of a person with his social environment as walking is an interaction of legs with a physical environment,"[60] *e.g.*, if society emphasizes the value of financial success, and the man of wealth is envied for his money and power, then persons will pursue this end.

It is inconsistent to say that morality *ought* to be social for "morals *are* social. The question of ought . . . is a question of better and worse *in* social affairs."[61] Rights and claims are a distinctly social phenomenon; they did not originate outside of society, but within it; moral pressures do not stem from ideals or absolutes, but empirically and actually from society. They are ideal only in the sense that they can be intelligently recognized and acted upon, similar to colors and canvas becoming ideal when they are used in ways that add meaning to life. Right is merely an abstract term for the many diverse specific concrete demands actively impressed on one by others; these one is obligated to accept, if for no other reason, at least for the sake of better living. Their authority is not an absolute principle or an inner categorical imperative, but the exigency of social demands and the efficacy of their insistencies. The right is subordinate to the good, but in the sense that it is the prescribed proper course for the attainment of good.

"If a man lived alone in the world there might be some sense in the question 'Why be moral?' were it not for one thing: No such question would then arise."[62] Approbation and condemnation are not abstract theoretical principles, but the response of society to one's conduct; one's acts affect others, and they respond in consequence to it. Approval and disapproval are social pressures imposed upon one as an inducement to think, desire, and act in a specific manner. "In this sense conduct and hence morals are social: they are not just things which *ought* to be social and which fail to come up to scratch. . . . Human interaction and ties are there, are operative in any case."[63]

Even the growth of individuality is via the social; the savage is not free; emancipation from one social situation is always followed by an introduction into another social order. Liberation from one set of social customs means initiation into another social group, but the larger and more progressive the society, the better. The broader the scope of stimuli that the community offers, the richer will be the opportunities, initiative, and endeavor of its citizens. Individual morals and social customs are synonymous; when individual morals conflict with social customs, then personal moral initiative may be the means of effecting a social reconstruction, but in any case "social institutions determine individual morality. Apart from the social medium, the individual would never 'know himself.' "[64]

Rights are social because they are accompanied by responsibility; although one is free to exercise his rights, it is a *responsible freedom*. A right to free speech implies the responsibility of respecting the rights of others, *i.e.*, not bringing any harm to them and giving them equal rights. Even the protection of one's rights is socially instituted and guaranteed. Murder, arson, theft, etc., are infringements upon one's rights and the person committing such is restrained by society because "the wrong, although done to one, is an expression of a disposition which is dangerous to all."[65]

If it were not for society man would live the life of a beast giving untamed satisfaction to his appetite of hunger, sex, etc.; social conditions are responsible for his human and moral nature; society awakens morality and intelligence in man. "Intelligence becomes ours in the degree in which we use it and accept responsibility for consequences. It is not ours by originality or by production. 'It thinks' is a truer psychological statement than 'I think.' Thoughts sprout and vegetate; ideas proliferate. . . . 'I think' is a statement about voluntary action.''[66] A dogmatic group or society restricts the critical powers of its individuals from forming, *i.e.,* inhibits the moral thoughtfulness and conscientiousness of its members. A wholesome society offers many opportunities for its citizens to engage in reflective thought and personal valuation. In any case morality does not stem from inner intuitive moral principles, but from society, for morality is essentially social. *"The very habits of individual moral initiative, of personal criticism of the existent order, and of private projection of a better order, to which moral individualists point as proofs of the purely 'inner' nature of morality, are themselves effects of a variable complex social order."*[67]

7. Evaluation of the Ethics of Dewey

John Dewey is unquestionably one of America's foremost philosophers; he was the only one fortunate enough to have bestowed on him the honorary title: *Dean of American Philosophers.* He has also earned the distinction of being one of the few Americans asked to give the Gifford Lectures in Scotland, which since have been published under the title: *The Quest for Certainty.* Furthermore, it can be safely said that he, more than any other philosopher, has had the greatest influence upon American education on all levels, and is one of the recognized founders of a distinctly American school of philosophy called Pragmatism which he later changed to Instrumentalism; a term he preferred and found more suitable to the philosophy he pioneered.

The belated and much needed emphasis on means was delayed until he brought it to the attention of the philosophical world and proved its worth, but of even greater service was his main objective, viz., integrating scientific beliefs and those of values. The Logical Positivists attempt to sever the two; it remained for Dewey to point out their relationship, and in the process, he humanized the sciences. Through his efforts, ethics was given a scientific basis by establishing an experimental basis for morality.

His emphasis on the social is both necessary and valuable, but to many it appears overdone; this is probably due to his Hegelian or Neo-Hegelian background in which such heavy stress is laid upon society at expense and loss to the individual. Santayana cited this objection: "In Dewey, as in current science and ethics, there is a pervasive quasi-Hegelian tendency to dissolve the individual into his social functions, as well as everything substantial and actual into something relative and transitional." In a sense, it is true that society gives the individual meaning and one's morals are derived from the social milieu, but it is extreme to claim they are entirely social. Morals must be due in considerable measure to human nature since animals lack morality, yet Dewey believes that if it were not for societal relations man would be reduced to the state of animal behavior, but it appears to be as much the case that moral beings created society as it is that society produced morals.

Dewey's emphasis on means is important, but overworked. Again, the reverse is equally valid, viz., the end gives direction and meaning as much as do the means, if not more so. At times Instrumentalism intimates that it matters little where you are going as long as you are going; the end is of minor import as long as one is progressing, but the question is begged: Going where?

8. Further Reading in the Philosophy of Dewey

It would be beyond our scope to list all of the writings of Dewey, consequently only his books have been selected for insertion in this section: *My Pedagogic Creed* (New York: E. L. Kellog and Co., 1897), *Psychology and the Philosophic Method* (Berkeley: University of California Press, 1899), *The School and Society* (Chicago: University of Chicago Press, 1903), *Logical Conditions of a Scientific Treatment of Morality* (Chicago: University of Chicago Press, 1903), *Studies in Logical Theory* (Chicago: University of Chicago Press, 1903), *Ethics* with James H. Tufts (New York: Henry Holt and Co., 1908, rev. ed. 1932), *The Influence of Darwin on Philosophy and other Essays in Contemporary Thought* (New York: Henry Holt and Co., 1910), *How We Think* (New York: Heath and Co., 1910, rev. ed., 1933), *Democracy and Education* (New York: Macmillan Co., 1916), *Essays in Experimental Logic* (Chicago: University of Chicago Press, 1916), *Creative Intelligence*, Dewey et al. (New York: Henry Holt and Co., 1917), *Reconstruction in Philosophy* (New York: Henry Holt and Co., 1920, rev. ed. 1949), *Human Nature and Conduct* (New York: Henry Holt and Co., 1922), *Experience and Nature* (Chicago: Open Court Publishing Co., 1925), *The Public and Its Problems* (New York: Henry Holt and Co., 1927), *The Quest for Certainty* (New York: Minton Balch and Co., 1929), *Art as Experience* (New York: Minton Balch and Co., 1934), *A Common Faith* (New Haven: Yale University Press, 1934), *Liberalism and Social Action* (New York: G. P. Putnam's Sons, 1935), *Experience and Education* (New York: Macmillan Co., 1938), *Logic The Theory of Inquiry* (New York: Henry Holt and Co., 1938), *Freedom and Culture* (New York: G. P. Putnam's Sons, 1939), *Theory of Valuation* (International Encyclopedia of Unified Science, Chicago: University of Chicago Press, 1939), *Intelligence in the Modern World*, ed. by Joseph Ratner (New York: The Modern Library, 1939), *Problems of Men* (New York: Philosophical Library, 1946), *Knowing and the Known* with Arthur Bentley (Boston: The Beacon Press, 1949).

NOTES

JOHN DEWEY

1. John Dewey, *Reconstruction in Philosophy* (New York: Henry Holt and Co., 1920), Ch. VII, "Reconstruction in Moral Conceptions."
2. *Idem.*
3. *Idem.*
4. *Idem.*
5. *Idem.*
6. *Idem.*
7. *Idem.*
8. *Idem.*
9. *Idem.*
10. *Idem.*
11. *Idem.*
12. *Idem.*
13. *Idem.*
14. John Dewey, *Problems of Men* (New York: Philosophical Library Inc., 1946), 213.
15. *Ibid.*, 214.
16. *Ibid.*, 216.
17. *Op. cit.*, "Reconstruction in Moral Conceptions."
18. *Idem.*
19. *Idem.*
20. *Idem.*
21. *Idem.*
22. *Idem.*
23. *Idem.*
24. *Idem.*
25. *Idem.*
26. *Idem.*
27. *Idem.*
28. John Dewey, *The Quest for Certainty* (New York: Minton, Balch and Co., 1929), 265.
29. *Ibid.*, 264.
30. *Ibid.*, 260.
31. John Dewey, "Theory of Valuation," *International Encyclopedia of Unified Science*, Vol. II, No. 4. (Chicago: The University of Chicago Press, 1939), 2.
32. *Ibid.*, 3
33. *Ibid.*, 8.
34. *Ibid.*, 9.
35. *Ibid.*, 22.
36. *Ibid.*, 22, 23.
37. *Ibid.*, 24.

38. *Idem.*
39. *Ibid.,* 29.
40. *Ibid.,* 31.
41. *Ibid.,* 35.
42. *Ibid.,* 36.
43. *Ibid.,* 41.
44. *Ibid.,* 44.
45. *Ibid.,* 45.
46. *Ibid.,* 47.
47. *Ibid.,* 48.
48. *Ibid.,* 53.
49. John Dewey and James H. Tufts, *Ethics* (New York: Henry Holt and Co., 1908), 209. Quotations cited from this book are restricted to the portion written by Dewey.
50. *Ibid.,* 211.
51. *Ibid.,* 440.
52. *Ibid.,* 442.
53. John Dewey, *Human Nature and Conduct* (New York: Henry Holt and Co., 1922), 278.
54. *Ibid.,* 279.
55. *Ibid.,* 280.
56. *Ibid.,* 282.
57. *Ibid.,* 283.
58. *Ibid.,* 287.
59. *Ibid.,* 316.
60. *Ibid.,* 318.
61. *Ibid,* 319.
62. *Ibid.,* 326.
63. *Ibid.,* 329.
64. Dewey, *Ethics, op. cit.,* 433.
65. *Ibid.,* 454.
66. Dewey, *Human Nature and Conduct, op. cit.,* 314.
67. Dewey, *Ethics, op. cit.,* 343.

ETHICAL REALISM

G. E. MOORE

It seems to me to be self-evident that knowingly to do an action which would make the world, on the whole, really and truly worse than if we had acted differently, must always be wrong.

(G. E. Moore)

1. Ideal Utilitarianism

George Edward Moore's school of ethical thought is termed *Ideal Utilitarianism* and is to be differentiated from the traditional mode of Utilitarianism. Its major departure is indicated in the following chief tenets of the school: (1) right action is equivalent to the *best possible consequences* obtainable from any given act; (2) *intrinsic good* is not limited to pleasure; (3) intrinsic good is an *organic unity*, viz., a *Gestalt*, in which the whole totals greater than the sum of its individual parts; (4) *indefinability of good*; (5) *ethical realism*.

Ideal Utilitarianism "may be summed up in two propositions (1) that the question whether an action is right or wrong always depends upon its *total* consequences, and (2) that if it is once right to prefer one set of *total* consequences, A, to another set, B, it must always be right to prefer any set precisely similar to B."[1] Inasmuch as moral action is dependent upon doing that act which brings about the best possible consequences, it would follow that it is also one's *duty*; but inasmuch as achieving the best possible consequences is equivalent to doing the *expedient* act, it would follow that duty and expedience are *coincident*. "An action is a *duty*, whenever and only when it produces the best possible consequences ... nothing is left to distinguish duty from expediency,"[2] *i.e.*, in that they always apply to the same actions, however, in other respects, a difference is possible.

The Ideal Utilitarian is opposed to the Intuitionist, such as Kant, who would claim that "justice ought to be done, even though the heavens should fall" and meaning by it "*however* bad the consequences of doing an act of justice might in some circumstances be, yet it always would be our duty to do it."[3] Moore argues, "It seems to me to be self-evident that knowingly to do an action which would make the world, on the whole, really and truly *worse* than if we had acted differently, must always be wrong."[4] Hence, if revealing the truth should issue in disastrous consequences it cannot possibly be one's duty to tell the truth; one would be under the obligation to lie, *e.g.*, it would be wrong for a physician to shock his patient to death by informing him of the gravity of the crisis through which the patient is passing. It would be moral to *steal* a gun from a man who intends to murder innocent persons. Therefore, it cannot be the case that there are obligations "which it *would* always be our duty to do or to avoid, *whatever* the consequences might be." The only obligation to which one is duty bound is that which "produces the best possible consequences."

In considering the best possible consequences, one must consider the means as well as the end, *i.e.*, one must select the best possible means to the best possible end. "The total results of an action always depend, not merely on the specific nature of the action, but on the circumstances in which it is done."[5]

2. The Right Act

The right act is that which produces the *best possible actual consequences*. The word *actual* is of critical importance in distinguishing the difference between a genuinely right act and those closely related to it, *e.g.*, to do an act because one believes sincerely that it will produce the best possible consequences is not necessarily the right act, for it may later turn out that it did not produce the best possible consequences; hence, right action does not depend upon *probable* consequences, *i.e.*, *predictable* results, but upon *actual* results.

It is apparent that right action cannot possibly depend upon motive, although good and evil motives are to be tallied in arriving at the total outcome of consequences. Furthermore, right action does not depend upon the intrinsic nature of the action, for this is only a fraction of the grand total set of consequences. Moore concludes: "the question whether an action is right or wrong *always* depends on its *actual consequences*."[6]

One must make a sharp distinction between what is *right and wrong action* on the one hand, and what is *morally praiseworthy* or blameworthy on the other. The right act is equivalent to that which produces the best possible actual consequences, not the act which one intended would produce the best. "What we should naturally say of a man whose action turns out badly owing to some unforeseen accident when he had every reason to expect that it would turn out well, is not that his action was right, but rather that *he is not to blame*."[7] One reason for not blaming the individual is that condemnation cannot serve any good purpose, moreover, it would likely produce harm, but this is not justification for asserting that he acted rightly. "I am inclined to think that in all such cases the man really did act *wrongly,* although he is not to blame, and although, perhaps, he even deserves praise for acting as he did."[8] Consequently, those persons are in error who are "strongly inclined to hold that they [right and wrong] do *not* depend upon the *actual* consequences, but only upon those which were antecedently *probable*, or which the agent had *reason* to expect, or which it was *possible* for him to *foresee*."[9] It is erroneous to "say that an action is *always* right, what its *actual* consequences may be, provided the agent had reason to expect that they would be the best possible; and always wrong, if he had reason to expect they would not."[10]

A peculiar paradox emerges, viz., that of being obligated to choose the wrong act, *e.g.,* one is obligated to select that action which produces the best possible actual consequences, but this is never known until the act has been consummated; consequently he must act in the light of the best *foreseeable* consequences which may not be the best actual. On the other hand, a person may commit an act intended to bring about disastrous consequences, but which inadvertently results in the best possible; such a person would be blamed, *i.e.*, censured for doing the right act, "and we are thus committed to the paradox that a man may really deserve the strongest moral condemnation for choosing an action, which *actually* is right. But I do not see why we should not accept this paradox."[111] This strange paradox engulfs the ill-fated individual who thought he was selecting the best possible consequences, which, unhappily, turned out to be otherwise. Although he committed a wrong act, he is still to be praised; in fact, "he will deserve the strongest moral blame if he does not choose the course in question, even through it may be wrong."[12] In spite of these objections, Moore concludes: "there is no conclusive reason against the view that our theory is right."[13]

The problem of doing the right act involves more than a *knowledge* of the best possible consequences, it is further complicated by one's *ability or inability* to execute the right act; he may be willing, but he may be powerless to proceed, *e.g.*, how is one to dispense with the problem of the man who knows what the best possible consequences are and is willing to proceed with their execution, but is impotent to do so? Moore believes that he has resolved this most serious of all the objections which have been raised heretofore with the reply: "Our theory . . . has not been maintaining, after all, that right and wrong depend upon what the agent absolutely *can* do, but only on what he can do, *if* he chooses. And this makes an immense difference."[14] Summarily, "a voluntary action is right whenever and only when its total consequences are *as* good intrinsically, as any that would have followed from any action which the agent *could have* done instead."[15]

3. The Doctrine of Ethical Realism

The doctrine of *ethical realism* is the belief that moral properties exist independent of human consciousness, *i.e.*, moral values exist in and of themselves alone, *sui generis*. These values are complex wholes, *Gestalten,* in which the wholes are greater than the sum of the individual parts taken separately. *"The value of the whole must not be assumed to be the same as the sum of the values of its parts."*[16] This whole or *Gestalt* is termed the *principle of organic unities*,[17] a concept borrowed from Hegel. An organic unity is a paradox inasmuch as *"the value of such a whole bears no regular proportion to the sum of the values of its parts."*[18] One reason for this paradox is that the elements of an organic unity are related telically; "to say that a thing is an 'organic whole' is generally understood to imply that its parts are related to one another and to itself as means to end; it is also understood to imply that they have a property described in some such phrase as that they have 'no meaning or significance apart from the whole.' "[19] If the foregoing is true, then one is entitled to formulate the following principle: *"The amount by which the value of a whole exceeds that of one of its factors is not necessarily equal to that of the remaining factor."*[20] If this principle is true, then an intrinsic value which is an organic unity, hence greater than the sum of its parts entitles one "always to add to the value of a whole which contains any one of them [parts], not only by adding more of that one, but also by *adding something else instead."*[21]

The nature of organic unities is sufficiently perplexing to cause one to query as to "Why should the parts be such as they are?" Moore answers: "Because the whole they form has so much value."[22] In fact, the isolated part is meaningless abstracted from the whole. " 'If you want to know the truth about a part,' we are told, 'you must consider *not* the part, but something else — namely the whole: nothing is true of the part, but only of the whole.' "[23]

Ethical values are of intrinsic worth, *i.e.,* they are valuable in and of themselves, inherently and essentially, even though at times they may serve to be of instrumental value as well; consequently, " 'right' and 'intrinsically good' are *not* subjective predicates,"[24] they are objective realities in their own right.

Although intrinsic values are not subjective, *i.e.,* they are not dependent for their existence upon the consciousness of any given individual, they are, nevertheless, involved in personal consciousness, for "nothing can be an intrinsic good unless it contains *both* some feeling and *also* some other form of consciousness;"[25] furthermore intrinsic value must also contain some amount of *pleasure*. Although pleasure is involved, a sharp distinction must be drawn to contrast this view with that of Hedonism or Utilitarianism, for those schools involve one "saying, for instance, that a world in which absolutely nothing except pleasure existed — no knowledge, no love, no enjoyment of beauty, no moral qualities — must yet be intrinsically better — better worth creating — provided only the total quantity of pleasure in it were the least bit greater, than one in which all these things existed *as well as* pleasure."[26] The hedonist is confronted with a *reductio ad absurdum* argument which proves destructive, if not fatal, to his system. Moore puts the argument in the form of an analogy; "It involves our saying that, for instance, the state of mind of a drunkard, when he is intensely pleased with breaking crockery, is just as valuable, in itself — just as well worth having, as that of a man who is fully realizing all that is exquisite in the tragedy of King Lear, provided only the mere quantity of pleasure in both cases is the same."[27] Bentham, and the other quantitative hedonists are taken to task for propounding the view that pleasures, of whatever kind, are alike except in their calculable amounts. "And if anybody, after clearly considering the issue, does come to the conclusion that no one kind of enjoyment is ever intrinsically better than another, provided only that the pleasure is both equally intense, and that, if we *could* get as much pleasure in the world, without needing to have any knowledge, or any moral qualities, or any sense of beauty, as we can get *with* them, then all these things would be entirely superfluous. . . . But it seems to me almost impossible that anybody, who does really get the question clear, should take such a view; and, if anybody were to, I think it is self-evident that he would be wrong."[28]

Moore believes in the ethical value of pleasure; moreover, nothing can be of any value *without* pleasure, but this must be contradistinguished from the position of the Hedonists and Utilitarians who claim that intrinsic value is always *in proportion* to pleasure. The fundamental question of ethics is: 'What things are goods or ends in themselves?' It would definitely be an error to assert that pleasure is the *sole* good, for the answer would have to lie in those things which, "if they existed by *themselves*, in absolute isolation, we should yet judge their existence to be good,"[29] *e.g.*, "the proper appreciation of a beautiful object is a good thing in itself."[30] The ethical problem requiring resolution is: What are the main elements included in such? To answer this would be the solution of the perennial ethical riddle, viz., what is intrinsic good? Moore contends, "things intrinsically good or bad are many and various ... most of them are 'organic unities' ... complex wholes, composed of parts which have little or no value in themselves. All of them involve consciousness of an object, which is itself usually highly complex and almost all involve also an emotional attitude towards this object ... goods are undoubtedly good, even where the things or persons loved are imaginary. ... Great evils may be said to consist either (a) in the love of what is evil or ugly, or (b) in the hatred of what is good or beautiful, or (c) in the consciousness of pain."[31]

In furnishing the foregoing, Moore believes that he has accomplished what philosophers have heretofore ignored, viz., the two major problems of ethics which only he has properly treated, viz., (1) Has it intrinsic value? and (2) Is it a means to the best possible end?

4. The Indefinability of Good

One feature in the ethical system of G. E. Moore that makes his moral philosophy unique is his insistence of *the indefinability of good*; it is not the *good* that is indefinable, but the *predicate good*. This difficulty emerges when one attempts to construct a proper definition of ethics, which must include properties "common and peculiar to all undoubted ethical judgments." The relevancy of the predicate good extends beyond *particular things,* it encompasses all *universal judgments* to which *goodness* may apply. "It must, however, enquire not only what things are universally related to goodness, but also, what this predicate, to which they are related, is: and the answer to this question is that it is indefinable or simple. . . . What is thus indefinable is not 'the good' but this predicate itself. 'Good,' then, denotes one unique simple object of thought among innumerable other; but this object has very commonly been identified with some other — a fallacy which may be called 'the naturalistic fallacy.' "[32]

The reason why *good* is indefinable is that it is a *simple notion, i.e.,* it is an ultimate term; all words are defined in terms of those that are more basic or fundamental, until one reaches the ultimate term by which others are defined; this ultimate term is, consequently, *simple* and *indefinable.* Only complex terms are subject to definition; their definitions consist in dividing the complexities into simpler terms, viz., by analysis, but simple terms are elements that cannot be subdivided, hence cannot be analyzed or defined. Although simple terms, such as good, are indefinable, they are nevertheless, *most significant*; this contention is easily demonstrated as in the case of another simple notion, viz., yellow.

Empirically, the color yellow defies all explanation; one can never convey the *experience* of the color yellow to a person who has never experienced it for himself. One may attempt to explain it scientifically in terms of light waves and where yellow is to be found in the color spectrum or color solid, but this certainly is not what is meant when one has an experience of the color yellow as is easily evidenced when one attempts to undertake to depict the experience of the color yellow to an individual who is color blind. The person who fancies that he has explained or defined the term yellow merely in terms of light waves, spectrum, etc., and not in terms of the experience sensed has confused the issue and fallen prey to the *naturalistic fallacy.* Scientific data concerning yellow is what a color blind person can see, but it certainly is not what is meant when one is viewing the color with enjoyment.

Notions such as *yellow* and *good* are simple, consequently, are not definable. Complex terms are composed of parts and are definable in terms of their molecular structure, but ultimately each is reducible to simplest parts, which can no longer be defined. It is in the foregoing sense that Moore claims good to be indefinable. "The most important sense of 'definition' is that in which a definition states what are the parts which invariably compose a certain whole; and in this sense 'good' has no definition because it is simple and has no parts."[33]

Inasmuch as good denotes a simple, unanalyzable, and indefinable quality, any attempt to define it almost invariably, and probably always, results in falling prey to the *naturalistic fallacy*. The reason is "that Ethics aims at discovering what are those other properties belonging to all things which are good. But far too many philosophers have thought that when they named those other properties they were actually defining good; that these properties, in fact, were simply not 'other,' but absolutely and entirely the same with goodness. This view I propose to call the 'naturalistic fallacy.'"[34]

In conclusion, it may be said that *the good* is definable; what is indefinable is *good itself*. To say, for example, that "Pleasure and intelligence are good" is to state a proposition, not a definition; even granting it the status of a definition, one would be defining *the good*, not *good itself*. "I do most fully believe that some true proposition of the form 'Intelligence is good and inteligence alone is good' can be found; if none could be found, our definition of *the* good would be impossible. As it is, I believe *the* good to be definable; and yet I still say that good itself is indefinable."[35] In the last analysis, "If I am asked 'What is good?' my answer is that good is good, and that is the end of the matter. Or if I am asked, 'How is good to be defined?' my answer is that it cannot be defined, and that is all I have to say about it,"[36] because good is simple, unanalyzable, hence indefinable.

5. Evaluation of Ideal Utilitarianism

There are those philosophers who define truth as *the definition of the real*; if this is the case, then to conclude good to be indefinable is tantamount to saying that it does not exist as a reality, inasmuch as reality is capable of definition. Moore could rebut with the defence that reality is not restricted to mere definition, inasmuch as experiences exist that cannot be harnessed by definition, viz., those that are simple, hence unanalyzable.

A much more serious and crucial objection pertains to the nature of the right act., viz., that action which results in the best possible actual consequences. The criticism is that it is impossible to do or even to know if one did perform such an act; the probability is that no one has even committed a single *objectively* right act although he may have been successful in accomplishing many *subjectively* right ones. After a single act is committed, its consequences continue indefinitely, in fact, endlessly; under such circumstances, how is one ever to know whether he ever did *one* single right act? Moore could countermand this animadversion by claiming it to be irrelevant, by claiming that it makes no difference whether or not one has performed a right act, it still remains a right act and it is one's duty to fulfill the obligation it entails. Nevertheless, the problem remains: Why should one be bound to an obligation that is impossible of fulfillment?

A final stricture involves the *reductio ad absurdum* argument, viz., obligating one to make unreasonable sacrifices. Moore writes: "It seems to me quite self-evident that it must always be our duty to do what will produce the best effects *upon the whole*, no matter how bad the effects upon ourselves may be and no matter how much good we ourselves may lose by it."[37] To carry such a premise out to its ultimate conclusions would implicate one in the obligation to surrender his life for vivisection and other experimental purposes which would eventuate in one's death, on the grounds that the marvelous consequences resulting would enable scientists to produce for the benefit of the remainder of mankind, cures of cancer, heart disease, brain tumor, and other maladies.

6. Further Reading in G. E. Moore

The bulk of Moore's philosophy, particularly his moral philosophy, may be found in *Principia Ethica* (1903), *Ethics* (1912), and *Philosophical Studies* (1922).

NOTES

G. E. MOORE

1. George Edward Moore, *Ethics* (London: Oxford University Press, 1912), 106.
2. *Ibid.*, 107.
3. *Ibid.*, 112.
4. *Idem.*
5. *Ibid.*, 110.
6. *Ibid.*, 121.
7. *Ibid.*, 119
8. *Ibid.*, 120.
9. *Ibid.*, 119.
10. *Idem.*
11. *Ibid.*, 121.
12. *Idem.*
13. *Idem.*
14. *Ibid.*, 123.
15. *Ibid.*, 140.
16. G. E. Moore, *Principia Ethica* (Cambridge: University Press, 1903), 28.
17. See *Principia Ethica*, chapter 1, section 18-22.
18. *Ibid.*, 27.
19. *Ibid.*, 31
20. Moore, *Ethics, op. cit.*, 151.
21. *Ibid.*, 152.
22. Moore, *Principia Ethica, op. cit.*, 32.
23. *Ibid.*, 34.
24. Moore, *Ethics, op. cit.*, 139.
25. *Ibid.*, 153.
26. *Ibid.*, 146.
27. *Ibid.*, 147.
28. *Idem.*
29. Moore, *Principia Ethica, op. cit.*, 187.
30. *Ibid.*, 189.
31. *Ibid.*, 223-225.
32. *Ibid.*, xii.
33. *Ibid.*, 9
34. *Ibid.*, 10.
35. *Ibid.*, 9
36. *Ibid.*, 6.
37. Moore, *Ethics, op. cit.*, 143.

ETHICAL IDEALISM

JOSIAH ROYCE

In loyalty, when loyalty is properly defined, is the fulfilment of the whole law. (Royce)

1. The Philosophy of Loyalty

(a) *The Ethics of Loyalty.* In the philosophy of Royce, all ethical principles, all virtues, all noble actions, hence all morality is reducible to *loyalty*. Loyalty is more than a good, it is a *supreme* good; it is the summation of all the virtues embodied in one. Loyalty is a value in and of itself, regardless of whether or not the cause to which it is devoted merits worth, *e.g.*, a loyal person is moral whether the cause to which he is committed is noble and beneficial to mankind or ignoble and detrimental to humanity. Loyalty is good wherever and in whomever it is found, the lofty or the lowly, the enlightened or the ignoramus, the intelligent or the subnormal, the cultured or the uncouth.

(b) *The Definition of Loyalty.* Loyalty is "*the willing and practical and thoroughgoing devotion of a person to a cause.*"[1] It is true that causes may conflict, but when this transpires, then one is obligated to be *loyal to loyalty*.

There are a number of prerequisites to loyalty: first of all, one must have a cause to which to be loyal; in the second place, he must *autonomously* choose the cause to which he intends to be loyal; he must do this *willingly* and with a *thorough* devotion so that he is completely committed to his cause; finally, his dedication to his cause must be expressed in a *sustained and practical way*, *e.g.*, "by acting steadily in the service of his cause." The foregoing can be illustrated by the loyal endeavors of the religious martyr, who freely chose his life's calling, completely dedicated his life to his noble cause, and steadfastly labored for his cause even to the portals of death. The same can be said of the loyalty of a ship's captain, who after his ship meets with disaster, busily engages himself in the task of saving the ship's company before considering his own safety; and, if necessary, perishes by going down with his ship.

The implications of loyalty are legion: Loyalty requires *self-control*; loyalty often demands *self-sacrifice*; loyalty implies a cause which is *personally valued*, sufficiently important to command one's devotion; loyalty implies *altruism*, the loyal individual is not interested in private advantage; loyalty is *social*, its cause includes other persons equally interested in the same cause.

(c) *The Need of Loyalty*. The human being has a fundamental need for loyalty; one needs to find causes to which to be loyal; such an endeavor necessitates the determination of what causes are worthy of loyalty. Loyalty is satisfying, not because it is pleasurable, but because it is a human need and longing, *e.g.*, "it is water that the thirsty man in the desert longs for, rather than pleasure, and rather than even mere relief from pain as such."[2] St. Augustine in his *Confessions* maintains that God has made man for Himself and man cannot find rest or peace except in God; the same can be said of loyalty. Loyalty does much for personality enhancement. "Whoever is loyal, whatever be his cause, is devoted, is active, surrenders his private self-will, controls himself, is in love with his cause, and believes in it.[3]

Loyalty is the *raison d'etre* of morality; it is the essence of duty. It is the answer to such questions as: "What do we live for?" "What is our duty?" "What is the true ideal of life?" "What is the true difference between right and wrong?" "What is the true good which we all need?" Loyalty is that which constitutes a duty; it is the reason for a duty being an obligation. Loyalty is the criterion of morality; "left to myself alone, I can never find out what my will is."[4]

The loyal personality culminates in a thoroughgoing sense of "an exaltation of the self, of the inner man, who now feels glorified through his sacrifice, dignified in his self-surrender, glad to be his country's servant and martyr,—yet sure that through this very readiness for self-destruction he wins the rank of hero."[5] In such one finds his salvation: "in this cause is your life, your will, your opportunity, your fulfilment."[6] Such a cause demands one's utmost, both in devotion and sacrifice,—"only a cause, dignified by the social unity that it gives to many human lives, but rendered also vital for the loyal man by the personal affection which it awakens in his heart, only such a cause can unify his outer and inner world. . . . Whatever cause thus appeals to a man meets therefore one of his deepest personal needs, and in fact the very deepest of his moral needs; namely, the need of a life task that is at once voluntary and to his mind worthy."[7] The sacrificial character of loyalty is noted in that it "discounts death, for it is from the start a readiness to die for the cause. It defies fortune; for it says: 'Lo, have I not surrendered my all? Did I ever assert that just I must be fortunate?' "[8]

In a world torn by turmoil and disaster, only the loyal can feel at home at peace; on the other hand, the seekers for power can never be at home or at ease; consequently, Napoleon's loyal soldiers won their goal when they died in his service, but he lost; the soldiers proved more fortunate than their leader. Loyalty is the only justification for sacrificial devotion. Royce concludes: "For the moment we have won our first distant glimpse of what I mean by the general nature of loyalty, and by our common need of loyalty."[9]

(d) *The Intrinsic Value of Loyalty.* Loyalty is a good, and a *supreme good,* regardless of the worthlessness of the cause upon which it is spent, be it magnificent or base. Loyalty, "be the cause worthy or unworthy, is for the loyal man a good, just as, even if his beloved be unworthy, love may in its place still be a good thing for a lover. And loyalty is . . . chief amongst all the moral goods of his life, because it furnishes to him a personal solution of the hardest of human practical problems, the problem: 'For what do I live? Why am I here? For what am I good? Why am I needed?' "[10]

The defence of loyalty as a value is most formidable; in fact, its opponent pays it homage, *e.g.*, in the act of attacking loyalty as a value, one is being loyal to what he believes is truth. Royce once had a critic attack him on this point by arguing that loyalty has been one of humanity's disastrous weaknesses and failings, inasmuch as tyrants have used the spirit of loyalty as a tool to gain their greedy evil objectives. Royce's rebuttal was that his "opponent's earnestness, his passion for the universal triumph of the individual freedom, his plainness of speech, his hatred of oppression, were themselves symptoms of a loyal spirit. . . . He spoke like a man who was devoted to that cause."[111]

Loyalty is a supreme good, "whatever be, for the world in general, the worth of his cause;"[12] it is "a supremely worthy personal attitude."[13] Inasmuch as loyalty is the supreme good, it would follow that a "mutually destructive conflict of loyalties is in general a supreme evil;"[14] international warfare between loyal soldiers is heinous, not because it "has hurt, maimed, impoverished, or slain men, as because it has so often robbed the defeated of their causes, of their opportunities to be loyal, and sometimes of their spirit of loyalty."[15] Life's worst evil is that which renders loyalty impossible, destroys it, or inhibits it. In principle, one should never oppose another's spirit of loyalty, only his blindness or ignorance to the cause to which he has pledged his allegiance. Should one attack another person's loyalty, he would commit the unpardonable sin of being *disloyal to loyalty*.

One needs no other virtue than loyalty, since *"all the commonplace virtues, in so far as they are indeed defensible and effective, are special forms of loyalty to loyalty."*[16] Virtues devoid of loyalty lack moral worth, *e.g.*, "benevolence without loyalty is a dangerous sentimentalism. Thus viewed, then, loyalty to universal loyalty is indeed the fulfilment of the whole law."[17] Loyalty in its supernal form is one that is capable of enlisting mankind's loyal individuals in the united cause of *loyalty to loyalty, i.e.,* the subjugation of private interests to a common universal cause, which ought to command one's complete devotion. Such a cause should be autonomously elected. "Since my loyalty never is mere fate, but is always also my choice, I can of course determine my loyalty."[18]

(e) *Loyalty to Loyalty.* Loyalty to loyalty is the culmination of the ethical philosophy of Royce. Ascension to this summit commences with a commitment to a cause, any cause, but preferably to a cause one has freely chosen, for this is his inalienable birthright. When loyal men are mutually engaged in conflicting causes, the moral mandate, which is also a dictate of conscience and will, dictates that men be *loyal to loyalty* above all else, *i.e.*, that they promote the sense of loyalty in human individuals. The foregoing may be stated in the form of a principle:

> This principle is now obvious. I may state it thus: In so far as it lies in your power, so choose your cause and so serve it, that, by reason of your choice and of your service, there shall be more loyalty in the world rather than less. And, in fact, so choose and so serve your individual cause as to secure thereby the greatest possible increase of loyalty amongst men. More briefly: *In choosing and in serving the cause to which you are to be loyal, be, in any case, loyal to loyalty.*[19]

Royce was enamored with a magnificent display of loyalty by the Speaker of the British House of Commons, when in January, 1642, under the reign of King Charles I, the king resolved to arrest specific members of the opposition party, by barging into the House of Commons with his guards and demanding that the Speaker identify the guilty persons. This was a high moment in English history; the speaker maintained genuine personal dignity and exemplified the quintescence of loyalty, when to the king's mandate he responded: "Mr. Speaker, do you espy these persons in the House?" the Speaker promptly fell on his knee before the King with the reply: "Your Majesty, I am the Speaker of this House, and, being such, I have neither eyes to see nor tongue to speak save as this House shall command; and I humbly beg your Majesty's pardon if this is the only answer that I can give to your Majesty."[20] The loyal attitude displayed by the Speaker of the House of Commons was a supremely worthy personal attitude and constitutes a supreme personal moral good in and of itself.

Although the foregoing behavior exemplifies the pinnacle of loyalty, it fails to furnish one with a criterion of causes worthy of loyal devotion. Causes purporting to be fitting candidates or objects of loyalty, qualify only when they are capable of joining "many persons into the unity of a single life. Their chief characteristic is that they must be *personal*; or *superpersonal*, if personality is defined in a purely human light. Causes worthy of one's enlistment are: "first, a friendship which unites several friends into some unity of friendly life; secondly, a family, whose unity binds its members' lives together; and, thirdly, the state, in so far as it is no mere collection of separate citizens, but such an unity as that to which the devoted patriot is loyal;"[21] fourthly, humanity, or that which binds all men together in a single cause of loyalty to loyalty; finally, all stable social relations capable of giving rise to causes that summon loyalty.

A tragic human predicament emerges as the result of *conflicting loyalties, e.g.,* loyal patriotic persons who find themselves in warfare against other loyal patriots. Loyalty, *per se,* is no criterion for detecting rightful causes, this is accomplished by an enlightened and autonomous will, viz., one freely chosen. Nevertheless, although conflicting causes may be evil, the loyalty prompting men to engage in such is noble and good; to attack or harm an individual's sense of loyalty is to commit sin against a spirit that is holy, "for such a sin is precisely what any wanton conflict of loyalties means."[22] Evil causes are distinguishable from those that are good: A cause is judged as good, "not only for me, but for mankind, in so far as it is essentially a *loyalty to loyalty,* that is, is an aid and a furtherance of loyalty in my fellows. It is an evil cause in so far as, despite the loyalty that it arouses in me, it is destructive of loyalty in the world of my fellows ... in so far as my cause is a predatory cause, which lives by overthrowing the loyalties of others, it is an evil cause, because it involves disloyalty to the very cause of loyalty itself."[23]

(f) *Loyalty as the Transmutation of all Moral Values.* Royce, borrowing some evolutionary ideas from Nietzsche, believes that ethics must undergo a transitional stage; the ethics of an earlier age is no longer suitable for an enlightened age; hence must be altered to the core for "time makes ancient good uncouth." Consequently, a modern revolt against moral traditions must be inaugurated; this is effected by a "transmutation of all moral values," *i.e.*, the displacement of antiquated forms of morality by the installation of *loyalty* as the only necessary essential moral quality.

Loyalty is the willing devotion of a self to a cause, but loftier forms of loyalty involve autonomous choice. Causes with loyalty appeal must be capable of fascinating, stirring, pleasing, arousing, and possessing one. Inasmuch as one may *choose* his loyalties, there need be no conflict of loyalties, provided he is *loyal to the universal loyalty of all mankind, i.e.,* "the universal loyalty of all mankind shall be furthered by the actual choices which each enlightened loyal person makes when he selects his cause."[24] Loyalty is not only a good, it is the *summum bonum.* Proper loyalties synthesize "private passion and outward conformity in one's life." One's major goal in life ought to be the practical serving of "the universal human cause of loyalty to loyalty," which is an integrated whole encompassing many causes in a developing system, so that loyalties can grow to maturity and new ones be annexed, hence there must be an evolutionary progress inherent in one's loyalty.

The better loyalties are *contagious, i.e.*, they spread to other persons. Loyalty is the summation of obligations, virtues, in fact, of all ethics: "My thesis is that *all those duties which we have learned to recognize as the fundamental duties of the civilized man, the duties that every man owes to every man, are to be rightly interpreted as special instances of loyalty to loyalty,*"[25] *e.g.,* justice, truth, benevolence, etc. are merely aspects of loyalty, "but justice, without loyalty, is a vicious formalism . . . benevolence without loyalty is a dangerous sentimentalism."[26]

Loyalty to loyalty has two characteristics: *decisiveness* and *fidelity*. General Robert E. Lee manifested these two qualities when he, at the culmination of his deliberations, decided to pledge his allegiance to the Confederate States. Like him, one must *"be loyal to loyalty, and to that end, choose your own personal cause and be loyal thereto."*[27] Hence, one must confront the moral command: *"Have a cause; choose your cause; be decisive."*[28] Commitments to loyalty cannot be postponed, indecision is anathema, one must accept the injunction: *"Decide, knowingly if you can, ignorantly if you must, but in any case decide, and have no fear."*[29] Royce concisely summarizes the entire matter:

> The conscience is the ideal of the self, coming to consciousness as a present command. It says, *Be loyal.* If one asks, *Loyal to what?* the conscience, awakened by our whole personal response to the need of mankind replies, *Be loyal to loyalty.* If, hereupon, various loyalties seem to conflict, the conscience says: *Decide.* If one asks, *How decide?* conscience further urges, *Decide as I, your conscience, the ideal expression of your whole personal nature, conscious and unconscious, find best.* If one persists, *But you and I may be wrong,* the last word of conscience is, *We are fallible, but we can be decisive and faithful; and this is loyalty.*[30]

2. Evaluation of the Ethics of Loyalty

It is commendable that Royce has given emphasis to a moral quality that has heretofore been grossly neglected, but it appears that the moral value of loyalty has been overestimated and fails to measure up to the pre-eminent status Royce has given it. Royce actually justifies the activities of the pirate, provided he is a loyal one. A Hitler and a Nero are moral, if their actions can be considered loyal. To support one's country by adhering loyally to the motto: "My country right or wrong," appears to be disloyal to moral laws, such as, justice, integrity, honesty, goodness, etc.

The same claims that Royce insists upon for loyalty can be equally applied to other noble qualities, *i.e.*, justice, integrity, honesty, goodness, etc. One can claim justice for the sake of justice, truth for the sake of truth, etc. The case for loyalty would be greatly strengthened if one were loyal to the cause of justice or the cause of truth, rather than a particular individual person or cause which implies partiality. Loyalty to the cause of justice, is a universal principle binding on all individuals, giving no recognition to privileged persons as would maintain in the case of loyalty. Loyalty's virtue and value consists in its cohering with other moral values.

3. Further Reading in the Philosophy of Royce

Royce's monumental work is: *The World and The Individual;* his foremost work in ethics giving his position in the philosophy of loyalty goes by that name, *The Philosophy of Loyalty,* but one may also find a brief review of ethical problems in the first part of his book: *The Religious Aspect of Philosophy.* A fine statement of his metaphysical position can also be found in his: *The Spirit of Modern Philosophy,* particularly the eleventh lecture. His epistemological emphasis may also be found in his Presidential Address at the third annual meeting of the American Philosophical Association; it is entitled, "The Eternal and the Practical," and published in *The Philosophical Review,* 1904.

NOTES

JOSIAH ROYCE

1. Josiah Royce, *The Philosophy of Loyalty* (New York: The Macmillan Company, 1908), 16.
2. *Ibid.*, 29.
3. *Ibid.*, 22.
4. *Ibid.*, 28.
5. *Ibid.*, 40.
6. *Ibid.*, 42.
7. *Ibid.*, 58, 59.
8. *Ibid.*, 90.
9. *Ibid.*, 48.
10. *Ibid.*, 57.
11. *Ibid.*, 61.
12. *Ibid.*, 101.
13. *Ibid.*, 105.
14. *Ibid.*, 116.
15. *Idem.*
16. *Ibid.*, 129, 130.
17. *Ibid.*, 146.
18. *Ibid.*, 120.
19. *Ibid.*, 121.
20. *Ibid.*, 104, 105.
21. *Ibid.*, 108.
22. *Ibid.*, 117.
23. *Ibid.*, 119.
24. *Ibid.*, 122.
25. *Ibid.*, 139.
26. *Ibid.*, 145, 146.
27. *Ibid.*, 183.
28. *Ibid.*, 187.
29. *Ibid.*, 189.
30. *Ibid.*, 195, **196.**

ETHICAL SUBJECTIVISM

DAVID HUME

The notion of morals implies some sentiment common to all mankind, which recommends the same object to general approbation.
The humanity of one man is the humanity of every one.
(Hume)

1. Ethics as Sentiment

All values, of whatever kind, naturally fall into one of two classifications, the useful or the agreeable, the *utile* or the *dulce;* hence morality or "Personal Merit" consists in possessing these mental characteristics, *i.e.*, to be useful or agreeable either to oneself or to others. "And as every quality which is useful or agreeable to ourselves or others is, in common life, allowed to be a part of personal merit; so no other will ever be received, where men judge of things by their natural, unprejudiced reason, without the delusive glosses of superstition and false religion. Celibacy, fasting, penance, mortification, self-denial, humility, silence, solitude, and the whole train of monkish virtues, neither advance a man's fortune in the world, nor render him a more valuable member of society; neither qualify him for the entertainment of company, nor increase his power of self-enjoyment."[1] The above mentioned series of pseudo-virtues belong in a catalogue of vices since they do no more than stultify the understanding, harden the heart, or sour one's disposition; they constitute a perversion of natural sentiments. Persons exhibiting such characteristics would scarcely be admitted into the intimacies of society, except the community of those who are as delirious and dismal as themselves.

For present purposes it will be hypothesized, "what surely, without the greatest absurdity cannot be disputed, that there is some benevolence, however small, infused into our bosom; some spark of friendship for human kind; some particle of the dove kneaded into our frame, along with the elements of the wolf and serpent."[2] Regardless of how weak these sentiments are in one, they are nevertheless capable of producing a preference for the good of mankind, *i.e.*, a preference for what is useful and serviceable to mankind, over that which is pernicious and dangerous to humanity. Such ability to favor discriminations of preference constitutes the power of making *moral* distinctions, *i.e.*, to experience sentiments of condemnation or approbation. "The notion of morals implies some sentiment common to all mankind, which recommends the same object to general approbation, and makes every man, or most men, agree in the same opinion or decision concerning it. It also implies some sentiment, so universal and comprehensive as to extend to all mankind, and render the actions and conduct ... an object of applause or censure, according as they agree or disagree with that rule of right which is established."[3]

Only the sentiments of humanity may be regarded as morally significant, that is, only those sentiments that are felt in common or for which there is consensus can be used as the foundation of a general system upon which to establish a theory of ethics based upon "blame or approbation." Sentiments that are personal, *i.e.*, individual, lack moral significance, only those possessing social content have moral value, *e.g.*, to label a person an *enemy* or *antagonist* stems from personal or selfish sentiments, hence such designations fall outside the moral domain, but to hurl epithets such as *vicious, odious,* or *depraved* is to express social sentiments, *i.e.*, one expects others to concur with his opinion or feeling.

Although moral distinctions are not derived from *reason*, nevertheless it does play a role in moral considerations;

particularly when one must deliberate concerning the usefulness of various sentiments, *e.g.*, when such encounter conflict or are open to controversy. The utilitarian application of the sentiment of justice, although it is as useful to society as benevolence, does at times create debates which are resolved only by reason. "But though reason, when fully assisted and improved, be sufficient to instruct us in the pernicious or useful tendency of qualities and actions; it is not alone sufficient to produce any moral blame or approbation. Utility is only a tendency to a certain end; and were the end totally indifferent to us, we should feel the same indifference towards the means. It is requisite a *sentiment* should here display itself, in order to give a preference to the useful above the pernicious tendencies. This sentiment can be no other than a feeling for the happiness of mankind, and a resentment of their misery; since these are the different ends which virtue and vice have a tendency to promote. Here therefore *reason* instructs us in the several tendencies of actions, and *humanity* makes a distinction in favour of those which are useful and beneficial."[4]

There are several arguments to defend the thesis that moral distinctions are not derived solely from reason; one is that reason adjudicates matter of fact issues, or those dealing with logical relations, not with sentiments or feelings. Reason may decide how, when, or where a crime has been committed, but sentiments remain unsolved through reason. "Examine the crime of *ingratitude*, for instance; which has place, wherever we observe good will, expressed and known, together with good offices performed, on the one side, and a return of ill-will or indifference, with ill-offices or neglect on the other: anatomize all these circumstances, and examine, by your reason alone, in what consists the demerit or blame. You never will come to any issue or conclusion."[5] The reason for this is that gratitude resides in the mind of the person experiencing the sentiment. The sentiment itself is not a crime to be analyzed by reason or justice, but the activity prompted from such passion, and it is this overt act that is subject to being scrutinized by reason in the light of justice. "Consequently, we may infer, that the crime of ingratitude is not any particular individual *fact;* but arises from a complication of circumstances, which, being presented to the spectator, excites the *sentiment* of blame, by the particular structure and fabric of his mind."[6] Nor is ingratitude subject to logical analysis by reason, for one may "twist and turn" the matter as he will, but to no avail since in moral matters one must have recourse to decisions of sentiment. To designate immoral actions such as ingratitude a crime leads only to complications, *e.g.,* a vain search for a criterion of right and wrong.

One cannot predicate moral turpitude of crime unless sentiments of disapproval are evoked in one. "The orator may paint rage, insolence, barbarity on the one side; meekness, suffering, sorrow, innocence on the other. But if you feel no indignation or compassion arise in you from this complication of circumstances, you would in vain ask him, in what consists the crime or villainy. . . . No satisfactory answer can be given . . . upon abstract hypothesis of morals; and we must at last acknowledge, that the crime or immorality is no particular fact or relation, which can be the object of understanding, but arises entirely from the sentiment of disapprobation."[7] If morality were not a matter of sentiment then natural objects and occurrences would be designated moral or immoral, *e.g.,* a falling tree that kills a human being could be regarded as immoral, or "a young tree, which overtops and destroys its parent, stands in all the same relations with Nero, when he murdered Agrippina; and if morality consisted merely in relations, would no doubt be equally criminal."[8]

The foregoing is conclusive proof that moral actions are alien to reason, but are entirely explicable in terms of sentiments and affections independent of the intellectual faculties. If an object is declared desirable, it must be based on the fact that it is in accord with human sentiment and affection. The intrinsic value of virtue, and its desirability, *suo jure,* without the necessity of reward other than the possession of its "dear sweet self alone," is predicated on the fact that "it is requisite that there should be some sentiment which it touches, some internal taste or feeling . . . which distinguishes moral good and evil, and which embraces the one and rejects the other. Thus the distinct boundaries and offices of *reason* and of *taste* are easily ascertained. The former conveys the knowledge of truth and falsehood: the latter gives the sentiment of beauty and deformity, vice and virtue. . . . Taste, as it gives pleasure or pain, and thereby constitutes happiness or misery, becomes a motive to action, and is the first impulse to desire and volition.'"[9] If it were not for taste, then a sentiment of blame or approbation would be an impossibility. In the final analysis the reason that one "pronounces characters and actions amiable or odious, praise-worthy or blameable; that which stamps on them the mark of honour or infamy, approbation or censure; that which renders morality an active principle and constitutes virtue our happiness, and vice our misery . . . depends on some internal sense or feeling.'"[10]

2. Moral Approbation as Social Opinion

It should now be apparent that the criterion of morality, *i.e.*, the distinction between a right and wrong act is *social opinion, sentiments* shared in common with the rest of society, or *social approbation*. The affection of humanity, *i.e.*, sentiments commonly shared with the rest of society, inasmuch as they are common to all men are alone the "foundation of morals, or any general system of blame or praise. One man's ambition is not another's ambition, nor will the same event or object satisfy both; but the humanity of one man is the humanity of every one, and the same object touches this passion in all human creatures. But the sentiments, which arise from humanity, are not only the same in all human creatures, and produce the same approbation or censure; but they also comprehend all human creatures; nor is there any one whose conduct or character is not, by their means, an object to every one of censure or approbation.'"[11] Passions of self-love, *i.e.*, selfish sentiments cannot provide a basis for ethics since such sentiments are not commonly shared, but produce different sentiments in each individual, *e.g.*, to exhibit a trait that affects only a solitary individual lacks moral significance, but to express tyrannical, insolent, or barbarous behavior fosters pernicious tendencies in conduct and creates a sentiment of repugnance and displeasure in others, accordingly has moral implications. "Whatever conduct gains my approbation, by touching my humanity, procures also the applause of all mankind, by affecting the same principle in them; but what serves my avarice or ambition pleases these passions in me alone, and affects not the avarice and ambition of the rest of mankind.'"[12] Sentiments that implicate humanity possess moral value, and command one's approval by touching one's humanity, but other passions cannot arouse moral concern. Consequently, neither personal approbation nor personal opinion is the criterion of moral right and wrong, but *social approbation* or social opinion; thus social approval determines moral conduct.

Personal merit, as previously stated, is that "quality of mind, which is *useful* or *agreeable* to the *person himself* or to *others,* communicates a pleasure to the spectator, engages his esteem, and is admitted under the honourable denomination of virtue or merit. Are not justice, fidelity, honour, veracity, allegiance, chastity, esteemed solely on account of their tendency to promote the good of society? . . . Can it be doubted, I say, that the tendency of these qualities to promote the interest and happiness of their possessor, is the sole foundation of their merit?"[13] Feelings which enhance the welfare of society are considered moral, but those which prove deleterious to the interests of society are condemned.

Moral approbation solicits one's obligation, both work towards the same end, viz., the happiness and welfare of the individual and of society, *e.g.*, a person who has any concern for his own happiness and welfare will find it in his best interests to exercise every moral duty, *i.e.*, the moral approbations of society. Practices pernicious to society's interests are not only immoral, but disadvantageous to the best interests of the individual. "What theory of morals can show, by a particular detail, that all the duties which it recommends, are also the true interest of each individual?"[14]

The subjectivity of ethics is further substantiated by the fact that personal subjective tastes are not subject to debate, but truth which exists objectively in the nature of things is debatable. "Truth is disputable; not taste: what exists in the nature of things is the standard of our judgement; what each man feels within himself is the standard of sentiment,"[15] *e.g.*, no one argues concerning another man's taste in beauty, but he may debate about the justice of his overt actions. The beauty of virtue and the deformity of vice are possible only because one acquires these proper representations of them by sentiment. "Extinguish all the warm feelings and prepossessions in favour of virtue, and all disgust or aversion to vice: render men totally indifferent towards these distinctions; and morality is no longer a practical study, nor has any tendency to regulate our lives and actions."[16]

3. The Criterion of Right Conduct (The Disinterested Spectator)

"The hypothesis which we embrace is plain. It maintains that morality is determined by sentiment. It defines virtue to be *whatever mental action or quality gives to a spectator the pleasing sentiment of approbation;* and vice the contrary."[17] Right and wrong conduct is determined on the basis of social subjectivism, *i.e.*, it is not a matter of personal opinion, but one of social opinion, group consensus, or one might even say morality is based on public opinion. It is a philosophy not too distant from the belief advocated by the expression: "When in Rome do as the Romans do." Nevertheless it is not personal opinion, *per se,* but the individual standing aside from the rest of society, observing its sentiments and actions as a disinterested bystander as it were, in order to determine what actions are considered moral or immoral, *i.e.*, what sentiments or actions are subject to social approbation. The innocent bystander may then proceed with the performance of those actions sanctioned by his particular society. All societies may not share the same opinion regarding moral sentiments, hence what is moral in one society may be immoral in another, *e.g.*, polygamy may be immoral in the Western world, but approved in the Middle East or elsewhere. Approbation or blame is not an activity of rational judgment, "but of the heart; and is not a speculative proposition of affirmation, but an active feeling or sentiment. . . . In moral decisions, all the circumstances and relations must be previously known; and the mind, from the contemplation of the whole, feels some new impression of affection or disgust, esteem or contempt, approbation or blame. . . . Nothing remains, but to feel, on our part, some sentiment of blame or approbation; whence we pronounce the action criminal or virtuous."[118]

The reason for this is that moral values are not external objects, such as tangible facts which are open to common inspection by individuals, but psychological states of feeling, wholly subjective in nature. "So that when you pronounce any action or character to be vicious, you mean nothing, but that from the constitution of your nature you have a feeling or sentiment of blame from the contemplation of it. Vice and virtue, therefore, may be compared to sounds, colours, heat and cold, which, according to modern philosophy, are not qualities in objects, but perceptions in the mind."[119]

4. Evaluation of the Ethics of Hume

The comments made pertaining to the ethical relativity of Westermarck are applicable here together with the following remarks: (1) Ethical subjectivism permits the existence of contradictory moral codes since the ethical sentiments of one society may be diametrically opposed to those of another, *e.g.*, moral opinion in one society may favor birth control whereas in another it may be considered reprehensible. According to the present ethic it would be moral for a person to practice birth control in the state where there are sentiments of approbation, but as soon as one crosses into a state where the social opinion censors birth control it would be immoral to practice it until one returned to his prior society. A society may oppose birth control in one generation but condone it in a subsequent one, does this mean that to practice birth control was immoral and became transformed into a moral practice when it became socially acceptable? This is what Hume's ethical theory intimates.

(2) Ethics according to the social subjectivist is reducible to a matter of statistics or vote, at least it is a psychological poll depending on the prevailing sentiment which is responsible for public opinion. Accordingly, slavery is moral provided sentiment favors the practice, but becomes immoral only when the tide of feeling respecting the practice expresses sentiments of disapproval.

(3) Since moral judgments depend upon emotional attitudes, viz., sentiments, then nothing may be considered morally good or evil until or unless one assumes an emotional attitude towards it. Consequently, if a child is hurt or a person tortured, it is an amoral situation until people express disdain, *e.g.*, the cruelties exhibited by Hitler and his regime could be considered moral since the German society displayed sentiments of approbation.

(4) Finally, this ethic lacks an adequate explanation for the moral reformer who runs counter to the sentiments of the group, except to condemn him inasmuch as his sentiments conflict with those of mass opinion. The logical impalatability of this ethical theory increases when one considers the fact that much of the prevailing moral sentiment of any age is the result of the past efforts of some moral reformer. Does not this system suggest that the sentiments of the moral reformer in his own day and time, since they were not accepted by the group were immoral? Consequently it was immoral for the former to have such sentiments, but in a subsequent time when they were approved as the direct result of the efforts of the moral reformer they became moral. This ethical theory implies that a moral reformer can never be considered moral during the initial process of reform, at least not until his sentiments become the prevailing sentiments of society. Is this not absurd?

5. Further Reading in the Philosophy of Hume

One who would enjoy pursuing the philosophy of David Hume further will find the following chief works of value: *A Treatise of Human Nature* (1739), *An Enquiry Concerning Human Understanding* (1748), *An Enquiry Concerning the Principles of Morals* (1751), *Dialogues Concerning Natural Religion* (1779).

NOTES

DAVID HUME

1. David Hume, *An Enquiry Concerning the Principles of Morals*, (1777), IX, 1.
2. *Idem.*
3. *Idem.*
4. *Ibid.*, Appendix I.
5. *Idem.*
6. *Idem.*
7. *Idem.*
8. *Idem.*
9. *Idem.*
10. *Ibid.*, I.
11. *Ibid.*, IX, 1.
12. *Ibid.*, IX, 2.
13. *Idem.*
14. *Ibid.*, IX, 2.
15. *Ibid.*, I.
16. *Idem.*
17. *Ibid.*, Appendix I.
18. *Idem.*
19. David Hume, *A Treatise of Human Nature* (1739), Bk. III, 1.

EDWARD WESTERMARCK

Moral judgments are ultimately based on emotions . . . all moral concepts are essentially generalizations of tendencies in certain phenomena to call forth moral approval or disapproval. (Westermarck)

1. Ethical Relativity

Westermarck has elected to label his brand of *ethical subjectivism*: "Ethical Relativity." It is a naturalistic ethic reducing all ethical phenomena to the state of *emotion*, his rationale being that ethical disputes remain indeterminate because they do not pertain to factual data or cognition, consequently, he "arrived at the conclusion that moral judgments are ultimately based on emotions, the moral concepts being generalizations of emotional tendencies."[1]

Westermarck was entranced with the origin of morality and devoted his two volume book to it and its development. It was the product of the upshot of many contentious discussions on the topic of morals which were never resolved. One debate, for example, revolved about the point as to "how far a bad man ought to be treated with kindness. The opinions were divided, and, in spite of much deliberation, unanimity could not be attained. It seemed strange that the disagreement should be so radical, and the question arose, whence this diversity of opinion? Is it due to defective knowledge, or has it a merely sentimental origin? And the problem gradually expanded. Why do moral ideas in general differ so greatly? And, on the other hand, why is there in many cases such wide agreement? Nay, why are there any moral ideas at all?"[2]

His deliberations terminated with the following conclusions: 1. Moral concepts, which constitute the bases of all moral judgments, are ultimately grounded on *moral emotions*. 2. Moral emotions are reducible to two basic types: *moral approval* and *moral disapproval* (indignation). 3. Emotions of moral approval form a subset of *retributive kindly emotion, i.e., gratitude;* emotions of disapproval form a sub-class of *resentment, e.g.*, anger, revenge, etc. 4. Since moral approval is a kind of retributive kindly emotion, *morality is relative, i.e.*, right or wrong action is an expression of *personal opinion, e.g., x* is right means "I approve of it" (personal approval). 5. Moral principles have *no objective validity* (ethical relativity *i.e.*, ethical subjectivism).

2. The Emotional Origin of Moral Judgments

Moral judgments are ultimately founded on emotions of *indignation or approval;* an individual designates an act or situation as evil if it evokes in him an expression of an unpleasant emotion, and judges it as right if it excites within him a pleasant emotion, *i.e.*, a sense of approbation. "Men pronounced certain acts to be good or bad on account of the emotions those acts aroused in their minds, just as they called sunshine warm and ice cold on account of certain sensations which they experienced, and as they named a thing pleasant or painful because they felt pleasure or pain."[3] A type of action, such as a good deed, is identified as good because it is apt to elicit a pleasant response (an emotion of approval); on the other hand, behavior censored as evil is condemned because it educes a feeling of distaste (an emotion of indignation). "Whilst not affirming the actual existence of any specific emotion in the mind of the person judging or of anybody else, the predicate of a moral judgment attributes to the subject a tendency to arouse an emotion. The moral concepts, then, are essentially generalizations of tendencies in certain phenomena to call forth moral emotions."[4]

3. The Nature of Moral Emotions

Ethical principles are founded on emotions, not all emotions, but only those that can qualify as a *moral emotion*. Moral emotions are *retributive;* these must be distinguished from all others which are of a non-moral character. The retributive emotions are dichotomized into those of approval and disapproval or indignation. In the class of retributive kindly emotions, there is to be found "nonmoral retributive kindly emotions." Moral emotions "differ from each other in points which make each of them allied to certain non-moral retributive emotions, disapproval to anger and revenge, and approval to that kind of retributive kindly emotion which in its most developed form is gratitude."[5] Westermarck, for purposes of elucidation supplies the following diagram:[6]

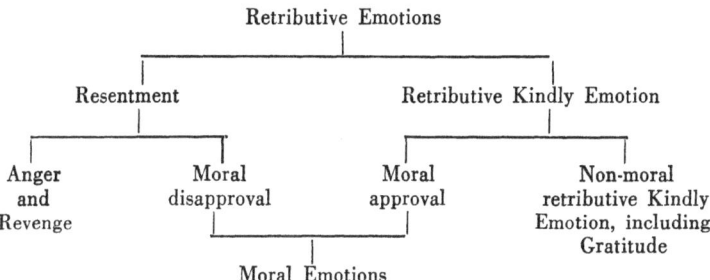

Note that moral disapproval is merely an offshoot of the feeling of resentment, and that resentment is essentially "an aggressive attitude of mind towards an assumed cause of pain,"[7] that is, it creates in one an unpleasant state of mind. Resentment is aggressiveness inverted or in disguised form; this emerged in the course of mental or social evolution. Anger and revenge, the emotions responsible for resentment, have been displaced at the higher stages of evolutionary moral development and superseded with the forgiveness of injuries as one's prime duty.

The law of retaliation and the principle of forgiveness are harmonious if not similar: forgiveness condemns nonmoral resentment and personal hatred; "forgiveness prohibits revenge, but not punishment." The *lex talionis* permitted one to take his revenge on all forms of resentment including impartial indignation. In fact, "according to the Laws of Manu, crime was so indispensably to be followed by punishment, that if the king pardoned a thief or a perpetrator of violence, instead of slaying or striking him, the guilt fell on the king."[8] The foregoing analysis indicates that *moral disapproval is a form of resentment,* and moral approval is to recompense by responding with a kindly emotion. viz., a *retributive kindly emotion,* such as *gratitude.*

For an emotion to qualify as a moral one, "our self condemnation and self approval must present the same characteristics as make resentment and retributive kindliness moral emotions when they are felt with reference to the conduct of other people,"[9] *e.g.,* remorse is experienced as the result of base and unjust actions, not from sacrificial acts prompted from a sense of duty or justice. Moral emotions exert greater force or command and a greater recognition when they possess a quality of generality about them, *i.e.,* when they are socially shared and widely accepted. In fact, moral principles have a social origin: "Society is the birthplace of the moral consciousness. The first moral judgments expressed not the private emotions of isolated individuals but emotions which were felt by the community at large. Public indignation is the prototype of moral disapproval and public approval is the prototype of moral approbation. And these public emotions are characterized by generality, individual disinterestedness, and apparent impartiality."[10] Emotions shared in common eventuate in what one fancies to be an objective moral value or principle, but actually they constitute a class of phenomena that the public at large has learned to respond to with kindred emotions. When a sufficient number of persons respond to a situation with like emotions, the situation is judged a moral one.

4. Ethical Subjectivism

Ethical relativity is *ethical subjectivism;* this section is devoted to emphasizing the subjectivistic elements in the ethics of Westermarck. Subjectivism is the belief that ethical good is some form of subjective experience without a corollary in objective reality. The subjectivist maintains that personal feeling is the ultimate criterion of what is right and good; it is the theory that relegates all moral data to subjective elements of experience. Ethical subjectivism is a view diametrically opposed to the position that moral value possesses objective validity, such as is found in the normative theories of ethics of Kant and others. The subjectivist believes that truth is a matter of opinion and that what one person believes is true, is true for him and what another person believes is true, is true for that person. Morality is relative to the person who thinks it to be so; some relativists believe that one cannot know good without knowing evil, or evil in the absence of good. Westermarck supports his relativity with such remarks as: "A mode of conduct which among one people is condemned as wrong is among another people viewed with indifference or regarded as praiseworthy or enjoined as a duty."[11]

Westermarck contends that ethical principles are grounded in emotions, hence are subjective expressions, of personal feelings on the part of the individual who confuses them with objectivity.

> A similar translation of emotional states into terms of qualities assigned to external phenomena is found in many . . . cases: something is "fearful" because people fear it, "admirable" because people admire it.[12] When we call an act good or bad, we do not *state* the existence of any emotional tendencies, any more than, when we call a landscape beautiful, we state any characteristics of beauty: we refer the subject of the judgment to a class of phenomena which we are used to call good or bad. But we are used to call them so because they have evoked moral approval or disapproval in ourselves or in other persons from whom we have learned the use of those words.[13]

Such is Westermarck's position and defence of his contention that moral values lack objectivity, viz., on the basis of their being essentially emotion, since emotion lacks objectivity. He contends: "In my opinion the predicates of all moral judgments, all moral concepts, are ultimately based on emotions, and that, as is very commonly admitted, no objectivity can come from an emotion."[14] Westermarck is satisfied that he has successfully shown that moral questions are not factual matters that can be debated with reference to objective data, but subjective states; moral values are reducible to states of feeling and personal or social opinion.

He proudly concludes his book, *Ethical Relativity* in a triumphant air: "I flatter myself with the belief that I have, in no small measure, given additional strength to the main contentions of this book: that the moral consciousness is ultimately based on emotions, that the moral judgment lacks objective validity, that the moral values are not absolute but relative to the emotions they express."[15]

5. Evaluation of Ethical Relativity

Relativity has been bombarded for over two millennia, ever since Socrates effectively attacked the philosophy of relativity expounded by Protagoras. The account is beautifully related in Plato's *Theatetus,* in which it is proved that the relativist's position is untenable due to its self-contradictory state, viz., if truth is a matter of opinion, then the person whose opinion it is that truth is objective and absolute would render his relativist opponent's stand false. *E.g.*, if Protagoras takes the stand that all truth is a matter of opinion and that what is true for him is true for him, and what is true for Socrates is true for Socrates, then Socrates can controvert by stating that in his opinion truth is objective or absolute and that Protagoras' position of subjectivism is false; Protagoras would then of necessity respond: "You are correct, Socrates." Plato happily puts it: "The best of the joke is, that Protagoras acknowledges the truth of their opinion who believe his opinion to be false; for in admitting that the opinions of all men are true, in effect he grants that the opinion of his opponents is true.'' Consequently, a consistent relativism is an impossibility.

If subjectivism were valid and truth were merely a matter of personal opinion then some very ludicrous and absurd conclusions would follow to destroy this thesis via the *reductio ad absurdum* argument. *E.g.*, someone judging the case of a man involved in a multiplicity of crimes such as murder, grand larceny, rape, etc., could dismiss the case with a two dollar fine and then levy life imprisonment to a second defendant who is merely guilty of a parking violation. If anyone were to object on the grounds that this constituted a gross miscarriage of justice, then the judge could reply that in his opinion he did what was right. The entire matter can be easily clarified by pointing out that a genuine principle of justice does exist and one is expected to adhere to it; it is true that often, and possibly always, one does not strike it on the head, but it is easily detectable when one is exceedingly remote from the mark or is disregarding the principle altogether as in the case of the unjust judge. However, if relativity is valid then grotesque results such as the foregoing could legitimately ensue. It would be far more coherent to claim that discrepancies about particular acts of justice are matters of opinion inasmuch as each approximates the principle of justice, but even under these circumstances, one must be closer to the truth than the others, even if he does not precisely hit the mark.

NOTES

EDWARD WESTERMARCK

1. Edward Westermarck, *Ethical Relativity* (New York: Harcourt, Brace and Co., 1932), xvii.
2. Edward Westermarck, *The Origin And Development of the Moral Ideas*, London: Macmillan and Co., 1912) vol. I, 1.
    In order to dispense with footnotes expeditiously, in subsequent citations, ET will be used for *Ethical Relativity*.
3. *Ibid.*, 4.
4. *Ibid.*, 4, 5.
5. *Ibid.*, 21.
6. *Idem.*
7. *Ibid.*, 73.
8. *Ibid.*, 77.
9. *Ibid.*, 107.
10. *Ibid.*, vol. II, 740.
11. *Ibid.*, 742.
12. See John Stuart Mill's proof of Utilitarianism.
13. ET, 114, 115.
14. *Ibid.*, 60.
15. *Ibid.*, 289.

ETHICAL NATURALISM

RALPH BARTON PERRY

In no case do we strive for, wish for, long for, or desire anything, because we deem it to be good, but on the other hand we deem a thing good, because we strive for it, wish for it, long for it, or desire it.[1]

(Spinoza)

1. Ethical Naturalism

Ethical Naturalism is that school of philosophical thought which reduces all ethics or value to the level of empiricism, *i.e.*, natural and social science; consequently, scientific laws of nature, including ethical value, are ruled invalid. The ethical naturalist regards moral propositions as derivatives of the empirical sciences, such as psychology, sociology, political science, etc., hence, ethical issues can be completely and satisfactorily answered on the findings of the natural or social sciences, solely. *Supernatural* phenomena, such as, autonomy, moral laws, telic and idealistic realities are denied any basis in the objective world; in other words, metaphysical realities lack significance, they are unwarranted and unnecessary hypotheses.

2. The Interest Theory of Value

Ralph Barton Perry's value theory is designated *Ethical Naturalism* because of its naturalistic reductionism, *i.e.*, assigning moral value to one's natural or psychological constitution, viz., *interest;* "that which is an object of interest is *eo ipso* invested with value. Any object, whatever it be, acquires value when any interest, whatever it be, is taken in it; just as anything whatsoever becomes a target when anyone whosoever aims at it."[2] Any neutral object may become valuable and does become a value at the moment a person expresses interest in it. Perry has algebraically formulated his thesis in the equation: "x is valuable=interest is taken in x."[3] According to this equation, it follows, that any object, real or imaginary, regardless of its ontological status, acquires value provided interest is expressed in it. "This is value *simpliciter,* — value in the elementary, primordial and generic sense."[4]

Philosophers, and others, have failed to disclose the nature of value in the generic sense because they have been too preoccupied with producing a scale of values; consequently, they have been victimized by the fallacy of compound questions. Their value theories are constructed to answer questions, such as: "What is uniquely valuable? What is superlatively valuable? What is reflectively or consciously valuable?" instead of answering the proper question posed by value theory: *"In what consists value in the generic sense?"* An accurate definition of value in its generic sense is: *"a thing — any thing — has value, or is valuable, in the original and generic sense when it is the object of an interest — any interest.* Or, *whatever is object of interest is ipso facto valuable."*[5] E.g., peace is highly valuable to those persons who express a deep interest in it, *i.e.,* for what it is, *per se,* for its attributes, consequences, implications, etc. To define *value* simply as *interest* is to commit a bi-verbal definition that begs the question, What is *interest?* Perry defines interest as *"a train of events determined by expectation of its outcome.* Or, *a thing is an object of interest when its being expected induces actions looking to its realization or nonrealization."*[6] E.g., peace is an object of interest when acts performed or events selected are conducive to peace.

The term *value, itself,* is an excellent word; its historical use implies duty, price, piety, utility, ideals, and codes, "at the same time it points toward that aspect of human life for which it is customary to employ the eulogistic-dyslogistic vocabulary. It points to other pointers, and borrows the ostensive meaning of such adjectives as 'good,' 'best,' 'right,' 'ought,' 'worthy,' 'beautiful,' 'sacred,' 'just,' and such nouns as 'happiness,' 'well-being,' and 'civilization'."[7] Furthermore, the term's grammatical convenience is noteworthy: it has substantive, adjectival, and verbal variants so that one may speak of *values,* of the *valuable,* and the act of *valuing.* The term suffers loss of some of its meaning when it is restricted to refer to concepts such as good, right, etc., only.

G. E. Moore erred when he asserted that certain words were *indefinable;* it would have been more appropriate to state that certain terms are not defined. The proof that value is definable is evidenced by the fact that it is herein defined, viz., "as *the relation of an object to a valuing subject.*"[8] One may find objections to this definition, such as, the charge that it is *circular* on the grounds that when an object is predicated to be good it is an object of positive interest, *e.g.,* "it is generally agreed that the goodness of drugs is questionable despite the intense craving of the addict; and it is usually concluded that the drug is bad because the craving is bad. It would seem to follow that in order that a thing shall be good it must be the object of a good interest, in which case 'good' is defined in terms of good."[9] Perry believes that this objection is counteracted with the recognition that an interest itself possesses value, *per se,* independent of whether its object is of positive or negative worth. The preceding statement unqualified implies that there can be *no bad interests,* but this is not the case, inasmuch as all interests are not on an equal par since certain ones are of higher worth than others. Consequently, no interest is bad, *per se,* but it is undesirable in the sense that it is a hindrance to the pursuit and fulfillment of the loftier interests, *i.e.,* an interest ought to be discarded if it inhibits the realization of an interest of greater worth. It now appears as though there exists a coherent system of interests similar to a hierarchy of goods, and if this is the case, then the grade of an interest is dependent upon its comprehensiveness, *i.e.*, important long range interests outrank the limited short range interests, hence the all-pervading or all-inclusive interest must be completely good.

Some critics mistakenly claim that various interests may clash by way of contradiction, but this cannot be true since interests do not contradict, but only *conflict*. Propositions are subject to contradictions, hence it is only when interests are stated as propositions that they may become self-contradictory. The apparent contradictoriness of interests stems from the omission of a frame or axis of reference, *e.g.*, it may appear contradictory to assert that an interest is *above and below* when one has neglected to specify above and below *what*. An interest can be both useful and ugly when properly specified, *e.g.*, an object of interest may be practically useful and aesthetically ugly or selfishly beneficent and socially injurious. If the foregoing is objected to on the grounds that this contradiction has been avoided by taking refuge in subjectivism or *relativism*, then, Perry's retort, is "Well, if one may be permitted a vulgarism, and so what?"[10] Nevertheless, this does not mean that *values are relative*, but rather, *relational;* consequently, a value may be conceived as absolutely valuable, independent of the value of any other object.

Interests are essentially objective; it is not the possessor of the interest that endues it with value, *i.e.*, it is not the person, the knower and judge of the interest that invests interest with value, any interest that is desired, liked, willed, loved, is good in and of itself alone. If this were not the case, then the individual would be considered the value, rather than interest, which would destroy the fundamental thesis herein, viz., that value is any object of interest. "When, however, value is defined in terms of interests, then *any* interest will satisfy the definition; and if I observe that anyone else likes, desires, loves, or wills a thing, then I am bound by the definition to judge it good. The evidence of its goodness or badness is the observable fact of interest, which is just as objective, and just as open to agreement, as any other fact of life or history."[11]

Certain interests have definite universal appeal and are of utmost import to humanity as a whole; when this is the case, such interests are referred to as *realms of value,* from which Perry's book derives its title. These "human enterprises and pursuits that have a claim to special attention because of their universality or importance are ... morality, conscience, politics, law, economy, art, science, education, and religion;"[12] such general interests spring from psychological *modes of interest,* viz., reflex, habit, instinct, hunger, appetite, feeling, pleasure, pain, emotions, etc.

Interest may be defined psychologically: *"An act is interested in so far as its occurrence is due to the agreement between its accompanying expectation and the unfulfilled phases of a governing propensity."*[13] An analysis of interest indicates that it is composed of a *governing propensity, i.e.,* a *determining tendency* or general *set* which is control of the individual organism as a whole at any given time. The second aspect of the definition involves *subordinate* or *auxiliary responses* by which the general propensity is executed. The third aspect of the definition implies that the subordinate responses are *tentative, i.e.,* they are chosen in the light of their anticipated results. Although this definition of interest is *teleological,* it has not been accomplished at the expense of any breach with *mechanism.*

3. The Criteria and Calculus of Value

Four criteria are employed as principles for the systematic gradation of values: *correctness, intensity, preference* and *inclusiveness.* Correctness is primarily a criterion of value, whereas the other three principles serve in the capacity of the commensurability of value; however, all four share in the dual function of qualifying interest, which is constitutive of value, and comparing values in such a manner as to preserve the generic purity and character, and prevent its adulteration with any new conception of value intrinsically discordant with the generic character. "In other words, there are two fundamental methods of criticism, the corrective method, and the quantitative method; the first expressed in the judgment, 'this value is founded on truth or error,' and the second expressed in the judgment, 'this value is greater or less'."[14] The latter method is used to calculate the magnitude of the interest or value which an object possesses, and the former serves in the determination of the accuracy of the interest, but does not predicate *more or less* and *better or worse* of its object.

The principle of the commensurability of values requires that values meet the standards of intensity, preference, and inclusiveness, *e.g.*, wine may be evaluated as the better object of interest than water provided: (1) the intensity of interest in the wine is greater, (2) the wine is preferred to water, and (3) the interest in wine is all-inclusive or has a greater inclusiveness than water.

(a) *The standard of intensity* is a measurement of the interest's value in terms of the object's ability to create an arousal, excitement, or strength of interest. It is an appeal to the cult of feeling, since it is measured in terms, such as, "listlessness," "ecstacy," "quickened sense of life," "high passion," "enthusiastic activity," as is exemplified in Pater's *Renaissance*:

> We have an interval, and then our place knows us no more. Some spend this interval in listlessness, some in high passions, the wisest, at least among the 'children of this world,' in art and song. For our one chance lies in expanding that interval, in getting as many pulsations into the given time. Great passions may give us this quickened sense of life, ecstacy and sorrow of love, the various forms of enthusiastic activity, disinterested and otherwise, which come naturally to many of us. Only be sure it is passion — that it does yield you this fruit of a quickened multiplied consciousness.

Intensity of interest "is a ratio of the elements which are acting under the control of the interest, to the totality of the elements of the organism."[15] Divided or conflicting interests and inattentiveness may be responsible for a reduction of interest. Intensity is "measured by the magnitude of the fraction rather than by that of its denominator;" consequently, "the whole-hearted play of the child is more intense than the half-hearted cooperation of his nurse, even though the one is the heart of an infant and the other the heart of an adult."[16]

(b) *The standard of preference* is appealed to when two objects are of the same intensity of interest. Preference is the distinguishing quality responsible for the breach between Bentham's egoistic hedonism and Mill's qualitative Utilitarianism; the one distinguishes humanity from the brute, the nobler joys from animal satisfactions. The important function of the principle of preference "is that it arranges the objects of any given interest in an order, relatively to one another, and in a manner that cannot be reduced either to the intensity or to the inclusiveness of the interest,"[17] *i.e.*, it measures in terms of a "distensive magnitude" or one of "qualitative difference."

(c) *The standard of inclusiveness* is invoked in the occurrence of an overlapping of interests, *i.e.*, where many interests are shared in common by a number of persons; it is essentially Mill's principle of "the greatest good of the greatest number," which is in turn based on the premise that the whole is greater than any of the parts of which it is composed. "Interest is added to interest in the same objects, and these objects derive augmented value from the summation of the interests taken in them."[18] Inclusiveness is the standard utilized in assimilating the various interests into one coherent system after having exploited to a maximum all of the standards of value.

4. The *Summum Bonum*

The standard of inclusiveness is the determinant of the *highest good,* by virtue of the peculiar role it plays in the definition of a hierarchy of values. "The greatest good will be the object of an all-inclusive and harmonious system of interests."[19] Such an all-inclusive and harmonious system of interests is an ideal object of an ideal will, viz., *an all-harmonious, all-benevolent, and enlightened unanimity.*

This is achieved through the harmonizing effect of love which is defined as a "favorable interest in the satisfaction of a second interest;" the second interest is another person. Love is free of selfishness; "love begins and ends abroad. That 'charity begins at home' is one of those many proverbs which have been coined by the devil to flatter human weakness. . . . Love, in other words, is an interested support of another's preexisting and independently existing interest."[20]

Many characteristics have been erroneously confused with love: it is neither approving nor censorious; it does not rebuke the immoral person nor rejoices in his merited punishment; it is not sex-love whose appetite feeds upon another individual as unloving as cannibalism. "The true quality of love is to be found in that sensitive imagination which can find its way into the secret sources of a man's joy and sorrow."[21] Love is essentially an interest in another which seeks to support and promote that person's achievement of desires or enjoyment, viz., interests. *Universal love* would be to assume the same attitude or disposition toward all mankind; this may be termed "an attitude of general kindly interest or amiability" or as Lincoln phrased it "with malice toward none, with charity for all," viz., the good Samaritan. Love is "a personal integration dominated by such a purpose [and] is known in the tradition of moral philosophy as 'good will'."[22]

Philosophically, love is *good will;* it is the precursor which ushers in the highest good. Good will is exemplarily rendered in Kant's *categorical imperative*: "Act on that maxim whereby thou canst at the same time will that it should become a universal law." Perry would revise this to read: "Cultivate that kind of will that is qualified to bring harmony through its universal adoption."[23] An all-benevolent will, viz., *love,* is the supreme virtue capable of contributing greatest to the fulfillment of the interests of all men; such a universal interest need not hamper individual interests for "the sentiment of humanity leaves to each man his own choices of individual perfection,"[24] resulting in the harmonious union of the two.

The *summum bonum,* viz., an all-harmonious, all-benevolent, and enlightened unanimity, is an ideal which is empirically unattainable, inasmuch as the "outstanding fact of life is conflict." The highest good, which is related to happiness, is not the "sheer satisfaction of maximum intensity, but, as Plato taught, an *order* of satisfaction, whose form is prescribed by reason."[25] There is no guarantee that the all-harmonious will, viz., the ideal, will be realized in heaven either; it appears then, the highest good is not an historical fact, "but a norm of legitimate aspiration." However, the realization of it would issue in *universal happiness,* and there are moments when man at his best seems to catch a spark of its realization, for there must be "a spark of God in man." Such moments are readily perceptible; "it is that moment of melting tenderness felt in the presence of beauty, or of chivalric devotion to a cause, or of compassion for the brave struggle and patient suffering of sentient creatures; when one is drawn into some major current of life, and when the joy that testifies to its unnatural exaltation . . . let the answer be found in those moments of perfected intercourse in which happiness is founded on generosity, and in which there is a sudden revelation of the meaning of marriage, of friendship, of human fellowship.[26] . . . Of all great gifts the commonest is loving-kindness: and of all great gifts, this is the greatest."[27]

5. Evaluation of the Ethics of Perry

One serious deterrent to Perry's value theory becoming a coherent system lies at the heart of his thesis, viz., *all value is interest,* hence there can be no bad interests, *i.e.,* no evil interests. The obvious fact is there are bad interests that prove deleterious and even devastating both to the individual manifesting the interest and those victimized by it, *e.g.,* a thief or a killer may have as his prime interest the robbery or murder of an individual who inhibits his free access to wealth and success, hence he commits robbery and murder to remove the obstacle frustrating his chance for opportunity and progress. Later, when the authorities apprehend him, he pays for his crime with his own life. Is this not sufficient proof of the possibility of bad interests, if not the existence of evil interests?

Perry's ethical naturalism falls squarely under the full brunt of the blow of G. E. Moore's *naturalistic fallacy*, viz., equating the physical properties of an object with the experiental object, *per se, e.g.*, the *experience* of sound is not to be confused with the *physical properties* of sound, such as sound waves, quanta, etc. Perry has committed precisely this error by reducing all value data to that of the natural sciences, viz., biology, psychology, etc., *e.g.*, all moral value is interest, all interest is biological; hence, all moral value is biological. However, it has never been successfully proved, scientifically or philosophically, that value is biological or physical; it appears to be a *sui generis*.

6. Further Reading in the Philosophy of Perry

Ralph Barton Perry wrote a number of works in the field of philosophy, but only those that pertain to value theory have been mentioned. His classic works are: *General Theory of Value*, (1926), and its sequel, *Realms of Value*, (1954), which is an expansion and revision of the "Gifford Lectures on Natural Religion" delivered from 1946 to 1948 at the University of Glasgow. An earlier book, *The Moral Economy*, (1909), is an expansion of the fundamental thesis found in his article entitled: "The Conception of Moral Goodness," published in the *Philosophical Review*, (1907). Two other articles: "The Quest of Moral Obligation," in the *International Journal of Ethics* (1911), and "The Definition of Value," in the *Journal of Philosophy, Psychology and the Scientific Method*, (1914), carry the same basic concept of value theory prevalent in his writings of a lifetime.

NOTES

RALPH BARTON PERRY

1. Spinoza, *Ethics*, Part III, Proposition IX, tr. by R. H. M. Elwes, 1901.
2. Ralph Barton Perry, *General Theory of Value* (Cambridge, Mass.: Harvard University Press, 1926), 115.
3. *Ibid.*, 116.
4. *Idem.*
5. Ralph Barton Perry, *Realms of Value* (Cambridge, Mass.: Harvard University Press, 1954), 3.
6. *Idem.*
7. *Ibid.*, 5.
8. Perry, *General Theory of Value*, op. cit., 122.
9. Perry, *Realms of Value*, op. cit., 11.
10. *Ibid.*, 12.
11. *Ibid.*, 13.
12. *Ibid.*, 14.
13. Perry, *General Theory of Value*, op. cit., 183.
14. *Ibid.*, 612.
15. *Ibid.*, 630.
16. *Idem.*
17. *Ibid.*, 635.
18. *Ibid.*, 645.
19. *Ibid.*, 659.
20. *Ibid.*, 677.
21. *Ibid.*, 678.
22. *Ibid.*, 679.
23. *Ibid.*, 682.
24. *Ibid.*, 683.
25. *Ibid.*, 687.
26. *Ibid.*, 691.
27. *Ibid.*, 692.

THOMAS HOBBES

Every man has a right to everything; even to one another's body. (Hobbes)

1. Might Makes Right

There exist two fundamental natural laws: (1) the right of nature; (2) the law of nature; the first entitles a man to preserve himself at all costs, in any manner; the second is an injunction against doing anything which may prove destructive to his life. "The *right of nature,* which writers commonly call *Jus Naturale,* is the liberty each man has, to use his own power, as he will himself, for the preservation of his own nature; that is to say, of his own life; and consequently, of doing anything, which in his own judgment, and reason, he shall conceive to be the aptest means thereto. . . . A *law of nature,* (*Lex Naturalis*) is a precept, or general rule, found out by reason, by which a man is forbidden to do, that which is destructive of his life, or takes away the means of preserving the same; and to omit, that, by which he thinks it may be best preserved."[1]

Man in his natural state, without the benefit of civil laws, is entitled to practice the law of the jungle, *i.e.,* "the law of tooth and claw." He has every right to plunder whomever he will and take whatever booty pleases him for *might makes right;* this is a person's natural birthright, consequently nothing can be considered unjust. Since the law of the jungle prevails, man is in a constant state of war, if not a violent outbreak of battle, at least a cold war. "To this war of every man against every man, this also is consequent; that nothing can be unjust. The notions of right and wrong, justice and injustice have there no place. Where there is no common power, there is no law, where no law, no injustice. Force and fraud, are in war the two cardinal virtues."[2] Since conditions of war prevail no morals or rules are countenanced, except those natural powers that a man can rally to his support. "And because the condition of man . . . is a condition of war of every one against every one . . . there is nothing that he can make use of, that may not be a help to him, in preserving his life against his enemies; it follows, that in such a condition, every man has a right to every thing; even to one another's body."[3]

Man has the natural right to behave as the beasts in the jungle do because he was created a belligerent being; his psychological constitution is geared to the jungle's law. "The desires, and other passions of man, are in themselves no sin. No more are the actions, that proceed from those passions, till they know a law that forbids them: which till laws are made they cannot know: nor can any law be made, till they have agreed upon the person that shall make it."[4] Man's fundamental, *i.e.,* original nature is evil, he cannot be trusted, nor does he trust anyone else. "It may seem strange to some man, that has not well weighed these things, that nature should thus dissociate, and render men apt to invade and destroy one another: and he may therefore, not trusting to this inference made from the passions, desire perhaps to have the same confirmed by experience. Let him therefore consider with himself, when taking a journey, he arms himself, and seeks to go well accompanied; when going to sleep he locks his doors; when even in his house, he locks his chests; and this when he knows there be laws, and public officers, armed, to revenge all injuries . . . what opinion he has of his fellow-subjects, when he rides armed; of his fellow-citizens, when he locks his doors; and of his children and servants, when he locks his chests. Does he not there as much accuse mankind by his actions, as do my words?"[5]

The characteristics of man's psychological nature responsible for his belligerent nature are: *competition, diffidence, glory.* His hunger for gain stems from a natural competitive constitution; his desire for safety emanates from diffidence, *i.e.*, distrust; his thirst for reputation is rooted in a natural disposition for glory. Each of these is used as a technique for conquering others, *e.g.*, "the first use violence, to make themselves masters of others men's persons, wives, children, and cattle; the second, to defend them; the third, for trifles, as a word, a smile, a different opinion, and any other sign of undervalue either direct in their persons or by reflexion in their kindred, their friends, their nation, their profession, or their name."[6] Man, a warfaring creature, is incessantly at war with his neighbor whether the battle is overt or repressed and covert; the latter, which is of the cold war mode is usually the type engaged, but it is a genuine conflict. "For war, consists not in battle only, or in the act of fighting; but in a tract of time, wherein the will to contend by battle is sufficiently known. . . . For as the nature of foul weather, lies not in a shower or two of rain; but in an inclination thereto of many days together; so the nature of war, consists not in actual fighting; but in the known disposition thereto, during all the time there is no assurance to the contrary."[7]

2. The Social Contract

In a situation which prevails under the code of an absolute ethics of power, no one can truly emerge the victor, inasmuch as the strongest physical man can be easily destroyed by the weakest with the use of a weapon, *e.g.*, a gun. Furthermore, men in groups are equal, even if they are not individual; consequently if a physically powerful man attacks a weak one, then the weak one may retaliate by recruiting others who for the sake of their own protection will unite in adherence to the principle: "United we stand divided we fall." However, if the strong man joins a group then the first group may use weapons, but if both groups increase the potency of their weapons to a great extent, *e.g.*, to the level of the atomic bombs of multimegaton weight, then war becomes an impossible enterprise, hence obsolete. In this sense men are equal:

"Nature hath made men so equal, in the faculties of body, and mind; as that though there be found one man sometimes manifestly stronger in body, or of quicker mind than another; yet when all is reckoned together, the difference between man, and man, is not so considerable, as that one man can thereupon claim to himself any benefit, to which another may not pretend, as well as he. For as to strength of body, the weakest has strength enough to kill the strongest, either by secret machination, or by confederacy with others that are in the same danger with himself."[8]

If man does not yield his right of nature and relinquish his prerogative under the law of nature, he will be faced with extinction, an alternative which he is unprepared for and incapable of accepting due to the nature of his psychological constitution. Man's instinct of self-preservation forbids any thought or recourse to annihilation; this drive is fortified with intense and potent "passions that incline men to peace ... fear of death; desire of such things as are necessary to commodious living; and a hope by their industry to obtain them."[9] Consequently, it is incumbent upon man to relinquish these rights of nature and substitute in their place one that is conducive to social co-existence and personal survival. Such is the "Fundamental Law of Nature; which is *to seek peace and follow it*. From this Fundamental Law of Nature, by which men are commanded to endeavor peace, is derived this second law; *That a man be willing, when others are so too, as far as for peace and defence of himself he shall think it necessary, to lay down his right to all things: and be contented with so much liberty against other men, as he would allow other men against himself.*"[10] Close examination of this second law will reveal that it is a modification of the Golden Rule; one is expected to be satisfied with as much right and liberty for his own enjoyment as he is willing to allow another. If men are not willing to accept this law, then it is tantamount to remaining in a condition of war.

Consequently, for the sake of peace and the safety of his own life, man must sue for peace by voluntarily resigning his Right of Nature and accepting in its stead, a *social con-*

tract. "The mutual transferring of right, is that which men call *contract.*"[11] The *social contract* is a "covenant of every man with every man, *I authorise and give up my right of governing myself, to this man, or to this assembly of men, on this condition, that thou give up thy right to him, and authorise all his actions in like manner.* This done, the multitude so united in one person, is called a *common-wealth,* in Latin *civitas.* This is the generation of that great LEVIATHAN or rather (to speak more reverently) of that *mortal god,* to which we owe under the *immortal God,* our peace and defence."[12] This great leviathan, king, or mortal god is entrusted with the task of enforcing the social contract, *i.e.,* he is empowered to oversee that the parties to the social contract live up to their agreement or else be punished. In exchange for his services, and in deference to his position, he enjoys the envied status of being above the law and free from its restraints, hence he need not abide by the laws levied upon the populace. "This person is called *sovereign,* and said to have *sovereign power;* and everyone besides, his *subject.* The attaining to this sovereign power, is by two ways. One, by natural force; as when a man makes his children, to submit themselves, and their children, to his government, as being able to destroy them if they refuse; or by war subdue his enemies to his will, giving them their lives on that condition. The other, is when men agree amongst themselves, to submit to some man, or assembly of men, voluntarily, on confidence to be protected by him against all others. This latter, may be called a political common-wealth, or common-wealth by *institution;* and the former a common-wealth by acquisition."[13]

In either type of commonwealth, however, the sovereign must have the requisite power to maintain peace and command the obedience of his subjects to the social contract. Should a change in circumstance occur whereby the sovereign has been overthrown by a greater power, then the new power by right of superior strength is entitled to enjoy the position heretofore held by the now displaced sovereign.

3. Natural Moral Law

An adherent of ethical naturalism believes that all morality originates from nature, not from a realm of non-natural values or moral laws. Hobbes true to this position has enumerated a set of moral laws which to him are genuine laws of nature; the first two have been listed above, viz., those which pertained to the transfer of one's rights to another, *i.e.*, the social contract. The rest are as follows.

3. The law pertaining to *justice*: "That men perform their convenants made."

4. The law of *gratitude*: "That a man who receives benefit from another of grace, endeavor that he which gives it, have not reasonable cause to repent of his good will."

5. The law of *compleasance (compliance)*: "That every man strive to accommodate himself to the rest."

6. Law of *pardon*: "That upon caution of future time, a man ought to pardon the offences past of them that repenting, desire it."

7. Law of *revenge*: "That in revenges, (that is, retribution of evil for evil), men look not at the greatness of the evil past, but the greatness of the good to follow."

8. Law of *contumely*: "That no man by deed, word, countenance, gesture, declare hatred, or contempt of another."

9. Law of *pride*: "That every man acknowledge other for his equal by nature."

10. Law regarding *arrogance* and *modesty*: "That at the entrance into conditions of peace, no man require to reserve to himself any right, which he is not content should be reserved to every one of the rest."

11. Law of *equity*: "That such things as cannot be divided, be enjoyed in common, if it can be; and if the quantity of the thing permit, without stint; otherwise proportionably to the number of them that have right."

12. Corollary of the law of *equity*: "That the entire right; or else (making the use of alternate), the first possession, be determined by lot. . . . Of lots there be two sorts, *arbitrary*, and *natural*. Arbitrary, is that which is agreed on

by the competitors: natural, is either *primogeniture* . . . or *first seisure.*"

13. Law of *safe conduct*: "That all men that mediate peace, be allowed safe conduct."

14. Law of *arbitration*: "That they that are at controversy, submit their right to the judgement of an arbitrator."[14]

All of these laws may be condensed into one which is simple and easily understandable, viz., the *Golden Rule*: "Do not that to another, which thou wouldst not have done to thy self."[15]

4. Evaluation of Ethical Naturalism

The greatest weakness in the system of Hobbes is the fact of his many unsubstantiated statements; many of his assumptions are ill grounded, viz., (1) the belief that man is not a social being by nature; (2) the doctrine of the depravity of man; (3) the claim that man is belligerent by natural constitution. Aristotle, believing that man's natural constitution is basically a peaceful one, noted that the Spartan nation fell in spite of its unfailing military might because the Spartans were ever geared for war and not for peace, hence in times of peace rusted as a sword in a scabbard.[16] If war were the natural state of man then persons would become adapted to it naturally, but war is an abnormal state capable of causing the strongest or healthiest minds to suffer a breakdown.[17]

Hobbes' claim that man is essentially evil is unsubstantiated except for the flimsy argument that one locks his doors because he does not trust his neighbor, and his chests at home because he does not trust the members of his family. Actually the average man is trustworthy, if it were not so, one could not conduct a properly operated or co-ordinated society at all. The thief is not typical of the average human being in society nor is the murderer; if one should even go to the extent of leaving his door wide open, the chances are that not one in a thousand would take advantage and commit theft. As for locking chests in one's home, this is necessary for the sake of privacy, if for no other reason; a locked desk drawer may contain very personal and private materials which would prove embarrassing and perhaps harmful if they were accidentally exposed to those who had no business with them.

If people were by nature evil and bellicose, then a social contract would never succeed operatively for any period of time as is evidenced by the behavior of criminal societies, *e.g.,* underworld gangsters; without mutual trust and honorable behavior there can be no society, but a state which is prevalent among the beasts of the jungle.

A. C. Ewing has a valid objection which he levels at all forms of ethical naturalism, viz., that all naturalistic definitions of moral value are unacceptable and evidently false on the basis that if they were true they could be discovered by science utilizing the standard scientific methods. Since they cannot be derived through the techniques of science then they cannot be natural phenomena, hence if they possess any reality at all, they must be non-natural, *i.e.,* idealistic.

5. Further Reading in the Philosophy of Hobbes

Those who care to investigate the philosophy of Hobbes further may consult the following works by him: *Human Nature* (1650); *De Corpore Politico* (1650); *Leviathan* (1651); *Of Liberty and Necessity* (1654); *De Corpore* (1655); *De Homine* (1658); *Behemoth* (1679).

NOTES
THOMAS HOBBES

1. Thomas Hobbes, *Leviathan* (1651), Part I, Ch. 14. To facilitate reading, the archaic spelling and words of Hobbes have been modernized throughout this section.
2. *Ibid.*, Part I, Ch. 13.
3. *Ibid.*, Part I, Ch. 14.
4. *Ibid.*, Part I, Ch. 13.
5. *Idem.*
6. *Idem.*
7. *Idem.*
8. *Idem.*
9. *Idem.*
10. *Ibid.*, Part I, Ch. 14.
11. *Idem.*
12. *Ibid.*, Part II, Ch. 17.
13. *Idem.*
14. *Ibid.*, Part I, Ch. 15.
15. *Idem.*
16. *Politics*, Bk. II, Ch. 9, (1271^b).
17. Cf. Robert White, *The Abnormal Personality, op. cit.*

MORITZ SCHLICK

Kindness, thou dear great name, that containest nothing in thee demanding loveless esteem, but prayest to be followed; thou dost not menace and needst not establish any law, but of thyself findest entrance into feeling, and willingly art revered; whose smile disarms all sister inclinations; thou art so glorious that we need not ask after thy descent, for whatever be thy origin it is ennobled through thee! (Schlick)

1. Ethical Naturalism

(a) *Analysis of Moral Value.* Moritz Schlick, although an adherent of the school of Logical Positivism,[1] has contributed to value theory, an ethic that differs markedly from the ethical skeptics or ethical nihilists, such as, A. J. Ayer. Faithful to the tradition of the Logical Positivists, Schlick reduces philosophical propositions, which naturally include moral principles, to non-entities; even scientific propositions are only definitions which "are in no way bound up with natural laws."[2] Nevertheless, Schlick is confident that he has successfully made some valid judgments in the area of ethics,[3] but these are not value judgments, instead they are scientific judgments, rightly belonging to the field of psychology. Philosophy, *per se,* is not a science; its function is to give meaning to scientific propositions. Whereas science is descriptive, *i.e.*, scientists relate, report, narrate, or recount facts, philosophy is *activity, i.e.,* behavior. The question arises as to the possibility of writing philosophical texts, since it is utterly impracticable to insert *activity* into a book. Schlick's reply is two-fold: First, communication of true scientific propositions is feasible; in the area of ethics, this is effected through the field of psychology. Second, some contribution has been made by way of philosophical activity (ethics); although these are not genuine propositions, they serve as "stimuli for the reader to carry out those acts by virtue of which certain propositions obtain a clear meaning."[4]

If ethics is to be meaningful, it must be a science, and the proper scope of its study is psychology; consequently, all ethical propositions are descriptive, not normative or absolute principles. If the philosopher is interested in ethical facts, he must content himself with being satisfied with descriptive data, but since this lies in the domain of psychological science and all else falls in the province of the moralist or reformer, consequently the philosopher must restrict himself to theoretical questions, for these are independent of human interest and lie in the legitimate sphere of the philosopher whose only proper goal is the pursuit of truth.

Ethics is not a question of norms and moral laws, but a discussion of the motives of conduct in general.[5] Ethics is a matter of inquiring into the causes, regularity, and order of human actions with a view towards arriving at the motives of moral action; "thus the central problem of ethics concerns the causal explanation of moral behavior."[6] Although this would restrict ethics to being a branch of psychology, it would be illegitimate to infer that ethics is devoid of all truth. Actually, the entire question is solely one of terminology. Nevertheless, not all psychological activity may properly be designated moral conduct; distinctions must be drawn between mere psychological *activity* and *conduct*. Conduct comprises actions which represent the decisions of life; they consist of moral activity or ethics, which is the substance out of which resolutions are constructed. Mere activity is external or superficial and often never reaches consciousness, whereas conduct implies acts of will, deliberations, and decisions. However, acts of will or choice are not invested with special powers, viz., will power, because the will's decisions are determined by diversity of motives.

The entire motivating process is termed by Schlick, "acts of will." When motives conflict, that idea emerging triumphant over all others is an *act of will,* which, in turn, is governed causally by the law of motivation. The motivating idea achieving ascendency over the remaining ones present, constitutes the individual's preference or *act of will.* In the last analysis, will is not a unique faculty or quality, *suo jure,* but part of the natural and causal motivation of human conduct, *i.e.,* it lacks autonomy. The will does not operate *motu proprio,* but by the "pleasure value" of an idea[7] which gives it its "motivative power."

(b) *Moral Value as Desire.* The law of motivation, viz., that which governs one's choice or will is determined by the stimulus which is most pleasant or least pleasant; the same maintains in instances of sacrifice, where the principle of psychological hedonism becomes operative, *e.g.,* proper breeding or rearing may prompt a young lady sacrificially to forego the desirable larger portion of cake for the smaller when it is offered to her because she mentally visualizes pleased or displeased parents with concomitant attitudes of praise or censure as the case may be. The "martyr accepts pain or death for the sake of an idea, a friend gives his life or 'happiness' for his friend . . . he desires to carry out or realize a definite goal."[8] The universal law governing all choice is that motive which has the "greatest degree of pleasant feeling connected with it."[9]

Desire is not to be equated with will; desire is mental, subjective, *imagined,* whereas willing implies *action* or conduct, but that which is imagined with the greatest quantity of pleasure is willed.

Schlick repudiates Egoistic Hedonism and denounces egoism as immoral. Egoism is not to be construed as a natural impulse, such as self-preservation, nor is it the will to pleasure; it may most accurately be defined as "inconsiderateness," at least this is the peculiar trait most characteristic of the egoist. "Egoistic volition is for us an example of immoral volition, volition that is condemned."[10] He censures egoism because of its inherent selfish characteristic which is the direct cause of harm to others "for its essence is just inconsiderateness with respect to the interests of fellow men, the pursuit of personal ends at the cost of those of others."¹¹

To adjudge an act immoral is to desire that it should not occur, *i.e.*, its occurrence would create unpleasantness. "The moral valuations of modes of behavior and characters are nothing but the emotional reactions with which human society responds to pleasant and sorrowful consequences that, according to the average experience, proceed from those modes of behavior and characters."¹²

The central point of morality is not a question of "What is demanded of me?" but rather a question of "How must I live to be happy?" Morality implies desire, not demand; it is not a question of what is *demanded* of you as a moral being, but a question of what you *desire* to do for others. A morality of desire is one of self-assertiveness, with an affirmative accentuation, whereas the morality of demand stresses the ethics of self-limitation, hence emphasizes the negative. The basic distinction between the two lies in the interpretation of the concept *good*. Good may be construed to mean *demand* (obligation) or *desire;* in its moral sense, the term refers to: (1) human decisions and (2) the approbations of society. Moral demands are the expressions of the desires of society, viz., social approbations, but good, interpreted as desire, terminates in the doctrine of Utilitarianism.

(c) *Ethical Relativity.* Schlick denies the existence of absolute values principally on the grounds that the term is devoid of meaning, but even if some significance could be detected enabling one to construct a hierarchy of values, the values would be of purely scientific interest, not of philosophical or moral concern.

> To my question, "What do these objective values mean to me?" the absolutist answers, "They constitute the guiding lines of your conduct! In setting up your goals of action you should prefer the higher to the lower." If I then ask, "Why?" the absolutist cannot give any answer. This is the decisive point, that because of his thesis of this independence of values, the absolutist has cut himself off from all possibility of giving any

other answer to my question, "What happens if I don't do it?" than "Then you don't do it, that is all!" Should he answer, "In that case you are not a good man," then we should know that this answer is relevant and can influence my action only if I desire ... to be a "good man," that is, only if it is presupposed that certain feelings are connected with that concept.[13]

Furthermore, value judgments do not possess the validity of logico-mathematical propositions, but this does not preclude the existence of values, it restricts their state to one that is relative to persons. To state that they also possess an absolute nature is to claim something unverifiable.

Are there worthless joys and valuable sorrows? The answer is *yes* since there is a pleasurable experience in certain sorrows and an undesirable experience in certain joys. The sole criterion or calculus of value is the joy which it promises.

(d) *Moral Value as Social Survival.* As to the question, "What is moral conduct?" the answer would be: "That conduct which society believes will best further its own welfare."[14] In respect to the question, "Why do persons act morally?" the reply would be: "Because the things which are useful to society make for the happiness of the individual."

The problem of moral responsibility is dismissed on the basis of the non-existence of the freedom of the will. Autonomy of will is a *pseudo-problem* which should never have entered the discussion of philosophers. The assignment of ethics is the explanation of moral behavior according to causal laws, not in terms of free will. Explanation has reference to laws, not to freedom of the will. Responsibility lies in motivation; consciousness of responsibility is "merely the knowledge of having acted of one's own desires."[15]

(e) *The Role of Kindness.* Not all conduct leads to value, hence one is not at liberty to behave indiscriminately. "Personality and kindness are the basic conditions of a valuable existence."[16] The Kantian hymn to duty may apply equally well to kindness:

Kindness, thou dear great name, that containest nothing in thee demanding loveless esteem, but prayest to be followed; thou dost not menace and needst not establish any law, but of thyself findest entrance into feeling, and willingly art revered; whose smile disarms all sister inclinations; thou art so glorious that we need not ask after thy descent, for whatever be thy origin it is ennobled through thee!"[17]

2. Critique of the Ethics of Schlick

Schlick appears to be attempting to effect a synthesis between ethics and the principles of Logical Positivism. Logical Positivism implies *value nihilism*, *i.e.*, all values including moral values, such as moral principles of right lack objective existence. Although Schlick has not conceded the validity of value judgments, he has yielded more than the average logical positivist has in value theory. He is not prepared to relinquish the reality of values, hence accepts the fact of value, but does not grant it validity equal to logico-mathematical propositions. Schlick offers no justifiable explication for this logical compromise *in re* values; the possibility of a dual system of validity subsists, one for logico-mathematical propositions and the other for value judgments.

Schlick is a psychological hedonist, but one of an unusual or unique type; the fact of his hedonism is indicated in statements such as: "If there were no pleasure and pain in the world there would be no values."[18] Furthermore, he has a peculiar concept of responsibility, for he denies the existence of any freedom of the will. What other philosophers have attributed to a free will, Schlick ascribes to motivation by causal psychological laws; this he maintains notwithstanding the fact that a person may be held consciously responsible for his actions. He defends his position on the presupposition that although one is motivated by causal psychological laws, he is nevertheless responsible for his behavior at the point of becoming aware of his actions, *i.e.*, at the moment one has conscious knowledge of having acted according to his own desires. The foregoing seems to imply that the psychologist or psychiatrist is in the most advantageous position for the pursuit of ethical goals or values since they are the experts in human motivation and behavior. The foregoing position is logically incongruous unless one postulates the validity of the doctrine of the freedom of the will, but inasmuch as Schlick repudiates the autonomy of will as a pseudo-problem, how can one possibly be responsible for his actions? If a human being is solely mechanistic, completely devoid of choice of any kind, then responsibility is meaningless.

In answer to the question: "Why should I be moral?" Schlick replies because it makes for individual happiness; furthermore, the same moral act that makes for the happiness of persons, also makes for the survival or enhancement of society. This is a most attractive and optimistic view for it suggests that the harmony of the individual's happiness and that of society's well-being have been foreplanned or designed in the nature of the universe. Such a view suggests the existence of God, but how is theism possible on the premises of Logical Positivism, since Logical Positivism implies metaphysical nihilism as well as value nihilism? Schlick has resolved the apparent contradiction by being a Positivist *in re* nature or science, but a Personalist *in re* persons and God.[19] Nevertheless, this need not be the case for Schlick since his positivistic principles are so defined that they encompass both concepts; he views verification as arbitrarily fixed definitions, therefore theism may be included among such definitions. He writes: "The possibility of verification does not rest on any 'experimental truth,' on a law of nature or any other general proposition, but is determined solely by our definitions, by the rules which have been fixed for our language, or which we can fix arbitrarily at any moment."[20]

Schlick is not very rigorous regarding the matter of logical consistency; not only does he attempt to reconcile theism with Logical Positivism, and the ethics of responsibility with positivistic principles, but he lays great stress on the freedom and ability of man to reconstruct and alter his personality morally, *i.e.*, invest itself of ethical qualities or moral value. At times it is difficult to see the difference between the ethical system of Schlick and that of the more conventional or traditional ethicists who maintain doctrines such as the freedom of the will and obligation. Although Schlick commendably estimates personality and kindness as prime values, it is perplexing to comprehend the logical compatibility of these values with Psychological Hedonism or the tenets of Logical Positivism.

3. Further Reading in the Philosophy of Schlick

With the exception of *Problems of Ethics,* Schlick's major publications have not, as yet, been translated into English. They are: *Allgemeine Erkenntnislehre,* Berlin (1925); *Gesammelte Aufsatze,* Wien (1938); *Problems of Ethics,* tr. Rynin, New York (1939).

NOTES

MORITZ SCHLICK

1. Schlick was the founder of the Vienna School of Logical Positivists.
2. Moritz Schlick, "Meaning and Verification," *Philosophical Review* (1936), 352.
3. Moritz Schlick, *Problems of Ethics*, tr. by David Rynin (New York: Prentice Hall, Inc., 1939).
4. *Ibid.*, xiv.
5. *Ibid.*, 27.
6. *Ibid.*, 28.
7. Schlick often uses the term idea as meaning motive.
8. *Ibid.*, 45.
9. *Ibid.*, 47.
10. *Ibid.*, 76.
11. *Ibid.*, 77.
12. *Ibid.*, 78.
13. *Ibid.*, 116, 117.
14. *Ibid.*, 160.
15. *Ibid.*, 155.
16. *Ibid.*, 205.
17. *Ibid.*, 208, 209.
18. *Ibid.*, 120.
19. On Zilzel's word, Schlick was a theist.
20. Schlick, "Meaning and Verification," *op. cit.*, 353.

ETHICAL SKEPTICISM AND VALUE NIHILISM (LOGICAL POSITIVISM)

A. J. AYER

Ethical judgments have no validity.
(Ayer)

1. The Emotive Theory of Ethics

Alfred Jules Ayer is perhaps the most persuasive writer of the emotivists and also the most radical. Furthermore, he is popular; his treatment of the emotive ethic, which is found in *Language, Truth and Logic,* has undergone nine printings and two editions since it was first published in 1936.[1] A J. Ayer (as he is commonly referred to in the philosophical world), wrote the book when he was relatively young, a feat that is rather rare in the philosophical community. His work is exactly as he says, "in every sense a young man's book, it was written with more passion than most philosophers would allow themselves to show;"[2] he attributes its popularity to that fact.

A. J. Ayer assumes an unusual position in the field of ethics; he has perhaps reached an extremity that cannot be exceeded, viz., *ethical skepticism.* He identifies his system with several names; in addition to his list are others, which are furnished by his colleagues and critics. When his treatise, *Language, Truth and Logic* was first published, he believed that his "theory of ethics might fairly be said to be radically subjectivistic,"[3] but when the book was revised, he preferred the appellation, *the emotive theory of values*.[4] *Emotive* is probably the better choice, inasmuch as he is anxious not to have his system confused with subjectivism for he claims that it has very little in common with traditional subjectivistic theories.

As far as Ayer is concerned, ethics are nonexistent; judgments cannot be passed on moral matters, ethics lie outside the realm of those propositions which can properly be called true or false, *i.e.*, ethical data are nonexistent, hence nothing can be predicated of them. In fact, he goes so far as to say that they are mere emotional experiences; expressions of morality are merely *ejaculatory, e.g.*, a person's statement about his emotional feelings or his moral attitude would carry no more *sensible* meaning than if he exclaimed *ouch, mmm, ugh, ow, etc.* The impossibility of value judgments does not rest in man's inability to fathom the complexity of the moral situation, but in the fact that values do not exist; inasmuch as they lie outside the domain of science, consequently have no significance. The most that can be said of morals is that they "are simply expressions of emotion which can be neither true nor false."[5] "Ethical concepts are pseudo-concepts and consequently indefinable."[6]

The treatment of ethics is divisible into the following four categories:

1. Propositions which express definitions of ethical terms;
2. Propositions describing the causes and phenomena of moral experience;
3. Exhortations to moral virtue;
4. Actual ethical judgments.

Although the study of ethics should have adhered to the above classification, hardly anyone has recognized it so; in fact, many writers in the field of ethics have interfused the above classes, consequently, "it is often very difficult to tell from their works what it is that they are seeking to discover or prove."[7] Historically, the treatment of ethics has fallen into one of the following four areas:

411

1. Propositions expressing definitions of ethical terms; this class alone can legitimately constitute the province of ethical philosophy.
2. Propositions describing the causes and phenomena of moral experience; such propositions, by right, ought to be relegated to the task of the psychologist or sociologist.
3. Exhortations to moral virtue. Strictly speaking, these are not propositions, but commands or ejaculations purported to stimulate moral action; such are foreign to philosophical or psychological enterprise, inasmuch as they are principally found in the pulpit.
4. Actual ethical judgments. These are non-cognitive judgments; they are emotive. Such in the past have been treated as genuine moral propositions by philosophers, but technically they do not belong in the field of ethical philosophy, inasmuch as they have emotive significance and want cognitive meaning. If they were cognitively significant, they would be the property of the scientist, but because they are emotive in nature, they are unclassified.

The philosopher mistakenly presumes his task to be one of constructing ethical judgments, whereas his true function is that of analyzing ethical terms with a view towards their classification. Ayer is satisfied that his efforts towards this end have been successful. He poses the problem as to whether or not statements of ethical value are convertible into statements of empirical fact; his investigatory efforts proved that "only normative ethical symbols, and not descriptive ethical symbols . . . are . . . indefinable in factual terms."[8] Since normative ethics, *i.e.*, a system that subscribes to objective universal moral laws, cannot be reduced to descriptive ethics, the way is open for the "absolutist" or "objectivist" view of ethics. Inasmuch as the "absolutist" ultimately bases his position on *a priori* propositions which are arrived at by "intellectual intuition," they cannot be substantiated by any valid criterion of truth, at least they cannot be empirically tested, hence are unverifiable. *Intellectual intuition* is not an adequate criterion "for it is notorious that what seems intuitively certain to one person may seem doubtful, or even false to another.'"[9] Certainty derived from intuition is merely psychological, hence reduced to subjectivity, and therefore unverifiable since it is incapable of undergoing any empirical or public test. Empirical verifiability, viz., the criterion of sense experience, *i.e.*, the belief that verification consists in subjecting an object to common or public sense inspection, is the only adequate test. Ayer desists from any logical affiliation with the subjectivist, at least this is his contention; his claim is that a subjectivist makes a statement or proposition about what he believes he is experiencing, whereas an emotivist refrains from making any statements, he merely emotes.

What then can be said of value judgments? First of all, they are unanalyzable inasmuch as there is no criterion by which they can be tested. Although emotivism is a complete repudiation of ethical absolutism or intuitionism, at this junction they are in agreement, since the emotivist believes that empirical facts are irrelevant to moral value. The absolutist or intuitionist that Ayer envisions is Kant; it is not that he is sympathetic with the Kantian belief in moral value, but with the conviction that no "relevant empirical test" for morality exists. His radical departure from the intuitionist consists in his designation of ethical concepts as pseudo-concepts; he accomplishes this deduction on the premise that the language used to express ethical concepts is normatively inconsequential, since words expressing value judgments are mere statements of fact. This can be demonstrated by the deletion of any value term without any corresponding alteration in the content, ethically or otherwise, *e.g.*, no moral difference maintains between the statements: "John is an habitual liar, therefore he is sinful," and "John habitually lies;" any detectable discrepancy is attributable to the emotional feeling of disdain possibly accompanying one, consequently all morality is reducible to emotion, viz., the expression of feeling, horror, delight, ejaculation, etc., *i.e.*, a certain psychological reaction.

> The presence of an ethical symbol in a proposition adds nothing to its factual content. Thus if

> I say to someone, "You acted wrongly in stealing that money," I am not stating anything more than if I had simply said, "You stole that money." In adding that this action is wrong I am not making any further statement about it. I am simply evincing my moral disapproval of it. It is as if I had said, "You stole that money," in a peculiar tone of horror, or written it with the addition of some special exclamation marks. The tone, or the exclamation marks, adds nothing to the literal meaning of the sentence. It merely serves to show that the expression of it is attended by certain feelings in the speaker.[10]

One can proceed from the foregoing premises to a systematic explanation of traditional codes of ethics and moral laws, *e.g.*, the Ten Commandments, as generalized statements couched in emotion. One cannot predicate truth or falsity to ethical codes, inasmuch as they are not judgments, but only emotive ejaculations, *e.g.*, the condemnatory remark, "Adultery is wrong," uttered with vehemence, is tantamount to the outcry, "Adultery!!!" in a loud exclamatory tone, or, as Ayer glibly states, by some other suitable convention. Truth or falsity cannot appropriately be designated to these statements. To enter into a harangue or disagreeable debate with someone concerning the immorality of an act is equivalent to admitting conflicting emotive feelings, but restricting the issue to this point alone; consequentially, it is reducible to a matter of psychological sentiment or mental constitution, and not a proper issue to be debated objectively or logically. The designation of certain types of acts as moral is simply to recognize that one's psychological make-up is such that he habitually reacts to a specific type of action in a given emotional manner. Hence, the impossibility of making factual statements in the realm of moral values where only moral sentiments are expressed; consequently, the preclusion of all argument.

> And the man who is ostensibly contradicting me is merely expressing his moral sentiments.

> So that there is plainly no sense in asking which of us is in the right. For neither of us is asserting a genuine proposition.[11]

The language or terms used to express ethical sentiment have a dual function: They serve to arouse feeling and to stimulate action. Furthermore, there are those that have the effect of commands:

> Thus the sentence, "It is your duty to tell the truth," may be regarded both as the expression of a certain sort of ethical feeling about truthfulness and as the expression of the command, "Tell the truth." The sentence, "You ought to tell the truth," also involves the command, "Tell the truth," but here the tone of the command is less emphatic. In the sentence, "It is good to tell the truth," the command has become a little more than a suggestion. And thus the "meaning" of the word "good," in its ethical usage, is differentiated from that of the word "duty" or the word "ought." In fact we may define the meaning of the various ethical words in terms both of the different feelings they are ordinarily taken to express, and also the different responses which they are calculated to provoke.[12]

The foregoing conclusions would indicate the absence of a criterion by which to test value judgments in the field of ethics. The intuitionist is mistaken in his belief in the possibility of the transcendence of empirical data, *i.e.*, metaphysical reality exists beyond the sense world, "independent of ordinary sense-experience." Ultimate reality simply does not exist in any form, consequently, moral values as truly real are sheer fanciful notions which possess no objective validity, but only an inner emotive impulse.

> But in the case of any given proposition we can say what makes it true simply by describing what would count as evidence for it.... This is a

415

matter of relating one symbol to another. It is a matter of establishing a set of semantic rules.[13]

For this reason, the ascription of truth or falsity to ethical codes is a misnomer since they are extra-judgmental and "sentences which simply express moral judgments do not say anything."[14] The reason for their cognitive insignificance is that they are feelings, emotions, sentiments, rather than *statements about* feelings, emotions, sentiments; "they are unverifiable for the same reason as a cry of pain or a word of command is unverifiable — because they do not express genuine propositions."[15] Could it be that Ayer, concerning the point in question had neglected to take into consideration the fact that psychologists can detect feigned cries from real ones?

2. Ethical Emotivism *vs.* Ethical Subjectivism

In order to comprehend the subtle differences existing between ethical emotivism and ethical subjectivism, it is important that distinctions be drawn between *expressions* of feeling and *assertions* of feeling; the former constitutes a psychological experience, and as far as the emotivist is concerned, it is the sum total of ethical data, whereas, the latter is a statement, hence is ethically inconsequential. This is the primary respect in which ethical emotivism differs from ethical subjectivism; subjectivists believe they are making statements of fact, when actually they are merely making statements about their emotive feelings. Should one interrogate: "Well, why not make statements about your emotive experiences? Are they not ethical judgments?" The subjectivist would countenance the validity of such statements as ethical judgments, but the emotivist would repudiate their validity with the expounder that statements about matters of fact are purely descriptive statements rather than value judgments, consequently should be consigned to the province of science such as the science of psychology which attempts to describe and make statements about emotional behavior. If this is true, then the subjectivist in ethics is not a philosopher in the sense that he is making value judgments in respect to ethical phenomena, but a usurper of the psychologist's prerogative by describing psychological phenomena and its causes, viz., interests, feelings, sentiments, emotions, etc.

Perhaps Ayer has overlooked the fact that true-false statements can be made about ejaculations, *i.e.*, the experiential locale to which moral data is restricted. Furthermore, he has failed to consider the claim of the hedonist in ethical theory who maintains that feelings of pleasure *per se*, are moral goods, and one has the right to enhance them with supplementary increments. The fundamental discrepancy existing between the emotive theory and the subjectivist theory of ethics is the persistent denial of the emotivist that the ethicist is stating any genuine proposition, whereas the subjectivist authenticates the verifiability of value judgments. Although the subjectivist withholds granting ethical codes any objectivity or absoluteness due to their non-empirical nature, he does, however, claim that value judgments are statements regarding one's own personal feelings and interests. The logical consequence from such a premise is that propositions expressing moral issues may be labeled either true or false, *i.e.*, such propositions would be true if the speakers did in fact have those experiences and false if the individual in question did not possess the feelings which he believed he was undergoing. Furthermore, such experiences are subject to empirical verification, logical discussion, and dispute, *e.g.*, should a person state categorically, "Deceit is dishonest," a second individual could take issue with it by maintaining that under extenuating circumstances, "To lie is moral;" hence a logical debate and discussion would ensue.

The distinguishing feature divorcing emotivism from subjectivism is the emotivist's belief that the subjectivist makes statements about his feelings, whereas the emotivist simply ejaculates or evinces them. In other words, one can express feelings without making statements about them; in fact, this is exactly what is done in ethics:

Thus I may simultaneously express boredom and say that I am bored, and in that case my utterance of the words, "I am bored," is one of the circumstances which make it true to say that I am expressing or evincing boredom. But I can express boredom without actually saying that I am bored. I can express it by tone and gestures, while making a statement about something wholly unconnected with it, or by an ejaculation, or without uttering any words at all. So that even if the assertion that one has a certain feeling always involves the expression of that feeling, the expression of a feeling assuredly does not always involve the assertion that one has it. And this is the important point to grasp in considering the distinction between our theory and the ordinary subjectivist theory. For whereas the subjectivist holds that ethical statements actually assert the existence of certain feelings, we hold that ethical statements are expressions and excitants of feeling which do not necessarily involve any assertions.[16]

The subjectivist in making ethical statements or judgments finds that it is often possible to make contradictory statements, particularly concerning debatable issues; emotivists escape such precarious predicaments for they desist from making any ethical statements whatever, in fact ethical judgments or value judgments are not subject to validation.

In the final analysis, all that can be said is, "We find that ethical philosophy consists simply in saying that ethical concepts are pseudo-concepts and therefore unanalyzable."[17] Pseudo-concepts or pseudo-propositions signify "a series of words that may seem to have the structure of a sentence but is in fact meaningless."[18]

3. Critique of the Ethics of Ayer

Ayer is unrivalled as the most radical of all the emotivists; in this estimation, ethics is an illegitimate study, deserving a place among the pseudo-sciences or occult studies for it does not qualify for a place in subjectivism or descriptive science, viz., psychology. It is obvious that in emotivism, one has reached the quintescence of *ethical nihilism,* the logical implications of which are staggering. *E.g.,* the atrocities that occur in wartime situations or the monstrous savagery and barbarity witnessed in civilian life would carry for the emotivist no moral significance; a person's malicious lies which result in violent injury to another are labelled morally opaque; Nazi hatred which resulted in torture and violent death to many innocent persons is regarded as morally neutral. Theoretically, for Ayer, these are not legitimate moral issues, "and we have, therefore, nothing to say to the guard in the concentration camp who prefers cruelty; we can only make noises expressive of our feelings of repulsion."[19] If one cares to moralize about such, he is merely emoting; his psychological constitution requires adjustment; since ethical behavior is merely impulsive ejaculations, the individual is in need of a psychiatrist.

Emotivism makes a mockery of anyone who sincerely attempts to achieve any level of moral distinction inasmuch as he is merely exchanging one set of ejaculations for another; the sorrowful fact is that one cannot be deemed any *better* than the other. The nerve of moral endeavor is completely demolished for one has no obligations or responsibilities, consequently the moral foundations upon which society and other interpersonal relations are built are annihilated, and man is reduced to an existence lower than the brute inasmuch as his nature has been perverted, psychologically and morally. To regard Nazi torture with moral indifference is an insult to the intelligence, for a man's reason forces him to face the facts of moral experience, whereas the emotivist's position of ignoring them in an ostrich-like manner would make a man intellectually dishonest by its insistence that one refuse to incorporate such dicta in his philosophy. C. I. Lewis registering complete disgust for the vile and contemptible position for any right-minded man to hold, writes:

> But this is one of the strangest aberrations ever to visit the mind of man. The denial to value-

apprehensions in general of the character of truth or falsity and of knowledge, would imply both moral and practical cynicism. It would invalidate all action; because action is pointless unless there can be some measure of assurance of a valuable result which it may realize. And this negation, if it be carried out consistently, likewise invalidates all knowledge; both because believing is itself an active attitude which should have no point if it were not better to be right than wrong in what one believes, and because knowledge in general is for the sake of action.[20]

A thoroughgoing skeptical position is untenable and self-defeating, for it is inherently self-contradictory. To fancy that no knowledge is possible is a tacit admittance that skepticism also is unknowable. The skeptic in ethics or value theory is in the same predicament: If value does not exist, ethically or otherwise, what makes Ayer's system of ethics any better or more accurate or right than any other? Ayer cannot possibly claim that his ethical ideas are right or even better than the next person's because he has destroyed the rule or criterion by which they are measured, viz., values such as *true, better, best, right, good,* etc. If one cannot possibly evaluate, *i.e.,* state one thing as being of greater value, better, more accurate, or right than another subjectively, objectively, or any other way, then Ayer cannot possibly claim pre-eminence or any other place of value for his position, since he has "killed the goose that laid the golden egg," *i.e.,* he has denied that which he needs to claim for himself and his philosophy, viz., value. Man is in what may be termed a *value-predicament;* he evaluates whether or not he cares to, because it is in his very nature so to do. "Our valuations ... pervade our whole experience, and affect whatever 'fact,' whatever knowledge we consent to recognize."[21] To state that value is emotive is to utter nothing but contradictions: In making the statement "value is emotive" one is in effect saying, " I *value* the emotivist's view concerning the philosophy of value as the *best* position on the subject;" which is tantamount to saying, "The most *valuable* philosophy denies the *existence of value.*" Does Ayer not see that in making such statements, he is in effect saying that his own philosophy is not of any value, *i.e.,* is no good or at least outside of the realm of goodness. He is admitting that the exhausting efforts he put forth in any endeavor; (such as the many books he has written), that even before he begins such a taxing and enterprising task, he knows it to be of *no value whatever.* His efforts, regardless of how industrious, how painstaking, how heartbreaking, how earnest, are of no value at all. His most noble act is as good as his most base; his most useless and wasteful act is no better than his most beneficial.

Ayer has confused a concomitant of ethics, viz., emotion, with ethical value, *per se.* To say that emotion is often involved in ethical issues is to make a correct observation, for ethical considerations are of utmost importance to most persons; consequently, one frequently becomes quickly and easily excitable, *i.e.,* emotional when ethical issues are at stake, but this does not entitle one to equate moral value with emotion, without doing violence to empirical data.

An embarrassing situation which Ayer attempts to reconcile pertains to the matter of ethical disputations. The problem is: If there are no valid ethical judgments, subjective or objective, why is it that men argue over ethical propositions? G. E. Moore employs this as an argument against ethical subjectivism.[22] In other words, if ethical judgments are subjective, why dispute about them at all? Ayer fancies that he has bypassed this difficulty by claiming that "one really never does dispute about questions of value."[23] If this is the case, then what is he doing and what does he think is being done here?

Barnes thinks that Logical Positivists "have sometimes spoken as though what is not a verifiable assertion is not meaningful."[24] Ayer is satisfied that he can successfully launch a counteroffensive by proving that arguments about ethical issues are actually debates about questions of fact. He writes:

What we attempt to show is that he is mistaken about the facts of the case. We argue that he has misconceived the agent's motive: or that he has misjudged the effects of the action, or its probable effects in view of the agent's knowledge. ... We do this with the hope that we have only to get our opponent to agree with us about the nature of the empirical facts for him to adopt the same moral attitude towards them as we do.[25]

Ayer does not see that this is precisely the whole ethical issue; these are the ethical judgments that are the subject of dispute, *e.g.*, a person believes that he has the correct data and true judgment about moral issues and attempts to convince his opponent. Ayer has the heart of the ethical problem in a nutshell and fails to recognize it. What can be more fundamental in ethics than the agent's motive? Ayer admits the fact of motives and their relevancy in ethical disputes; he accepts it as a cognitive judgment, but fails to recognize its moral value.

Probably nowhere in the history of ethical thought is there any greater display of temerity or a more radically extreme explanation of moral actions as in the ethical skepticism of Ayer. Emotivism is a highly unreasonable position to maintain, for it results in absurd conclusions when it is carried out in practice or when its implications are considered. Ayer claims that there is no difference between the statement, "You acted wrongly in stealing that money," and "You stole that money." The only distinction in the two statements is that one has emotional overtones, *i.e.*, it was prompted by emotion. Ayer is in effect saying that there is absolutely no moral difference between whittling on a pencil with a jack-knife and torturing one's best friend with the same knife. They are simply two different acts; if one is disturbed about the latter act, he is merely expressing a bit of emotion and mistakes it as a moral issue.

Joad observes, "If I consistently believe that the statement, 'stealing is wrong,' does no more than express an emotion of horror at stealing, it will presently cease to express the emotion of horror. Not to put too fine a point on it, I shall cease to believe that stealing is wrong."[26] S. L. Hart condemns such indifference to value as "mental derangement and moral callousness."[27] The only conceivable reason for Ayer's maintenance of such a perverse theory of moral value is that he *esteemed* his philosophy of Logical Positivism so *valuably* that he condescended to accept any ethical theory which was in harmony with his philosophy regardless of the absurd degradation to which he might descend. For Ayer to contemplate Nazi atrocities and then conclude that ethics is merely the misuse of language or a non-existent entity is simply to refuse to face the realities of experience and to deny the facts of moral experience.

In conclusion, it may be added that emotivism fails to satisfy the pragmatic test; it is not practicable for everyday use. One could not commit himself to such an ethic, *i.e.*, he could not put it into operation without encountering serious contradictions, *e.g.*, to practice such an ethical scheme would result in the loss of one's friends and the eventual ostracism from one's society. Even an emotivist would not want another ethical skeptic as his friend, but would prefer a person who believed in moral values and was committed to them, in preference to a fellow emotivist who fails to make any moral distinction between aiding a friend and stealing from him, comforting a friend and torturing him, or saving a drowning person and raping a helpless individual. Even a proponent of ethical skepticism would refrain from committing himself to emotivism as his regular program of practice. In the final analysis, it becomes apparent that society would become disrupted to the point of peril, should its members embrace emotivism in its laws, customs, mores, or folkways.

4. Further Reading in A. J. Ayer

Two major books by Ayer are: *Language, Truth and Logic* which was first published in 1936, and *The Foundations of Empirical Knowledge,* 1940. In 1947, he published *Thinking and Meaning*. He has published numerous articles, some of which are: "Atomic Propositions," *Analysis,* 1933; "A Demonstration That Metaphysics is Impossible," *Mind,* 1934; "The Criterion of Truth," *Analysis,* 1935; "Truth by Convention," *Analysis,* 1936.

NOTES

A. J. AYER

1. The edition used herein is a 1949 printing; several printings have appeared since then.
2. Alfred Jules Ayer, *Language, Truth and Logic* (London: Victor Gollancz Ltd., 1946), 109.
3. *Idem.*
4. *Ibid.*, 20.
5. *Ibid.*, 103.
6. *Ibid.*, 113.
7. *Ibid.*, 103.
8. *Ibid.*, 108.
9. *Ibid.*, 106.
10. *Ibid.*, 107.
11. *Ibid.*, 108.
12. *Idem.*
13. *Ibid.*, 28.
14. *Ibid.*, 108.
15. *Ibid.*, 109.
16. *Ibid.*, 109, 110.
17. *Ibid.*, 112.
18. A. J. Ayer, "A Demonstration that Metaphysics is Impossible" in *Mind*, 1934, 335.
19. C. E. M. Joad, *Critique of Logical Positivism* (London: Victor Gollancz, Ltd., 1950), 119.
20. C. I. Lewis, *An Analysis of Knowledge and Valuation* (LaSalle: The Open Court Publishing Co., 1946), 366.
21. F. C. S. Schiller, *Humanism* (London: Macmillan and Co., 1903), 10.
22. See G. E. Moore, *Philosophical Studies*, "The Nature of Moral Philosophy" (London: Kegan Paul, Trench, Trubner and Co., Ltd., 1922).
23. Ayer, *Language, Truth and Logic, op. cit.*, 110.
24. Winston H. F. Barnes, "Ethics Without Propositions," *Proceedings of the Aristotelian Society*, Supp., (1948), 5.
25. Ayer, *op. cit.*, 111.
26. Joad, *op. cit.*, 146.
27. Samuel L. Hart, *Treatise on Values* (New York: Philosophical Library, Inc., 1949), 63.

BERTRAND RUSSELL

Ethics . . . contains no statements, whether true or false, but consists of desires of a certain general kind.
(Russell)

"Values" lie wholly outside the domain of knowledge.
(Russell)

1. Ethical Skepticism

Bertrand Russell in his book entitled: *Religion and Science*, offers a view of value theory amazingly similar to that of A. J. Ayer; but this should not come as too surprising since Russell has announced that he is a member of the *positivistic* school of thought,[1] for Russell also, ethical value lies outside the domain of judgment and as such lacks cognitive meaning, hence is neither true nor false. The findings of his deliberations are concisely stated:

> I conclude that, while it is true that science cannot decide questions of value, that is because they cannot be intellectually decided at all, and lie outside the realm of truth and falsehood. Whatever knowledge is attainable, must be attained by scientific methods; and what science cannot discover mankind cannot know.[2]

Although Russell appears to speak of a domain of ethics, viz., outside the realm of science, it is not a cognitively valid realm since ethical principles and values lack any criteria of truth, hence truth or falsity cannot be predicated of them. Values do not transcend scientific boundaries to a privileged cognitive region of absolute truths beyond the reach of science.

425

Since science remains silent about the question of values, then nothing valid may be attributed to them, consequently, ethical judgments are impossible. He admits "the fact that science has nothing to say about 'values' . . . but when it is inferred that ethics contains truths which cannot be proved or disproved by science,"[3] this he denies.

In ethical matters one is destitute in providing proof; this is evidenced by the fact that proof, both scientific and intellectual is lacking. Although decided ethical disagreement exists which possesses practical import, it nevertheless is deficient in logical and scientific importance. Practical ethics are essentially matters of personal opinion, emotively prompted. This accounts for the reason why one believes his opinions to be correct and motivates him to persuade others to his own opinion. Ultimately, "we have no means, of a scientific or intellectual kind, by which to persuade either party that the other is in the right . . . they are all emotional, not intellectual."[4]

The experience of obligation is not grounded in ethical data, but emotional experience, *e.g.*, when a person says, "I *ought* to do so and so," what he means is, "This is the act towards which I feel the emotion of approval."[5]

Russell shares the belief with men of religion who insist that values lie outside the domain of science, but a discrepancy arises between them when he claims that it is precisely for this reason that they exceed the bounds of knowledge. " 'Values' . . . lie outside the domain of science, as the defenders of religion emphatically assert . . . but I draw the further conclusion, which they do not draw, that questions as to 'values' lie wholly outside the domain of knowledge."[6] Furthermore, whenever a statement is made regarding ethical judgments, one is merely giving vent to his emotions rather than engaging in a discussion whose facts possess objective validity independent of one's personal opinion.[7]

Persuading one's opponent to share ethical views is not proof that it has been accomplished on objective grounds as though one were in possession of absolute truth concerning values, but rather that one has been successful in winning his opponent to his own way of thinking by eliciting kindred emotions. The extent of success is limited to emotional sentiments evoked and shared. "Every attempt to persuade people that something is good (or bad) in itself, and not merely in its effects, depends upon the art of rousing feelings, not upon an appeal to evidence."[8] A preacher's success in persuading his congregation to accept and adhere to the principles he is presenting lies solely in his ability to excite in his congregation emotions that he shares in the matter.[9] Geiger interprets this as a "taste-plus-power." ethics.[10]

What one erroneously terms *moral value* is, in reality, merely an emotional response; consequently, when an object excites an emotional reaction in a person, that individual, in turn, seeks to proselytize others to respond to the same stimulus with an equivalent emotion.

> When a man says, "this is good in itself," he *seems* to be making a statement, just as much as if he said, "this is square" or "this is sweet." I believe this to be a mistake. I think that what the man really means is: "I wish everybody to desire this," or rather "Would that everybody desired this."[11]

Russell interprets this statement as merely the declaration of a personal wish and its generalization, and the heightening of the wish to the status of desire: a wish possesses a personal connotation, whereas a *desire* denotes *universality*. A sizable measure of the confusion in ethics results from the peculiar interfusion of the *particular,* viz., *wishes,* with the *universal,* viz., *desires. Particulars, i.e.,* wishes, are not assertions since they are incapable of comprising an affirmation, "it is logically impossible that there should be evidence for or against it, or for it to possess either truth or falsehood.[12] On the other hand, universals, *i.e.,* desires, are statements of the optative mood, consequently possess cognitive significance since they constitute statements regarding a person's state of mind and as such can be either true or false. *E.g.,* if a person makes a statement in accord with his state of mind, then his statement is true, but if he makes a false statement about his state of mind, then he is in error. Nevertheless, as Russell accurately notes, such matters are not proper subject matter for the province of ethics, but are relegated to the field of psychology or biography. Since wishes are not even assertions, but expressions, they lack all cognitive qualification. To epitomize:

> Ethics . . . contains no statements, whether true or false, but consists of desires of a certain general kind. . . . Science can discuss the causes of desires, and the means of realizing them, but it cannot contain any genuinely ethical sentences, because it is concerned with what is true or false.'"[13]

Russell appears to be in agreement with A. J. Ayer in respect to the function of language; they concur in that language has two basic purposes: *descriptive* and *emotive*. Russell designates the emotive aspect of language, *expression;* the descriptive or cognitive use of language he terms *communication*. "Language has two primary purposes, expression and communication. In its most primitive form it differs little from some other forms of behavior. A man may express sorrow by sighing, or by saying, 'Alas!' or 'Woe is me!' He may communicate by pointing or by saying, 'Look!' "[14]

Communication's primary purpose is to impart information, but it serves in the dual capacity of raising questions and issuing commands. On the other hand, the expressive use of language serves to vent emotions, imperatives, and interjections, but the two types or use of language overlap, at times. The emotive or expressive use of language serves in the additional capacity of influencing the behavior of others as has been adequately noted earlier.[15]

2. Russell's Critique of his Own Theory of Moral Value

Russell, himself, registers dissatisfaction with his ethical skepticism; not only has he furnished valid objections to his own theory, but he has recognized the validity of some of the objections advanced by those who are unsympathetic with his views.

One discrepancy arises from the unsuccessful attempt to reconcile his theoretical ethical skepticism with the practical ethics of Russell, the moral reformer, *i.e.*, in value theory he claims to be an ethical emotivist or ethical subjectivist, but in practice, and at times in theory, an ethical objectivity is maintained.[16] *E.g.*, the fundamental thesis of his ethical nihilism is that moral values are non-existent, yet he finds himself ill-content to abandon moral values. His books, *Marriage and Morals* treats ethics from a non-emotive perspective, but in *What I Believe,* he expresses provocation at those persons, indifferent to moral issues, who refuse to recognize certain phenomena as immoral, particularly is he disturbed with clergymen who "condone cruelty and condemn innocent pleasure, they can only do harm as guardians of the morals of the young."[17] For an ethical skeptic, viz., Russell, the foregoing is logically incongruous.

Another logically incompatible statement appears in his *History of Western Philosophy*: he writes that one "cannot prove that it is bad to enjoy . . . the infliction of cruelty,"[18] yet elsewhere he writes: "Pleasure in the spectacle of cruelty horrifies me, and I am not ashamed of the fact that it does."[19] To the foregoing may be added his conclusion in the section on ethics in his: *Philosophy,* "The good life is one inspired by love and guided by knowledge,"[20] not to mention the many press reports expressing his indignant attitude regarding social ethics and values, such as, his declaration that the heads of nations possessing the atomic bombs are more evil than Hitler for they have the power to exercise greater destruction. Although the preceding statements are logically inconsistent, Russell is not prepared to relinquish any of them. Nevertheless, conscious of his logical incompatibility, he says:

> I am accused of inconsistency,[21] perhaps justly, because although I hold ultimate ethical valuations to be subjective, I nevertheless allow my-

self emphatic opinions on ethical questions. If there is any inconsistency, it is one that I cannot get rid of without insincerity.[22]

The foregoing unquestionably implies that Russell is persuaded in the existence of moral value, particularly from the fact that his refusal to be insincere is indicative of moral concern which is further supported by his insistence on maintaining value judgments on ethical questions.

Can it be that Russell is not completely persuaded about the validity of his ethical skepticism for he remarks that he has no intention of yielding his *right* to express himself on moral issues? Obviously, a *moral right* is discordant with a *positivistic* value theory, yet he states: "I am not prepared to forego my right to feel and express ethical passions; no amount of logic, even though it be my own, will persuade me that I ought to do so."[23] This statement not only suggests a repudiation of ethical nihilism, but a rejection of the validity of the principles of Logical Positivism. The matter is further embellished by the remark: "I am no more prepared to give up all this than I am to give up the multiplication table."[24] Russell believes that the confusion and inconsistency found in his ethical philosophy are due to the subjectivity of ethical evaluations. He is correct in thinking so for a subjectivistic value theory is inherently self-contradictory, the reason being that the person who offers a subjectivistic theory of value is in effect asserting the objectivity of values. The subjectivist is in effect saying that his own value theory is the *right one,* or at least the *best* one, *i.e.,* the most valuable independent of what one's subjective opinions, thoughts, or desires are. *Right* and *best* are *not* only value terms, but terms implying objectivity.

Russell's claim to subjectivism rests on the contention that the property *truth* is inapplicable to ethical judgments, *i.e.,* value judgments are not independent of what persons may or may not think about them. Two difficulties emerge at this point: the first being that value judgments *possess* objectivity, hence are capable of the property called truth, *e.g.,* the value judgments: "One ought to do what is right" and

"One ought to do what is best" are objectively true independent of particular personal opinion. Granted that wide differences of opinion may exist as to the particular right or best course of action, these do not affect its validity. Scientists often disagree concerning the nature of an object without denying its existence; furthermore, nothing is completely independent of a person's thoughts regarding it.[25]

Russell shares some of the foregoing conclusions for he suggests that subjective opinions have objective validity when he writes:

> Suppose, for example, that someone were to advocate the introduction of bull-fighting in this country. In opposing the proposal, I should *feel,* not only that I was expressing my desires, but that my desires in the matter are *right.*[26]

Russell holds that in making the above statement, he is not guilty of any inconsistency; how the claim can be supported without logical abuse to the term *right* is difficult to understand nor does he offer any explanation. *Right* implies objectivity or truth in moral matters, but how is it possible simultaneously to be completely objective and subjective regarding one and the same fact of experience? Furthermore, the possibility of being right is precluded by the "standards" of Positivism and Subjectivism which deny *rightness* or truth in moral questions.

Russell fancies that he has not been guilty of logical inconsistency, but he is not reticent in expressing doubts and dissatisfaction for he comments, "While my own opinions as to ethics do not satisfy me, other people's satisfy me still less."[27] A final observation is probably worth mentioning, viz., Russell, fundamentally, is not an ethical subjectivist, at least this is not true of the morals to which he has committed himself for in practice he has abandoned ethical skepticism. He arrives at the conclusion: "What is horrible I will see as horrible," *i.e.,* what is in truth horrible, irrespective of what people's opinions happen to be, Russell will make the *judgment of moral value* that it is in *truth* horrible.

3. Further Reading in the Philosophy of Russell

Some of the works of this prolific writer are: *Philosophical Essays,* 1910; *The Problems of Philosophy,* 1912; *What I Believe,* 1925; *Philosophy,* 1927; *Marriage and Morals,* 1929; *Religion and Science,* 1935; *Power: A New Social Analysis,* 1938; "Reply to Criticisms," in Paul Arthur Schilpp, (ed.), *The Philosophy of Bertrand Russell,* 1944; *A History of Western Philosophy,* 1946; *Human Knowledge: Its Scope and Limits,* 1948; *Authority of the Individual,* 1949; *Unpopular Essays,* 1950; *Human Society in Ethics and Politics,* 1954; *Fact and Fiction,* 1961; and the monumental work with Alfred North Whitehead, *Principia Mathematica,* 1913.

NOTES

BERTRAND RUSSELL

1. See Bertrand Russell, *History of Western Philosophy* (New York: Simon and Schuster, 1946), 836.
2. Bertrand Russell, *Religion and Science* (London: Oxford University Press, 1935), 243.
3. *Ibid.*, 223.
4. *Ibid.*, 230.
5. Bertrand Russell, *Philosophy* (New York: W. W. Norton Co., Inc., 1927), 226.
6. Russell, *Religion and Science, op. cit.*, 230.
7. Bertrand Russell, "Reply to Criticisms" in Paul Arthur Schilpp, *The Philosophy of Bertrand Russell* (Evanston: Northwestern University, 1944), 723.
8. Russell, *Religion and Science, op. cit.*, 235.
9. Russell, "Reply to Criticisms," *op. cit.*, 724.
10. George R. Geiger, "Values and Inquiry" in Ray Lepley, *Value: A Cooperative Inquiry* (New York: Columbia Univ. Press, 1944), 94.
11. Russell, *Religion and Science, op. cit.*, 235.
12. *Ibid.*, 237.
13. *Idem.*
14. Bertrand Russell, *Human Knowledge: Its Scope and Limits* (New York: Simon and Schuster, 1946), 59.
15. See part 2, chapter 1 of *Ibid.*
16. See C. E. M. Joad, *Critique of Logical Positivism* (London: Victor Gollancz, Ltd., 1950), 122.
17. Bertrand Russell, *What I Believe* (New York: E. P. Dutton and Co., 1925), 47.
18. Russell, *History of Western Philosophy, op. cit.*, 834.
19. Russell, "Reply to Criticisms," *op. cit.*, 720.
20. Russell, *Philosophy, op. cit.*, 235.
21. Russell writes in reference to Buchler's accusation of him. Cf. Justus Buchler, "Russell and the Principles of Ethics," in Schilpp, *The Philosophy of Bertrand Russell, op. cit.*, 513 ff.
22. Russell, "Reply to Criticisms," 720.
23. *Idem.*
24. *Idem.*
25. Cf. Ralph Barton Perry's treatment of "the ego-centric predicament."
26. Russell, "Reply to Criticisms," *op. cit.*, 724.
27. *Idem.*

CHARLES L. STEVENSON

The resolution of an ethical argument requires a resolution of disagreement in attitude, and so requires that the attitude of one party or the other (or both) be changed or redirected. (Stevenson)

1. The Non-Cognitive Theory of Ethics

Similar to, yet distinguishable from the emotive theory of ethics, Stevenson's ethical philosophy purports that moral disputes are both expressive and persuasive; they hold a legitimate place in philosophy. "It is certainly mandatory that the term 'emotive' . . . be kept as a tool for use in careful study, not as a device for relegating the non-descriptive aspects of language to limbo."[1] Although ethical utterances do not convey knowledge, they do function in the capacity of moral imperatives designed to win a kindred attitude in one's disputant. In factual or scientific disputes, differences of opinion arise concerning the accuracy of data or evidence, but two persons engaged in a moral argument are unable to resolve their differences because they are not based on objective data. *E.g.*, a disagreement in length may be resolved with a ruler since it is an objective factual matter, but a difference of opinion on a moral question lacks an objective criterion capable of settling the issue. It is worth nothing that although morality is a subjective attitude, nevertheless objective facts can and do alter such attitudes; consequently as new facts are brought to light, one's attitude toward moral issues changes. In like manner one can convert another to his own moral preference by supplying facts new to him and capable of modifying or changing entirely his moral attitude.

The non-cognitive ethical position expressed here differs from the emotive theory of Ayer by emphasizing that moral conflicts, if not conflicts in belief, are genuine conflicts of attitude, not merely an ejaculation or an evincing. Consequently, ethical discussions are significant, their meaning is pertinent to attitude, accordingly moral disputes are disagreements in attitude. However, this system is not to be misconstrued with Hedonism, nor is ethics to be construed with psychological science, despite the fact that "ethical principles" are expressions of attitude. This theory takes a dim or skeptical view regarding ethical principles or the concept of obligation; a value claim constitutes no more than an attitude of condemnation.

Ethical statements are not descriptive, hence cannot be relegated to psychology; they are imperative in nature and elicit a change of attitude. Consequently, to solicit a change of attitude in an individual is to be engaged in a moral endeavor; all such moral concern falls into the province of ethical value, not the field of psychology. The psychologist's activity is restricted to a description of the facts which demarcates his interest in the matter from that of the moralist who seeks to invoke an alteration in one's attitude.

2. Ethics as Attitude

Stevenson summarizes his position:

> When a man is making an evaluative decision he is trying to resolve a conflict in his attitudes. For his beliefs serve as intermediaries between his attitudes, and by uniting them in new ways may alter their combined strength. The resolution of his conflict, then will intimately depend upon his beliefs, which themselves will be of great variety.
> An emotive conception of ethics — one that takes the ethical terms to express or evoke attitudes — may at first seem to ignore the beliefs that are in question. The present paper argues that it

does not: that it allows an intelligible place for them all. And it argues that any non-emotive analysis will be likely to fail in that respect: it will be unable to introduce all the cognitive topics that are relevant; so it will either be incomplete or else obtain completeness at the cost of being too simple.[2]

Stevenson's primary ethical task is twofold: the clarification of the meaning of ethical terms and the equally important self-imposed assignment of presenting methods and systems of verification of value judgments.

The central problem in normative ethics does not concern agreement or disagreement in belief, but it is one of agreement or disagreement in attitude. There is a dual implication inherent in this statement: (1) ethics is fundamentally a matter of attitude; (2) ethical controversies do not revolve about objective facts, but exhortations designed to alter attitude; however facts may be employed in such endeavors. Furthermore, there is a valid place for intellectual enterprise in ethics since ethical controversies involve both disagreement in belief as well as disagreement in attitude. Stevenson's intent is not that of eliminating beliefs from their rightful place in ethical thought, but to introduce attitudes within the scope of ethics. Attitudes and beliefs are at the root of all ethical problems; both play a major role and must be understood in their reciprocal relationship. Since ethical disagreements are one of attitude, then for a person to say, "This is wrong!" does not signify that he is disputing a norm, but that he is saying: " 'This is wrong' means *I disapprove of this; do so as well;*" also " 'This is good' means *I approve of this; do so as well;*" or " 'He ought to do this' means *I disapprove of his leaving this undone, do so as well.*"[3] The *meaning* of any ethical statement pertains to an agreement or disagreement in *attitude,* but agreement or disagreement in *belief* pertains to an *analysis of methods.*

Two objectively contradictory statements may both be subjectively true, *e.g.,* when two individuals engage in a dispute, one may approve and the second disapprove of some matter; each may be correct for each is describing his own state of mind, since their states of mind differ, then each may be uttering a correct statement, yet mutually contradictory. Similarly, one can distinguish between ethical and scientific statements: ethical statements possess imperative connotations, consequently result in agreements and disagreements in attitudes, but this procedure employed regarding normative ethics is not to be confused with psychological and scientific statements about ethics. "Ethical statements cannot be taken as fully comparable to scientific ones. They have a quasi-imperative function which, poorly preserved by the working models, must be explained with careful attention to emotive meaning; and they have a descriptive function which is attended by ambiguity and vagueness, requiring a particularly detailed study of linguistic flexibility. Both of these aspects of language are intimately related to ethical methodology."[4] It may be said that normative ethics is emotive and subject to agreement and disagreement in respect to attitude, but descriptive meaning or descriptive ethics is scientific; nevertheless, both are related. The emotive meanings of words are expressions or symptoms of emotions, *e.g.*, laughs, sighs, groans, etc.; interjections give vent to emotions or attitudes, but terms describing emotions denote them. The habitual use of particular words is responsible for one's mode of emotional expression or attitude, consequently, interjectional expressions result from force of habit, *e.g.*, "for one who assorts mail, 'Connecticut' may cause only a toss of the hand, but for an old resident it may bring a train of reminiscences."[5]

The function or purpose of emotive or normative ethics is that of soliciting a certain attitude or in redirecting one's attitude; often the value term *good* does no more than "indicate agreement or disagreement in attitude." However, emotive terms, such as *good* do not always express exhortation, often good is used to mean *effective*, etc.; other times *good* conveys an informative meaning, *e.g.*, "This is good writing paper." The outcome of an analysis of normative ethics indicates that the statement: "This is good" is equivalent to saying, "I approve of this; do so as well." "Do so as well" suggests a discrepancy in attitude, not one of objective fact. The term *good* as it is used here contains an emotive meaning, not a factual one. To say that "x is good" is identical to saying, "psychologically, I approve of x and hope to influence you to do so as well." Hence, the goal or purpose of ethical judgments is to influence, guide, or remold attitudes.

Emotive ethics falls in the province of morals or values, not in the field of psychology; the psychologist's responsibility is to show how attitudes influence, *i.e.*, to show the cause and effect relations of attitudes, but the moralist's concern is to influence, modify, or change them. The psychologist describes how attitudes are changed; the moralist accepts the assignment of actually carrying it out. The descriptive endeavor is scientific (psychology), whereas the emotive (ethics) is an active engagement in executing the findings of the scientists. The former entails the academic knowledge of how the attitudinal changes are wrought, the latter the administration of the principles gained through science to the end of manipulating attitudinal changes. "An ethical judgment is not a psychological statement; that is granted. A characterization of its emotive meaning in psychological terms serves to distinguish it from a psychological statement, not to make one. It exerts its influence upon attitudes in a much more direct way than any statement of science, and lends itself to a different sort of agreement and disagreement."[6]

3. The Resolution of Ethical Disputes

Inasmuch as ethics is a matter of attitude, it would follow that resolution of ethical disputes and problems is reducible to harmonizing discordant attitudes. To convert another would entail redirecting or changing his attitude to bring it into line with one's own. "The resolution of an ethical argument requires a resolution of disagreement in attitude, and so requires that the attitudes of one party or the other (or both) be changed or redirected."[7]

Among the number of ways by which attitudes are altered is by effecting changes in belief through the utilization of psychology and persuasion. Persuasion, which is of particular importance, "depends on the sheer, direct emotional impact of words — on emotive meaning, rhetorical cadence, apt metaphor, stentorian, stimulating, or pleading tones of voice, dramatic gestures, care in establishing *rapport* with the hearer or audience, and so on."[8] Persuasion is neither rational nor irrational, but non-rational for its methods exceed the rational in the sense that it is not concerned with belief. *Rational* methods relate to belief, while *irrational* methods pertain to fallacious reasoning, but *non-rational* methods are concerned with attitudes; non-rational methods of persuasion are primarily employed in the emotive use of words. One may utilize these same techniques for the purpose of self-persuasion as well, or else he may effect a self-persuasion by projecting himself into a social setting and fancying himself in debate with another, preferably a superior. Occasionally, when one is trying to persuade another, it is not always the other person he really wishes to convince, but *himself*. The art of persuasiveness extends to terms aptly defined, *e.g.*, a "persuasive definition" is one "which gives a new conceptual meaning to a familiar word without substantially changing its emotive meaning, and which is used with the conscious or unconscious purpose of changing, by this means, the direction of people's interests."[9]

Validity is without relevancy to persuasion or attitudes, *e.g., one cannot speak of a valid or invalid* attitude. "To evaluate or recommend an ethical method (whenever validity can have no bearing on the case) is to moralize about the ways of moralists."[10] One may speak of attitudes being valid only in the sense that one says "That is true" when referring to agreement in attitude rather than in belief.

Stevenson's primary concern is with the method of ethics, not with moralizing; he distinguishes himself from the moralist by being occupied with the method of ethics, rather than with ethical judgments or even description, for the person who condemns the judgments of the moralist is himself moralizing, accordingly becomes or assumes the prerogative of the moralist. Propagandists are moralists since they are engaged in the activity of indoctrination.

4. The Dual Function of Language

Stevenson, like a number of other emotivists, attributes a dual function to language: one of its purposes is to communicate beliefs; this is its scientific function. The second use is to incite attitudes or persons to action, to give vent to feelings, or to create moods; this latter function constitutes the emotive use of language, *i.e.*, it is concerned with interjections, oratory, poetry, etc. The latter function is termed *dynamic*, and the former, *descriptive*, *e.g.*, "Hydrogen is the lightest known gas" illustrates the descriptive use; "When a person cuts himself and says 'Damn' his purpose is not ordinarily to record, clarify, or communicate any belief. The word is used dynamically."[11]

To recapitulate Stevenson's non-cognitive theory of ethics, it may be said that morals are a matter of attitudes and persuasion; "ethical judgments have quasi-imperative force, because of their emotive meaning. They influence people's attitudes, rather than describe what these attitudes already are."[12] The ethicist's responsibility is the study of the methods of ethics, while psychologists determine the cause and effect of behavior or attitudes, *i.e.*, they explore the most effective manner by which to change one's attitudes. The moralist is the one who assumes the assignment of effecting these changes in attitudes. Fundamentally, the entire process is a non-rational one, *i.e., an emotive one.*

5. Critique of the Ethics of Stevenson

A fine critique on the ethics of Stevenson is offered by Richard Brandt, whose paper "The Emotive Theory of Ethics"[13] was read as part of a symposium on the emotive theory of ethics at the 1949 meeting of the eastern division of the American Philosophical Association. Brandt's critique was preceded by Stevenson's paper: "The Emotive Conception of Ethics and Its Cognitive Implication." Perhaps the greatest inadequacy of the ethical theory of Stevenson, and this objection holds true for other emotivists as well, is the fact that he does not venture to offer any valid or cogent argument for the support of his position, particularly in support of Positivism's fundamental thesis. Too often, he merely declares his position by simply stating facts without support; consequently one has the feeling of reading a creed that has been announced in *ipse dixit* fashion, rather than a thesis presented with adequate defence and ground. Some statements lack any support whatever.

The essence of Stevenson's ethical theory is: Moral decisions are resolutions of conflicts of attitude. The statement taken by itself is correct, the objection is to the dismissal of moral value on this basis. Granted that one's moral decisions are of sufficient concern and import to affect his attitude and his entire personality as well, this does not entitle one to delimit moral value to attitude. Furthermore, why does one attempt to resolve conflicts of attitude in a moral situation? Is it not because the attitudes themselves are of moral value? They are of supreme moral import to many individuals.

Stevenson contends that the central problem of normative ethics is not one of agreement and disagreement in *belief*, but one of agreement or disagreement in *attitude*. Two difficulties emerge at this point: first, since beliefs can and do mold attitudes, they are implicated in morals; second, attitudes, *per se*, possess moral value, *e.g.*, an attitude of contempt or hatred which motivates one to indulge in murder becomes moral turpitude as well as crime, delete the attitude and the act is reduced to manslaughter, or even a lesser charge. To argue that ethics is a matter of attitude is not to eject it from the realm of the moral, but to place it squarely in its center. A wholesome or good attitude is capable of enhancing the welfare of oneself and others.

Although Stevenson does recognize to some degree a place for beliefs in his system, nevertheless he does not stress the full import of the efficacy of beliefs in forming, molding, and altering attitudes. A child on his way to the store to buy some ice cream may become quite despondent in attitude as a result of having lost his money with which to make the purchase. His attitude of despondency may be transformed into joy and hope should one convince him of the belief that the money will definitely be found.

Stevenson's claim that "x is wrong" is equivalent to "I disapprove of this; do so as well,"[14] is not an accurate analysis of the case; often what is meant is "I disapprove of x because I ought (obligation) to; and experience an obligation to enlighten you concerning the matter." The difficulty here is due to the failure of distinguishing between what is *in fact* transpiring and the *principle* behind what is taking place; his analysis was one of scientific description, not a philosophical evaluation. Joad adds: "Why *moral* approval and disapproval, if there is no uniquely *moral* factor in the universe to be at once the source and object of the moral feelings which are our response to it."[15]

His analysis of the term *good* indicating that it is devoid of all factual meaning and possesses only an emotive one is objectionable, *e.g.*, he claims *good* means "I approve of this; do so as well;" hence *good* is merely an attitude, not an objective fact, it has subjective connotation only. Although moral good is an attitude, this does not necessarily imply that it is subjective, *e.g.*, an attitude that is good for one person may be good for all; conversely one that is undesirable for one person may be detrimental for all as is keenly recognized in the field of psychiatry today.

6. Further Reading in the Philosophy of Stevenson

Stevenson's classic work is: *Ethics and Language* (1944), but other important writings are: "The Emotive Meaning of Ethical Terms," in *Mind* (1937), "Persuasive Definitions," in *Mind* (1938), "Ethical Judgments and Avoidability," in *Mind* (1938).

NOTES

CHARLES L. STEVENSON

1. Charles L. Stevenson, *Ethics and Language* (New Haven: Yale University Press, 1944), 79.
2. C. L. Stevenson, "The Emotive Conception of Ethics and Its Cognitive Implication," *Bulletin of the Eastern Division of the American Philosophical Association* (1949), 7.
3. *Op. cit.*, *Ethics and Language*, 21.
4. *Ibid.*, 36.
5. *Ibid.*, 43.
6. *Ibid.*, 108.
7. *Ibid.*, 139.
8. *Idem.*
9. C. L. Stevenson, "Persuasive Definitions," *Mind* (1938), 331.
10. *Op. cit.*, *Ethics and Language*, 158.
11. C. L. Stevenson, "The Emotive Meaning of Ethical Terms," *Mind* (1937), 21.
12. C. L. Stevenson, "Ethical Judgments and Avoidability," *Mind* (1938), 49.
13. Richard Brandt, "The Emotive Theory of Ethics," *Philosophical Review* (1950), 305-319.
14. *Op. cit.*, *Ethics and Language*, 21.
15. C. E. M. Joad, *Critique of Logical Positivism* (London: Victor Gollancz, Ltd., 1950), 131.

For this alone is lacking even unto God
To make undone the things that have once been done.

(Agathon)

INDEX

A

Adultery, (see sex)
Aesthetic, 50, 298-303
Agape, 188-189
Ambition, 25
Amoral, 48-49
Anger, 184, 206
Anxiety, 190-191
Appetite, 81-82
Approbation, 335
Aristippus, 138-139
Aristotle,

B

  Politics, 2
  Man's nature, 5
Beatitudes, 181-184
  Defined, 182
Benevolence, 81-82
Bentham's dictum, 110
Brotherhood, 193-197

C

Categorical Imperative, 51-53
  Defined, 52
  Dewey's version, 333
  Perry's version, 388
Censoriousness, 191-192, 204
Character 35-36
Choice, 17ff., 33
Christian love, 188-189
  Mandate, 194
Classical Intuitionism, 76ff.
Compassion, (see pity)

Condemnation, 335
Conscience, 79-81, 83-85, 128
Contemplation, 5, 8ff.
Contentment, 147-148
Continence, 30
Courage, 20, 165, 206, 266
Cynicism, 152-154
Cyrenaics, 138-139

D

Death, 283-285
Decalogue, 171-174
Deontological ethics, 57-59, 101
Desire, 148
Dignity, 55-57, 194-197
Divorce, 184-186
Duty, 58-59, 88-90, 129, 331-333, 341
  As loyalty, 353

E

Egoistic Hedonism, 98-99, 127
Equity, 34, 129
Eternal Recurrence, 256, 263
Ethical
  Disputes, 438-440
  Inquiry, 318-321
  Naturalism, (def.), 381; 396-397
  Realism, 341-350
  Relativity, 373-379
  Salvation, 285-288
  Skepticism, 410-418
  Subjectivism, 376-378
Ethics,
  As attitude, 435-438
  As sentiment, 362-366

445

Defined, 2ff., 100-101
Dialectical, 294-298
Egoistic Hedonism, 269
Emotivism, 410-416
Evolutionary Naturalism, 269
Naturalism, 237ff., 253
Non-cognitive, 434ff.
Of Loyalty, 352-359
Of Pity, 288-292
Subjective, 368
Survival, 264-266
Taste-plus-power, 427
Evil, 208-210, 221-223, 239-245, 281-283, 324
  As parasitic, 63-64, 210
  As positive, 281-283
  Problem of, 322-323
Evolutionary Naturalism, 269

F

Free will, 16, 210-212, 309-313
Friendliness, 26-28, 142, 303

G

Gentleness, 26
Gestalt, 345, 387
Golden mean, 10
Golden rule, 175-177, 192-193, 398
Good
  Aquinas, 221-223
  Aristotle, 5ff.
  Dewey, 324
  Kierkegaard, 303ff.
  Moore, 347-349
  Nietzsche, 239-245
  Spencer, 269, 271
Good life 201-203
  (see also *good*)
Great Commandment, 175-177, 193-194
Greatest Happiness Principle, 126

H

Habit, 13ff.
Happiness, 3, 5, 6-9, 82, 123-126, 130-131, 212, 225-227

Hedonism, 8, 346-347
Hedonistic Calculus, 101-105
Hedonistic Paradox, 134

I

Ideal Utilitarianism, 341-342
  Defined, 45, 341
  Compared with Intuitionism, 45
Idiopsychological Ethics, 87-88
Immortality, 284
Individual, 306-310
Instrumental value, 56
Intellect 224-225
Intelligence
  Defined, 318
Interim Ethics, 204-205
Intuitionism
  Defined, 44
Irrationalism, 313-314

J

Justice, 31-34, 126, 128-129, 174-175, 267

K

Kindness, 405-406
Kingdom of Ends, 57

L

Lamarckian Theory, 267-268
Lex Talionis, 128, 174-175, 205, 375
Liberality, 21-22
Love, 199-201, 388
  Defined, 388
Loyalty, 352-359
  Defined, 352

M

Magnanimity, 23-25
Magnificence, 22-23
Meek, 183

Meliorism, 323
Merit, 92-93
Metaphysics of ethics, 66-67
Moderation, 10, 167
Moral, 14
    Conceptions, 321-324
    Emotions, 374-376
    Evolution of, 266-268
    Growth, 324-325
    Nihilism, 244
    Reconstruction, 423
    Responsibility, 324
    Skepticism, 425-428
    Standards, 331-333
Morality, 2
    As approbation, 366-368
    As social, 333-336
    Genealogy of, 237-242
    Master, 242-245
    Slave, 242-245
Moral law, 47, 203-204
    Natural, 396-398
Moral motivation, 48-49, 92-94
Moral Science
    Definited, 319
Moral Value
    Analyzed, 401-403
    As desire, 403-404
    As survival, 405-406
Murder, 184
Mysticism, 300-301

N

Naturalistic fallacy, 348-349, 390
Nature, 24, 208-209
    Fundamental law of, 395

O

Oathtaking, 186-187
Obligation, 59-60, 331-333
Optimism, 269-272
Organic unity, 345
Ostentation, 189-190

P

Pantheism, 310

Peace of mind, 147-148
Peripatetic school, 2
Persuasive definition, 439
Pessimism, 271, 276-283, 295, 322
Pity, 251, 253
Plato, 378-379
Pleasure, 101-105
Potentiality, 302
    (see Self-Realization ethics)
Power, ethics as, 253-256
Practical reason, 65-66
    Primacy of, 65-66
Protagoras, 378
Prudence, 49-51
Psychological Hedonism, 98, 269-272
    Defined, 269
Purity of Heart, 206, 303-306

Q

Qualitative Hedonism, 99-100
Quantitative Hedonism, 98

R

Reason, 10
Resentment, 247
Resignation, 150-151
Retaliation, 187-188
Right Act,
    Aristotle, 12ff.
    Aristotle's definition, 12, 13
    As might, 392-394
    Hume, 368-369
    Martineau, 90-92
    Mill, 123-126
    Moore, 342-344
    Spencer, 269
Rights, 331-333

S

Sanction, 105-108, 127-128
    Defined, 127
Scotus, John Duns, 224
Self, 310-313
Self-affirmation, 252

Self-control, 147-353
Selfishness, 126-127
Self-knowledge, 165-166, 300-301, 335
Self-love, 81-82, 305
Self-preservation, 269
Self-Realization Ethics, 1ff., 220-227
　Definition, 3ff.
Sermon on the Mount, 181-193
Sex, 154-155, 225-227, 247, 255
　Adultery, 33, 184-186, 205, 235, 278
Shame, 30
Sin, 233-235
　Definition, 233
　Mortal, 233-235
　Venial, 233-235
Slavery, 37-38
Social Contract, 394-396
Social Ethics, 68
Socrates, 149, 225, 301, 308-310, 378
Socratic Dialectic, 159-162
Socratic Method, 158-162
Soul, 15ff.
Spencer's dictum, 270
Stealing, 54-55
Stoicism, 146, 206
Suicide, 146, 212, 283-285, 301
Summum bonum
　Aquinas, 221-223
　Aristotle, 5ff., 62
　Augustine, 212-213
　Bentham, 101, 110
　Dewey, 322
　Epicurus, 141-142
　Kant, 62
　Loyalty as, 358
　Mill, 123-126
　Perry, 387-389
　Royce, 354, 358

T

Temperance, 21
Temptation, 111-113
Ten Commandments, 171-174, 200-201
Truthfulness, 29

U

Unmoral, 49
Utilitarianism, 97-137, 323
　Defined, 121, 346
　Mill's proof of, 129-131

V

Value,
　Absolute, 238
　Calculus of, 385-387
　Criteria of, 385-387
　Defined, 329, 382
　Interest theory of, 381-385
　Loyalty as, 354-356
　Revaluation of, 248, 256
　Theory, 325-331
Vice, 10-12
　Butler, 77
Virtue, 10-12
　Aquinas' definition 227
　Aristotle, 13, 19ff.
　Augustine, 213-215
　Butler, 77
　Epictetus, 151-152
　Intellectual, 34-35
　Kant, 60-62
　Lombard's definition, 227
　St. Paul, 199-201
　Seven Cardinal Christian, 227-233
　Socrates, 163-165
　Theological, 230-233
　The Four Cardinal, 228-229
Volition

W

Will, 53-55, 224-225, 303ff., 310-313
402-403
　Autonomy of, 46ff., 405
　Unconquerable, 148-150
Wittiness, 29-30

www.ingramcontent.com/pod-product-compliance
Lightning Source LLC
Chambersburg PA
CBHW031305150426
43191CB00005B/86